LOGIC
FOR
PHILOSOPHERS

Sources in Contemporary Philosophy
Frank A. Tillman, *Consulting Editor*

LOGIC
FOR
PHILOSOPHERS

Richard L. Purtill
Western Washington State College

HARPER & ROW, PUBLISHERS

New York, Evanston, and London

LOGIC FOR PHILOSOPHERS
Copyright © 1971 by Richard L. Purtill

LIBRARY OF CONGRESS CATALOG CARD NUMBER: 70-127341

To
RUDOLF CARNAP
Philosopher
Logician
Teacher

CONTENTS

Appendixes

Preface
MAINLY FOR TEACHERS

How is this logic book different from the many other logic books now available? Part I, which covers propositional logic, syllogistic logic, set theory, and first-order predicate logic is obviously not much different from many other modern logic books in the material covered. The outstanding difference is that I have tried to use material from philosophical sources with as little modification as possible, both in examples and in exercises. The advantages of this for philosophy majors and minors is obvious, but it should also add interest and increase motivation for students who are not majoring in philosophy. The very artificial examples usually found in introductory books often have very little resemblance to any real arguments encountered inside or outside of philosophy, and most students are well aware of this. Not that I have avoided artificial examples altogether: When first learning a technique, it is better to focus attention on form rather than content. As soon as it is feasible, however, I try to show how the techniques which have been learned can be applied to arguments of some interest and importance. As sources of examples and exercises, I have used, where possible, philosophical works, such as the Platonic dialogues, which the philosophy student will encounter early in his studies.

There are other innovations, major and minor, in Part I. For example, after introducing the student to a new set of symbols, I first ask him to translate statements from symbols to English, just as in learning a foreign language we usually first translate from the other language to English before attempting the more difficult task of translating from English to the other tongue. Again when presenting implications and equivalences, I try to give them in a logical and memorable order rather than in the usual helter-skelter grouping.

Some of my innovations may strike you as mistaken. In those cases I ask you to consider carefully the reasons for your objections. You may, for example, feel that I dismiss the so-called paradoxes of material implication too easily. One critic said that the students will "wonder what all the fuss was about." But I feel this criticism is misguided. Beginning students have no idea that there is a problem here. Is it better to explain material implication in such a way that no problem arises or first to create, then explain away, a difficulty? I find the first course more reasonable. Another example: You may feel that I depart from standard logical usage by using Carroll diagrams rather than Venn diagrams and "Every S is P" rather than "All S are P" for A statements. But where, outside of an introductory logic book, will a student ever encounter a Venn diagram? He will encounter syllogisms in some major works of philosophy, but the Greeks and medievals used the "Every . . . " form rather than the "All . . . " form, and even the occasional modern who uses or mentions syllogistic arguments may use this form. The habitat of the so-called standard syllogism is again mainly the introductory text.

In places where my approach may seem overcomplicated, I have what seem to me to be good reasons for the complication. For example, in Chapter 1 connectives are defined by what I call a *matrix,* which is essentially a truth table arranged in a somewhat more compact way. There are several reasons for using this device. One reason is that it enables me to postpone a discussion of variables until the next part. Beginning students are easily confused and dismayed by having to digest too many unfamiliar ideas at once, and until they have some idea of how connectives work, it is hard to convey to them an adequate understanding of variables. Once the student is familiar with matrices used for definition, similar devices can be used in later chapters, saving time and confusion. You may find, incidentally, that your students have encountered similar matrices in "new math" courses, where they are used to explain operations such as addition and multiplication. I use Euler diagrams in Chapter 3 because experience has shown that they are heuristically valuable. They help the student to see what is wrong with an invalid syllogism and what is right with a valid one.

However in Chapter 5 I use Carroll diagrams because I want to give the student an example of a mechanically applicable diagrammatic technique.

The Carroll diagrams have several advantages over the Venn diagrams which are generally used. (Venn diagrams have been provided as an alternate for those who prefer them.) The shape of cells in Venn diagrams is often somewhat misleading to beginners, suggesting for example that the outer cells represent larger classes than the inner cells. Also a purely practical matter that is not without its importance is that it is often hard to show markings in the inner cells of a Venn diagram clearly, either on the blackboard or on paper. Also the Carroll diagrams can be extended easily to four or more classes, which is almost impossible with Venn diagrams.

The reason for the complications in the instantiation and generalization rules in Chapter 5 is philosophical: The several versions I give of that UI and EG reflect philosophically important differences. In other ways, these rules are less complicated than those usually given; for example, the flagging of variables by accent marks makes automatic the application of certain restrictions which must be added to other rules.

Finally, some innovations in Part I are justified by their interest or utility; for example, the inference rules for class logic in Chapter 4 or the simplified dispoof method in Chapter 5. No innovation has been made simply to be different. All of them are made for what I believe are sound reasons.

The material in Part II is almost never found in introductory texts. Some of it has not made its way even into advanced textbooks. The material on second-order predicate logic in Chapter 6 gives the student some tools necessary for dealing with many philosophically interesting arguments. I have found the material on modal logic in Chapter 7 to be interesting to students and not unduly difficult for them. Furthermore, there are a number of philosophically interesting applications of modal logic—I have drawn some examples from my own published papers. Deontic and epistemic logic, which are presented in Chapter 8, can hardly yet be called developed branches of logic. Nevertheless, they are potentially so valuable to philosophy that I think they deserve discussion in a logic text for philosophy students.

In Chapter 9 an effort is made to draw together and formalize some techniques used by philosophers of ordinary language. Not all such techniques can be dealt with formally. I have stuck to those which can. Finally, in Chapter 10 is a brief survey of certain areas related to logic, such as probability theory and philosophy of language, as well as certain subjects that are traditionally part of logic, such as definition.

Throughout the book I have tried to give a great many exercises (there are about 1000) and have given answers to all the even-numbered problems. Thus, there is a good deal of material on which the student may practice. He can test himself on the even-numbered items, and the teacher can test him on the odd-numbered ones.

For each major subdivision of the book, there is a section on philosophical applications and one on philosophical difficulties in that area of logic. The sections on difficulties make no claim to be exhaustive, but they should serve to start classroom discussion. The sections on applications offer an opportunity to demonstrate the application of logical techniques to philosophical material of some interest, but, again, they are only a beginning, and should be supplemented in class.

There is very little material on mathematical logic in the sense of study of logic itself as a formal system. It is essential that graduate students in philosophy have such a course, and even undergraduates may profit from a course of this kind. However, it makes a very bad *first* course in philosophy, in my view. Consider the way in which a first course in statistics is taught to social scientists. An understanding of concepts and a mystery of techniques is emphasized, rather than a mathematical justification of these techniques. I think logic is as much the philosopher's natural tool as statistics is the social scientist's. Not every problem in philosophy can be attacked by means of formal logic, any more than every problem in the social sciences is amenable to statistical procedures. However, more problems than we think may be open to investigation by formal logic.

Depending on the interests of the instructor and the purpose of the course, material may be chosen from the various chapters of this book to make up a variety of courses. For example, a course mainly concerned with modern developments in formal logic might deal only with Chapters 1, 2, 5, 6, 7, and 8. A more traditionally oriented course, mainly concerned with deductive logic, might use Chapters 1 through 5. Teachers who wish to say something about informal logic and scientific method as well as about deductive logic can use Chapters 9 and 10 together with some selection from Chapters 1 through 5, for example, Chapters 1 through 3 or Chapters 1, 2, and 5. Some teachers may wish to omit syllogistic logic in its traditional treatment; they may omit Chapter 3 and still find some treatment of syllogistic arguments in Chapters 4 or 5. Some may wish to omit the material on class logic in Chapter 4; others may find it especially interesting. If Chapters 1 through 5 are used for an introductory course, Chapters 6 through 10 can be used for an intermediate or advanced course. Some chapters must be read if certain other chapters are to be understood. Thus Chapter 2 depends on Chapter 1, Chapter 5 depends on 2, and Chapter 6 depends on 5. Chapter 7 depends on 2, and Chapter 8 depends on both 7 and 5. Chapters 3, 4, 9, and 10, are each relatively independent. There will be some cross-references other than those mentioned, but these can be ignored, briefly explained by the instructor, or left for the student to check.

I myself have covered all of the material in this book in one very swiftly moving one-quarter course, whose enrollment consisted mainly of philosophy majors and minors. At another time and place, with a somewhat different class enrollment, I have taken two semesters to cover the same material. All of the material has been used in classes at two state colleges. I will welcome any criticisms or suggestions for improvement from teachers who use this book.

I am happy to acknowledge the help I have received from various sources in completing this book. Typing of the manuscript was largely paid for by the Research Office at Western Washington State College, who also gave me grants in aid during two summers. I wish to thank especially Mrs. Jane Clark and the staff of the Research Office for their work on the manuscript. I also received help from the Departments of Philosophy at Western Washington State College and at San Francisco State College, where I spent a year as a visiting professor, and I wish to thank the departmental secretaries at Western and SFSC, especially Mrs. Mary Sutterman at Western. Professor Paul Snyder of Temple University pointed out several errors and weaknesses in Chapters 7 and 8, and Professor Hugh Lehman of the University of Guelph and Professor Arthur Benson of Los Angeles State College have read the manuscript with care and attention, giving me the benefit of their experience and good sense on many points, large and small. I have not always been convinced by my critics, and any weaknesses or inadequacies that remain can be laid at no one's door but my own. Finally. I wish to thank Mr. Les Elliot, Mr. James Clark, Miss Karen Judd, and Mrs. Kathleen MacDougall, all of Harper & Row.

It seems to me that logical techniques could be much more widely used than they are at present in attacking philosophical problems. The hopes expressed by such great philosopher-logicians of the last generation as C. I. Lewis, Bertrand Russell, and my own teacher, Rudolf Carnap, that modern logical techniques would achieve important results in philosophy have largely not been fulfilled. It seems to me that this is at least partly due to the way students of philosophy are introduced to logic. Whether or not the approach taken in this book will prove to be an improvement, only time will tell.

R.L.P.

Introduction
MAINLY FOR STUDENTS

This is a book about formal logic, with philosophical applications. In this respect it is like a book about, for example, statistics with applications in psychology. Just as statistics cannot be used in attacking every psychological problem, so formal logic cannot be used in attacking every problem in philosophy. On the other hand, just as it is difficult or perhaps impossible to understand modern psychology without a knowledge of statistics, so formal logic is becoming increasingly essential to understanding modern work in philosophy.

We are interested, then, in learning to use formal logic as a tool for working on philosophical problems. For the philosophy student, this provides a good reason for using this book to study logic. Many students in the average logic class, however, are not philosophy students. What about them? This depends somewhat on their motivations. Some of them, although they are not philosophy majors or minors, are interested in philosophy. They took the course because of an interest in philosophy rather than because of an interest in logic. Others will become interested in philosophy through logic. Some of my best students began this way.

Other students take logic courses to improve their reasoning ability. Perhaps they intend to become lawyers or go into other fields where clear thinking and argumentation are important. These students will probably not use all of the techniques which they will learn from this book, but they may be able to use some of them. At any rate they will get a good deal of practice in analyzing statements and arguments. Also they will gain some knowledge of, and perhaps respect for, two important fields of intellectual endeavor—logic and philosophy. If they are to learn logic, they must see how it applies to some kind of problems: Philosophical problems, besides being interesting and important, offer a great deal of scope for logical techniques.

The student who is looking for an easy or amusing course will probably be disappointed in a course which uses this book. If he is to pass the course or do well in it, he is likely to have to work harder than he wishes. Although the problems discussed are interesting and important, the book is not intended to provide amusement or entertainment.

Since some students may begin the study of logic with only a vague idea of what logic is, I will give a very brief and sketchy discussion of this and related points. Since the whole book is intended to show what logic is, these introductory remarks will at best begin to give you some idea of the nature and scope of logic.

Briefly, then, logic is the science concerned with the analysis of statements and arguments. The first stage of analysis is generally clarification: making sure exactly what is being stated or asserted or just what argument or proof or justification is being presented. In general, logic is not concerned with the truth or falsity of statements, except in those cases where the statement is of a kind that is always true or always false regardless of its subject matter. Such statements are called logical truths or logical falsehoods, and they are part of the subject matter of logic.

In logic it is extremely important to distinguish between cases where we are *using* a sentence to make a statement, say, or to ask a question, and cases where we are *mentioning* or talking *about* a sentence. For example, if I say that logic is useful for philosophy I have expressed an opinion, said something true or false. If, however, I merely use the sentence "Logic is useful for philosophy," as an example of a sentence which is in English or which has an abstract noun for a subject or which is about logic, I have *not* asserted the sentence; I have not used it to express an opinion or state something which is true or false. It would be very odd if we could not quote, mention, or discuss statements without asserting them. Of course, we might not be sure on a given occasion whether a given writer or speaker was using or mentioning a sentence, but the distinction itself is clear enough.

In ordinary writing we indicate that we are mentioning or quoting an expression by putting it within quotation marks or by setting it off typographically from the body of what we are saying. Since such devices as quotation marks or indention are used also for other purposes, their use in logic can be confusing. However, it seems better in an introductory book to stick to familiar patterns where possible rather than to introduce new conventions unnecessarily. So we will use the ordinary methods to indicate when we are mentioning or quoting English sentences, and we will use the same quotations marks or indentions, when we are mentioning or quoting statements in logical symbolism. We will, however, be somewhat more free in using the device of setting off a mentioned expression on a separate line than is usual in ordinary English prose; especially we will do this for short expressions more often than is usual in ordinary prose. (When we mention rather than use names and symbols which stand for names, we will sometimes use the usual devices, such as quotes, but we will omit quotes, especially with symbolic expressions, where no confusion is likely to arise.)

One other matter should be mentioned at this point: words for talking about words. I use the term *expression* as my most general term: Sentences, phrases, and sometimes even single words are referred to as expressions. I use the term *statement* to refer to complete declarative sentences or the act of uttering such sentences. Such terms as *proposition* or *standard form statement*, are technical terms. They are defined where they first occur and are listed in the Index. As is usual in ordinary English usage, I may sometimes for stylistic or other reasons use the wider term for the narrower, for example, "expression" for "statement."

By an *argument* we will mean a set of statements such that one or more of them, which we will call the *premise* or *premises*, may be offered as proof of, or evidence for, another of the statements, which we will call the *conclusion*. (In some trivial arguments, the conclusion simply repeats one of the premises.) In logic we are usually interested in whether the conclusion *follows from* the premises, rather than in whether the conclusion is true. When we say that the conclusion follows from the premises, we mean that, *if* the premises are true, the conclusion must necessarily be true. If the conclusion follows from the premises, the argument is called a *valid* argument. If the conclusion does not follow, the argument is called *invalid*. If the argument is valid and the premises are true, then, of course, the conclusion is true. Valid arguments with true premises are sometimes called *sound* arguments or, less frequently, *cogent* arguments. Just as in learning mathematics we are usually concerned with learning how to calculate properly and don't care whether the data used in an example or exercise is accurate, so in logic we are concerned with learning how to reason correctly (that is, how to argue validly), and don't care whether our premises are true.

Formal logic is that part of logic for which we are able to give relatively clear and simple rules and techniques for analyzing statements and arguments. It is not the same as what I will call *mathematical logic*, which is concerned with logic as a system rather than with its application to particular arguments. We sometimes speak of *informal* logic as that area of logic in which we cannot give many or any rules or techniques for analyzing arguments. In my view, the student should begin logic by studying formal logic, rather than either mathematical or informal logic.

There are many subdivisions of formal logic, which we can think of either as parts of a larger system or as somewhat independent systems. In general, I will speak in this second way, as if the logics that we consider are independent systems. Although some logical systems are to some extent competitive or incompatible, all of the systems discussed in this book are compatible. In fact, we can think of what we are doing here as the gradual development of more and more powerful and flexible tools for analyzing statements and arguments. Although we will occasionally retrace our steps, each completed system includes all of the previous ones.

The main line of the book is developed in the odd-numbered chapters, 1, 3, 5, 7, and 9. Each of these introduces a new logical system which is developed or expanded in the following even-numbered chapter. In each of the odd-numbered chapters the first section introduces the basic machinery of the system. The following sections discuss ways of finding which statements in the system are logically true or logically false, which statements mean the same thing as (or come to the same thing as) others, and which arguments can be shown to be valid or invalid in the system. In a final section either philosophical applications or philosophical difficulties of the system are discussed. Of the even-numbered chapters, Chapter 2, which introduces the basic techniques of proof, is the most important for understanding later chapters. Chapters 1 through 5 cover most of the material usually dealt with in introductory logic books, while Chapters 6 through 10 describe interesting and important developments in logic that are seldom encountered at an introductory level.

After each section of each chapter there are exercises, except for the sections on philosophical difficulties which have suggestions for further reading. There are a great many exercises, placed more or less in order of difficulty, and the answer to almost all of the even-numbered exercises are given in the back of the book. Thus you can gain experience in dealing with logical problems by working as many even-numbered exercises as you like, and you will be able to check immediately to see if your answers are correct. At the beginning of the answer sections a few typical problems are worked out in detail. The most important symbols and rules used in the book are summarized in the final appendix, in the pages just preceding the indexes. There is an index of symbols which tells you where each symbol is first introduced and discussed and a similar index for rules.

Any student who has suggestions for improving the book is encouraged to write to me in care of the publishers. My thanks are due to my own students who have directly or indirectly helped me to make this a better book.

R.L.P.

Part I
BASIC LOGIC

Chapter 1
PROPOSI-
TIONAL
LOGIC

We begin with propositional logic, since, though it is not the earliest sort of logic to be noticed and systematized by philosophers, it is by far the simplest variety of logic. Actually it is of quite respectable antiquity; many of its important rules were discovered by the Stoic philosophers as early as the fourth century B.C. However, the modern development of propositional logic (which began in the nineteenth century with the English logician George Boole) has one great advantage over its classical and medieval predecessors in that we now have a simple and flexible symbolic "shorthand" which makes the rules of propositional logic easy to understand and use. Consider the rule which we will learn to write as

$$((p \supset q) \cdot (q \supset r)) \supset (p \supset r).$$

It was well known to the Stoics, but *they* had to express it in this way: "If, if the first then the second and if the second then the third, then, if the first then the third." Whether or not you are comfortable with algebraic looking

3

symbolism like that above (and if you are not, you may be one of the people this book is written for), you will learn that it is a great time-saver and con-fusion-preventer. It may help you to know that propositional logic is basically simple to the point of being simple minded: All of its essential manipulations are about as complex as performing the operations of addition and multipli-cation where the only numbers you have to deal with are ones and zeros. If you can do that, then there is no reason why you cannot do all the essential operations of propositional logic.

It may strike you as surprising that so simple a system can be worth studying or that it can be applicable in any way to philosophy. However, in the earlier sections of this chapter you will find some examples and exercises taken from actual philosophical contexts, and in section 1.5 you will find a discussion of the applicability and limits of propositional logic.

1.1 OPERATORS AND CONNECTIVES

The simplest part of the propositional logic consists of combining *simple propositions* into *compound propositions* and determining the *truth value* (that is, the truth or falsity) of the resulting compounds. By a *proposition* we mean any expression, in any language, which is definitely true or definitely false. This excludes, first, all meaningless expressions, second, all expressions which are meaningful but are not capable of being either true or false (such as questions and commands), and, finally, all statements which look as if they are capable of being true or false but which for some reason cannot be definitely classed as one or the other (for example, statements about non-existent things).

Propositions

A proposition is simple if it cannot be broken down into other propositions without loss of meaning. For example, "Alice and May are tired" can be broken down into "Alice is tired, May is tired," but "Alice and May are sisters" cannot be broken down without loss of meaning. Later in this book, when we look at the internal structure of statements in more detail, we will be able to discuss this point with more precision. For propositional logic, however, when we are satisfied that our propositions are simple ones, we need take no further interest in their internal structure: Propositions are the unanalyzed "atoms" of propositional logic.

For our future convenience we will lay down the following convention: In working with statements in English, we abbreviate these statements by substituting for the statement a single capital letter of the Roman alphabet, generally but not necessarily the initial letter of a key word in the sentence. Thus instead of "The Gryphon is looking at Alice," we might write "G"; instead of "The Mock Turtle is looking at Alice," we might write "M." Of course, with only twenty-six letters and millions of propositions, we will have to reuse the same letter to stand for different propositions in different examples. Thus, we should always give a "dictionary," showing what propositions our letters stand for in various examples. We will use the symbol "#" to mean "stands for" or "abbreviates," so that we will write, for example, "A # Alice is a girl" meaning that "A" stands for "Alice is a girl."

Notice that the whole idea of propositions demands that there be an effective test for truth and falsity and that every proposition *by definition* has a determinate truth value. If a statement or expression lacks a definite truth value, then it is not a proposition as we define propositions, and propositional logic cannot deal with it.

In addition to propositions, propositional logic contains another basic element—operators on propositions. Propositions are like the sticks in a Tinker Toy set; without the round spools or connector blocks, you can do very little with the sticks. Operators are like the connector blocks; by adding them to propositions we get more complex structures. Most operators do, in fact, connect propositions and will be called *connectives*. But some operators do something to a single proposition. It is rather like putting one stick into one connector block: It can then stand up where previously it could only lie in a horizontal position.

Truth-Functional Operators

The subject which we now call propositional logic allows only operators which have the quality of being *truth functional*. By a truth-functional operator we mean one such that the following condition is met: In order to know the truth value of the proposition resulting from applying the operator to a proposition or propositions, *all* we need to know is the definition of the operator and the truth value of the proposition(s) to which it was applied.

Many interesting operators on propositions are not truth functional, and in due course we will look at some of these. Perhaps no operator or connective in English is purely truth functional, but some come quite close.

Conjunction

The word "and" for example when it connects two propositions forms a compound proposition which is true only if both of the propositions it joins are true. For example, the compound proposition "Alice is sitting under the tree, and Alice's sister is reading a book" is true only if "Alice is sitting under the tree" and "Alice's sister is reading a book" are both true. If Alice isn't under the tree *or* if her sister isn't reading *or* both, then the compound statement is false. So our first truth-functional connective will be similar to "and" in English (and also to some uses of "but" and "although" and "however"); it will be *defined* as a connective which forms compound propositions which are true only in the case when both of the propositions joined by it are true.

5

We will use symbols, rather than words for our connectives; and our symbol for this connective that is like "and" will be a dot written between two propositions. Thus if

$$A \# \text{Alice is sitting under the tree}$$

and

$$B \# \text{Alice's sister is reading a book}$$

then A · B can be read as "Alice is sitting under the tree, and Alice's sister is reading a book."

One convenient way of remembering what our connectives mean in terms of truth and falsity is to give a *matrix* like Matrix 1.1. T and F stand

MATRIX 1.1

		Value of second proposition	
	·	T	F
Value of first	T	T	F
proposition	F	F	F

for true and false, of course, and by looking in the appropriate row and column we can see the truth value of a compound proposition whose component propositions are joined with · for various truth values of those component propositions. If, for example, the first proposition is true and the second is false, the value of the compound proposition, which is circled

MATRIX 1.2

·	T	F
T	T	Ⓕ
F	F	F

in the matrix 1.2, is false. If both components are false, the compound is false (Matrix 1.3), and so on.

MATRIX 1.3

·	T	F
T	T	F
F	F	Ⓕ

At this point we have to notice that the truth-functional connective · doesn't do everything that "and" does in English. For often "and" in English has the force of "and then" or "and so." In our original example it wouldn't affect the truth values if we switched the clauses and said "Alice's sister is reading a book and Alice is sitting under the tree." But of course, in "Alice slipped into the pool of tears and Alice got wet," we definitely affect the meaning and the truth value of the sentence if we switch clauses. Here "and" means both "and then" and "and so," so that "Alice got wet and Alice slipped into the pool of tears" gives quite a different picture of both the temporal and causal sequence.

The fact is that we must simply realize that truth-functional connectives are more limited than the English connectives which more or less correspond to them. The whole meaning of a truth-functional connective is given by its truth matrix while the whole meaning of an English connective often contains elements that are not truth functional. So long as we realize this and don't expect more from truth-functional connectives than they can do, we shall have no major difficulties.

Disjunction

The connective "or" in English is a bit more slippery than "and." For one thing, sometimes it means "one thing or the other but not both." When the Queen tells the Duchess "Either you or your head must be off, and that in about half of no time," she adds "Take your choice." The Duchess can (and does) save her head by taking her departure. On the other hand sometimes "or" means "one or the other and perhaps both"; e.g., "Why is Alice with the baby? Well, either the baby is crying or the Duchess has gone to play croquet with the Queen" (and possibly for both reasons).

For reasons that will become clearer later on, we will use the more inclusive sense of "or." The truth-functional connective v which is our substitute for "or" is so defined that if two simple statements are joined with v, the resulting compound is true if either of the simple propositions is true or if both of the simple propositions are true; the resulting compound is false only if both simple propositions are false. That is, its matrix definition is as is shown in Matrix 1.4.

MATRIX 1.4

v	T	F
T	T	T
F	T	F

The compound proposition "Alice is minding the baby or the baby is crying," then, is true under any of the following conditions:

1. Alice is minding the baby and it is crying.
2. Alice is minding it, but it isn't crying.
3. Alice isn't minding it, but it is crying.

and false only if

4. Alice isn't minding it and it isn't crying.

7

This is true of course only if we interpret the "or" here as having the same effect as v. Actually the English compound proposition "Alice is minding the baby or the baby is crying" might be interpreted as meaning "Alice minds the baby, or it cries, but not both." In English fairly often there is some ambiguity about which of the two senses of "or" is meant. Since v always means the inclusive "or," one often has to decide which sense of "or" is meant before translating an English statement into the symbols of propositional logic.

Negation

Another example of a truth-functional operator is the phrase, "It is false that. . . ." Suppose I know that "Alice is a curious child" is true; then of course I know that "It is false that Alice is a curious child" is false. And if I know that "Alice is a curious child" is false, of course "It is false that Alice is a curious child" is true.

The word "not" inserted at the appropriate point in the sentence works the same way. If "Alice is falling" is true, then "Alice is not falling" is false, and if "Alice is falling" is false, then "Alice is not falling" is true.

Our operator to do the job of "it is false that" and "not" will be ~ (read "not . . ." or "it is false that . . ."). Since ~ is an operator which is not a connective (that is, it operates on a single proposition instead of connecting two propositions), the matrix will be even simpler (Matrix 1.5). That is, if proposition A is true, ~A is false, and if A is false, ~A is true.

MATRIX 1.5

~	
T	F
F	T

At this point it is necessary to introduce another kind of symbol, which will avoid ambiguity if we mix ~ and v or either of them with the symbol · for "and." Thus to avoid the ambiguities involved in such expressions as

$$A \lor B \cdot C$$

or

$$\sim A \cdot B$$

we will use parentheses as punctuation marks.

The general principle which governs parentheses for punctuation or grouping are the following:

1. A ~ standing in front of a letter negates only that proposition, while a ~ in front of an expression in parentheses negates the whole compound statement within those parentheses.

MATRIX 1.7

⊃	T	F
T	T	F
F	?	?

But if ⊃ is to be a truth-functional connective, the lower line of Matrix 1.7 will never do: We *must* be able to determine the truth value of the compound from the truth value of its component simple propositions. So there must be T's and F's on this line. But how should these be arranged?

Suggestion 1. We could put two F's, as in Matrix 1.8. But then ⊃ would have the same definition as · has.

MATRIX 1.8

⊃	T	F
T	T	F
F	F	F

Suggestion 2. We could put T and F as in Matrix 1.9. But then the truth

MATRIX 1.9

⊃	T	F
T	T	F
F	T	F

value of the compound would depend entirely on the second proposition regardless of the truth value of the first proposition. The best English equivalent of such a connective would not be "if A then B," but rather something like "B whether or not A."

Suggestion 3. A similar objection applies to putting an F and a T (Matrix 1.10). This suggestion amounts to saying that the baby cries if Alice minds

MATRIX 1.10

⊃	T	F
T	T	F
F	F	T

it but also that it cries *only* in case Alice is minding it. Even if I am alleging that Alice's presence causes the crying, I am willing to concede that other things may cause it to cry too.

Thus the only matrix remaining for ⊃ is Matrix 1.11. Although Matrix

MATRIX 1.11

⊃	T	F
T	T	F
F	T	T

1.11 is not ideal, we shall see in Chapter 2 why and how this matrix definition of ⊃ is a workable one for our purposes.

Equivalence

Matrix 1.10 of Suggestion 3 does represent a useful truth-functional connective, although for ⊃ it is not adequate. Sometimes we wish to say that two statements are true and false under the same conditions, for example, "Alice is minding the baby if the Duchess is playing croquet and only if she is." If it is true that the Duchess is playing croquet, then it is true that Alice is minding the baby. If the Duchess isn't playing croquet, then Alice isn't minding the baby. For this sort of connective, the Matrix 1.10 is just the one we need. Its nearest English equivalent is the phrase "if and only if," and ≡ is its symbol. The new connective is defined by Matrix 1.12.

MATRIX 1.12

≡	T	F
T	T	F
F	F	T

Terminology

Technical terms are often useful in avoiding cumbersome circumlocutions. The following will be useful in our discussion. For any two propositions, A and B:

~ A is called the *denial* or *negation* of A, and sometimes we refer generally to "a denial" or "a negation," as in "A negation is always true if the statement which it denies is false."

A · B is called the *conjunction* of A and B or simply "a conjunction."

A v B is called the *disjunction* of A and B or simply "a disjunction."

A ⊃ B is called the *implication* of B *by* A or "an implication." A is called the *antecedent* of the implication and B the *consequent* of the implication.

A ≡ B is called the *equivalence* of A and B or simply "an equivalence."

The components of a conjunction are called *conjuncts*; the components of a disjunction are called *disjuncts*; and the components of an equivalence are called *equivalents*. Since we rarely need to distinguish between the first term and the second term in a conjunction, disjunction, or equivalence, there is no established terminology for distinguishing them.

Table 1.1 summarizes our truth-functional operations and their matrix definitions.

TABLE 1.1

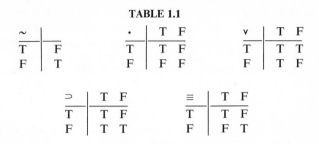

~	
T	F
F	T

·	T	F
T	T	F
F	F	F

v	T	F
T	T	T
F	T	F

⊃	T	F
T	T	F
F	T	T

≡	T	F
T	T	F
F	F	T

EXERCISES 1.1

A. (1) Translate from symbols to English, using the following dictionary:

A # Alice minds the baby   B # The baby cries

C # The Cheshire Cat makes trouble

1. A · (B · C)
2. (A · B) · C
3. ~(A · B) · C
4. A · ~(B · C)
5. A · (B v C)
6. (A ⊃ B) · C
7. ~(A ⊃ B) · C
8. A ⊃ ~(B · C)
9. A ⊃ (B v C)
10. (A ⊃ B) v C

(2) Determine the truth value of the ten compound propositions above if A and C are true and B is false.

B. Translate the following into compound statements using the connectives discussed in this section and the following dictionary:

A # The Red Queen is angry   B # The White Knight is bewildered

C # Alice is crowned queen

1. Alice is not crowned queen, and either the Red Queen is angry or the White Knight is bewildered.
2. Alice is crowned queen if and only if the Red Queen is not angry and the White Knight is not bewildered.
3. Either the Red Queen is angry and the White Knight is not bewildered or she is not angry and Alice is not crowned queen.
4. If the Red Queen is angry, then either the White Knight is bewildered or Alice is not crowned queen.
5. If the Red Queen is angry, then the White Knight is bewildered and, if she is not angry, Alice is crowned queen.

C. Express the following as compound statements using the connectives discussed in this section. Use letters as abbreviations for simple propositions, and give your own dictionary. (Source: Plato, *Lysis*.)

1. If friends have everything in common, then one of you can be no richer than the other if you say truly that you are friends.
2. If you are in the condition of a slave and cannot do what you like, you will not be happy.
3. If your father and mother love you and wish that you should be happy, no one can doubt that they are very ready to promote your happiness.

4. If your father or mother want anything read or written, you would be the first person in the house who is summoned.
5. If the Great King has an eldest son, who is Prince of Asia, and you and I go to him and establish to his satisfaction that we are better cooks than his son, he will entrust to us the prerogative of making soup and let us put in anything we like, rather than the Prince of Asia who is his son.
6. If the son of the king has bad eyes, the king will not allow the son to touch his own eyes if he thinks the son has no knowledge of medicine.
7. If we are supposed to have a knowledge of medicine, he will allow us to open the eyes wide and sprinkle ashes upon them if he supposes that we know what is best.
8. If we understand the subject, everyone will trust us and we may do as we please, and no one will interfere with us; but, if we do not understand the subject, not everyone will trust us—they will hinder us as far as they can and not let us do as we please.
9. If you are wise, all men will be your friends and kindred and you will be useful and good, but, if you are not wise, this will not be true.
10. If the wise are not seekers of wisdom and those hardened in ignorance are not seekers of wisdom, then the seekers of wisdom must be neither the wise nor the hardened in ignorance but those who realize their own ignorance and wish to cure it.

1.2 TAUTOLOGIES, CONTRADICTIONS, AND CONTINGENTS

At this point we will introduce the following convention: the small letters of the Roman alphabet, beginning usually with p but using as much of the alphabet as necessary, will be used as *variables*. A variable is not itself a proposition, but any proposition can be put in its place. It may help you to think of a variable as a labeled box which can be filled with any proposition so long as each box with the same label has the same proposition put in it. Now, since we don't know what proposition we'll put in the box (i.e., replace the variable with), we don't know whether it will be true or false, and we have to consider all the possibilities. In order that we may be sure that we have considered all the possibilities, we write down a *truth table*: an exhaustive tabulation of all the possible combinations of truth values. The truth table for one variable is quite simple:

$$p$$
$$T$$
$$F$$

This merely says that you can put either a true proposition or a false one in box p. However, with two variables, p and q, we get complications. For this, we use Truth Table 1.1, which represents the fact that we could put a true proposition in box p and a true proposition in box q or a true one in the first and a false one in the second or a false one in the first and a true one in the second or false propositions in both.

14

TRUTH TABLE 1.1

p	q
T	T
T	F
F	T
F	F

Logical Forms of Propositions

We can find the *logical form* of any compound proposition by replacing all of its propositions by propositional variables (using a different variable for each different simple proposition), leaving its connectives and parentheses (if any) untouched. In a way, it doesn't matter *which* propositional variables we use. To give the logical form of A · B, we might write

$$p \cdot q \quad \text{or} \quad q \cdot p$$

because both simply mean "some proposition *and* another (possibly but not necessarily different) proposition." To avoid confusion, we will introduce the following convention: In reducing any compound proposition or group of compound propositions to its logical form, we will always use p to replace each occurrence of the first proposition and replace each new proposition with a new letter, in alphabetical order. Each proposition which occurs more than once will be replaced by the same propositional variable each time it is replaced. Thus the logical form of

$$A \cdot (B \supset C)$$

or of

Alice will mind the baby, and, if the baby cries, then the Cheshire Cat will make trouble.

is $\qquad p \cdot (q \supset r)$.

The logical form of

$$(A \vee B) \cdot (D \supset A)$$

or of

Either Alice will mind the baby or the baby will cry, and also if the Duchess plays croquet, Alice will mind the baby.

is $\qquad (p \vee q) \cdot (r \supset p)$, and so on.

15

It can be seen that two compound propositions with very different meaning and truth value can have the same logical form. Logical forms themselves are, of course, not propositions, for they are neither true nor false. The statement p · q is like "something and something else" or "blank and another blank." It says nothing, so says nothing true or false.

Substitution Instances of the Logical Forms

Besides reducing propositions to their logical form, we can take a given logical form and make a proposition with that logical form by replacing the variables with actual propositions. Such a proposition is said to be an *instance* or a *substitution instance* of the logical form. Thus

$$A \cdot B \qquad B \cdot C \qquad C \cdot D$$

Alice minds the baby, and the baby cries.
The baby cries, and the Cheshire Cat makes trouble.
The Cheshire Cat makes trouble, but the Duchess goes to tea with the Queen.

are all substitution instances of the form p · q.

Now, while propositional forms have no truth value of their own, we can specify the possible truth values of substitution instances of a given form. We can do this by drawing up a truth table which shows all possible combinations of true and false propositions which could be substituted for the variables of a given form and, for each line of the truth table, figuring what would be the truth value of a compound proposition of the form in question. Thus the line in Truth Table 1.2 means that, if we substitute true

TRUTH TABLE 1.2

p	q	r	$(p \supset q) \vee r$
T	T	T	T

propositions for p, q, and r, then an expression of the form $(p \supset q) \vee r$ would be true.

The general formula for writing truth tables for any number of variables is as follows: write out the variables in alphabetical order across the top (Truth Table 1.3). The number of lines needed will be 2^n where n is the number of variables. Thus for 3 variables we need $2^3 = 8$ lines.

TRUTH TABLE 1.3

	p	q	r
1			
2			
3			
4			
5			
6			
7			
8			

Start in the right-hand column and alternate T's and F's (Truth Table 1.4).

TRUTH TABLE 1.4

	p	q	r
1			T
2			F
3			T
4			F
5			T
6			F
7			T
8			F

Then move to the next column left and alternate pairs of T's and F's (Truth Table 1.5). Then go to the next column and double the numbers of T's

TRUTH TABLE 1.5

	p	q	r
1		T	T
2		T	F
3		F	T
4		F	F
5		T	T
6		T	F
7		F	T
8		F	F

and F's which are alternated (Truth Table 1.6) and so on as long as necessary.

TRUTH TABLE 1.6

	p	q	r
1	T	T	T
2	T	T	F
3	T	F	T
4	T	F	F
5	F	T	T
6	F	T	F
7	F	F	T
8	F	F	F

If the table is correctly drawn, the first (horizontal) line will be all T's, the last line all F's, and the leftmost column will be evenly divided, the first half T's, the second half F's.

Truth Tables of the Propositional Forms

To draw the truth table of a propositional form which has *n* variables, first write a truth table for *n* variables. Then for each line figure the value of the propositional form as if the variables were propositions with the values appearing under them for that line and as if the propositional form was a compound proposition. Since we have a number of lines to figure out in this way, we will figure out the value of each compound and write the result under the connective, crossing out the values which we have used. Suppose we wish to test

$$((p \supset q) \cdot p) \vee ((r \supset {\sim}q) \cdot r)$$

For line 1 in our example, we would first write the values for each variable under the appropriate variable, getting the values from the columns under p, q, and r. (We will call these the "reference columns" and separate them from the compound form to be tested by a vertical line.)

p	q	r	$((p \supset q) \cdot p) \vee ((r \supset {\sim}q) \cdot r)$
T	T	T	T T T T T T

We would then figure the value for any negated variables. (We have one in this case.) We write the value under the ~ sign and cross out the value used by putting a check *below* it. (This leaves it legible if we need to check for mistakes.)

p	q	r	$((p \supset q) \cdot p) \vee ((r \supset {\sim}q) \cdot r)$
T	T	T	T T T T FT T
			✓

We then figure the values for each compound statement. We cannot get the value of the whole statement until we get the value of the disjuncts (though of course one true disjunct will make the whole disjunction true), nor can we get the value of

$$(p \supset q) \cdot p \qquad \text{until we know that of} \qquad p \supset q$$

nor of

$$(r \supset {\sim}q) \cdot r \qquad \text{until we know the value of} \qquad r \supset {\sim}q$$

So we do $p \supset q$ and $r \supset {\sim}q$ first. At each stage we write the value of the expression beneath the connective, crossing out the values we have used to get that value.

```
p   q   r  |  ((p ⊃ q) · p) v ((r ⊃ ~q) · r)
T   T   T  |   T T T   T      T F FT    T
               √   √           √  √√
```

We then get the value of the two disjuncts

```
p   q   r  |  ((p ⊃ q) · p) v ((r ⊃ ~q) · r)
T   T   T  |   TT  TTT         TT FT  FT
               √√  √  √         √√ √√   √
```

and finally the value of the disjunction

```
p   q   r  |  ((p ⊃ q) · p) v ((r ⊃ ~q) · r)
T   T   T  |   TT TTT   T     TF FT  FT
               √√ √ √√          √√ √√  √√
```

The final value which is not crossed out is the value of the compound for that line of the truth table. Proceeding this way for each line we get Truth Table 1.7. (After this, we will put a check under each *column* as it is used, instead of checking every value as it is used. See, for instance, Truth Table 1.8.)

TRUTH TABLE 1.7

	p	q	r	((p ⊃ q) · p) v (r ⊃ ~q) · r)
1	T	T	T	TT T TT T TF FT FT
				√√ √ √√ √√ √√ √√
2	T	T	F	TT T TT T FT FT FF
				√√ √ √√ √√ √√ √√
3	T	F	T	TF F FT T TT TF TT
				√√ √ √√ √√ √√ √√
4	T	F	F	TF F FT F FT TF FF
				√√ √ √√ √√ √√ √√
5	F	T	T	FT T FF F TF FT FT
				√√ √ √√ √√ √√ √√
6	F	T	F	FT T FF F FT FT FF
				√√ √ √√ √√ √√ √√
7	F	F	T	FT F FF T TT TF TT
				√√ √ √√ √√ √√ √√
8	F	F	F	FT F FF F FT TF FF
				√√ √ √√ √√ √√ √√

Some propositional forms are such that, no matter what propositions you substitute for their variables, you must get a true proposition. One example of such a form is p v ∼p, and we can see that it has this property by writing Truth Table 1.8. Thus we see that, whether the proposition sub-

TRUTH TABLE 1.8

	p	(p v ∼p)
1	T	T T F T
2	F	F T T F
		√ √√

stituted for p is true or false, any proposition of the form p v ∼p is true. A more complicated example is ((p · q) ⊃ p), which has Truth Table 1.9.

TRUTH TABLE 1.9

	p	q	(p · q) ⊃ p
1	T	T	T TT T T
2	T	F	T FF T T
3	F	T	F FT T F
4	F	F	F FF T F
			√ √√ √

Again, no matter what values the propositions substituted for p and q have, any compound proposition of the form (p · q) ⊃ p is true.

Terminology

Logical forms with this property are called *tautologies*. Logical forms with the opposite property, that any substitution instance of them is *false*, are called *contradictions*. By substituting the symbol · for the v, we can make our previous example, the tautology p v ∼p, into the contradiction p · ∼p. (A truth table for this form will have a solid line of F's in its remaining column, that is, the column left uncrossed out after we have used the value of each subexpression to get the value of the whole expression.) Logical forms which are neither contradictions nor tautologies have some true substitution instances and some false ones. The remaining column of the truth tables for this kind of logical form will have a mixture of T's and F's. These forms are called *contingent* forms. The usual terminology makes the word *contingent* an adjective and the words *tautology* and *contradiction* nouns. This leads to very cumbersome phrases such as "Is this form a tautology, a contradiction, or a contingent *form*?" or "Are these forms contingent, tautolog*ous*, or contradic*tory*?" I find this annoying and will use the words tautology, contradiction, and contingent as both nouns and adjectives. Thus I will speak of *a contingent* or of *tautology forms* and *contradiction forms*. Purists may object, but these are technical terms and rather ugly anyway—they may as well be made more manageable.

EXERCISES 1.2

A. Determine by truth tables whether the following are tautologies, contradictions, or contingents:

1. p · p
2. p ∨ p
3. p ⊃ p
4. p ≡ p
5. p · ~p
6. (p · r) ⊃ (q ∨ t)
7. (p ∨ r) ≡ (q ∨ r)
8. (p ⊃ r) ⊃ (q ⊃ r)
9. (p ≡ r) ≡ (q ≡ r)
10. (p · r) · (q · ~r)

B. Translate the following statements into symbolism, giving your own dictionary. Then determine whether they are tautologies, contingents, or contradictions.
1. If Alice is a Queen, Alice is not a boy.
2. If Alice is a boy, she is not a girl.
3. Alice is either a Queen or not a Queen.
4. If Alice and the White Knight are in the wood, then Alice is in the wood.
5. Alice and the White Knight are in the wood, but Alice is not in the wood.

C. The first five of the following sentences are logically true, the second five logically false. Can they be written as truth-table tautologies and contradictions? If so, give a translation into symbolism and show by truth-table that the proposition is a tautology or contradiction. If not, discuss briefly why not. Ignore phrases in parentheses. (Source: Lewis Carroll, *Through the Looking Glass*.)

1. Everybody that hears me sing this song—either it brings the tears into their eyes, or else. . . . Or else it doesn't, (you know).
2. If you think we're waxworks, you ought to pay. If you think we're alive, you ought to speak. You either think we're alive or that we're waxworks, so you ought to pay or speak.
3. If it was so, it might be, and if it were so, it would be, but as it isn't, it ain't. That's logic.
4. I sit out here alone because there's nobody with me.
5. There are three hundred and sixty-five days in a year, and you have one birthday, so you have three hundred and sixty-four unbirthdays.
6. The White King turned cold to the end of his whiskers, but he didn't have any whiskers.
7. The King will never forget the horror of that moment, but he will forget it unless he makes a memorandum, and he doesn't make a memorandum (since Alice took his pencil).
8. I could show you hills, in comparison with which this one would be a valley.
9. If you rejoice in something, then you're not afraid of it; Alice rejoices in insects, but is afraid of them.
10. Alice knows her name begins with an *L*.

1.3 EQUIVALENCES

We now come to some useful applications of the machinery which we have been building up. The first application is the notion of *logically equivalent* propositions.

Tautology and Equivalence

A proposition is logically equivalent to another (so far as propositional logic is concerned) if and only if the logical form of their equivalence is a tautology. It is important to write the two expressions with an equivalence sign between them before computing the logical form. Of course A ⊃ B is not equivalent to ∼C v D even though if we took their logical forms in isolation, they could be p ⊃ q and ∼p v q, which are equivalent forms. Writing

$$(A \supset B) \equiv (\sim C \vee D)$$

and *then* replacing the propositions with variables makes this clear for, when we come to C and D, we replace them with r and s since p and q have been used for A and B. Of course, (p ⊃ q) ≡ (∼r v s) is not a tautology. On the other hand A ⊃ B is equivalent to ∼A v B since we can write

$$(A \supset B) \equiv (\sim A \vee B)$$

replace the constants by variables, and get the tautology

$$(p \supset q) \equiv (\sim p \vee q)$$

If the logical form of the equivalence of two compound propositions is a tautology, then the two propositions "come to the same thing" or in one restricted sense "mean the same thing." Thus with the truth-functional connective ⊃, A ⊃ B and ∼B ⊃ ∼A come to the same thing: If we can assert one then we can assert the other, and if we deny one we must deny the other. This can be seen by taking the logical form of each statement and seeing they are equivalent. The logical form of

$$A \supset B \quad \text{is} \quad p \supset q$$

If we merely considered ∼B ⊃ ∼A in isolation, we might write its logical form as ∼p ⊃ q. But we are considering it in connection with A⊃B and so will use the same variables for each occurrence of A and B in the two propositions. Thus the logical form of

$$\sim B \supset \sim A \quad \text{will be} \quad \sim q \supset \sim p$$

On testing (Truth Table 1.10), we find the equivalence is a tautology, so the

TRUTH TABLE 1.10

	p	q	$(p \supset q) \equiv (\sim q \supset \sim p)$
1	T	T	T T T T F T F
2	T	F	T F T T T F F
3	F	T	F T T T F T T
4	F	F	F T F T T T T
			✓ ✓ ✓ ✓ ✓ ✓

propositions are equivalent. While not everyone immediately sees this equivalence, it was recognized and used by philosophers even before the development of propositional logic.

For example, in the *Meno* Plato has Socrates and Meno agree that, if virtue can be taught, then there must be teachers of virtue. Socrates then argues that "conversely," if there are no teachers of virtue, then virtue cannot be taught. (The argument is actually somewhat more complicated as we will see later.) We let

$$V \# \text{ Virtue can be taught}$$
$$T \# \text{ There are teachers of virtue}$$

Socrates is arguing from $V \supset T$ to $\sim T \supset \sim V$, making use of the equivalence

$$(p \supset q) \equiv (\sim q \supset \sim p)$$

Negation of a Negation

Another equivalence which is rather useful is the equivalence between any proposition and the negation of its negation. Since the negation of a proposition is false when that proposition is true, then the negation of that negation will be true when the original proposition is true (Truth Table 1.11),

TRUTH TABLE 1.11

p	$\sim(\sim p)$
T	T F T
	✓ ✓

and similarly, when the original proposition is false, its negation will be true, and the negation of the negation false (Truth Table 1.12). For any

TRUTH TABLE 1.12

p	$\sim(\sim p)$
F	F T F
	$\checkmark$ $\checkmark$

proposition A, therefore, $\sim(\sim A)$ will always have the same truth value as A since the equivalence $p \equiv \sim(\sim p)$ is a tautology (Truth Table 1.13).

TRUTH TABLE 1.13

p	$\sim(\sim p) \equiv p$
T	T FT T T
F	F TF T F
	$\checkmark$ $\checkmark\checkmark$ $\checkmark$

After this we will omit the parentheses and write $\sim \sim p$ rather than $\sim(\sim p)$ since no confusion is likely to result.

Of course few people will bother to say "not-not-A" when they mean to say "A." In fact, double negatives in ordinary usage have a number of uses, not all of which agree with our truth-functional double negation. One use which is quite close to the truth-functional double negation is that in which we take two expressions which are contradictory* and assert one by denying the other. Two expressions are contradictory if it is true that, if one is true, then the other must be false and, if one is false, the other must be true. If we assume, as Plato seems to have done, that "the All is one" and "the All is a plurality" are contradictory statements, then the following argument from the *Parmenides* rests on double negation: "You [Parmenides] assert in your poem that the All is one. . . . Zeno asserts it is not a plurality. . . . Each expresses himself in such a way that your arguments seem to have nothing in common, though really they come to very much the same thing."

We might go on illustrating equivalences with examples from actual philosophical arguments, but, even if we could find an example for each equivalence, this might confuse and would certainly lengthen our task. What we will do, instead, is give a listing, with comments, of a number of useful equivalences, which we will then be able to use in our further work.

Useful Equivalences

Let us begin with the simplest case. The simplest propositional form consists merely of a single propositional variable, p, standing alone. The

---

* If a conjunction is a contradiction, of course its conjuncts are contradictory. However, if two expressions are contradictory, this cannot always be shown by propositional logic alone, as in the example above.

following equivalences hold between p and seemingly more complex forms.

E 1 $p \equiv \sim\sim p$ E 3 $p \equiv (p \vee p)$

E 2 $p \equiv (p \cdot p)$ E 4 $p \equiv (\sim p \supset p)$

The first equivalence, E 1, is simply the "cancelling out" of two negatives, discussed above, and E 2 and E 3 are clear enough. For any proposition A, if A is true, both $A \cdot A$ and $A \vee A$ would have two true components and be true. If A is false, they would have two false components and be false. They are therefore true or false under the same conditions that A is.

More puzzling is E 4, so much so that the medievals called one version of it the *consequentia mirabilis* or, roughly, "the astounding implication." However, it works out by truth table: If A is true, then $\sim A$ is false, making $\sim A \supset A$ true by the definition of $\supset$. If A is false, then $\sim A$ is true, making $\sim A \supset A$ an implication with a true antecedent and a false consequent and therefore false. So, surprising as it seems, $\sim A \supset A$ is true and false under the same conditions as A and is therefore equivalent to it. There is no simple expression with $\equiv$ as its main connective which is equivalent to p. For example, $p \equiv p$ is a tautology, and $p \equiv \sim p$ is a contradiction.

Very often the denial of a complex form can be understood better by looking at some equivalent form. Two interesting equivalences using $\sim p$ are

$$E \ 5 \quad \sim p \equiv (p \supset \sim p)$$

which is the negative form of the *consequentia mirabilis* mentioned above, and

$$E \ 6 \quad \sim p \equiv (p \supset (q \cdot \sim q))$$

which we will discuss later. The following equivalences illustrate the point that, with the connectors $\cdot$ and $\vee$, the *order* of the two propositions does not matter:

E 7 $(p \cdot q) \equiv (q \cdot p)$ and   E 8 $(p \vee q) \equiv (q \vee p)$

Frequently useful are the equivalences

E 9 $\sim(p \cdot q) \equiv (\sim p \vee \sim q)$ and   E 10 $\sim(p \vee q) \equiv (\sim p \cdot \sim q)$

which are sometimes called De Morgan's Rules after a logician who did not discover them but who emphasized their usefulness. If we have a negation of a conjunction or disjunction it is often useful, as we will see, to replace the negation by its equivalent according to E 9 or E 10. This is sometimes called "moving the negation sign inside the parentheses" or "demorganing" the expression.

The expressions equivalent to $p \supset q$ are more complex than those equivalent to p and $\sim p$:

$$E\ 11 \qquad (p \supset q) \equiv (\sim q \supset \sim p)$$
$$E\ 12 \qquad (p \supset q) \equiv (\sim p \lor q)$$
$$E\ 13 \qquad (p \supset q) \equiv \sim(p \cdot \sim q)$$

The expressions E 11 and E 12 represent the first equivalences we discussed in this section while E 13 shows that you can express the idea of $\supset$ by using $\sim$ and $\cdot$ as well as by $\lor$. For any two propositions A and B, A $\supset$ B is false only if A is true and B is false, and is true otherwise. But this is true of $\sim A \lor B$ and $\sim(A \cdot \sim B)$ also. Since propositions are equivalent if they are true and false under the same conditions, these forms are equivalent.

It is also useful to know a simple expression for the negation of implications:

$$E\ 14 \qquad \sim(p \supset q) \equiv (p \cdot \sim q)$$

The following equivalences show that we can get expressions that are true and false under the same conditions as $p \equiv q$ in a number of ways:

$$E\ 15 \qquad (p \equiv q) \equiv (q \equiv p)$$
$$E\ 16 \qquad (p \equiv q) \equiv ((p \supset q) \cdot (q \supset p))$$
$$E\ 17 \qquad (p \equiv q) \equiv ((p \cdot q) \lor (\sim p \cdot \sim q))$$

Another interesting fact about $\equiv$ is shown by

$$E\ 18 \qquad (p \equiv q) \equiv (\sim p \equiv \sim q)$$

Similar equivalences do *not* hold for $\cdot$ and $\lor$. Neither

$$(p \lor q) \equiv (\sim p \lor \sim q) \qquad \text{nor} \qquad (p \cdot q) \equiv (\sim p \cdot \sim q)$$

is a tautology; hence these expressions are not equivalent.

The negation of an equivalence can be formed in two ways:

$$E\ 19 \qquad \sim(p \equiv q) \equiv (\sim p \equiv q)$$
$$E\ 20 \qquad \sim(p \equiv q) \equiv (p \equiv \sim q)$$

These two equivalences

$$E\ 21 \qquad (p \cdot (q \cdot r)) \equiv ((p \cdot q) \cdot r)$$
$$E\ 22 \qquad (p \vee (q \vee r)) \equiv ((p \vee q) \vee r)$$

illustrate the point that in expressions with only *and*s or only *or*s punctuation is unimportant. A similar equivalence does *not* hold for $p \supset (q \supset r)$. Interestingly enough such an equivalence does hold for $p \equiv (q \equiv r)$, but it is not used often enough to add to our list of rules. The equivalence that does hold for $p \supset (q \supset r)$ is

$$E\ 23 \qquad (p \supset (q \supset r)) \equiv ((p \cdot q) \supset r)$$

Finally the three equivalences

$$E\ 24 \qquad (p \cdot (q \vee r)) \equiv ((p \cdot q) \vee (p \cdot r))$$
$$E\ 25 \qquad (p \vee (q \cdot r)) \equiv ((p \vee q) \cdot (p \vee r))$$
$$E\ 26 \qquad ((p \supset q) \cdot p) \equiv (p \cdot q)$$

show some useful reshuffling that is possible with such forms.

Eventually all of these equivalences should be as familiar to you as the multiplication table. It should help to remember them in logical order: first the p group, then the p . . . q group, then the p . . . q . . . r group. In each group the order of operators is $\sim$; $\cdot$; $\vee$; $\supset$; $\equiv$; then mixtures of operators.

The negations are parallel to the nonnegative equivalences. All the equivalences are presented in Table 1.2. Many of the equivalences have traditional names, which are given for future reference, together with convenient abbreviations.

Notice that there are only 18 names for equivalences, since some similar ones are grouped under the same name. The word *material* in such names as "Definition of Material Implication" or "Definition of Material Equivalence" warns us that there are other sorts of implication and equivalence, some of which we will consider later.

TABLE 1.2

Equivalences

Name	Symbolization
E 1 Double Negation (DN)	$p \equiv \sim\sim p$
E 2 Repetition (Rep)	$p \equiv (p \cdot p)$
E 3 Repetition (Rep)	$p \equiv (p \vee p)$
E 4 Consequentia Mirabilis (CM)	$p \equiv (\sim p \supset p)$
E 5 Negative Consequentia Mirabilis (NCM)	$\sim p \equiv (p \supset \sim p)$
E 6 Reductio (Red)	$\sim p \equiv (p \supset (q \cdot \sim q))$
E 7 Commutation (Com)	$(p \cdot q) \equiv (q \cdot p)$
E 8 Commutation (Com)	$(p \vee q) \equiv (q \vee p)$
E 9 De Morgan's Rules (DeM)	$\sim(p \cdot q) \equiv (\sim p \vee \sim q)$
E 10 De Morgan's Rules (DeM)	$\sim(p \vee q) \equiv (\sim p \cdot \sim q)$
E 11 Transposition (Transp)	$(p \supset q) \equiv (\sim q \supset \sim p)$
E 12 Definition of Material Implication (DMI)	$(p \supset q) \equiv (\sim p \vee q)$
E 13 Definition of Material Implication (DMI)	$(p \supset q) \equiv \sim(p \cdot \sim q)$
E 14 Negation of Material Implication (NMI)	$\sim(p \supset q) \equiv (p \cdot \sim q)$
E 15 Commutation (Com)	$(p \equiv q) \equiv (q \equiv p)$
E 16 Definition of Material Equivalence (DME)	$(p \equiv q) \equiv ((p \supset q) \cdot (q \supset p))$
E 17 Definition of Material Equivalence (DME)	$(p \equiv q) \equiv ((p \cdot q) \vee (\sim p \cdot \sim q))$
E 18 Complimentarity (Comp)	$(p \equiv q) \equiv (\sim p \equiv \sim q)$
E 19 Negation of Material Equivalence (NME)	$\sim(p \equiv q) \equiv (\sim p \equiv q)$
E 20 Negation of Material Equivalence (NME)	$\sim(p \equiv q) \equiv (p \equiv \sim q)$
E 21 Association (Assoc)	$(p \cdot (q \cdot r)) \equiv ((p \cdot q) \cdot r)$
E 22 Association (Assoc)	$(p \vee (q \vee r)) \equiv ((p \vee q) \vee r)$
E 23 Exportation (Exp)	$(p \supset (q \supset r)) \equiv ((p \cdot q) \supset r)$
E 24 Distribution (Dist)	$(p \cdot (q \vee r)) \equiv ((p \cdot q) \vee (p \cdot r))$
E 25 Distribution (Dist)	$(p \vee (q \cdot r)) \equiv ((p \vee q) \cdot (p \vee r))$
E 26 Absorption (Abs)	$((p \supset q) \cdot p) \equiv (p \cdot q)$

The use of equivalence for simplification can be illustrated in several ways. For example, the simplest form of tautology is $p \vee \sim p$, and any tautology, no matter how complicated, is equivalent to it. Similarly the simplest form of contradiction is $p \cdot \sim p$, and any contradiction form is equivalent to it. (Note: It may help you to know that no form can be either a tautology or a contradiction unless it has at least one repeated variable.) Many complex contingents are reducible to simple forms such as

$$p \cdot q \qquad p \vee q \qquad (p \supset q) \cdot r$$

This may sometimes help to make a complex, confusing piece of discourse much simpler and easier to understand. However, the details of the techniques are fairly complex for simplifying expressions by replacing them with simple equivalents, and these details are of little use in most philosophical contexts. Therefore they are not discussed here but in Appendix A at the back of the book.

If the equivalence of two forms is a tautology, then we may always replace either form with the other, for doing so will always give us a form true and false under the same conditions as the replaced form. It follows from this that we may always replace a proposition with an equivalent proposition, since this replacement will always result in the same truth value, no matter what the truth value of the component propositions. Equivalents, thus, allow *substitution*, and in fact we can state a general rule, the *Replacement Rule*: Any proposition or part of a compound proposition may be replaced by a logically equivalent proposition.

EXERCISES 1.3

A. Determine by truth tables whether the following propositional forms are equivalent:
1. $p \cdot q$ and $\sim(\sim p \vee \sim q)$
2. $p \vee q$ and $(\sim p \supset \sim q)$
3. $p \supset q$ and $\sim(\sim q \cdot (p \vee p))$
4. $p \equiv q$ and $(p \cdot q) \vee (\sim p \cdot q)$
5. $p \cdot \sim q$ and $\sim(p \supset q)$
6. $\sim p \vee (q \cdot r)$ and $p \cdot (q \equiv r)$
7. $(p \cdot (q \vee r)) \vee (r \cdot (q \cdot \sim p))$ and $(p \vee (q \equiv r)) \cdot (r \vee (q \vee \sim p))$
8. $(p \cdot (q \vee r)) \vee (r \cdot (q \cdot \sim p))$ and $((p \cdot q) \vee (p \cdot r)) \vee ((r \cdot \sim p) \cdot q)$
9. $(\sim p \cdot (q \equiv r)) \vee ((\sim r \cdot \sim q) \cdot p)$ and $((\sim q \equiv \sim r) \cdot \sim p) \vee (p \cdot \sim(r \vee q))$
10. $(\sim p \cdot (q \equiv r)) \vee ((\sim r \cdot \sim q) \cdot p)$ and $(\sim p \cdot (\sim q \vee \sim r)) \vee (\sim r \cdot (\sim q \cdot p))$

B. Translate the following pairs of statements into compound propositions, giving your own dictionary and using propositional connectives. Then test by truth table to see if they are equivalent.
1a. If Alice says a thing, she means it.
  b. If Alice means a thing, she says it.
2a. The Hatter and either the Dormouse or the Hare had tea with milk.
  b. The Hatter and the Dormouse had tea with milk and so did the Hare.
3a. Either the Hatter and the Dormouse had jam or the Hatter and the Hare had jam.
  b. The Hatter had jam and either the Hare or the Dormouse had jam.
4a. It is not true that if you eat treacle you will be ill.
  b. You eat only treacle, and you will not be ill.

5a. If you can draw water from a water well, then, if you live in a treacle well, you can draw treacle.

b. If you live in a treacle well and can draw water from a water well, then you can draw treacle from a treacle well.

C. Translate the following pairs of statements into symbolism giving your own dictionary, and test for equivalence by truth table. (Source: Plato, *Laws.*)

1a. If a man intentionally does an unholy act, either he disbelieves in the existence of the gods or else he believes that they will not punish evildoing.

b. If a man believes in the existence of the gods and believes that they punish evildoing, then he will not intentionally do an unholy act.

2a. If the gods exist, they will punish evildoing only if they are just.

b. The gods will punish evildoing unless they are nonexistent or unjust.

3a. If the gods exist, then it will be possible to prove their existence by reasonable arguments.

b. Either the existence of the gods can be proved by reasonable arguments or the gods do not exist.

4.a If a thing is changed by something else, it cannot be the beginning of change.

b. If a thing is the beginning of change, it cannot be changed by something else.

5a. If all things were at rest and nothing was able to move itself, then motion would not begin.

b. If motion begins, all things were at rest but something was able to move itself.

6a. If something has life, it has a soul, and, if it has a soul, it is self-moving.

b. If something is self-moving, it has a soul, and, if it has a soul, it has life.

7a. A thing is a soul if and only if it is self-moving.

b. A thing is not a soul if and only if it is not self-moving.

8a. If soul is what is self-moving and what is self-moving is the origin of change, then soul is the origin of change.

b. It cannot be true both that soul is not the origin of change and also that soul is what is self-moving and that what is self-moving is the origin of change.

9a. If soul is the origin of all change, then it is the origin of good and evil.

b. If soul is not the origin of good, then it is not the origin of all change.

10a. Either one soul is the origin of both good and evil, or one soul is the origin of good, another of evil.

b. If one soul is not the origin of both good and evil, then one soul is the origin of good, another of evil.

1.4 IMPLICATIONS

When we come to cases where the logical form of the implication of one proposition by another is a tautology, we come to the heart of propositional logic—the reason it is worth study by philosophers. For the logical form of an implication can be a tautology only if in all cases where the antecedent is true the consequent is also true. Thus if we have an implication and know that its logical form is a tautology and know also that its antecedent is true, then we know that its consequent is also true.

Now we can know which implications are tautologies by purely mechanical means—by drawing up truth tables. Thus if we gain factual information showing that the truth of the antecedent of an implication whose form is a tautology, then we can be sure that the consequent of that implication is factually true also.

Valid Arguments

To put it in another way, the technique of testing an implication to see if its form is a tautology gives us a supply of valid arguments. A valid argument is one which cannot have true premises and a false conclusion. This is just what is guaranteed by the fact that the implication is a tautology: when its antecedent consists of the premises of the argument and its consequent is the conclusion of the argument.

Valid arguments are important because they enable us to use the information which we have to gain new information. If we fail to draw correct inferences from the information we have, we are forced to go to additional work to get information which we already have in implicit form.

Just as we had the Replacement Rule for equivalences which are tautologies, we can now give the following *Inference Rule*: If an argument is written as an implication, so that the premises joined by the symbol · are the antecedent and the conclusion is the consequent and the resulting implication is a tautology, then the argument is *valid* (that is, if its premises are true then its conclusion must be true). Thus, when we are justified in asserting the premises of a valid argument we are justified in asserting the conclusion.

The simplest and most common form which is a tautology when written as an implication is the form*

$$p \supset q$$
$$\underline{p}$$
$$q$$

That is, if we know the truth of a conditional statement and also that its antecedent is true, then we know that its consequent is true. We construct the implication form of this argument by joining the premises $(p \supset q)$ and p by the symbol · and making this expression the antecedent of a conditional with the q as the consequent. Of course, we add appropriate punctuation to avoid ambiguity, giving us first

$$(p \supset q) \cdot p \quad \text{and finally} \quad ((p \supset q) \cdot p) \supset q$$

---

* Note that the rule separates premises from conclusion and suggests that the premises add up to the conclusion as in the form 2

$$\frac{2}{4}$$

It may be worthwhile to look at a detailed truth table for this form (Truth Table 1.14). Notice that there is no line in which we have a T for both of the

TRUTH TABLE 1.14

	p	q	$((p \supset q) \cdot p) \supset q$
1	T	T	T T T T T T
2	T	F	T F F F T T F
3	F	T	F T T F F T T
4	F	F	F T F F F T F
			√ √ √ √ √ √

premises and an F for the conclusion. Where we have a T for both premises we have a T for the conclusion, and where we have an F for the conclusion we have an F for one premise or both. Thus the inference is valid, for we have looked at all cases and found none where the premises could be true and the conclusion false.

Modus Ponens

Most common forms of inference (and this is a very common one) have traditional names. The name of this one is *modus ponens*, and it is so simple an argument form, that it is often not spelled out in philosophical arguments. Here is a somewhat simplified example of *modus ponens* from Plato's dialogue *Meno* which will illustrate several points.

> *Socrates:* We have admitted that a thing cannot be taught of which there are no teachers?
> *Meno:* We have.
> *S.:* And there are no teachers of virtue to be found anywhere?
> *M.:* There are not.
> *S.:* Then virtue cannot be taught?
> *M.:* Not if we are right in our view.

Notice that Socrates puts one of his points in a general form: "*a thing* cannot be taught. . . ." In due course we will be able to analyze this sort of case more fully. For present purposes we can regard his argument as:

> If there are no teachers of virtue, then virtue cannot be taught.
> There are no teachers of virtue. Therefore virtue cannot be taught.

This is an example of *modus ponens*. Notice that both the antecedent and the consequent are negative. This does not alter the fact that this is an example of *modus ponens*. If we give the dictionary

T # There are teachers of virtue   V # Virtue can be taught then the argument can be symbolized

$$(\sim T \supset \sim V)$$
$$\underline{\sim T}$$
$$\sim V$$

If we remember that the variables are like boxes which can be filled with any proposition, compound or simple, negated or not, then we can visualize the argument as shown in Argument 1.1. In fact, Socrates' argument is more

ARGUMENT 1.1

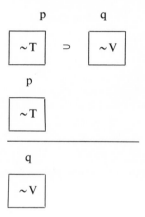

complex than we have noted. He mentions learners as well as teachers of virtue, and his argument is more nearly expressed as

> If there are no teachers and no learners of virtue, then virtue cannot be
>   taught.
> There are no teachers and no learners of virtue.
> Therefore virtue cannot be taught.

If we add to our dictionary

$$L \ \# \ \text{There are learners of virtue}$$

then the argument is

$$(\sim T \cdot \sim L) \supset \sim V$$
$$\underline{\sim T \cdot \sim L}$$
$$\sim V$$

But this is still *modus ponens* since even compound propositions can be "put in the box," that is, substituted for variables (Argument 1.2).

ARGUMENT 1.2

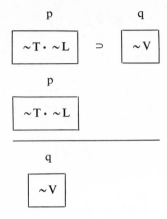

Modus Tollens

Another implication which can be shown by truth table to be a tautology is

$$((p \supset q) \cdot \sim q) \supset \sim p$$

The traditional name of this implication is *modus tollens*. Written in the other way it is

$$\frac{\begin{array}{l} p \supset q \\ \sim q \end{array}}{\sim p}$$

An example of *modus tollens* is the following excerpt from Plato's *Parmenides*: "*Socrates*: Zeno, you say that if things are a plurality they must be both like and unlike. But that is impossible. . . . And so . . . it is also impossible that things should be a plurality." Let

P ＃ Things are a plurality
L ＃ Things are both like and unlike

Then the argument is

$$\frac{\begin{array}{l} P \supset L \\ \sim L \end{array}}{\sim P}$$

if we regard "it is impossible" as simply a strong denial, and this is an instance of *modus tollens*.

Actually *modus tollens* could be eliminated as an independent argument form. Instead of writing the argument in the way we did, we could substitute

$$\sim L \supset \sim P \qquad \text{for} \qquad P \supset L$$

giving as our justification the equivalence

$$(p \supset q) \equiv (\sim q \supset \sim p)$$

(Transposition) and the Replacement Rule. Then the form would be

$$\frac{\begin{array}{c} \sim L \supset \sim P \\ \sim L \end{array}}{\sim P}$$

which is *modus ponens*. This can always be done, so, in a way, we don't need *modus tollens*. However, it is convenient to retain it in order to avoid the extra steps involved in using Transposition and the Replacement Rule.

Disjunctive Syllogism

Another theoretically replaceable but practically useful variant of *modus ponens* is the form

$$\frac{\begin{array}{c} p \vee q \\ \sim p \end{array}}{q}$$

which written as an implication is $((p \vee q) \cdot \sim p) \supset q$.

Its traditional name is *Disjunctive Syllogism*. A moderately complicated example of it occurs in the *Meno*. Socrates has shown to Meno's satisfaction that a slave boy has knowledge of certain principles of geometry. Socrates then gets Meno to grant that either the boy learned these principles at some time since his birth or else he has a knowledge which was not acquired during his lifetime. Since Meno is in a position to know that the boy has never, since birth, had any opportunity to learn geometrical principles, he is forced to admit that the boy has knowledge not acquired in this life. Let

L # The boy's knowledge was acquired during his lifetime
N # The boy has knowledge not acquired in this life

The argument can then be symbolized as an instance of Disjunctive Syllogism:

$$\frac{\begin{array}{l} L \vee N \\ \sim L \end{array}}{N}$$

However, by using the Replacement Rule, Double Negation, and the Definition of Material Implication we could replace L in L ∨ N by ∼ ∼ L using Double Negation. Then we replace ∼ ∼ L ∨ N by ∼ L ⊃ N, using Definition of Material Implication. The form would then again be *modus ponens*:

$$\frac{\begin{array}{l} \sim L \supset N \\ \sim L \end{array}}{N}$$

Hypothetical Syllogism

Another traditionally recognized pattern of argument is the *Hypothetical Syllogism*:

$$\frac{\begin{array}{l} p \supset q \\ q \supset r \end{array}}{p \supset r}$$

Written as an implication it is

$$((p \supset q) \cdot (q \supset r)) \supset (p \supset r)$$

It occurs fairly often in philosophical contexts, either alone or in connection with other arguments. To return to the *Meno*, at one point Meno states as his opinion that some men desire evil. Socrates gives an argument which can be reconstructed as follows:

If a man desires evil, he desires what is hurtful to its possessor.
If he desires what is hurtful to its possessor, he desires what brings misery to himself.
(Therefore) If a man desires evil, he desires what brings misery to himself.

Let

E # A man desires evil
H # A man desires what is hurtful to its possessor
M # A man desires what brings misery to himself

When the argument is symbolized, it gives an instance of Hypothetical Syllogism:

$$E \supset H$$
$$H \supset M$$
$$\overline{E \supset M}$$

Socrates then gets Meno to agree that man does not desire what brings misery to himself so that Meno retracts his original opinion that some men desire evil. This is, of course, *modus tollens*:

$$E \supset M$$
$$\sim M$$
$$\overline{\sim E}$$

In fact, the combination of Hypothetical Syllogism and *modus tollens* is rather frequent in philosophy: Starting from an assumption, a philosopher tries to show that the assumption leads by a series of implications to a false conclusion, and therefore the assumption is false.

Constructive and Destructive Dilemmas

Two related argument forms which we will consider together are called respectively *Constructive Dilemma* and *Destructive Dilemma*. Writing them side by side shows their similarities and dissimilarities:

C.D.		D.D.	
	$p \supset q$		$p \supset q$
	$r \supset s$		$r \supset s$
	$\underline{p \ \lor \ s}$		$\underline{\sim q \lor \sim s}$
	$q \ \lor \ s$		$\sim p \lor \sim r$

The two dilemmas have obvious similarities to *modus ponens* and *modus tollens*. If we knew that the proposition substituted for p was true or that the proposition substituted for r was true or that both were, Constructive Dilemma would simply be one or more instances of *modus ponens*. However, since we don't know whether the propositions substituted for p or r or both are true, we can say only that either the propositions substituted for q or s or both are true. Similar remarks apply to Destructive Dilemma and *modus tollens*. Just as *modus tollens* could be reduced to *modus ponens* by using Transposition and the Replacement Rule, so any instance of Destructive Dilemma could be reduced to Constructive Dilemma by using Transposition on both implications.

Written as an implication, Constructive Dilemma is

$$(((p \supset q) \cdot (r \supset s)) \cdot (p \lor r)) \supset (q \lor s)$$

and Destructive Dilemma is

$$(((p \supset q) \cdot (r \supset s)) \cdot (\sim q \lor \sim s)) \supset (\sim p \lor \sim r)$$

Checking them out requires a truth table for four variables, which has 2^4 or 16 lines.

Dilemma arguments are fairly common in philosophy. The following dilemma occurs as part of a more complex argument in the *Parmenides*. Zeno poses the following dilemma to Socrates, as being against the theory of Forms:

Either things receive the whole Form or things receive parts of Forms.

If things receive the whole Form, the Form will be separated from itself (by existing at different times and places). If things receive parts of Forms, the Form is divided.

Since a believer in the theory of Forms presumably must take one of the two alternatives presented (that things receive Forms wholly or partially) he seems to be faced with the embarrassing consequence that the Forms are either divided or separated from themselves, which Socrates does not wish to admit.

EXERCISES 1.4

A. Prove the validity or invalidity of the following arguments by truth table.

1. $\sim B \supset \sim A$

    $\underline{A}$

    B

2. $B \equiv \sim A$

    $\underline{\sim A}$

    B

3. $\sim (A \cdot B)$

    $\underline{A}$

    $\sim B$

4. $\sim B \supset \sim A$

    $B \equiv \sim C$

    $\underline{A}$

    $\sim C$

5. $\sim A \lor B$

    $B \equiv C$

    $\underline{A}$

    $\sim C$

6. $\sim (A \equiv B)$

    $\underline{\sim C \supset \sim B}$

    $\sim A \supset C$

7. $\sim A \lor B$

    $C \supset D$

    $\underline{A \supset C}$

    $\sim B \supset D$

8. $A \supset B$

    $B \equiv C$

    $\underline{\sim C \lor D}$

    $\sim D \supset \sim A$

9. $((A \lor B) \lor C) \supset D$

    $\underline{B}$

    D

10. $A \equiv B$
     $C \equiv D$
     $\underline{\sim(\sim A \cdot \sim C)}$
     $B \vee D$

B. Translate the following arguments into symbolism, giving your own dictionary, and test for validity by truth table.
1. The players will not be executed if the king pardons them, and he did pardon them, so they will not be executed.
2. If the Mock Turtle doesn't begin, he can't finish. He did finish, so he must have begun.
3. If the hedgehogs walk away, then Alice chases them, and, if she chases them, the flamingo uncurls. So, if the flamingo uncurls, the hedgehog has walked away.
4. Either the Queen won or someone was beheaded. Since the Queen did not win, someone was beheaded.
5. The Queen and Alice cannot both win. Since the Queen didn't win, Alice did.

C. Symbolize, giving a dictionary, and test for validity by truth table. (Source: Plato, *Euthyphro, Apology.*)
1. If piety were what is pleasing to the gods, then a certain action would be both pious and impious. Therefore, it is not true that piety is what is pleasing to the gods.
2. If the gods love courage, it is pious. Therefore, if courage is pious, then the gods love it.
3. If the gods love courage, it is pious, and, if courage is pious, then the gods love it. Therefore, the gods do not love courage if and only if it is not pious.
4. If Euthyphro is pious, he is just. If he is just, he is pleasing to the gods. Therefore, if he is pleasing to the gods, he is pious.
5. If the service which we pay to the gods is like the service the trainer pays to his horses, then we will improve and benefit the gods by our service. But, if we improve or benefit the gods by our service, the gods stand in need of us and depend on us. However, the gods do not stand in need of us. Therefore, the service we pay to the gods is not like that the trainer pays to his horses.
6. If our services to the gods are like those services a slave does for his master, the gods profit in some way from our services. If they profit from our services, they owe us something. But our services to the gods are not like those a slave does for his master. Therefore, the gods owe us nothing.
7. If our worship of the gods is like a business transaction, then we must gain something and so must the gods. But, if the gods gain something, they are benefited by us. But we cannot benefit the gods. Therefore, our worship is not like a business transaction.
8. If Socrates were like the philosophers described by the comic poets, he would speculate about the heavens and try to make the weaker case appear

stronger. But Socrates neither speculates about the heavens nor tries to make the weaker case stronger. Therefore, he is not like the philosophers described by the comic poets.

9. If prejudices have risen against Socrates and he has not been doing what the comic poets describe, then he must have been doing something out of the ordinary. But he has not been doing what the comic poets describe. Therefore, he must have been doing something out of the ordinary.

10. If no one is wiser than Socrates, then Socrates must be very wise or others must not be as wise as they appear. But Socrates is not very wise. Therefore, others must not be as wise as they appear.

1.5 PHILOSOPHICAL DIFFICULTIES

Elementary logic bristles with philosophical difficulties—so many that we will save some problems for later chapters which might well have been raised in this first chapter. One source of many philosophical difficulties is the concept of truth. The words *true* and *false* were used without explanation in the earlier parts of this chapter as if we understood well enough what we were talking about when we talked about truth and falsity—and so we do for many purposes.

To give a philosophical account of truth and falsity, however, is not at all easy. We can do no more here than mention some of the main theories. References for further reading are given at the end of this section. Three important theories about the nature of truth are the coherence theory, the verification theory, and the correspondence theory.

The *coherence theory* says that a proposition is true if it is consistent with other propositions which we hold or are prepared to assert. This theory is perhaps suggested by mathematics and is most plausible as an account of mathematical truth. Its most serious difficulty is the apparent possibility of holding a system of propositions which are consistent with one another but unrelated to reality. The coherence theory thus appears to underrate in questions of truth the importance of "the world" or reality.

The *verification theory* and the closely related *pragmatic theory* of truth say that for a statement to be true it must be provable. Certainly any proposition which can be proved to be true is true, but can all propositions which are true be proved to be true? We can think of many statements which would seem to be obviously either true or false but which cannot in practice be proved to be one or the other. For example, it would be a rare person who could decide the truth or falsity of: "The seventeenth sentence I spoke after waking up, a week ago today, contained the word *and*." This forces us to introduce the idea of provability in principle, which has many accompanying problems.

The *correspondence theory* says that a proposition is true if it agrees with, or corresponds with, reality or "the way things are." It has some claim to be the commonsensical theory of truth, but it is full of difficulties. What precisely do we mean by "agrees" or "corresponds with"? What is it exactly that the true proposition "I have a handkerchief in my pocket" corresponds with? If that seems to be answerable, with what does the true proposition "I don't have a picture of my mother in my pocket" correspond?

The Truth-Value Condition

Insofar as possible, we have tried not to favor any particular theory of truth in our uses of words like true or false in this book. However, in Section 1.1 we laid down a condition which limits the applicability of propositional logic, which can be restated as follows:

Condition 1. A simple proposition must have a determinable truth value; that is, it must be definitely true or definitely false.

As we pointed out at the time, this means that propositional logic is unable to deal with expressions whose truth or falsity cannot definitely be determined.* Propositional logic does not require that truth or falsity be determined in any special way, for example, by coherence with other statements, correspondence with reality, verification by sense experience. Propositional logic does require that a clear decision can be made about which expressions are true and which are false.

Notice also that, except in the case of tautology forms and contradiction forms (which are true and false respectively no matter what propositions we substitute for the variables), propositional logic itself gives us no information about the truth or falsity of propositions. Once we determine from some source outside of propositional logic that certain propositions are true or false, we can use this information to determine the truth or falsity of compound propositions or of propositions equivalent to or implied by the original propositions. Unless we have some propositions of known truth value as starting points, however, we cannot determine the truth or falsity of any proposition except compound propositions which have tautology or contradiction forms. Thus propositional logic is in a sense incomplete or, if you like, parasitic; propositional logic is of no use to us unless we know something besides propositional logic.

Propositional logic is parasitic or incomplete in another sense, too. The propositions which we symbolize and work with are all borrowed from natural languages or in some cases from a technical language such as that of mathematics. Thus propositional logic as we have developed it is not a language which could exist independently of any other language (as, for

---

* Some philosophers have discussed the possibility of a logic with values other than truth and falsity. These many-valued logics are discussed briefly in Appendix D.

example, English could). To call propositional logic a language at all is seriously misleading. The joke "Speak some logic" or "Say something in logic" has a serious point; there is nothing which we can say using only symbols proper to propositional logic. For example, even the tautology $p \vee \sim p$ is not itself a proposition, only the form of a proposition.

Another problem related to truth and falsity is this: We said in Section 1.1 that we could deny the proposition "Alice is falling" either by saying "It is false that Alice is falling" or by saying "Alice is not falling." There are difficulties about this. If I say "Alice is falling" I am talking about Alice and saying of her that she is falling. But if I say "'Alice is falling' is true" or "It is true that Alice is falling" I *seem* at any rate to be saying something somewhat different. I seem to be talking about the proposition "Alice is falling." and saying of it that it is true. This has the same truth value as "Alice is falling," but does it have the same meaning? Similarly, "Alice is not falling" seems to be about Alice. On the other hand "'Alice is falling' is false" or "It is false that Alice is falling" seems to be about a proposition. There seem, in fact, to be subtle differences in meaning between "Alice is not falling" and "It is false that Alice is falling" and "It is not true that Alice is falling."

Because of the complexities involved in these differences of meaning, most logic books use some phrase such as "it is not the case that" to indicate negation or denial. This practice has not been followed in this book for two reasons.

1. Hardly anyone outside of logic books ever uses the rather archaic and formal phrase "it is not the case that . . ." to indicate denial. If a phrase of this kind is used at all, "it is false that . . ." is overwhelmingly the most popular, followed probably by "it is not true that. . . ."

2. Using "it is not the case that . . ." doesn't really avoid the difficulty. "It is not the case that . . ." is merely a rather stilted way of saying "it is false that . . ." or "it is not true that. . . ." If "It is false that Alice is falling" is about a proposition rather than about Alice, so is "It is not the case that Alice is falling."

In restricted formal systems it is possible to make a distinction between an *object language* in which one talks about a subject matter, and a *metalanguage* in which one talks about the object language. If talk about truth or falsity is talk about propositions, then "true" and "false" belong to the metalanguage, and it would be a mistake to use "it is false that," which is a metalanguage statement, as equivalent to "not-A," which is a proposition in the object language. However, in this book we are interested in using propositional logic to analyze statements and arguments in ordinary language. In natural languages such as English we talk about objects and propositions in the same language and use, for example, "It is false that Alice is asleep" and "Alice is not asleep" more or less indiscriminately to deny "Alice is asleep." Since we are interested in propositional logic as a means of symbolizing statements and arguments in natural languages and since the truth value of "it is false that A" is always the same as that of "not A," we will follow ordinary usage by regarding the two expressions as the same for most purposes.

Another philosophical problem is that which has been masked by the use of the word "proposition." This is the problem of what it is that is said to be true or false, what is the "carrier" of truth or falsity. Sentences—words put together to express a completed assertion—are one possible candidate, but this solution raises major difficulties, for the same sentence can be used at one time and be true and at another time and be false. "The President of the United States was born in Texas" was false in 1946, true in 1966. Utterances, sentences spoken or written on a given occasion, are another promising candidate. But several utterances may seemingly express the same truth, for example, "My son is sick" or "My patient is ill" or "I am ill," as said on the same occasion by Jones' mother, Jones' doctor, and Jones.

It has thus seemed to some philosophers that something other than sentences or utterances of sentences was needed as the vehicle of truth or falsity. Various accounts have been given of this entity, and various names have been given to it, including the name proposition. However, the term proposition as we use it in this book can be taken to mean *whatever* it is that is true or false, leaving to further philosophical discussion to determine what it is that is the carrier of truth or falsity—whether sentences, utterances, meanings of sentences, uses of sentences, or whatever it may be.

Again, this avoidance of the issue fails to solve all of our problems. If we look at the way that language is ordinarily used, we find that it is in many cases impossible to determine the truth or even the full meaning of a proposition without knowing something of the context in which it was uttered.

The Independence Condition

However, propositional logic owes its present form to mathematically oriented logicians, and context is relatively unimportant to the truth or meaning of mathematical expressions. Thus propositional logic is founded on the basically somewhat unrealistic supposition that propositions can be taken as separate units and their truth or falsity determined in isolation. This produces the second important limitations on the applicability of propositional logic, which can be stated as:

Condition 2. The meaning and truth value of a simple proposition must be determinable without reference to context, background, etc.

We will call this the *independence* condition.

One thing made necessary by the independence requirement is the elimination of cross-references between propositions by means of pronouns such as he, she, or it. Thus "Alice will mind the baby or she will not mind it" must become "Alice will mind the baby or Alice will not mind the baby." (In later chapters we will examine more powerful systems of logic which permit a greater degree of cross-reference.)

The Truth Value of Compound Propositions

The final restriction on the applicability of propositional logic which we will discuss here can be expressed as follows:

Condition 3. The truth value of a compound proposition must be determinable solely from the truth values of the simple propositions of which it is composed plus the definitions of the operators.

Many operators on propositions are not truth functional in this way and thus cannot be expressed in propositional logic. Take, for example, the operators "He said . . ." and "He believes. . . ." From the truth or falsity of a given proposition, A, we cannot determine the truth or falsity of the statement that a given person said "A" or of the statement that a given person believes A. Similarly the connective ". . . because . . ." as it functions between descriptions of events is not truth-functional; for example, "Alice is wet because Alice fell into the pool of tears." Even if it is true that Alice is wet and true that she fell into the pool of tears, she may not be wet *because* she fell into the pool of tears. (For example, she might have been wet before she fell in or fallen in without getting wet and later gotten wet for some other reason.)

On the other hand, many connectives that are not truth functional have a truth-functional aspect: Their logic can be partially described in truth-functional terms. If A is true and B is not, then "A because B" would be false. Also, "A because B" in many cases means "A is true because B is true" and implies that both A and B *are* true. So a partial truth table for "because" would be as shown in Truth Table 1.15. This table suggests

TRUTH TABLE 1.15

	p	q	p because q
1	T	T	?
2	T	F	F
3	F	T	F
4	F	F	F

that, if we had to do the best we could to symbolize "A because B" with a truth-functional connective, then A · B would be the least unsatisfactory.

A good deal of the philosophical discussion of truth-functional connectives has centered on the "paradoxes of material implication." That is, on the respects in which the symbol $\supset$ is unlike many uses of "if . . . , then" in ordinary English. The main oddities concern cases in which we know the truth or falsity of some proposition and, because of this, can assert conditional statements in which that proposition appears as antecedent or consequent. If we know that a proposition A is false, then any compound proposition A $\supset$ B is true, no matter what the meaning or truth value of B. Similarly if we know that A is true, then any compound proposition B $\supset$ A is true, no matter what B is. Again for any two propositions A and B which are both known to be true or both known to be false, the compounds A $\supset$ B, B $\supset$ A, and A $\equiv$ B all hold true.

All of this seems odd or paradoxical only if we forget how little truth-functional connectives actually assert. For example, all that A $\supset$ B says is that *if* A is true then B is, so that, if we know that A is false or that B is true, we know all that is necessary to assert A $\supset$ B since, if A is known to be false, we don't have to worry about what would be the case if it were true, and, if B is known to be true, it will obviously be true if A is true.

These seeming paradoxes do emphasize the wide separation between $\supset$ and many ordinary uses of "if . . . , then," and, insofar as they do this, they are a useful reminder of the limitations of truth-functional connectives. However, truth-functional connectives have one virtue that cannot be denied: No proper use of valid inferences or equivalences based on truth-functional connectives will ever lead from true premises to a false conclusion.

Thus, as we go on to more adequate logical techniques, we leave safe ground behind us. Though many arguments which are valid in stronger systems of logic cannot be shown to be valid in propositional logic, when we have shown that an argument is valid in propositional logic, it can be relied on not to lead us from truth into falsity.

READING LIST

The following book contains a number of interesting contemporary articles on theories of truth, together with a bibliography on other contemporary discussions:

Pitcher, G.   *Truth* (Prentice-Hall, Englewood Cliffs, N.J.), 1964.

This next book discusses at length some of the difficulties of translating ordinary language into logical symbolism:

Strawson, P. F.   *Introduction to Logical Theory* (Methuen & Co., London, U.K.), 1952.

The following sections of the best modern history of logic give you some historical background on propositional logic:

Kneale, W., and Kneale, M.   *The Development of Logic* (Oxford University Press, New York), 1962, chapter 3, esp. sections 1, 3; chapter 4, esp. section 5; chapter 8, esp. section 1; chapter 9, esp. sections 1, 2, 3.

Further discussions of some points raised in this section may be found in the following books of readings in the philosophy of logic:

Jager, R.   *Essays in Logic* (Prentice-Hall, Englewood Cliffs, N.J.), 1963.

Copi, I., and Gould, J.   *Readings on Logic* (The Macmillan Company, New York), 1964.

Copi, I., and Gould, J.   *Contemporary Readings in Logical Theory* (The Macmillan Company, New York), 1967.

Chapter 2
PROOFS
AND
DISPROOFS

It is necessary to mention briefly the reasons for studying the proof techniques in this section. From the point of view of propositional logic they are unnecessary, since everything that can be decided about the validity of arguments in propositional logic can be decided by truth tables. From the point of view of philosophy they could be said also to be unnecessary, since in philosophy as opposed to mathematics, we rarely find long and complicated trains of deductive reasoning.

However, it is worthwhile studying proof techniques from both points of view. From the point of view of propositional logic, although proof techniques are not strictly necessary they are extremely convenient. To check for validity, an argument involving half a dozen statements would need a truth table of 2^6 or 64 lines, and any truth table this big is likely to be unwieldy. (It can be done by computer, but a computer is not always available.) More important, in later sections we will find ourselves unable to use truth tables though still able to use proof techniques, so that practice in doing proofs where we can check our results by truth table is valuable. From the philosophical point of view, we do find some important philosophical arguments which depend on proofs of a fair degree of complexity. Even if these are relatively infrequent, the facility in deductive reasoning developed by doing proofs can be a useful asset in philosophical investigation. It is, in fact, helpful to be able to handle arguments of a greater degree of complexity than any we expect to meet, on the principle that one can do an easier task more quickly and accurately if one is prepared to do a harder task.

2.1 DIRECT PROOFS

Argument Forms

For doing long proofs, we will need several nontraditional but convenient argument forms which can be shown by truth table to be valid. They are

$$\frac{p \cdot q}{p} \quad \text{and} \quad \frac{p \cdot q}{q}$$

which are called *Simplification*, and

$$\frac{p}{p \vee q}$$

which is called *Addition*. The first two cause no special problems. Simplification merely says that, if we know two statements to be true, we know either of them separately to be true. Addition is more puzzling—but of course it could never give us true premises and a false conclusion. If the premise is true then any disjunction with the premise as a component will be true no matter what the other disjunct is. This, as we will see, is a convenient principle.

We need also at this point one other argument form, *Conjunction*, which is difficult to state as an implication which is a tautology. Its form is

$$\frac{\begin{array}{c} p \\ q \end{array}}{p \cdot q}$$

That is, if we know two separate facts to be true, we can assert that the first *and* the second are true. Of course if A is true and B is true, A · B could never be false. When we try to write this in implication form however, we get only the rather uninformative

$$(p \cdot q) \supset (p \cdot q)$$

Notice that this is the perfectly acceptable result of taking the two premises of the argument, joining them with the symbol · and putting a ⊃ between the conjoined premises and the conclusions. But the resulting implication is uninformative rather than enlightening, whereas, for example,

$$((p \supset q) \cdot p) \supset q$$

is not similarly uninformative about the form

$$
\begin{array}{l}
p \supset q \\
\underline{p} \\
q
\end{array}
$$

All of our implications can now be laid out in either of two forms. Argument forms are shown in Table 2.1; the corresponding tautologous implications are shown in Table 2.2.

TABLE 2.1

Argument Forms

Variations of Modus Ponens

A 1 Modus Ponens (MP)

$$
\begin{array}{l}
p \supset q \\
\underline{p} \\
q
\end{array}
$$

A 2 Modus Tollens (MT)

$$
\begin{array}{l}
p \supset q \\
\underline{\sim q} \\
\sim p
\end{array}
$$

A 3 Disjunctive Syllogism (DS)

$$
\begin{array}{l}
p \lor q \\
\underline{\sim p} \\
q
\end{array}
$$

Other Conditional Arguments

A 4 Hypothetical Syllogism (HS)

$$
\begin{array}{l}
p \supset q \\
\underline{q \supset r} \\
p \supset r
\end{array}
$$

A 5 Constructive Dilemma (CD)

$$
\begin{array}{l}
p \supset q \\
r \supset s \\
\underline{p \lor r} \\
q \lor s
\end{array}
$$

A 6 Destructive Dilemma (DD)

$$
\begin{array}{l}
p \supset q \\
r \supset s \\
\underline{\sim q \lor \sim s} \\
\sim p \lor \sim r
\end{array}
$$

TABLE 2.1—*continued*

Convenient Transformations

A 7	Simplification (Simp)	$p \cdot q$	
		p	
A 8	Simplification (Simp)	$p \cdot q$	
		q	
A 9	Addition (Add)	p	
		$p \vee q$	
A 10	Conjunction (Conj)	p	
		q	
		$p \cdot q$	

TABLE 2.2

Tautologous Implications

A 1 $((p \supset q) \cdot p) \supset q$
A 2 $((p \supset q) \cdot \sim q) \supset \sim p$
A 3 $((p \vee q) \cdot \sim p) \supset q$
A 4 $((p \supset q) \cdot (q \supset r)) \supset (p \supset r)$
A 5 $(((p \supset q) \cdot (r \supset s)) \cdot (p \vee r)) \supset (q \vee s)$
A 6 $(((p \supset q) \cdot (r \supset s)) \cdot (\sim q \vee \sim s)) \supset (\sim p \vee \sim r)$
A 7 $(p \cdot q) \supset p$
A 8 $(p \cdot q) \supset q$
A 9 $p \supset (p \vee q)$
A 10 $((p) \cdot (q)) \supset (p \cdot q)$*

Replacement and Inference Rules

This set of argument forms (Tables 2.1 and 2.2) together with the equivalences given earlier, the Replacement Rule, and the Inference Rule, will enable us to establish the validity of any argument which can be shown to be valid by truth tables. To do this, we proceed systematically in the following way: we write down the premises of the argument in symbolic form, numbering each one. To the right of the premises we write the conclusion to be proved. We then proceed to build a bridge between premises and conclusion, using our argument forms, equivalences, and rules. We number each line, and,

* It may help to emphasize with punctuation that "p" and "q" in A10 are originally separate.

when we get a line which is the same as the desired conclusion, we have completed a *Direct Proof* of the conclusion.

We must now restate the Replacement Rule and Inference Rule more carefully. As applied to proofs they will read as follows:

Replacement Rule (RR): If we have a proof in which a proposition A occurs as a line or part of a line, we may write a proposition B as a line or part of a line which is otherwise the same as the line in which A occurs provided that the logical form of the equivalence A ≡ B is one of the equivalences listed in Section 1.3 (or in subsequent lists of logical equivalences). The new line will be justified by citing the number of the line in which A occurs, the name of the equivalence, and RR.

Inference Rule (IR): If we have a proof in which A (or A and B or A and B and C) are lines, then we may write a proposition, D, as a line provided that the logical form of A ⊃ D (or of (A · B)) ⊃ D or of ((A · B) · C) ⊃ D) is one of the tautologous implications listed in Section 2.1 (or in subsequent lists of logical implications). The justification of the new line will consist of the number(s) of the line(s) A or A and B or A and B and C, the name of the implication, and IR.

For example, consider the following argument, which occurs in the *Parmenides*.

If things participate in Forms, then either the whole Form is received, or part of the Form is received.
If part of the Form is received, then the Form is divided.
If the whole Form is received, then the Form is separated from itself (by existing at different times and places).
Forms can neither be divided nor separated from themselves.
Therefore things do not participate in Forms.

Let   F # Things participate in Forms
                  P # Part of the Form is received
                  W # The Whole Form is received
                  D # The Form is Divided
                  S # The form is Separated from itself

Then the premises are as given in 1–4 below and the conclusion is ∼F.*

$$
\left.
\begin{array}{ll}
1 & F \supset (W \lor P) \\
2 & P \supset D \\
3 & W \supset S \\
4 & \sim(D \lor S)
\end{array}
\right\} \sim F
$$

---

* Note the brace which ties together the premises and points to the conclusion. We will use this form in the future for proofs.

We first use De Morgan's rules to put premise 4 in a more convenient form, writing

$$5 \qquad \sim D \cdot \sim S$$

We show our justification for this line by citing the previous line used, the equivalence used, and the fact that the Replacement Rule is used. We do this in shorthand:

$$5 \qquad \sim D \cdot \sim S \qquad 4, \text{DeM, RR}$$

We then detach the two components of line 5, using Simplification and the Implication Rule:

$$6 \qquad \sim D \qquad 5, \text{Simp, IR}$$
$$7 \qquad \sim S \qquad 5, \text{Simp, IR}$$

We then use *modus tollens* twice:

$$8 \qquad \sim W \qquad 7, 3, \text{MT, IR}$$
$$9 \qquad \sim P \qquad 6, 2, \text{MT, IR}$$

Since *modus tollens* needs two premises, we must cite two lines. We then use Conjunction to put lines 8 and 9 together

$$10 \qquad \sim W \cdot \sim P \qquad 8, 9, \text{Conj, IR}$$

and use De Morgan's Rules in the opposite direction

$$11 \qquad \sim (W \vee P) \qquad 10, \text{DeM, RR}$$

and finally *modus tollens* again:

$$12 \qquad \sim F \qquad 11, 1, \text{MT, IR} \qquad \text{Q.E.D.}$$

The abbreviation Q.E.D., *quod erat demonstrandum* or "what was to be demonstrated," is a traditional end to proofs of this kind. It is a convenient, though not strictly necessary, way of indicating that we have reached the conclusion of a proof.

Contradictions

Interestingly enough, given the proof techniques we have so far, it is possible to show that, if we start from a contradiction or from self-contradictory premises, we can prove any arbitrary statement at all. Suppose, for example, we started from the contradiction A · ~A and wished to prove some arbitrary and quite unrelated statement, B. The proof would go like this:

1	A · ~A }	B	
2	A	1, Simp, IR	
3	A v B	2, Add, IR	
4	~A	1, Simp, IR	
5	B	3, 4, DS, IR	Q.E.D.

This emphasizes the importance of not admitting any inconsistencies into a logical argument since, if we can prove a contradiction, we can prove anything whatsoever, as we have just seen.

Some further worked-out proofs will be found in the answers to the even-numbered problems after this section. There is no way to lay down mechanical rules for doing proofs of the kind we are doing in this section. Proofs in propositional logic are simple enough so that some rather complicated automatic proof techniques, involving a different sort of rules from those that we are using, can, in fact, be given. Such techniques are not available for some of the interesting kinds of logical systems we will study later, however, and one object of doing proofs in propositional logic is to gain experience in doing proofs which will be useful later. Some rules of thumb which may help you until you have more experience with proofs can be given.

1. Look for premises with one or more letters in common and see if these imply some statement which will be useful in proving your conclusion.

2. If nothing can be done with the premises as they are, see if some of them would be more useful if replaced by equivalent expressions.

3. It is often useful to work backwards from the conclusion; for instance, in the above example from the *Parmenides* you might reason; "If I had ~(W v P), I could prove ~F. If I had ~D, I could prove ~P, and if I had ~S, I could prove ~W. Then join ~P and ~W to make ~W · ~P, which is equivalent to ~(W v P). I can get ~D · ~S from ~(D v S) by De Morgan's Rules. So there I am."

However, useful as such rules of thumb are, only experience, trial, and plenty of error, learning from mistakes, will enable you to finally master the art of constructing proofs.

EXERCISES 2.1

A. Provide direct proofs for the indicated conclusions.

1. C ⊃ (N v A)
   N ⊃ S
   A ⊃ S   } ~C
   S ⊃ ~D
   D

2. D ⊃ (R v L)
   ~R   } ~D
   ~L

3. $L \supset (I \supset D)$
   $\sim D$
   L $\Big\}$ $\sim I$

4. $L \supset (\sim D \supset \sim I)$
   $\sim D$ $\Big\}$ $\sim I \vee \sim L$

5. $\sim S \supset \sim R$
   $S \supset M$
   $\sim M$ $\Big\}$ $\sim R$

6. $L \supset (D \supset E)$
   $\sim E$ $\Big\}$ $\sim L \vee \sim D$

7. $D \supset (R \vee L)$
   $\sim R$
   $\sim L \vee \sim D$ $\Big\}$ $\sim D$

8. $C \supset V$
   $N \supset \sim V$ $\Big\}$ $N \supset \sim C$

9. $N \supset \sim C$
   $D \supset N$ $\Big\}$ $D \supset (\sim C \vee B)$

10. $\sim P \supset \sim R$
    $P \supset S$
    $\sim S$ $\Big\}$ $\sim R$

B. Using the following dictionary,

A # Alice has reached the last square   C # Alice was crowned queen
B # Alice was bound for the last square   D # Alice met Humpty Dumpty

symbolize and provide direct proofs for the following:

1. If Alice was not crowned queen, then Alice has not reached the last square. Alice has reached the last square. Therefore Alice was crowned queen.
2. Alice was bound for the last square if and only if she has not reached the last square. But she has reached the last square. Therefore she was not bound for the last square.
3. It is not true both that Alice has reached the last square and that she was bound for it. She has reached it; so she was not bound for it.
4. If Alice was not bound for the last square, she didn't reach the last square. She was crowned queen if and only if she reached the last square. She was crowned queen; so it follows she was bound for the last square.
5. Either Alice wasn't bound for the last square or she met Humpty Dumpty. She reached the last square if and only if she was bound for it; so, if she didn't meet Humpty Dumpty, she didn't reach the last square.

C. Give direct proofs for the following. (Source: Plato, *Phaedo.*)

1. If Socrates did not believe that when he dies he will be in the company of gods and good men, he would do wrong in not objecting to death. If he does believe this, he would not do wrong in not objecting to death. Therefore, either he does believe it and would not do wrong in not objecting to death or he does not believe it and would do wrong in not objecting to death.
2. If death is the separation of the soul from the body, then, if the soul can exist apart from the body, the soul becomes free of the body through death. Therefore, if it is not true that the soul becomes free of the body through death, then either death is not the separation of the soul from the body or else the soul cannot exist apart from the body.
3. If the body is a hindrance to the soul, then it is good for the soul to be free of the body. If this is true, then death is not to be feared. But, if in

the knowledge of the highest things the soul is deceived by the body, the body is a hindrance to the soul. But the soul is deceived by the body in this way. Therefore, death is not to be feared.

4. If it is impossible in company with the body to know anything purely, one of two things follows: Either true knowledge is possible nowhere or only after death. But, if partial knowledge can be had in this life, then true knowledge is possible somewhere. But we can have partial knowledge in this life. Therefore, if true knowledge was not possible after death, then it would not be impossible in company with the body to know anything purely.

5. If death is a freeing of the soul and if philosophy seeks to free the soul, then, if you are truly a philosopher, you will not fear death. But death *is* a freeing of the soul, and this *is* what philosophy seeks. Therefore, if you fear death you are not truly a philosopher.

6. If the soul is destroyed when the body is destroyed, then death is to be feared, but, if the soul is not destroyed when the body dies, there is hope. Of course the soul is either destroyed when the body is, or it is not. So it follows that, if there is no hope, death is to be feared.

7. If people are questioned properly, then they show knowledge not acquired during this life. They could not do this if they had not acquired their knowledge in a previous life. If they acquired their knowledge in a previous life, it can be proved that the soul can exist independent of the body. Thus, if people are questioned properly, then it can be proved that the soul can exist independent of the body.

8. If we recognize some things as equal and some as unequal, then we must know what equality itself is. But, if nothing in our sense experience is the same as equality itself, either we don't know what equality itself is or we don't acquire this knowledge by sense experience. If we don't acquire this knowledge through sense experience, then we were born having some knowledge. Since we do recognize some things as equal and some as unequal, and, since nothing in our sense experience is the same as equality itself, it follows that we were born having some knowledge.

9. If the soul is like a tune played on a musical instrument, then it could not exist before the body existed. But, if the argument from recollection is a good one, then the soul did exist before the body existed. If the soul did exist before the body existed, it could exist before the body existed. Therefore, either the argument from recollection is not a good one or the soul is not like a tune played on a musical instrument.

10. If the soul is immortal, fear of death is out of place. But, if the soul outwears many bodies but at last wears out itself, the soul is not immortal. If the soul is like the eternal Ideas, however, it is immortal. But the soul is like the eternal Ideas. So, therefore, it is not true that the soul outwears many bodies but at last wears out itself, and fear of death is out of place.

2.2 DISPROOFS

Nothing could be more frustrating than to spend a great deal of time and effort trying to do a proof only to finally discover that the argument was invalid after all. So in this section we will give a few techniques by which one can check to see if an argument is, in fact, invalid. One way to do this is simply a full-scale truth-table method. Suppose we have the following invalid argument form:

$$p \supset q$$
$$q \supset r$$
$$\underline{\sim p}$$
$$\sim r$$

We can show by Truth Table 2.1 that the argument is invalid:

TRUTH TABLE 2.1

	p	q	r	$(((p \supset q) \cdot (q \supset r)) \cdot \sim p) \supset \sim r$
1	T	T	T	T T T T T T T F F T T F T
2	T	T	F	T T T F T F F F F T T T F
3	T	F	T	T F F F F T T F F T T F T
4	T	F	F	T F F F F T F F F T T T F
5	F	T	T	F T T T T T T T T F F F T
6	F	T	F	F T T F T F F F T F T T F
7	F	F	T	F T F T F T T T T F F F T
8	F	F	F	F T F T F T F F T F T T F
				√ √ √ √ √ √ √ √ √ √ √√

On lines 5 and 7 we have F's under the main connective. So the implication form of the argument is not a tautology, and the argument is thus invalid. However, this was a great deal of work, and there are simpler ways of showing the invalidity of the argument.

One shortcut would simply be to ignore all those lines of the truth table for which the conclusion $\sim r$ is true, for only the case where the premises are true and the conclusion false will show that the argument is invalid. We need consider only the cases in which r is true, since only then would the conclusion $\sim r$ be false.

Shortcuts

However, though this saves some work (and a few other shortcuts of this sort can be suggested), the method is still cumbersome. A technique which is much shorter, but which is not purely mechanical, is the following.

1. Write out the argument:

$$A \supset B$$
$$C \supset D$$
$$\underline{\sim A}$$
$$\sim C$$

2. Assume that the conclusion is false:

$$A \supset B$$
$$C \supset D$$
$$\underline{\sim A}$$
$$F$$
$$\sim C$$

3. Try to find a consistent assignment of truth values for which all the premises are true. Start with the simplest premise, in this case $\sim A$.

$$A \supset B$$
$$B \supset C$$
$$TF$$
$$\checkmark$$
$$\underline{\sim A}$$
$$F$$
$$\sim C$$

Since we have made C false and $\sim A$ true, C must, to be consistent, be true, and A must be false.

$$F$$
$$A \supset B$$
$$T$$
$$B \supset C$$
$$TF$$
$$\checkmark$$
$$\underline{\sim A}$$
$$F$$
$$\sim C$$

$A \supset B$ and $B \supset C$ will be true whether B is true or false. So it can be either. Thus there are two cases where we have true premises and a false conclusion

T   T

F T   F F

√ √   √ √

A ⊃ B   A ⊃ B

T   T

T T   F T

√ √   √ √

B ⊃ C   B ⊃ C

T   T

~A   ~A

―――   ―――

F   F

~C   ~C

and these correspond exactly to lines 5 and 7 of the truth table. However you need only one such case to prove the invalidity of the argument.

Whenever you are in any doubt about the validity of an argument, you can set up the premises for a proof and try to find an assignment of truth values which makes the premises true and the conclusion false. If you can find no such assignment, the argument is valid, or else you have missed some possible assignment of values. When the argument is sufficiently complex to make this a real possibility, a truth-table check is the safest and may save time in the end.

EXERCISES 2.2

A. Check the validity or invalidity of the following arguments by the shortcut method. If valid, give a proof.

1. ~P ⊃ ~J }
   J   } P

2. (C · ~P) ⊃ A }
   ~P   } A

3. B ⊃ W
   W ⊃ F } B
   F

4. J ⊃ (W ⊃ ~P)
   G ⊃ W } G ⊃ ~P
   J

5. ~B ⊃ (P v (K v G)) }
             } (P v (K v G))
   ~B

6. E ⊃ ~B
   S ⊃ E } ~B
   ~S

7. C ⊃ (E ⊃ U) }
            } ~C ⊃ E
   ~U

8. ~F ⊃ ~P
   F v N } ~P
   ~N

9. R ⊃ C
   C ⊃ E   } ~R v ~E
   ~C

10. ~C ⊃ ~F
    B   } ~F · ~C
    B ⊃ ~C

B. Symbolize and check for validity by the shortcut method. If valid, give a proof. Use the same dictionary as for Exercise 2.1B.

1. If Alice reached the last square, then either she was bound for the last square or she met Humpty Dumpty. If she was bound for the last square, then she was crowned queen. If she met Humpty Dumpty, she was crowned queen. So, if she reached the last square, she was crowned queen.

2. If Alice reached the last square, either she was bound for it or she met Humpty Dumpty. She wasn't bound for it, nor did she meet Humpty Dumpty. So she didn't reach the last square.

3. If Alice didn't reach the last square, she wasn't bound for it. If she did reach the last square, she was crowned queen. She wasn't crowned queen. Therefore she was bound for the last square.

4. If Alice reached the last square, then, if she was bound for it, she was crowned queen. She wasn't crowned. So she didn't reach it.

5. If Alice reached the last square, then either she was bound for it or she was crowned queen. She wasn't bound for it. Either she didn't reach it or she wasn't crowned queen. So she didn't reach it.

C. Symbolize and check for validity by the shortcut method. If valid, give a direct proof. Give your own dictionary. (Source: Spinoza, *The Ethics.*)

1. If substance is conceived through itself, then a conception of it can be formed independently of any other conception.
   If a conception of substance can be formed independently of any other conception, then substance is prior to its modifications.
   ───────────
   If substance is prior to its modifications, it is conceived through itself.

2. Either substance is produced by something internal or by something external.
   It is not produced by anything external, and, if it is produced by something internal, it is its own cause.
   ───────────
   Substance is its own cause.

3. Either substance is finite or it is infinite
   If it were limited by something else, it would be finite.
   It is not limited by something else.
   ───────────
   Substance is infinite.

4. If substance can be divided into parts, then either the parts would retain the nature of substance or they would lose the nature of substance.
   The parts would not retain the nature of substance.
   The parts would not lose the nature of substance.
   ───────────
   Substance cannot be divided into parts.

5. If the parts of a divided substance were substances, they would retain the nature of substance.

If the parts of a divided substance were substances, a substance could be made up of other substances.

It is false that a substance could be made up of other substances.

It is false that the parts of a divided substance would retain the nature of substance.

6. If the parts of a divided substance were not substances, they would not retain the nature of substance.

If the parts of a divided substance were substances, a substance could be made up of other substances.

It is false that a substance could be made up of other substances.

It is false that the parts of a divided substance would retain the nature of substance.

7. If the parts of a divided substance would lose the nature of substance, then, if a substance were divided, a substance could be destroyed.

It is false that a substance could be destroyed.

It is false that the parts of a divided substance would lose the nature of substance.

8. If the parts of a divided substance would lose the nature of substance and a substance could be divided, then a substance could be destroyed.

A substance could not be destroyed.

A substance could not be divided.

9. If the parts of a divided substance would lose the nature of substance, then, if a substance were divided, a substance could be destroyed.

It is false that a substance could be destroyed.

Either it is false that the parts of a divided substance would retain the nature of substance, or it is false that substance could be divided.

10. If a substance could be divided, either the parts would retain the nature of substance or they would lose the nature of substance.

It is false that the parts would retain the nature of substance.

Either it is false that the parts would lose the nature of substance, or it is false that a substance could be divided.

A substance could not be divided.

2.3 CONDITIONAL PROOFS

The technique which we will now describe is essentially a device for shortening and simplifying proofs. It will be presented as an additional rule, with the same status as the Inference Rule and the Replacement Rule. As we will see, however, it differs from the previous two rules in several important respects. It can be stated as follows:

Rule of Conditional Proof (*RCP*). At any point in a proof, any proposition A may be put down as a line of the proof with the justification

Assumption for Conditional Proof (ACP) provided that an asterisk is placed to the left of the number of that line. (This will be called starring the line.) Each line which cites that line is similarly starred, and each line which cites a starred line is starred. Starred lines may cite also premises or previous lines obtained from the premises.

The assumption may be *dismissed* after any starred line as follows: If the assumption is a proposition A and the last starred line is a proposition B, we may write an *un*starred line A ⊃ B, citing *all* starred lines so far (in the style: first starred line, dash, last starred line) and the justification, Rule of Conditional Proof (e.g., 5–12, RCP). No starred line may be the conclusion of an argument and no starred line may be cited after its assumption is dismissed.

The justification for this rule is as follows: If by assuming a proposition A we can prove, together with certain premises, another proposition B, then we have shown that, if those premises are true, then if A is true, then B is true. This is exactly what writing A ⊃ B as a line of the proof asserts: that on those premises, if A is true, then B is true. The Rule of Conditional Proof is in theory eliminable: With our previous rules and the listed equivalences and implications, we could always avoid using RCP at the cost of greater (sometimes much greater) complication.

Although the chief use of RCP is to prove propositions of the form p ⊃ q, we can use it also to establish conclusions of other forms. For example, a proposition of the form p ∨ q can be proved by proving ~p ⊃ q by RCP and then using DMI and DN. A proposition of the form p ≡ q can be proved by using two separate conditional proofs to establish p ⊃ q and q ⊃ p and then using DME. Finally, a conclusion of the form p or of the form ~p can be established by proving ~p ⊃ p or p ⊃ ~p or p ⊃ (q · ~q) by RCP and using CM or NCM or Red, respectively.

The case in which we make an assumption, prove a contradiction from it, and go on to derive a conclusion of the form ~p by use of the equivalence

$$\sim p \equiv (p \supset (q \cdot \sim q))$$

(Reductio) is in most logic books given the status of a separate rule, called Indirect Proof or Reductio Proof. It has obvious analogies with traditional *reductio ad absurdum* proofs in philosophy and mathematics. However, it is unnecessary to make it a separate rule, apart from reasons of tradition, since the use of RCP with NCM or Red can always take the place of such a separate rule. It is, however, a useful proof strategy to make the denial of a line we wish to prove an assumption for conditional proof, derive a contradiction, and thereby prove the denial of the denial of the line we wish to prove, which is equivalent by DN to the line we want. Such a proof is often easier to devise than a direct proof of the same line.

Conditional Proofs within Conditional Proofs

We can also have conditional proofs within conditional proofs. In this case we have *double* (or triple, or more—but this becomes cumbersome) starred lines and, in dismissing assumptions, go from double starred lines to single starred lines (or from triple to double, and so forth.)

An example of a proof which would be rather complicated as a direct proof but which can be done more simply as a conditional proof is Proof 2.1.

PROOF 2.1

From	Prove
1 C ⊃ (N v A)	
2 N ⊃ S	D ⊃ ~C
3 A ⊃ S	
4 S ⊃ ~D	
*5 D	ACP
*6 ~ ~D	5, DN, RR
*7 ~S	6, 4, MT, IR
*8 ~A	7, 3, MR, IR
*9 ~N	7, 2, MT, IR
*10 ~N · ~A	8, 9, Conj, IR
*11 ~(N v A)	10, DeM, RR
*12 ~C	11, 1, MT, IR
13 D ⊃ ~C	5–12, RCP Q.E.D.

Another long proof can be done by RCP as shown in Proof 2.2.

PROOF 2.2

From	Prove
1 D ⊃ (R v L)	
2 ~R	~D
3 ~L v ~D	
*4 D	ACP
*5 R v L	1, 4, MP, IR
*6 L	2, 5, DS, IR
*7 L ⊃ ~D	3, DMI, RR
*8 ~D	6, 7, MP, IR
9 D ⊃ ~D	4–8, RCP
10 ~D	9, NCM, RR Q.E.D.

Finally the proof from the *Parmenides* done in Section 2.1 can be shortened by the use of RCP as shown in Proof 2.3.

PROOF 2.3

From	*Prove*

1 F ⊃ (P v W)
2 P ⊃ D
3 W ⊃ S   ~F
4 ~(D v S)
*5 F   ACP
*6 P v W   5, 1, MP, IR
*7 D v S   2, 3, 6, CD, IR
8 F ⊃ (D v S)   5–7, RCP
9 ~F   . 8, 4, MT, IR   Q.E.D.

EXERCISES 2.3

A. Provide a conditional proof for the following:

1.   A ⊃ B
     B ≡ D   ~A
     ~D

2.   E ⊃ (F v G)
                       H ⊃ (~F ⊃ G)
     ~E ⊃ ~H

3.   (J · K) ⊃ L
     M ⊃ J   (M · N) ⊃ L
     ~K ⊃ ~N

4.   ((P v Q) · R) ≡ S
                       T ⊃ S
     T ⊃ (Q · R)

5.   U v ~V
     W ≡ V   ~X v V
     ~W ⊃ ~X

6.   A ⊃ (B ⊃ C)
                       (D · B) ⊃ C
     ~D v A

7.   (E v F) ⊃ (G · H)
                       ~E
     ~H · F

8.   (~J v ~K) ⊃ ~L
                       M ⊃ (J · K)
     ~M v L

9.   N ≡ O
     ~O ≡ ~P   N ⊃ Q
     Q v ~P

10. (R v S) ⊃ U
                       S ⊃ V
     ~V ≡ ~U

B. Translate the following arguments into compound propositions and check for validity. If valid, give a conditional proof.
1. Either the Mock Turtle has a sorrow or it's all his fancy (but not both). If the Gryphon is right, it's all his fancy. So, if the Mock Turtle has a sorrow, the Gryphon is not right.
2. The Gryphon and the Turtle cannot both be right. If the Mock Turtle is right, he has a sorrow. The Gryphon is right. So the Mock Turtle doesn't have a sorrow.
3. If the Mock Turtle was once a real turtle and is now a mock turtle, then he must have changed. He is now a mock turtle. So if he didn't change he was not once a real turtle.
4. If the Mock Turtle could afford extras, he could take either French or washing. He couldn't take French, so he must not have been able to afford extras.
5. Either you know what "to uglify" means or, if you know what "to beautify" means, you are a simpleton. You are not a simpleton, so either you don't know what "to beautify" means or you do know what "to uglify" means.

C. Symbolize these arguments, and show that the conclusion follows from the premises by a conditional proof or a direct proof, whichever is easier. (Source: Plato, *Crito* and *Apology*.)
1. Crito is practicing athletics. He will either pay attention to the trainer's opinion or pay attention to the opinion of the multitude, but not to both. If he pays attention to the opinion of the trainer, he will fear the trainer's blame and welcome the trainer's praise. If he pays attention to the multitude, he will fear the blame and welcome the praise of the multitude. If he does not pay attention to the trainer's opinion, he does harm to himself. Therefore, if he pays attention to the opinion of the multitude, he has done harm to himself and has feared the blame and welcomed the praise of the multitude.
2. Socrates will not do what is wrong. If he returns evil for evil, he will do wrong. If he breaks an agreement with the state because he has been unjustly condemned, he will return evil for evil. Therefore, if by making his escape he will be breaking an agreement because he has been unjustly condemned, he will not make his escape.
3. If the Laws of Athens enabled Socrates' parents to marry and to raise and educate Socrates, then the Laws are even more to be respected than his parents. If they are, then, if he attempts to destroy the Laws, this would be as bad as attempting to destroy his parents. The Laws of Athens did enable Socrates' parents to marry and to raise and educate Socrates. If Socrates attempts to escape, he will attempt to disobey the Law. Therefore, if disobeying the Law is the same as destroying the Law, then, if Socrates attempts to escape, this would be as bad as attempting to destroy his parents.
4. If Socrates did not approve of the Laws of Athens, he could have either emigrated from Athens or tried to have the Laws changed. If he neither emigrated nor tried to have the Laws changed, then Socrates agreed to obey the Laws. It is not true that Socrates emigrated from Athens.

Therefore, if he did not try to have the Laws changed, then he approved of the Laws and agreed to obey them.

5. If Socrates breaks the Law and escapes, then his friends will suffer. If he escapes and emigrates to a nearby city, he will be regarded as an enemy if he is a lawbreaker. Therefore, if escaping is breaking the Law, then, if Socrates escapes, he will be regarded as an enemy or else his friends will suffer.

6. If Socrates avoids well-governed cities, his life will not be worth living. If he goes to Thessaly, he will become a laughingstock and will not be able to bring up his children well. Therefore, if escaping means that Socrates will go to Thessaly or will avoid well-governed cities, then, if his life is worth living, his children will not be well educated.

7. If Socrates escapes, then things will not be better for him in this world, and, when he comes to the next world, he will come as a lawbreaker. If Socrates is persuaded by Crito, he will escape. If things will not be better for him in this world, he will not be happy in this world, and, if he comes to the next world as a lawbreaker, he will not be happy in the next world. Therefore, if Socrates is persuaded by Crito, he will be unhappy both in this world and in the next.

8. Either death is a complete extinction and the dead man feels nothing, or death is a change and migration for the soul from this place to another place. If the dead man feels nothing, then eternity is like a night of dreamless sleep, and death is a blessing. If death is a change and migration from this place to another and if, as they say, all the dead are in that place, then we shall be with the great men of the past, and death is a blessing. Thus, if, as they say, all the dead are in that place, then death is a blessing.

9. If Socrates meets the souls of the great after death, he will cross-examine them. If he cross-examines them, then, if the dead die no more, he cannot be put to death for cross-examining them. If he cannot be put to death for it, he can spend eternity cross-examining the souls of the great and will be eternally happy. Thus, if the dead die no more, then, if Socrates meets the souls of the great after death, he will be eternally happy.

10. If no evil can happen to a good man either living or dead, then Socrates' death is not an evil. If his death is not an evil, his "signal" would not have warned him to act differently at his trial, and he would have no reason to be angry with his accusers or those who condemned him. Thus, if Socrates did have reason to be angry with his accusers, this would mean that it was false that no evil can happen to a good man, either living or dead.

2.4 LOGICAL SYSTEMS

If you take another course in logic after this one, it will very likely be a course in *mathematical* logic. The mathematical approach to logic emphasizes logic itself as an abstract system. Mathematical logicians are interested in developing logical systems in an orderly fashion, beginning with a few basic assumptions called *axioms*. The axioms are assumed without proof (at least without proof within the system being developed), but other propositions called *theorems* can be proved by using the axioms and certain rules of inference. Usually the rules of inference are kept to a minimum, although sometimes derived rules are used, which bear somewhat the same relation to the basic rules as theorems do to axioms.

To present an axiomatic theory in a systematic way, mathematical logicians frequently present first the basic vocabulary of the system, then give *formation rules*, which tell which combinations of the basic vocabulary are permissible. Axioms are usually given next, then *inference rules*, which tell which manipulations are allowable. Inference rules are ideally such that, if one starts with axioms or already derived theorems and proceeds according to the inference rules, he will always get statements which are true if the axioms are true. If the axioms are consistent and the inference rules lead only to theorems which are true if the axioms are, then the system is *consistent*. This is, of course, vital since, if a contradiction exists in the axioms or is provable from them, then anything is provable.

Mathematical logicians are interested also in *completeness*. There are various technical versions of this notion, but, informally, we usually have some body of truths which we wish to make provable from a set of axioms, for example, all truth-table tautologies in propositional logic. In many systems it is possible to show that every one of a certain class of truths is provable from a few simple axioms; such systems are *complete*. In some fairly complex systems it can be shown that there are truths statable in the system which are not provable in the system. Such systems are *incomplete*.

Given a set of axioms, we may wonder if any of them are redundant in the sense that some axiom could be proved as a theorem from others. If this is not the case, the axioms are *independent*. Notice that independence is a characteristic of the *axioms*, whereas completeness and consistency are properties of the system as a whole.

The *Principia* System

One famous set of axioms for propositional logic is that given in *Principia Mathematica* by Bertrand Russell and A. N. Whitehead. I will give a slightly modified version of this system. The axioms are

$$
\begin{array}{ll}
\text{A 1} & (p \lor p) \supset p \\
\text{A 2} & q \supset (p \lor q) \\
\text{A 3} & (p \lor q) \supset (q \lor p) \\
\text{A 4} & (p \lor (q \lor r)) \supset (q \lor (p \lor r)) \\
\text{A 5} & (q \supset r) \supset ((p \lor q) \supset (p \lor r))
\end{array}
$$

The letters p, q, and r are taken as dummies or stand-ins for any proposition you like rather than as variables. Thus, for example, A 3 says in effect "For any two propositions p and q, it is true that $(p \lor q) \supset (q \lor p)$."

The first rule of inference in the *Principia* is

PIR 1. Whatever follows from a true propositon is true.

As applied to "dummy" propositions, this means that, if we have p as a line of a proof and p implies q, then we can write q as a line. This rule is thus like our Inference Rule in some respects. Since one way of knowing that p implies q is to have p $\supset$ q as a line in the proof, this rule resembles also *modus ponens*.

The second rule is the following:

PIR 2. Any proposition is a theorem which is derived from an axiom or theorem by uniform substitution of occurrences of simple or compound propositions for occurrences of simple propositions in the original axiom or theorem.

To keep track of substitutions, we adopt the following convention: When we substitute a proposition p for a proposition q in an axiom or theorem, we will write "Subst p/q" as justification. (Of course p must replace *every* occurrence of q.)

In addition to the axioms and inference rules, we have one definition

$$PD 1 \qquad p \supset q = \text{def} \sim p \vee q$$

with the understanding that we may substitute the definition for the expression defined. We will cite PIR 1 as justification for this on the principle that, of course, if a proposition is true a proposition resulting from substituting, a definition for a defined expression will be true also. There are two formation rules for the *Principia* system:

FR 1   If p is a proposition, so is $\sim$p.
FR 2   If p and q are propositions, so are p $\vee$ q and p $\cdot$ q.

The *Principia* system is *complete* in the sense that every truth-table tautology of propositional logic can be proved from the axioms using the rules of inference. Also it can be shown to be *consistent*. The axioms as given are not *independent*, however, since it was shown after the publication of *Principia* that A4 could be derived from the other four axioms. An example of a proof in the *Principia* system is the following:

Prove: q $\supset$ (p $\supset$ q)
1   q $\supset$ (p $\vee$ q)   Axiom 2
2   q $\supset$ ($\sim$p $\vee$ q)   1, Subst $\sim$p/p
3   q $\supset$ (p $\supset$ q)   2, PD 1, PIR 1

Some other examples are given as Exercises 2.4A.

Natural Deduction System

A quite different approach to systematizing propositional logic is the so-called natural deduction type of system, based on the work of G. Gentzen. In these systems the basic principle is that of proofs without premises in which we arrive at theorems by the principle that a proposition is a logical truth if it can be derived as a conclusion in a proof with no premises at all. This sounds odd, but consider the following case.

Suppose that we had the Rule of Conditional Proof, *modus ponens*, and Simplification as rules in a system and wished to show that Hypothetical Syllogism was a logical truth. It could be done as in Proof 2.4. With no premises at all, we were able to derive the conclusion in Proof 2.4, thus

PROOF 2.4

Prove: $((p \supset q) \cdot (q \supset r)) \supset (p \supset r)$

*1	$(p \supset q) \cdot (q \supset r)$	ACP
*2	$p \supset q$	1, Simp
*3	$q \supset r$	1, Simp
**4	p	ACP
**5	q	4, 2, MP
**6	r	5, 3, MP
*7	$p \supset r$	4–6, RCP
8	$((p \supset q) \cdot (q \supset r)) \supset (p \supset r)$	1–7, RCP Q.E.D.

showing that, in any system in which MP, Simp, and RCP are rules, HS is a logical truth.

Notice that we did not cite the Inference Rule: In this kind of development, one has a number of *independent* rules which are used to derive logical truths. Some so-called natural deduction systems start with no logical truths at all, but with enough rules to derive any desired logical truth.

In such a system, equivalences function as two-way inference rules, for example, Double Negation is seen as a rule enabling us to infer $\sim\sim p$ from p but also to infer p from $\sim\sim p$. Each equivalence is thought of as an independent rule of this sort; the Replacement Rule is not cited.

Logical Truth and Falsehoods

In this book we will make no attempt to develop propositional logic as an axiomatic system. We will, however, add Substitution to our battery of rules and use it on occasion in later chapters. We will also sometimes use the technique of proofs without premises to show that certain statements are logical truths. This will be especially useful when we get beyond propositional logic and can no longer use truth-table techniques. Our main aim, however, will always be to analyze statements and arguments, using whatever logical tools are most convenient. The techniques used in this book are designed with this purpose in mind. We will also add a special rule for definitions:

Definition Rule (DR): For any two propositions p and q, if p = def q, then it is a logical truth that p ≡ q.

We will not discuss separately ways of discovering whether propositions are logical falsehoods, since the denial of any logical truth is a logical falsehood, and the denial of any logical falsehood is a logical truth. Thus, if we wish to know whether a statement is a logical falsehood, we can see if its negation is a logical truth.

The exercises at the end of this chapter are intended to give you some feel for the process of proving theorems in axiomatic and natural deduction systems.

EXERCISES 2.4

A. Consider a system in which you have the following axioms and definitions:

Ax 1	(p ∨ p) ⊃ p	Ax 2	q ⊃ (p ∨ q)
Ax 3	(p ∨ q) ⊃ (q ∨ p)	Ax 4	(p ∨ (q ∨ r)) ⊃ (q ∨ (p ∨ r))
Ax 5	(q ⊃ r) ⊃ ((p ∨ q) ⊃ (p ∨ r))		

D 1   p · q = def ~(~p ∨ ~q)
D 2   p ≡ q = def (p ⊃ q) · (q ⊃ p)
D 3   p ⊃ q = def (~p ∨ q)

Rules of inference: PIR 1, PIR 2 (Substitution)

Prove as theorems the following:

1.	(p ⊃ ~p) ⊃ ~p	2.	q ⊃ (p ⊃ q)
3.	(p ⊃ ~q) ⊃ (q ⊃ ~p)	4.	(p ⊃ (q · ~r)) ⊃ (q ⊃ (p · ~r))
5.	(q ⊃ r) ⊃ ((p ⊃ q) ⊃ (p ⊃ r))	6.	(p ⊃ q) ⊃ ((q ⊃ r) ⊃ (p ⊃ r))
7.	p ⊃ (p ∨ p)	8.	p ⊃ p
9.	~p ∨ p	10.	p ⊃ ~ ~p

B. Consider a system without axioms but with the following rules of inference: Conjunction, Simplification, Addition, *modus ponens*, Rule of Conditional Proof, plus the two-way inference rules: Commutation, Association, Repetition, Double Negation, De Morgan's Rules, Definition of Material Implication, and Definition of Material Equivalence. Prove as theorems, by proofs without premises, 1–10 in Part A above.

C. Symbolize the following axioms, giving your own dictionary. (Source: Spinoza, *Ethics.*)
1. If A is the cause of B, then B can be understood by means of A.
2. If A has nothing in common with B, B cannot be understood by means of A.
3. If A and B have something in common, they have the same nature or the same attributes.

4. If A and B have the same nature or attributes, they are the same.
5. If A and B are distinct things, they are not the same.

Use the axioms, plus the techniques of propositional logic to prove the following as theorems:

6. If A has nothing in common with B, then A cannot be the cause of B.
7. If A and B are distinct things, then they have neither the same nature nor the same attributes.
8. If A and B are distinct things, then they have nothing in common.
9. If A and B are not the same, A cannot be the cause of B.
10. If A is the cause of B, then A and B are not distinct things.

2.5 PHILOSOPHICAL APPLICATIONS

One major way in which formal logic can be useful in philosophy is this: It enables us to put philosophical arguments into a form which is valid so that we know that, if the premises of the argument are true, the conclusion is true. We can then concentrate our attention on the problem of whether or not the premises are true. Another benefit is, that if the conclusion is to follow from the premises, these must contain all the statements which are necessary to prove that conclusion; we cannot ignore or fail to notice some assumption which is necessary for the proof, for if a necessary premise is missing, the proof will not be valid.

The Deductive Form

We may have various motives for thus formalizing a philosophical argument. In the exercises at the end of previous sections those taken from Spinoza were examples of arguments cast in deductive form in order that their conclusions could be established. Wanting to assert some seemingly paradoxical conclusions, Spinoza tried to demonstrate that they followed deductively from acceptable premises. Another philosopher might put arguments into deductive form in order to refute them. In each case he might argue that one or more of the premises are simply false or are misused or misunderstood in the argument.

Comparatively few philosophers give their arguments in the form of deductive arguments, but in many cases we can clarify an argument by putting it in such a form. Consider, for example, the following argument from St. Augustine's *City of God*:

> Let us examine, then, this fear of foreknowledge which led Cicero to attempt to deny it. ... He argues thus: If all that is future is foreknown, each event will occur in the order in which it is foreknown that it will occur. But if things happen in this order, the order of things is foreknown for certain in the mind of God who foreknows them. But if the order of events are known for certain, then the order of causes is foreknown for certain—since nothing can happen without a preceding efficient cause.

If, however, the order of causes by which all happens is known for certain, then, he says, all that happens happens by fate. But if this is so, nothing is left to our own power, and, therefore, there is no choice in our will. But, he goes on, once we admit this, all human life comes topsy-turvy; laws are made in vain; there is no point in reproaches or in praise, in scolding or in exhortation; there is no ground in justice for rewarding the good or punishing the wicked.

Thus his motive for rejecting foreknowledge of the future was to avoid unworthy, absurd, and dangerous implications for human society. He narrows down the choices ... to these alternatives, *either* the power of choice *or* foreknowledge.

Let us formalize this in propositional logic, giving the symbolized argument and the dictionary in parallel columns as shown in Proof 2.5.

PROOF 2.5

Argument	Dictionary
Premises:	
1 $F \supset E$	F $\#$ All that is future is foreknown
	E $\#$ Each event will occur in the foreknown order
2 $E \supset O$	O $\#$ The order is known for certain by God
	C $\#$ The order of causes is known by God
3 $O \supset C$	H $\#$ All that happens happens by fate
	N $\#$ Nothing is left to our own power
4 $C \supset H$	W $\#$ There is no choice in our will
5 $H \supset N$	L $\#$ Laws are made in vain
6 $N \supset W$	P $\#$ Reproaches and praise are pointless
7 $W \supset (L \cdot (P \cdot G))$	G $\#$ Justice and punishment are groundless

Conclusion:

$$F \supset (L \cdot (P \cdot G)) \quad \text{or} \quad \sim F \vee (L \cdot (P \cdot G))$$

The proof would be quite simple:

Argument	Justification of steps	
8 $F \supset O$	1, 2, HS, IR	
9 $F \supset C$	8, 3, HS, IR	
10 $F \supset H$	9, 4, HS, IR	
11 $F \supset N$	10, 5, HS, IR	
12 $F \supset W$	11, 6, HS, IR	
13 $F \supset (L \cdot (P \cdot G))$	12, 7, HS, IR	
14 $\sim F \vee (L \cdot (P \cdot G))$	11, DMI, RR	Q.E.D.

Cicero, Augustine argues, chose to deny the consequences of lack of the power of free choice and was therefore bound to deny foreknowledge. That is, taking $F \supset (L \cdot (P \cdot G))$ as true, Cicero asserted $\sim(L \cdot (P \cdot G))$ and so by *modus tollens* asserted $\sim F$. Indeed, if we admit Premises 1–7 and assert that God has foreknowledge, we are bound to assert

$$L \cdot (P \cdot G)$$

simply by *modus poneus*:

$$\frac{\begin{array}{l} F \supset (L \cdot (P \cdot G)) \\ F \end{array}}{L \cdot (P \cdot G)}$$

Augustine evades the conclusion by admitting some premises but denying one, thus breaking the chain of argument at a crucial point. He denies that, if the order of causes is foreknown by God, then everything happens by fate. His *reason* for denying this is that among the causes foreknown by God are human wills, so that some things are determined by human will rather than by fate:

> Our main point is that, from the fact that to God the order of all causes is certain, there is no logical deduction that there is no power in the choice of the will. The fact is that our choices fall within the order of the causes, which is known for certain to God and is contained in His foreknowledge—for human choices are the causes of human acts.

Attacking the Premises

Whether from the philosophical point of view this is a satisfactory answer to the dilemma of determinism is a question which belongs to philosophy rather than logic. But formalizing the argument makes several things clear: Augustine can (and seemingly does) assert to the truth of Premises 1–3 and 5–7. By denying the truth of Premise 4 he effectively breaks the connection between foreknowledge and lack of free choice. Anyone who, like Augustine, wishes to avoid the conclusion of this argument must, like Augustine, deny Premise 4 or else deny the truth of some other premise. Granted that God has foreknowledge, it seems difficult to deny either that events will occur in the foreknown order or that that order and the corresponding order of causes are foreknown. These ideas seem to be involved directly in the notion of foreknowledge. Similarly, once fate is admitted, free will seems to be ruled out with the consequences described by Cicero. So Augustine has attacked the argument at the only possible point, has cut the chain at its weakest link.

So propositional logic makes precise what Augustine is and is not denying and why he attacks the argument at the point that he does. It leaves to philosophy the crucial point as to whether his reasons for rejecting Premise 4 are satisfactory.

It is fairly rare to find an argument so easily formalized, however. Consider the complete argument in the final part of Plato's *Meno*. We have seen that one important part of this argument is:

If virtue can be taught then there are teachers and learners of virtue.

There are neither teachers nor learners of virtue.

Therefore virtue cannot be taught.

However, what support does Socrates give for his assertion that there are no teachers or learners of virtue? Examination of the dialogue shows that the evidence that he cites for this is that the Sophists, who claim to teach virtue, notoriously fail to do so and that the greatest and noblest Athenians have failed to teach their own children virtue. Why does *this* show that there are no teachers of virtue at all? Here we need to fill in the argument. Sophist and citizen, paid teacher and parent—evidently Socrates has in his mind some public-private or professional-amateur division. We might conjecturally reconstruct his argument as follows:

If there are teachers of virtue, then either there are professional teachers of virtue or there are amateur teachers of virtue.

If there are professional teachers of virtue, then the Sophists will be teachers of virtue.

If there are amateur teachers of virtue, then the noblest Athenians will be teachers of virtue to their children.

The Sophists are not teachers of virtue.

The noblest Athenians are not teachers of virtue to their children.

Therefore, there are no teachers of virtue.

In addition to this argument Socrates explicitly states at one time:

If there are learners of virtue, then there are teachers of virtue.

Let us now put the whole argument together as shown in Proof 2.6. Notice

PROOF 2.6

Argument	Dictionary
Premises:	
1 $V \supset (T \cdot L)$	V # Virtue can be taught
	T # There are teachers of virtue
2 $L \supset T$	L # There are learners of virtue
3 $T \supset (P \vee A)$	P # There are professional teachers of virtue
	A # There are amateur teachers of virtue
4 $P \supset S$	S # The Sophists are teachers of virtue
5 $A \supset N$	N # The noblest Athenians are teachers of virtue to their children
6 $\sim S$	
7 $\sim N$	
Conclusion:	
$\sim V$	

PROOF 2.6—*continued*

Argument	Justification of steps
Proof:	
8 ~A	5, 7, MT, IR
9 ~P	4, 6, MT, IR
10 ~P · ~A	8, 9, Conj, IR
11 ~(P ∨ A)	10, DeM, RE
12 ~T	11, 3, MT, IR
13 ~T ∨ ~L	12, Add, IR
14 ~(T · L)	13, DeM, RE
15 ~V	14, 1, MT, IR Q.E.D.

several things about this argument. First, Premise 2 and in fact all references to learners of virtue are strictly unnecessary to the argument. By saying that if virtue can be taught there must be *both* teachers and learners of virtue. Socrates has made it unnecessary to say anything about learners of virtue, if we can show that there are no teachers of virtue. For, if there are *no* teachers, there are obviously not *both* teachers and learners. Plato may or may not have realized this—it is much easier to see in the formalized version of the argument. Second, from Premises 1–5 it would be possible to prove

$$V \supset (S \vee N)$$

"If virtue can be taught then either the Sophists are teachers of virtue or the noblest Athenians are teachers of virtue to their children." Putting the argument this way makes it clear how much rests on these two cases.

Finally, although the argument is valid and some of its premises are unobjectionable, some of them are definitely questionable. Let us begin by granting the truth of Premises 6 and 7. Whether the Sophists or the noble Athenians were able to teach virtue is a matter for historical rather than philosophical research, and we will presume that Socrates knew what he was talking about on these points.

Premise 3 also seems to be satisfactory: Professional and amateur seem to exhaust the possibilities sufficiently (any teacher will be one or the other), though strictly speaking we might raise the question of how these terms are defined and whether some teacher might not be professional from one point of view and amateur from another.

However, Premises 4 and 5 are quite questionable. Are the Sophists the *only* candidates for professional teachers of virtue? How about those like Ion, who claim to teach virtue from the pages of Homer? What about religious leaders and priests? Surely Euthyphro would be confident of his ability to teach virtue. Agreed, Socrates in other dialogues argues against these pretensions. But should they not at least be mentioned in the *Meno*? Again, are men like Pericles, Socrates' examples of noble Athenians, most likely to be successful in teaching their children virtue? As public figures their family may be sacrificed to their public duties. In addition, a father famous for virtue can sometimes be a hindrance rather than a help to virtue, as witness the old proverbs about parsons' sons. What about good but not famous men. Are they more successful in bringing up virtuous children? In fact, what about Socrates' own children?

In raising these sorts of questions we have really left the realm of formal logic. But the questions may serve as examples of the philosophical questions which can be raised about the parts of a philosophical argument once they are set down as premises of a valid argument.

Premise 2, as we have seen, is unnecessary. Premise 1 would seem to be true by definition: If a thing is teachable, there must be teachers of it. Here we can make a not unimportant distinction. A thing may be teachable in principle without ever having been taught. For example, the newest discoveries in physics or biology might be the sort of thing which can be taught, but as a matter of fact they might not yet have *been* taught, and there might *now* be no teachers of them. So Socrates has failed to notice a possibility that perhaps could be dismissed but surely should be mentioned—that virtue might be in principle teachable but for some reason it had not yet been taught.

We might raise also questions about what it means to teach virtue. Someone can learn tennis from excellent teachers without becoming a good player, perhaps because he is uncoordinated. Might not, for example, the Sophists be excellent teachers of virtue whose pupils for some reason fail to profit from instruction?

Steps in Analysis

Returning to formal logic, let us remind ourselves of the steps followed in analyzing this argument by means of propositional logic.

1. Wherever it was said that B was true *because* A was or that, if A was true, then B was, etc., we put A $\supset$ B as a premise.

2. When some proposition A or its denial $\sim$A was asserted as true, we simply wrote A or $\sim$A, as the case might be, as a premise.

3. Where words such as *either*, *both*, *and*, or *or* occur, we symbolize them with the appropriate truth-functional connectives.

4. We then seek to prove the desired conclusion from the premises as set down. If additional premises are necessary to provide a valid argument, we supply them.

5. We can then turn to philosophical arguments about the truth of the premises.

These techniques are far from being a universal method in philosophy. In a way, the real philosophizing begins *after* the formalization of the argument ends. However, they do serve to clarify arguments and to make clear what is the real point at issue. Though this is not the last step in philosophy, it is certainly the first.

DISCUSSION QUESTIONS

1. Discuss any cases in Section 1.1 where the result of translation into the symbols of propositional logic seemed to change the meaning or truth value of a sentence in English.

2. Discuss any cases in Section 1.2 where the result of translation into symbols and testing by truth table seemed to give results which conflict with your judgment of the English sentence (e.g., a sentence which does not seem self-contradictory in English is shown by truth table to be a contradiction after translation or a sentence which seems to be logically true in English is not a truth table tautology).

3. Comment on any cases in Section 1.3 where the result of translation and test conflict with your judgment as to whether English sentences are equivalent.

4. Do all of the arguments discussed in Section 1.4 seem intuitively valid to you? Can you construct an argument which is valid by truth-table test but seems odd or invalid in English?

5. Discuss what exactly is going on if an argument is condemned as unclear or invalid because it cannot be shown to be valid in propositional logic.

6. In the proofs you have done, could every step be restated in ordinary language and justified to someone who knew no logic? If not, give examples of difficulties.

7. Have the paradoxes of material implication and equivalence caused any difficulties in your proofs? If so, give examples.

8. In the philosophical examples, were there any cases where some of the meaning was lost by translation into propositional logic? If there were, give examples.

9. What limitations have you found in propositional logic? How might these be eliminated?

10. In your reading outside this class, find examples of arguments which can be symbolized and tested in propositional logic.

Chapter 3
SYLLOGISTIC
LOGIC

The area of logic which we are now about to investigate was the first to be developed systematically and has been, until fairly recently, the most used and most useful variety of logic. It was first investigated by Aristotle in the fifth century B.C. and is often called Aristotelian or traditional logic. Because the theory of the syllogism is at the heart of Aristotelian logic, we will refer to it as syllogistic logic. This kind of logic was put to philosophical uses by Aristotle himself and was used extensively by medieval and other philosophers. Despite the more sophisticated logical tools available today, syllogistic logic can often be the most convenient method for analyzing certain philosophical arguments.

The system described in this chapter is a modern version of syllogistic logic. This version differs in some ways from other modernizations of Aristotle's system, and some of the differences from other modern systems are noted. It is hoped that the system described here is sufficiently convenient and flexible to justify its departures in some respects from conventional ways of treating syllogistic logic.

3.1 STANDARD FORM STATEMENTS

The expressions in syllogistic logic which correspond to the propositions of propositional logic are in some respects less restricted, though in other respects more restricted, than those propositions. Therefore we will use a wider term, speaking of *statements* rather than of propositions. We will be especially concerned with *standard form statements*, which are subject-predicate expressions having one of the six forms in Table 3.1. "Some" is regarded as meaning "at least one" and includes "many," "most," etc., which we have no way of expressing in standard form statements.

TABLE 3.1

A	Every . . . is	A′	*. . . is . . . .
E	No . . . is	E′	*. . . is not . . . .
I	Some . . . is		
O	Some . . . is not		

* The subject term here designates an individual.

The letters A, E, I, O, A′, and E′ are convenient shorthand ways of referring to the statements. Thus, instead of saying that a statement is of the form "Every . . . is . . .," we will say "an A statement." The A and E statements are called *universal* statements. The I and O statements are called *particular* statements, while the A′ and E′ statements are called *singular* statements. The A, A′, and I statements are called *affirmative* statements, while the E, E′, and O statements are called *negative*. Thus the six statement forms can be described as in Table 3.2.

TABLE 3.2

A	Universal Affirmative	A′	Singular Affirmative
E	Universal Negative	E′	Singular Negative
I	Particular Affirmative		
O	Particular Negative		

Standard Form Statements

Notice that, whereas in propositional logic propositions were treated as unanalyzed units and our concern was with compound propositions formed from these units, in syllogistic logic we pay attention to the internal structure of statements. Thus we will need constants to stand for actual subject terms and predicate terms (such as "man" or "living thing") which can be fitted into the standard patterns to make standard form statements. Also we will need variables to stand for subject terms and predicate terms when we want to talk about statement *forms*. We will use the following conventions:

1. All small letters except *s* will stand for designations of individuals, for example

> p # Plato   a # the author of this book
> f # the first man to land on the Moon

2. All capital letters except *S*, *P*, and *M* will stand for expressions other than designations of individuals which can serve as subjects or predicates when inserted into standard forms, for example,

> R # (a) rich person   A # (an) author   W # (a) woman

Indefinite articles can be supplied or dropped to make grammatical English sentences. It would be convenient in some ways to make an indefinite article part of the form, for example,

> Every . . . is a . . . .   Some . . . is not a . . . .

However, since we will sometimes wish to use terms such as "rich" rather than "a rich person," or "red" rather than "a red thing," it would be inconvenient to make the indefinite article part of the standard form. Greek and Latin, in which a good deal of the development of syllogistic logic was done, are inflected languages in which the idea of the indefinite article is included in the noun or adjective so that this problem did not arise for Aristotle or the medievals.

For our purposes we will distinguish between a *strict* and a *loose* version of our standard form statements. In the stricter version we will use predicate terms which could also appear in the subject position if the accompanying indefinite article were dropped, for example, (*a*) *rich person*, (*a*) *running man*, or (*a*) *white thing*. In the looser version we will use predicate terms, such as adjectives or the verbal gerundives, which could not appear in the subject position, for example, *rich, running*, or *white*. Examples of the two forms are shown in Table 3.3. Adding words to make a loose form into a strict one will be called *standardizing* the predicate.

TABLE 3.3

Strict	*Looser*
Every writer is a rich person	Every writer is rich
Some writer is a running man	Some writer is running
Some book is not a white thing	Some book is not white

3. The letters *S*, *P*, *M*, and *s* will be variables marking gaps into which any subject or predicate term may be inserted. The small *s* marks gaps into

which only designations of individuals may be inserted; the capitals mark gaps into which names of individuals may *not* be inserted. Using these variables we can rewrite the standard statement forms as shown in Table 3.4.

TABLE 3.4

A	Every S is P	A′	s is P
E	No S is P	E′	s is not P
I	Some S is P		
O	Some S is not P		

Examples of standard form statements, using the dictionaries given above as examples, would be

Every A is R   No A is R   Some W is not A   Some R is W
  p is not W   a is not R

Notice that

Some W is not f   No R is p   p is not f

are *not* standard form statements since we do not allow standard form statement in which the name of an individual (or the negation of the name of an individual) appears as the predicate term.

Classes

In a widely accepted interpretation of the standard form statements, developed long after Aristotle, them are regarded as statements about classes or groups of things. Thus "Every S is P" is interpreted to mean the same as "Every member of the class of things each of which is an S is a member of the class of things each of which is a P." The statement "No S is P" is interpreted to mean the same as "No member of the class of things each of which is an S is a member of the class of things each of which is P. The statement "Some S is P" is interpreted to mean the same as "Some member of the class of things each of which is an S is a member of the class each of which is a P." The statement "Some S is not P" is interpreted to mean the same as "Some member of the class of things each of which is an S is not a member of the class of things each of which is a P. "The statement "s is P" is interpreted as "s is a member of the class of things each of which is a P" and "s is not P" as "s is not a member of the class of things each of which is a P."

The class interpretation of standard form statements enables us to give diagrammatic presentation of standard form statements as shown in Figure 3.1.

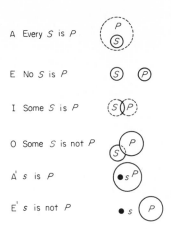

A   Every *S* is *P*

E   No *S* is *P*

I   Some *S* is *P*

O   Some *S* is not *P*

A' *s* is *P*

E' *s* is not *P*

Figure 3.1

Distribution of Terms

Notice that individuals are represented as dots (heavy ones so as to be visible). This suggests the indivisibility of individuals: they can be in a class or out of it, but not partly in a class. Classes are represented as circles, which can be completely within other circles, completely outside them, or partly inside or outside other circles. Some circles have solid lines, and some have dotted lines, to indicate what is called the *distribution* of terms.

A term which says something about every member of a class is said to be distributed; one which says something about only some (less than all) members of a class is said to be undistributed. Consider the statement, "Every author is a rich person" (which is unfortunately untrue). It says something about every author but not about every rich person. In statements of this form the subject term is *distributed* while the predicate term is *undistributed*. On the other hand, the statement "No author is a rich person" (also untrue) says something about every author (that he is not rich) and about every rich person (that he is not an author). Thus both subject and predicate terms are distributed. The statement "Some author is rich" (which is true) says nothing about every author or about every rich person; thus both its subject term and its predicate term are undistributed.

As you can see in Figure 3.1, the terms which are distributed are represented by circles which have solid lines, while the terms which are undistributed are represented by circles which have completely or partly dotted lines.

We notice, however, that the predicate term of "Some authors are not rich" should be distributed if this symbolism is carried out. That the predicate must be distributed is in fact what logicians say about statements of this form. This can be puzzling at first acquaintance. The justification for describing as

81

distributed the predicated term of statements of the form "Some *S* is not *P*" is as follows: A term is said to be distributed in a statement if the statement tells us something about everything of that sort or every member of that class. If the predicate term of a statement like "Some author is not a rich person" were *not* distributed, we would be saying in effect "Some authors are not *some* rich persons." But this would be true whether all authors were rich or none were or whether some were and some weren't.

Suppose, for example, that all authors were rich. Still some author, say Ernest Hemingway, would not be *some* rich man, say John Paul Getty. Similarly in almost any situation "Some author is not *some* rich person" would be true. It would be false only if there were one author and one rich person who were the same person. What we really want to say is that some author is different from *every* rich person. This is what we are insisting on when we say that the predicate term is distributed in a statement like "Some authors are not rich persons."

Finally, the subject term is distributed in a statement of the form "*s* is *P*," and both the subject and predicate are distributed in a statement of the form "*s* is not *P*." The reason here is that an individual is either wholly within a class or wholly outside it. Thus we are saying that every (that is, the only) *s* is included in the class *P* or else that every (that is, the only) *s* is completely outside the class *P* and thus every member of the class *P* is different from *s*.

One convenient way to indicate that a term is distributed is to circle it: thus we can summarize what we have said about distribution by circling the distributed terms in the standard forms (Table 3.5).

TABLE 3.5

A	Every $\widehat{S}$ is *P*	A′	$\widehat{s}$ is *P*
E	No $\widehat{S}$ is $\widehat{P}$	E′	$\widehat{s}$ is not $\widehat{P}$
I	Some *S* is *P*		
O	Some *S* is not $\widehat{P}$		

If a statement in ordinary English can be translated into standard form at all, it can be translated by a series of steps, in which we ask questions like the following:

1. Is it about an individual?
2. Is it affirmative?
3. Is it universal?

We can show the result of asking these questions by the flow chart in Figure 3.2. Finally we ask:

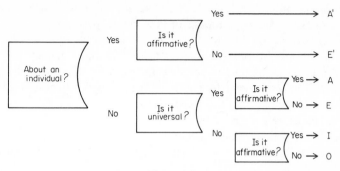

Figure 3.2

4. What term is the subject and what is the predicate?

Try this process with a simple statement: "Bears like honey."

1. About an individual?   No (not A′ or E′)
2. Universal?   Yes (not I or O)
3. Positive?   Yes (not E; so A)
4. What are the subject and predicate terms?
   Subject: bear; predicate: a creature who likes honey.

Final form: "Every bear is a creature who likes honey." The diagam is shown in Figure 3.3.

Figure 3.3

Labels and Symbols

A word about the labeling of diagrams: Although the *terms* we are using are singular, for example, "(a) bear," the class names on our diagrams will be in the plural. The class of things each of which is a bear is more conveniently and concisely referred to as the class of bears, or simply as "Bears." Thus, when a statement like "Every bear is a lover of honey" is given a class interpretation, it becomes "The class of bears is included in the class of lovers of honey" or "Bears are among the lovers of honey." Of course it would be absurd to label a circle representing a class with a singular term, and there is

83

no need to use circumlocutions such as "class of things each of which is a bear" rather than "Bears," at least for labeling purposes.

Notice that to fit the statement into our very restrictive standard form we had to (1) change the plural subject "bears" to the singular "(a) bear," which can appear before the "is" of the standard form; (2) change the original predicates ". . . likes honey" to a term "(a) thing which likes honey," which can appear after the "is" of the standard form.

In some cases we may have to do more. For example, "Honey is what a bear likes" seems to mean the same as "Bears like honey," but, to some people, "Honey" might appear to be the subject; and "bear," the real subject, is buried.

In this case I have to ask "What is the subject that I am talking *about*?" Bears? Honey? What am I *saying* about the subject?" The answer is often somewhat arbitrary and will depend to a great extent on our purpose in analyzing the sentence.

In many cases insistence on singular forms leads to rather unnatural sentences, but in other cases consistent use of the plural leads to equally strained sentences. Any attempt to be precise and rigorous by using a few rigid forms where ordinary language has a multiplicity of expressions is bound to run into some difficulties. The forms we use have disadvantages, but they have fewer disadvantages for our purposes than any of the alternatives.

It will be useful to have also a convenient shorthand for writing standard form statements. This shorthand is unlike the symbolism of propositional logic in that it is merely a convenient way of writing expressions in English, not a symbolism with independently defined symbols. We use pairs of parentheses written between letters for our symbolic forms, but since the parentheses are not being used as parentheses, we will call them *curves*. A left parenthesis, (, is called an *outcurve*, a right parenthesis,), is called an *incurve*. We symbolize the six standard form statements (Tables 3.2 and 3.5) shown in Table 3.6.

TABLE 3.6

Every S is P	S))P	s is P	s))P
No S is P	S)(P	s is not P	s)(P
Some S is P	S()P		
Some S is not P	S((P		

Notice several features of this notation: the left-hand curve indicates universal (incurve) or particular (outcurve). The right-hand curve indicates positive (incurve) or negative (outcurve). Distributed terms can be told at a glance because every distributed term is in the hollow of a curve; that is, the curve adjacent to it curves in such a way that if the curve were extended into a circle the circle would enclose the letter, for example

$$(\overset{\frown}{S}))P$$

Undistributed terms, on the other hand, are on the outside of a curve. If you think of the curves as representing parts of circles, the symbolism reminds you of the diagrams we considered earlier (Figure 3.1). In Figure 3.4, you

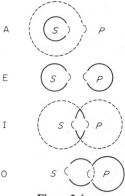

A

E

I

O

Figure 3.4

have to think of the right-hand curve as being part of a larger circle which encloses the circle of which the left-hand curve is part. For O, you have to think of the left-hand curve as part of a circle smaller than that of which the right-hand curve is part and as intersecting it. This is merely a suggestion to help you remember the symbolism. Its drawbacks are that the curvature has to be interpreted differently for A and O forms, and there is no natural extension of this picture to A' and E'. Other advantages of this symbolism will appear in due course.

EXERCISES 3.1

A. For the following statements (a) classify the statement as A, E, I, O, A', or E'; (b) give the subject and predicate terms; and (c) indicate which terms are distributed. (Source: Lewis Carroll, *Symbolic Logic.*)
1. No fat creature runs well.
2. Some greyhound is not fat.
3. Some sweet thing is liked by children.
4. Every person in the house is ill.
5. No Frenchman likes plum pudding.
6. Every Englishman likes plum pudding.
7. No portrait of a lady satisfies her.
8. Some old miser is not thin.
9. John is in the house.
10. Some judge does not exercise self-control.

B. Given the following dictionary translate the following symbolic statements into colloquial English.

A # (an) admiral	a # Andrew
B # (a) beer drinker	b # Bill
C # (a) courageous person	c # Charles
D # (a) dangerous person	d # David

1. A))B
2. B)(C
3. C)(A
4. D()B
5. b))D
6. B()A
7. a)(D
8. D))B
9. C((B
10. d)(A

C. Translate into standard form statements. (Source: A. A. Milne, *Winnie the Pooh.**)

1. Rabbits always live in holes.
2. Pooh always liked a little something at eleven o'clock in the morning.
3. Rabbit will never be able to use his front door again.
4. Wedged bears are comforted by sustaining books.
5. All Rabbit's friends and relations went head over heels.
6. Woozles are sometimes hostile animals.
7. Buzzing sounds are made by bees.
8. Some bees were suspicious.
9. The bees in the tree were all suspicious.
10. Every little cloud always sings aloud.

3.2 IMMEDIATE INFERENCE

Once we have put a statement into standard form we can more or less mechanically determine that certain other statements are true and false under the same conditions as our original statement. This enables us to give for syllogistic logic something like the table of equivalences that we gave for propositional logic.

Conversion

Traditionally, however, these equivalences have been regarded somewhat differently—as transformations which can be applied to standard form statements. There is no real difference in the two points of view; we can say either that "No *S* is *P*" is equivalent to "No *P* is *S*" or that "No *S* is *P*" can be transformed into "No *P* is *S*" and vice versa. When regarded as a permissable transformation, this process of switching the position of subject and predicate is called *conversion,* and the *converted* form is called the *converse*. Only E and I statements can be converted, so that we can give Table 3.7.

---

* Quotes and paraphrases from the book *Winnie the Pooh* by A. A. Milne. Copyright 1926 by E. P. Dutton & Co, Inc. Renewal, 1954 by A. A. Milne. Used by permission of the publishers.

TABLE 3.7

Standard Form Statement		Converse
A	Every *S* is *P*	None
E	No *S* is *P*	No *P* is *S*
I	Some *S* is *P*	Some *P* is *S*
O	Some *S* is not *P*	None
A′	*s* is *P*	None
E′	*s* is not *P*	None

Of course we *can* switch subject and predicate in an A, O, A′ or E′ statement, but by doing so we do not get a statement which is true and false under the same conditions as the original. We can see the reason for this in two ways, by diagram and by considering distribution. The diagram of "Every S is P" is shown in Figure 3.5, and only the subject term is distributed. If we at-

Figure 3.5

tempted to get from "Every *S* is *P*" to "Every *P* is *S*," we would be arguing from the fact that the *S* circle is in the *P* circle to the statement that the *P* circle was contained in the *S* circle. We would be going from a statement which said something about every *S* but not something about every *P* to a statement which said something about every *P*. An example makes it clear how absurd it would be to regard such a transformation as legitimate: We could argue from "Every woman is human" to "Every human is a woman."

In an E statement, on the other hand, both subject and predicate are distributed, and the diagram (Figure 3.6) can equally be read as showing that

Figure 3.6

the *S* circle is outside of the *P* circle or that the *P* circle is outside the *S* circle. An example would be the passage from "No mother is a male" to "No male is a mother."

Similarly in an I statement both subject and predicate are *un*distributed, and the diagram (Figure 3.7) shows either that the *S* circle is partly in the

Figure 3.7

P circle or that the *P* circle is partly in the *S* circle. Thus "Some women is a doctor" implies and is implied by "Some doctor is a woman."

Finally, in an O statement only the predicate is distributed. The diagram (Figure 3.8) shows that part of *S* circle is outside of the *P* circle. Unfortunately

Figure 3.8

it suggests also that part of the *P* circle is definitely outside the S circle, which is misleading. The point here is that we don't know about the rest of the *S* circle and its relation to the *P* circle. It may turn out that the *S* circle does not overlap at all with the *P* circle (Figure 3.9), or that the *S* circle completely

Figure 3.9

includes the *P* circle (Figure 3.10), or that they partially overlap, as our stan-

Figure 3.10

dard diagram suggests (Figure 3.8). If it were not too much trouble, it might be preferable to use a diagram like Figure 3.11 for O statements. Since we

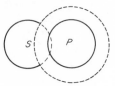

Figure 3.11

don't know which of these situations obtains, we cannot convert O statements. For example it would be silly to try to argue from "Some woman is not a wife" to "Some wife is not a woman."

The reason that A' and E' statements cannot be converted is that this would involve putting individual names in the predicate position, which cannot occur in a standard form statement.

Negation

If we allow the introduction of negative terms such as "nonwoman" or "nonauthor," we can describe two other sorts of "immediate inference." Negative terms will be formed by prefixing *non-* to a word or, in some cases, by inserting the phrase "a thing which is not." (For example, to form the negative of "a person who likes coffee," we must write "a thing which is not a person who likes coffee.") Negatives are so interpreted in Aristotelian logic that either a term or its negative applies in any given case. "Nonwoman" includes not only men and bears but also such things as inanimate objects, and abstractions. Similarly a person who has never tasted coffee, a chair, and the square root of 144 all come under the description "a thing which is not a person who likes coffee." Negative terms are thus highly peculiar: They apply to everything *except* a certain class of things. The medievals called such terms by a name which can be translated as "infinite name" or "infinite term," which suggests this peculiarity. (This terminology seems to have been introduced by a mistranslation of Aristotle, whose Greek word for such terms meant merely "*indefinite* names" or *indefinite* terms.")

Symbolically we will represent negative terms in the following way: We will give the positive term in our dictionary, for instance,

$$C \mathbin{\#} \text{(a) person who likes coffee}$$

and put a bar over the letter to represent the negative term. This is called *negating* the term, and such a term is said to be *negated*. Thus $\bar{C}$ would be "a thing which is not a person who likes coffee."

Negative terms have the following effect on distribution: A negated term is *not* distributed if it is in a position where a nonnegated term would be distributed, and a negated term *is* distributed if it is in a position where a nonnegated term would not be distributed. Thus, for example, in "Every $\bar{S}$ is $\bar{P}$," the term S is *not* distributed and P, on the other hand, *is* distributed.

Contraposition

With this rule in mind, we can show the validity of two new immediate inferences in which the subject and predicate are switched and both are negated. If we go from

$$\text{Every } S \text{ is } P \qquad \text{to} \qquad \text{Every } \bar{P} \text{ is } \bar{S}$$

S remains distributed and P remains undistributed. Similarly, if we go from

Some S is not P to   Some $\bar{P}$ is not $\bar{S}$

S remains distributed and P remains undistributed. However, if we go from

No S is P to   No $\bar{P}$ is $\bar{S}$

S and P which were distributed both become undistributed, and, if we go from

Some S is P to   Some $\bar{P}$ is $\bar{S}$

S and P which were undistributed become distributed. The point is that the negation and interchange of positions have the effect of keeping the distribution quality the same for each term. This is important because, if a transformation makes a term distributed which was formerly undistributed, we are concluding something about all of a class when we have information about only part of it, which is unjustified. If a distributed term becomes undistributed, we have a weaker statement, which is not equivalent to the one we began with. We can now give Table 3.8 for these inferences, which shows the *contraposition*.

TABLE 3.8

Standard Form Statement	Contrapositive
A Every S is P	Every $\bar{P}$ is $\bar{S}$
E No S is P	None
I Some S is P	None
O Some S is not P	Some $\bar{P}$ is not $\bar{S}$
A′ s is P	None
E′ s is not P	None

The reasons for not allowing contraposition for A′ and E′ statements again involves the fact that individual names cannot appear in the predicate position. Notice that those which have contrapositives are those which lacked converses, A′ and E′ excepted.

Obversion

There is another form of immediate inference, which can be applied to all standard form statements. It is called *obversion*, and the formula is somewhat complex. The formula is "Change the quality, but not the quantity of the proposition and negate the predicate." This means that you must change a

90

universal affirmative (A) to a *universal* negative (E) and vice versa, or a particular affirmative to a particular negative and vice versa, or an individual
affirmative to an individual negative and vice versa. That is, the formula can
be expanded as shown in Table 3.9 and the predicate negated. This formula

TABLE 3.9

Original Statement	Change to	Original Statement	Change to
A	E	A′	E′
E	A	E′	A′
I	O		
O	I		

gives us the transformations in Table 3.10. You can check each case and see

TABLE 3.10

	Standard Form Statement	Obverse
A	Every S is P	No S is $\bar{P}$
E	No S is P	Every S is $\bar{P}$
I	Some S is P	Some S is not $\bar{P}$
O	Some S is not P	Some S is $\bar{P}$
A′	s is P	s is not $\bar{P}$
E′	s is not P	s is $\bar{P}$

that distribution is preserved. We can sum up our results so far in Table 3.11.

TABLE 3.11

	Standard Form Statement	Converse	Contrapositive	Obverse
A	Every S is P	——	Every $\bar{P}$ is $\bar{S}$	No S is $\bar{P}$
E	No S is P	No P is S	——	Every S is $\bar{P}$
I	Some S is P	Some P is S	——	Some S is not $\bar{P}$
O	Some S is not P	——	Some $\bar{P}$ is not $\bar{S}$	Some S is $\bar{P}$
A′	s is P	——	——	s is not $\bar{P}$
E′	s is not P	——	——	s is $\bar{P}$

Every valid immediate inference preserves distribution, and every immediate inference is in fact an equivalence, so that one can go, for example,

from a standard form statement to its obverse or from the obverse to the original form.

A useful feature of the symbolic notation introduced earlier is that forms which *convert* have symmetrical curves

$$S)(P \qquad S()P$$

and forms which contrapose have asymmetrical curves

$$S))P \qquad S((P$$

The bar notation can of course be used with our symbolic forms, so Table 3.11 in symbolic form is Table 3.12.

TABLE 3.12

Statement	Converse	Contrapositive	Obverse
$S))P$	——	$\bar{P}))\bar{S}$	$S)(\bar{P}$
$S)(P$	$P)(S$	——	$S))\bar{P}$
$S()P$	$P()S$	——	$S()\bar{P}$
$S))P$	——	$\bar{P}((S$	$S(($\bar{P}$

The bars must be understood as reversing the rule that a letter in a hollow represents a distributed term and vice versa. Several other forms of immediate inference related to these just discussed have been described by traditional logic. For example, the *inverse* of a statement $S))P$ would be $\bar{S}))\bar{P}$ and so on. None of those other forms seems to me sufficiently useful to discuss here. We will find a use for Conversion, Obversion, and Contraposition in later sections in dealing with certain syllogistic arguments.

Squares of Opposition

Another kind of immediate inference can be described as follows: For any standard form statements with the same subject and predicate, either the A statement or the O statement will be true, but not both, and similarly either the E statement or the I statement will be true, but not both. Accordingly A and O statements with the same subject and predicate are *contradictories:* They have the same relation as a proposition and its negation in propositional logic. This means that from the truth of one we can infer the falsity of the other, and from the falsity of the one we can infer the truth of the other. One way of expressing this is the diagram shown in Figure 3.12, called a *partial square of opposition.*

The universal statements are above in Figure 3.12, the particular below, the affirmative at the left, the negative at the right. The diagonal lines which

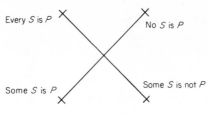

Figure 3.12

cross to make an X and have X's at their ends suggest conflict or opposition. The contradictory of any statement can be found by following the diagonal line from that statement to the opposite corner of the square.

The next step is extremely crucial. *If* there exist things to which the subject term applies *and* things to which the predicate term applies, then, if an A statement is true, the I statement with the same subject and predicate is also true, and, if the I statement is false, then the A is also false. Also, if an E statement is true, then the O statement with the same subject and predicate is true, and, if the O statement is false, so is the E.

But this condition is not always fulfilled, so the restriction is necessary. Consider, for example, the statement "No woman is a witch." Most people would feel this is true, since no witches exist. Without our restriction, we could infer from the truth of "No woman is a witch" the truth of "No witch is a woman," by conversion, then infer "Some witch is not a woman," which sounds as if we were saying that witches *did* exist!

Similar problems arise with A and I. Suppose a man says, "Every trespasser on my land is a person who is going to be prosecuted." This may be true, even if there have been no trespassers so far. But he should not be able to infer, "Some trespasser on my land is a person who is going to be prosecuted," and, using conversion, "Some person who is going to be prosecuted is a trespasser on my land," either of which might falsely suggest that there had been trespassers already.

Therefore we can allow the inference of I statements from A and of O from E (with the same subject and predicate, of course), only subject to the condition mentioned. (And it is not a matter of logic whether the condition is fulfilled.)

This relation between A and I and between E and O is usually called *subalternation*, and we put it on the square of opposition as shown in Figure 3.13. The arrows remind us that the relation is directional, and the asterisks

Figure 3.13

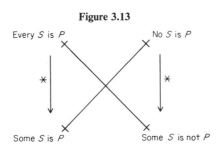

remind us that the relation is subject to a condition. When this condition is satisfied, we will say that subalternation *holds.*

Now if subalternation holds, so do two other relationships. First, if the subalternation condition is satisfied, A and E statements with the same subject and predicates cannot both be true since, if the A statement is true, its contradictory, the O statement with the same subject and predicate, will be false and, if the O is false, so is the E. Similarly if the E is true, then the I is false, and therefore the A is false too. Thus, though A and E statements with the same subject and predicate can both be false (for instance, "Every woman is a mother" and "No woman is a mother"), they cannot both be true. This relationship is called *contriety,* or *contrariety,* and A and E are *contraries.*

Secondly, I and O are *sub*contraries. An I and an O with the same subject and predict may both be true ("Some woman is a mother" and "Some woman is not a mother") but cannot both be false if subalternation holds: If an I statement is false, its contrary the E statement is true and thus the O statement, which is the subaltern of the E, is true.

Similarly if we assume that the O is false, then the A will be true and thus its subaltern, the I, will be true. So, if I is false, O is true and, if O is false, I is true, and they can never both be false. This gives us finally the *complete square of opposition,* shown in Figure 3.14. The asterisks remind us that all

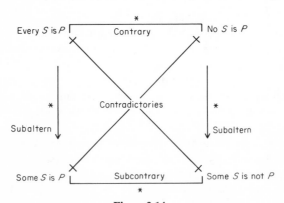

Figure 3.14

relations except contradiction hold subject only to a condition. The symbol ⌐ for contraries and the symbol ⌐ for subcontraries remind us of their position in the square. We can use them outside of the square and give Table 3.13.

We can see that the square of Figure 3.14 is more compact than is Table 3.13, but the table reminds us that each standard form statement has three relations, and the only relation shared by all four is contradiction. The relation between I and A and between O and E can be expressed also by saying

TABLE 3.13

Every S is P	⌐	*No S is P
Every S is P	×	Some S is not P
Every S is P	⟶	*Some S is P
No S is P	⌐	*Every S is P
No S is P	×	Some S is P
No S is P	⟶	*Some S is not P
Some S is P	⌐	*Some S is not P
Some S is P	×	No S is P
Some S is P	⟵	*Every S is P
Some S is not P	⌐	*Some S is P
Some S is not P	×	Every S is P
Some S is not P	⟵	*No S is P

that A is the *super*altern of I and E the *super*altern of O. We can express all these relations using propositional logic as in Table 3.14. In fact we can use these definitions, together with standard propositional logic argument forms (such as MP, MT, DS) to reach conclusions about the truth or falsity of

TABLE 3.14

(p × q) ≡ (p ≡ ~q) or (~p ≡ q)	
(p ⌐ q) ≡ (~p v ~q)	
(p ⌐ q) ≡ (p v q)	
(p ⟶ q) ≡ (p ⊃ q)	
(p ⟵ q) ≡ (q ⊃ p)	

some standard form statements on the basis of information about the truth or falsity of others with the same subject and predicate.

Also we can set out the first sort of immediate inferences as a table of equivalences (Table 3.15). We can then regard our maneuvers with conversion, obversion, and contraposition as cases which are covered by an extended Replacement Rule for equivalences.

TABLE 3.15

Every S is P	≡	Every $\bar{P}$ is $\bar{S}$
	≡	No S is $\bar{P}$
No S is P	≡	No P is $\bar{S}$
	≡	Every S is $\bar{P}$
Some S is P	≡	Some P is S
	≡	Some S is not $\bar{P}$
Some S is not P	≡	Some $\bar{P}$ is not $\bar{S}$
	≡	Some S is $\bar{P}$

Is it legitimate to mix syllogistic and propositional logic in this way? It is, so long as the restrictions on both forms are observed. For example, facts such as the contrariety of A and E statements are not part of the machinery of propositional logic and must be introduced as *premises* in a propositional argument.

Our symbolic forms gives us the following help with square of opposition relationships. In contradictories, both curves face opposite ways:

$$S))P \times S((P \qquad S)(P \times S()P$$

In contraries and subcontraries the right-hand curves face opposite ways:

$$S))P \frown S)(P \qquad S()P \frown S((P$$

Thus the symbolism expresses the fact that contradictories are opposite in both quality and quantity, whereas contraries and subcontraries are alike in quantity but unlike in quality.

EXERCISES 3.2

A. (1) For each of the following statements give the converse or contrapositive, depending on which is equivalent to the original statement. (2) Give the obverse of each of the following statements. (Source: Lewis Carroll, *Symbolic Logic.*)
1. Every wasp is unfriendly.
2. Every unfriendly creature is unwelcome.
3. No old rabbit is greedy.
4. Every black rabbit is greedy.
5. Some eggs are hard-boiled.
6. No egg is uncrackable.
7. No antelope is ungraceful.
8. Every graceful creature delights the eye.
9. Every well-fed canary sings loud.
10. No canary is melancholy who sings loud.

B. For each of the following groups of statements, indicate if you can which are true and which are false if the starred statement above the group is true.

    *Some ambushes are surprising.
1. Some surprising things are ambushes.
2. No ambushes are surprising.
3. Some nonambushes are not surprising.
4. Some ambushes are not unsurprising.
5. No surprises are ambushes.
    *No person with a balloon is a person who can be uncheered.
6. No person who can be an uncheered person is a person with a balloon.
7. Some person with a balloon is a person who can be uncheered.
8. Some person who can be uncheered is not a person with a balloon.
9. Every person who can be uncheered is a person without a balloon.
10. No person who can be uncheered is a person without a balloon.

3.3 SYLLOGISMS

Immediate inference gives us a certain insight into the structure of standard form statements, but it is not of much direct use. Syllogistic arguments, on the other hand, have been extensively used by many philosophers since Aristotle first developed syllogistic logic. Much of medieval philosophy, for example, becomes much more accessible if you have a good grasp of syllogistic logic. Even in modern philosophical writing, as we shall see, you will encounter arguments which are in syllogistic form or can be put in this form.

Syllogistic Form

A syllogism is an argument consisting of three standard form statements, two of which are the premises of the argument and the other of which is the conclusion of the argument. By definition, a syllogism has three terms. Of these three terms, one called the *middle term*, appears in both premises but not in the conclusion. Another of the three terms, called the *minor term*, appears in one premise and is the subject of the conclusion. The remaining term, called the *major term*, appears in one premise and is the predicate of the conclusion. The premise in which the major term appears is called the *major premise*, that in which the minor term appears is called the *minor premise*. By convention, syllogisms are written as follows.

> major premise
> minor premise
> _____
> conclusion

For example, consider the following syllogism.

> Every bear is a lover of honey.
> Pooh is a bear.
> _____
> Pooh is a lover of honey.

"Bear" is the middle term, "Pooh" the minor term, "a lover of honey" the major term. The order of premises is major premise first, minor premise second. Since the middle term may be either subject or predicate in either major premise or minor premise, and major premise, minor premise, and conclusion can be A, E, I, O, A' or E' statements, there are $6 \times 2 \times 6 \times 2 \times 6 = 864$ distinguishable syllogisms. Since for many purposes A' and E' statements may be treated like A and E statements, it is more usual to say that there are $4 \times 2 \times 4 \times 2 \times 4 = 256$ separable syllogisms. Of this very large number, only a comparative handful are valid argument forms. Of the invalid forms, some are extremely unconvincing and would probably deceive no one while others are quite similar to valid arguments and frequently take people in. Again, of the valid arguments, some are more obviously good arguments than others. So if a person is presented with an argument in

97

syllogistic form, it is by no means easy to decide intuitively whether the argument is good or bad.

In this section we will present two techniques for deciding the validity of arguments in syllogistic form. The first technique consists of a set of rules. Every valid syllogism satisfies all of these rules, and every invalid syllogism breaks at least one of them. The rules can be quickly and easily applied and are a completely mechanical technique for separating valid from invalid syllogistic arguments. However it is not always easy to see why a syllogism which breaks the rules is invalid. Therefore we will give a second technique which is by no means so easily applied and is not mechanically applicable in the way in which the rules are but which gives a much greater insight into the reason for the validity or invalidity of a particular syllogistic argument. This second technique consists of a diagrammatic method which is an extension of the diagrams already used for immediate inference.

Syllogistic Rules

We will first state the rules, then apply them to sample arguments to show the validity or invalidity of sample arguments. Then at this stage we will introduce the diagrammatic techniques to illustrate and illuminate the decisions reached by the rules.

The first step in checking an alleged syllogistic argument for validity is to make sure it *is* a syllogism; that is, that it has two premises and a conclusion, that it has only three terms, and that no term occurs twice in the same statement. It may be necessary also to rearrange the order of statements so that the conclusion is at the end and, less important, that the major premise comes first and the minor premise comes second.

If there are more than two premises, the argument may be a *sorites* or chain of syllogisms, which we will discuss in Section 3.4. If there is only one premise, the missing premise may be obvious or easy to supply. In this case the argument is called an *enthymeme*, and such arguments also are discussed in Section 3.4. Mere lack of standard order does not affect the validity of a syllogism, though it may lead to confusion.

However, if there are more than three terms we may have a fallacious argument which looks like a syllogism but is not. Such arguments can be extremely misleading, especially if they use a term in two different senses or use different terms which seem to be synonymous but are not. For example, consider the two seemingly syllogistic arguments

> Every angel is a nonmaterial being.
> My wife is an angel.
> _____
> My wife is a nonmaterial being.

and

> Every poor person is a public responsibility.
> Every college professor is a person who always needs more money.
> _____
> Every college professor is a public responsibility.

In the first argument "angel" is used first literally, then metaphorically. In the second argument "poor person" and "person who always needs more money" might appear synonymous, but are not. We will call arguments of this kind "pseudo syllogisms" and will be on our guard against them.

If the syllogism is a genuine one, it is valid if and only if it satisfies the conditions in all the following rules.

1. Not more than one premise is negative.
2. Not more than one premise is particular.
3. The conclusion is negative if and only if one premise is negative.
4. The conclusion is particular if and only if a premise is particular.
5. The middle term is distributed at least once.
6. If a term is distributed in the conclusion, it is distributed in a premise.

(The condition of Rule 2 is redundant but convenient, as is part of the condition in Rule 4.)

The rules are arranged in such a way that those points which are easier to check come first. Looking only at the premises, we see whether these satisfy conditions in Rules 1 and 2. Then we look at the conclusion, and check the premises to see if conditions in Rules 3 and 4 are met. Finally, we can draw distribution circles around terms. If the middle term is circled, the condition of Rule 5 is satisfied. If a term is circled in the conclusion, it must be circled in a premise to satisfy the condition of Rule 6. The flow chart in Figure 3.15 indicates the sequence.

Remember! *All* you need to know in order to know what terms are distributed is their position (in the subject or predicate) and the type of statement in which they appear. For your convenience we reproduce here (Table 3.16) the distribution table that was originally given as Table 3.5. The circles indicate distributed terms.

TABLE 3.16

A	Every $\widehat{S}$ is P	A′	$\widehat{s}$ is P
E	No $\widehat{S}$ is $\widehat{P}$	E′	$\widehat{s}$ is not $\widehat{P}$
I	Some S is P		
O	Some S is not $\widehat{P}$		

Diagramming a Syllogism

With the set of six rules that are presented in the flow chart of Figure 3.15, we can decide mechanically whether a syllogistic argument is valid or not. We want to understand also why the syllogism is a good or bad argument, and for this the diagrams are useful. To diagram a syllogistic argument, we use the same diagrams introduced in the last section (Figure 3.1). We first diagram the major premise, which involves a circle for the middle term and

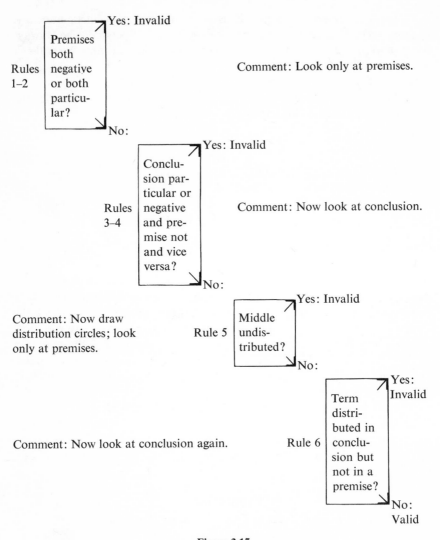

Figure 3.15

one for the major term. Then, *using the same circle for the middle term* we diagram the minor premise. If the argument is valid, diagramming the major and minor premises automatically produces a diagram of the conclusion. Consider this valid argument:

> No pig is fond of bathing.
> Piglet is a pig.
> _____
> Piglet is not fond of bathing.

We diagram the major premise, then the minor, using the same circle for the middle term (Figure 3.16). Since Piglet is inside the "Pigs" circle and that

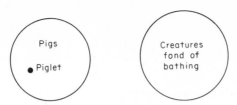

Figure 3.16

circle is completely outside the "Creatures fond of bathing" circle, Piglet must be completely excluded from the class of creatures fond of bathing.

However, suppose that both premises were negative, breaking Rule 1, as in

> No pig is fond of bathing.
> Pooh is not a pig.
> ───────────────
> Pooh is not fond of bathing.

We diagram (Figure 3.17) the major (short for "major premise") as before.

Figure 3.17

But when we come to diagram the minor (premise) we can put Pooh anywhere we like so long as it is outside the "Pigs" circle. Thus the diagram of Figure 3.18, which makes the premises true and the conclusion false, is *possible.*

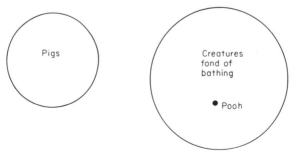

Figure 3.18

The difficulty here is that the two negative premises both tell us where something is not, so to speak, and this leaves us without a connection between major and minor terms. Similarly, knowing that Pooh is not at Owl's house, and that Piglet is not where Pooh is, leaves us uncertain as to whether Piglet is at Owl's house or not. No matter what conclusion we try to reach, the two negative premises cannot give us any connection between the major term and the minor term.

A syllogism which breaks Rule 2 will always break some other rule also, so Rule 2 will not be discussed separately. Rule 2 is included only because it is easy to check whether both premises are particular, and this can save time and trouble.

Rule 3 says, in effect, that, if an argument has one negative premise, it has a negative conclusion, and, if it has a negative conclusion, it has one negative premise. Consider this example, which violates the condition of Rule 1:

> Every bear is fond of honey.
> Piglet is not fond of honey.
> ──────────────────────────
> Piglet is a bear.

If we diagram the premises we diagram *a* conclusion, but it *cannot* be an affirmative one (Figure 3.19). Since Piglet is outside the "Creatures fond of

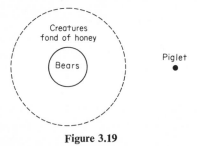

Figure 3.19

honey" circle, he *cannot* be inside the "Bears" circle. Similarly we cannot reach a negative conclusion from two positive premises.

> Every bear is fond of honey.
> Pooh is a bear.
> ──────────────────────────
> Pooh is not fond of honey.

The diagram (Figure 3.20) is the one we have already seen. Since Pooh must be inside the "Bears" circle and the "Bears" circle must be inside the "Creatures fond of honey" circle, Pooh *cannot* be outside of the "Creatures fond of honey" circle.

Rule 4 has two parts. The part that says that a syllogism with a particular premise must have a particular conclusion is like Rule 2, convenient and dispensable—if a syllogism breaks this part of Rule 4, it will also break other

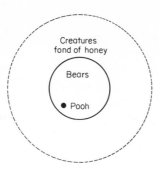

Figure 3.20

rules. The part of Rule 4 that says that a syllogism with a particular conclusion must have one particular premise is not dispensable, but is somewhat controversial. Some logicians seem to have assumed that every simple* class with which they dealt would have at least one member. This enabled them to draw some inferences forbidden by our Rule 4, for example:

> Every bear is fond of honey.
> Every bear is a lazy creature.
> ———————————————
> Some lazy creature is fond of honey.

This is intuitively convincing, for if bears are both lazy and fond of honey, then obviously at least one creature is both lazy and fond of honey. However if we allow arguments of this kind, we open the door to arguments like this:

> Every creature fond of honey is fond of sugar.
> No square circle is fond of sugar.
> ———————————————
> Some square circle is not fond of honey.

The first premise is probably empirically true, the second is trivially true, but the conclusion sounds as if we were saying that there exist square circles and that these have likes and dislikes about foods. The problem is that we often use a universal or individual negative statement because we think that the predicate class is empty. We say "No woman is a witch" because we think there are no witches. We say of a given individual, "John is not perfect" no matter how much we admire him, just because we think no one is perfect, and so on. But when we say "Some *S* is not *P*" we do seem to be asserting the existence of *S*'s.

There are three ways out of this difficulty. First, we might restrict syllogistic logic to cases where all simple classes had members. This would unduly restrict the scope of syllogistic logic. Second, we might take Aristotle's way

* A simple class is one defined by a single property. See Chapter 4 for further discussion of simple and compound classes.

out of this difficulty, which was to regard *all* negative statements about non-existent things as true, including particular negatives. This is confusing and distorts our ordinary use of "some . . . not . . ." statements. Finally, we might allow certain inferences only where we were sure that all simple classes had members. What we will do is to regard the intuitively valid argument above as justified by deriving "Some bear is a lazy creature" from "Every bear is a lazy creature" by subalternation. The condition that the class of bears and of lazy creatures have members is, of course, fulfilled. The resulting syllogism

> Every bear is fond of honey.
> Some bear is a lazy creature.
> ────────────────────────────
> Some lazy creature is fond of honey.

is quite valid by our rules. (The argument about square circles above cannot be saved by this method since we know that this class has no members.) Consider the syllogism used for illustration earlier.

> Every bear is fond of honey.
> Pooh is a bear.
> ────────────────────────
> Pooh is fond of honey.

We diagram the major premise in Figure 3.21, and then diagram the minor

Figure 3.21

premise (Figure 3.22). We see that Pooh is necessarily in the "Creatures fond of honey" circle.

Figure 3.22

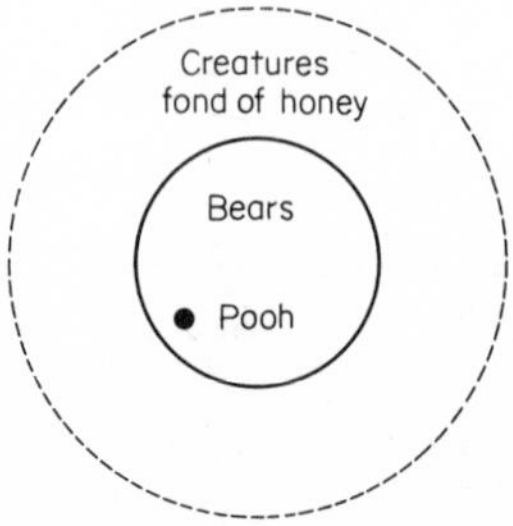

Notice that in this diagram the middle term is literally in the middle, and its role is obviously that of connecting the minor term with the major term.

Now consider what happens when Rule 5 is broken and the middle term is not distributed. We give an example of a syllogism with an undistributed middle term by reversing subject and predicate in the major premise of our previous argument.

> Every creature fond of honey is a bear.
> Pooh is a bear.
> _____
> Pooh is fond of honey.

We diagram the new major premise first (Figure 3.23). When we come to

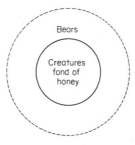

Figure 3.23

diagram the minor premise, we are not forced to make a diagram of the conclusion. We can put Pooh in the "Bears" circle without putting him in the "Creatures fond of honey" circle (Figure 3.24). This diagram shows that

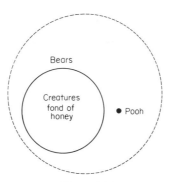

Figure 3.24

the premises of our syllogism can be true and yet the conclusion false. The difficulty lies precisely in the fact that we lack enough information about the middle term: In this case it fails to do its job of connecting the major and minor terms. The statement that every honey lover is a bear, even if true, would not tell us whether every bear was a honey lover. If we cannot be sure of this, the fact that Pooh is a bear does not ensure that he is a honey lover, for, if there *may* be some bears who are not honey lovers, Pooh *may* be one of them. Thus an undistributed middle term cannot do its connecting job properly.

Finally, if Rule 6 is broken, the diagrams again give us some insight into the sort of breakdown which takes place. Consider the syllogism

> Every bear is a creature fond of honey.
> Every creature fond of honey is a creature fond of sugar.
> ──────────────────────────────
> Every creature fond of sugar is a bear.

The diagram is shown in Figure 3.25. The syllogism is invalid because

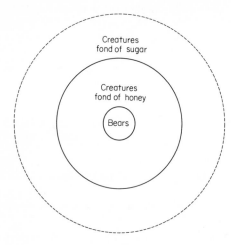

Figure 3.25

"creature fond of sugar" is distributed in the conclusion but not in the pre-mise. The diagram makes this fairly clear; the "Creatures fond of sugar" circle is on the outside, and we know nothing about all of this class, whereas the conclusion tries to say something about every member of the class. The same point is clear in a negative example.

> No bear is fond of acorns.
> Some friend of Piglet is a bear.
> ──────────────────────────────
> Some creature fond of acorns is not a friend of Piglet.

Figure 3.26

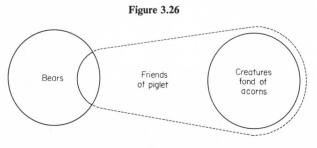

The diagram is shown in Figure 3.26. Note that, since we don't know all of what the class of Piglet's friends includes, it *might* include *all* acorn lovers. The conclusion needs to say something about every friend of Piglet, but this is a class we lack complete information on: For all we know all acorn lovers are Piglet's friends. So, in general, a term distributed in the conclusion but not in the premise shows up fairly clearly in the diagram.

We have tried briefly to show how the breaking of each rule leads to mistakes which can be spotted when we draw the diagram for the fallacious syllogism. This becomes much clearer as you work with syllogisms, seeing how, in each case that a rule is broken, the diagram reflects the fact that the conclusion does not follow from the premises.

We can write out syllogisms in symbolic form, and this (besides saving space) makes it very easy to check the rules. If the middle term is not in the hollow of a curve, Rule 5 is broken; if a term is in the hollow of a curve in the conclusion but not in a premise, Rule 6 is broken. Two particular premises give a

$$($$

backwards 3 pattern $($

on the left, for example

$$S((M$$
$$\underline{M()P}$$

Two negative premises give the same pattern on the right:

$$S)(M$$
$$\underline{M((P}$$

With practice, it is possible to detect many invalid patterns at a glance.

EXERCISES 3.3

A. Test by rules, putting in standard form when necessary. (Source: Lewis Carroll, *Symbolic Logic*.)

1. No doctor is enthusiastic.
    You are enthusiastic.
    _____
    You are not a doctor.

2. Every dictionary is useful.
    Every useful book is valuable.
    _____
    Every dictionary is valuable.

3. No miser is unselfish.
    Every person who saves eggshells is a miser.
    _____
    No unselfish person saves eggshells.

4. Some candle gives very little light.
    Every candle is meant to give light.
    _____
    Some thing meant to give light gives very little.

5. Every person eager to learn works hard.
   Some of these boys work hard.
   ___
   Some of these boys are eager to learn.

6. Every lion is fierce.
   Some lion does not drink coffee.
   ___
   Some creature that drinks coffee is not fierce.

7. Some epicures are not generous.
   Every one of my uncles is generous.
   ___
   No uncle of mine is an epicure.

8. Some cravats are not artistic.
   Every artistic thing is a thing I admire.
   ___
   Some cravats are not things I admire.

9. No miser is generous.
   Some old men are ungenerous.
   ___
   Some old men are misers.

10. No fossil can be crossed in love.
    Some oyster can be crossed in love.
    ___
    No oyster is a fossil.

B. Put the following arguments into standard syllogistic form and test for validity. Ignore phrases in parentheses. (Source: Duns Scotus, *Ordinatio*.)

   1. The knowledge of pure spirits is the most noble because it has to do with the noblest class of things and whatever knowledge has to do with the noblest class of things is the most noble.

   2. No natural knowledge of the properties of pure spirits is possible unless we know naturally the subjects which have these properties. Since we cannot know these subjects naturally, we cannot know the properties of pure spirits naturally.

   3. [Against this I argue that] we can know naturally any necessary truths whose terms we can know naturally. All necessary revealed truths are necessary truths whose terms we can know naturally. Therefore they are truths we can know naturally.

   4. No contradiction is possible unless terms are being used in the same way. Theologians and philosophers contradict one another. Therefore they use terms in the same way.

   5. Whatever is ordered toward some end toward which it is not disposed must be gradually disposed for this end. Man is ordered to an end for which he is not disposed. Therefore he needs to be gradually disposed to possess this end.

   6. Any being which uses an imperfect instrument is subject to the limitations of that instrument. Man in using his intellect is using an imperfect instrument. Therefore, he is subject to the limitations of that instrument.

   7. Every natural passive faculty has some corresponding natural agent. The possible intellect is a natural passive faculty. Therefore it has some corresponding natural agent.

   8. Speculative acquired sciences perfect the speculative intellect. Metaphysics is a speculative acquired science. Therefore metaphysics perfects the speculative intellect.

   9. Anyone capable of knowing first principles can know naturally the conclusions embodied in them. Man is capable of knowing first principles. Therefore he can know naturally the conclusions embodied in them.

10. Every agent who acts knowingly needs a distinct knowledge of his destiny or end. Man acts knowingly. So Man needs a distinct knowledge of his destiny or end.

3.4 SORITESES AND ENTHYMEMES

Consider the following passage from *Winnie the Pooh* by A. A. Milne:*

One day when Winnie-the-Pooh was out walking, he came to an open place in the middle of the forest, and in the middle of this place was a large oak-tree, and, from the top of the tree, there came a loud buzzing noise.

Winnie-the-Pooh sat down at the foot of the tree, put his head between his paws and began to think.

First of all he said to himself: "That buzzing noise means something . . . and the only reason for making a buzzing noise that *I* know of is because you're a bee."

Then he thought another long time and said: "And the only reason for being a bee that I know of is making Honey."

And then he got up, and said: "And the only reason for making honey is so as *I* can eat it." So he began to climb the tree.

Now the thinking processes of the astute bear cannot be expressed as a *single* syllogism. But they can be expressed as a *chain* of syllogisms in this fashion:

P 1   The top of this tree is a place where there is a buzzing sound.
P 2   Every place where there is a buzzing sound is a place where there are bees.

C 1   The top of this tree is a place where there are bees.
P 3   Every place where there are bees is a place where there is honey.

C 2   The top of this tree is a place where there is honey.
P 4   Every place where there is honey is a place where there is something for me to eat.

C 3   The top of this tree is a place where there is something for me to eat.
P 5   Every place where there is something for me to eat is a place I want to go.

C 4   The top of this tree is a place where I want to go.

And so, as the story says, he began to climb the tree. Notice several things about this example.

First, the syllogisms are linked in such a way that C 1, the conclusion of P 1 and P 2, is one of the premises of the second syllogism; C 2, the conclusion of the syllogism by C 1 and P 3, is one of the premises of the third syllogism, and so on. This is what we mean by calling it a *chain* of syllogisms.

* Quotes and paraphrases from the book *Winnie the Pooh* by A. A. Milne. Copyright 1926 by E. P. Dutton & Co., Inc. Renewal, 1956 by A. A. Milne. Used by permission of the publishers.

Second, if the whole chain is to be a valid syllogism chain or *sorites*, then each syllogism composing the chain must be valid. If the sorites as a whole is to be sound, each premise must be true. Thus to check the validity or soundness of a sorites we check the validity or soundness of the syllogisms which make it up.

Finally, we may notice that at several points we had to expand the reasoning as presented by the author. Although P 1 was not expressed as part of Pooh's reasoning, it is obvious from the context. Nor is P 5 expressed either, but it is obvious to anyone who knows Pooh. Furthermore, the subsidiary conclusions, C 1, C 2, and C 3 are not stated in the original, but were derived from premises which are stated as we reconstructed the argument. Also, the final conclusion, C 4, is not stated verbally, but is implied by the bear's actions. Thus the reconstructed argument makes explicit much that is unexpressed or understood in the original.

Solving a Sorites

Soriteses in logic books are amusing puzzles which require a certain amount of ingenuity to work out, especially if the premises are expressed informally. But essentially they can be solved by a mechanical process, even if the premises are given in scrambled form. One simply pairs off any premises which have a common term and then draws the conclusion which can be validly drawn from the paired premises. The resulting conclusion should have a term in common with one of the remaining premises. One then draws the conclusion from this pair, and so on until all the premises are exhausted. The resulting conclusion will be the conclusion of the whole sorites. Take, for example, the following sorites, invented by Lewis Carroll.

> P 1   Babies are illogical.
> P 2   No one who can manage a crocodile is despised.
> P 3   Illogical persons are despised.

Both P 2 and P 3 have the common term "despised." If we interpret them as universal statements, the first syllogism becomes:

> P 3   Every illogical person is a despised person.
> P 2   No crocodile-manager is a despised person.
> ------
> C 1   No crocodile-manager is an illogical person.

Now C 1 has the term "illogical (person)" in common with the original P 1 (which we again interpret as an A statement). Thus the second syllogism is:

> C 1   No crocodile-manager is a despised person.
> P 1   Every baby is a despised person.
> ------
> C 2   No baby is a crocodile manager.

110

We can discover what conclusion follows from the premises by application of the rules. Since P 2 and P 3 are universal, the conclusion must be universal, by Rule 6. Since P 2 is negative, the conclusion must be negative, by Rule 2. Since the order of subject and predicate doesn't matter in an E statement, either C 1 or its converse follow from P 1 and P 2.

Suppose that, instead of pairing P 2 and P 3, we had paired P 1 and P 3, which have the common term "illogical." Our chain would then have been:

P 3	Every illogical person is despised.
P 1	Every baby is an illogical person.
C 1	Every baby is despised.
P 2	No crocodile-manager is despised.
C 2	No baby is a crocodile-manager.

This is an equally good sorites. Traditional logic books give certain rules about the order and arrangement of premises within a sorites. These are completely unimportant unless one wishes a particular artificial arrangement of premises. For example, if one insists that the major term of the final conclusion occur in the major premise of the first syllogism and the minor term of the final conclusion occur in the minor premise of the final syllogism, one has what is called an *Aristotelian sorites*. Our second try at the sorites about the baby is Aristotelian. No substantive purpose is served by such niceties, however, and we shall ignore them for our purposes. Two rules that cannot be ignored are the following:

SR 1   Only one of the original set of premises can be negative, because it appears in the final version of the sorites.

SR 2   Only one of the original premise set can be particular or individual.

If either of these rules is broken, we get a syllogism somewhere in the chain with two negative premises or two particular premises or two individual premises or one particular and one individual premise, and no syllogism with these combinations is valid. The qualification in SR 1 is intended to cover cases where an original premise is negative but, by obversion or contraposition and double negation, appears as positive when we formalize the argument.

Once one grasps the relatively simple principles involved, soriteses (this plural of sorites was coined by Carroll) are not very difficult to handle. Lewis Carroll invented dozens of moderately amusing soriteses for use in teaching logic. Since these are in the public domain, almost all logic books steal at least some of the easier ones for use as exercises. The second set of exercises for this section gives some of Carroll's soriteses. The given solutions are in symbolic form for the sake of compactness, and dictionaries are given in the exercises.

Solving an Enthymeme

The other topic which we will briefly examine in this section is that of enthymemes. An *enthymeme* is a syllogistic argument with either the major premise, the minor premise, or the conclusion omitted. A valid enthymeme is one for which the missing part can be supplied so that the result is a valid syllogism. An invalid enthymeme is one such that we can find no standard form statement which added to the enthymeme will make it a valid syllogism. A Type 1 enthymeme is one which needs a major premise supplied. A Type 2 needs the minor premise supplied, and a Type 3 needs a conclusion supplied.

Stricly speaking, the original premise sets of soriteses have one Type 3 enthymeme which, when converted to a syllogism, makes another premise into a Type 3 enthymeme, and so on. We sometimes speak of an *enthymatic sorites*, a sorites which has at least one premise missing which cannot be derived as a conclusion from other premises. Usually the missing premise or premises must be few in number and fairly obvious; otherwise the line between an enthymatic sorites and a fallacious argument disappears. (Given almost any random collection of standard form statements we could with sufficient ingenuity link them into a sorites by adding enough additional premises.) The sorites about Pooh and the bees with which this section opened can be regarded as an enthymatic sorites.

If a enthymeme is valid, the missing part can be discovered mechanically by application of the rules. If it is a Type 3 enthymeme, we proceed as we did with soriteses. If it is a Type 1 or a Type 2 enthymeme, we proceed as follows. First, we identify the conclusion. It then follows that the middle term is the term in the premise which does not appear in the conclusion. The other term in the premise will be either the subject of the conclusion, in which case the major premise is missing, or the predicate of the conclusion, in which case the minor premise is missing. We now know which premise is missing and what terms it contains. Then, reasoning from the quality, quantity, and distribution of the conclusion and premise, we fill in the form of the missing premise. For example, suppose we have the enthymeme:

> Piglet is a friend of Pooh.
> ———————————————————
> Piglet is a friend of Christopher Robin.

Suppose that context enables us to identify the second statement as the conclusion. Therefore "a friend of Pooh," which does not appear in the conclusion, must be the middle term. "Piglet" is the subject of the conclusion. So we are missing the major premise. The major premise must contain the middle and major terms, "friend of Pooh" and "friend of Christopher Robin." Since the conclusion is individual affirmative, the missing premise must be universal affirmative. Since the middle is not distributed in the minor premise, it must be distributed in the missing major. Thus the missing premise is:

> Every friend of Pooh is a friend of Christopher Robin.

Any enthymeme which is valid can be reconstructed by this method. If an enthymeme is invalid, the attempt to reconstruct it will lead to impossible or conflicting demands. For example, the enthymeme

> Every friend of Christopher Robin is a friend of Pooh.
> _____
> Some relation of Rabbit is a friend of Christopher Robin.

is invalid if the second statement is the conclusion. The middle would have to be "friend of Pooh." Since the conclusion is particular affirmative, the missing minor premise must also be particular affirmative. Since "friend of Pooh" is not distributed in the major, it must be distributed in the minor; but this conflicts with the previous requirement for, if the missing minor is an I statement, the middle cannot be distributed in it since neither the subject nor the predicate of an I statement is distributed. So the enthymeme is invalid.

EXERCISES 3.4

A. Find the conclusion of the following syllogisms. If there is no valid conclusion write "invalid." (Source: Lewis Carroll, *Symbolic Logic*.)

1. Pain is wearisome;
   No pain is eagerly wished for.

2. All medicine is nasty;
   Senna is a medicine.

3. Some unkind remarks are annoy-ing;
   No critical remarks are kind.

4. No tall men have nervous tics.
   Some Dons have nervous tics.

5. All philosophers are logical;
   An illogical man is always obsti-nate.

6. John is industrious;
   All industrious people are happy.

7. These dishes are all well cooked;
   Some dishes are unwholesome if not well cooked.

8. No exciting books suit fever-ish patients;
   Unexciting books make one drowsy.

9. No pigs can fly;
   All pigs are greedy.

10. When a man knows what he's about, he can detect a sharper;
    You and I know what we're about

B. Find the conclusions of the following soriteses, and reconstruct the chain of syllogisms. (Source: Lewis Carroll, *Symbolic Logic*.)

Note: Several things about these Carroll soriteses need explaining. The term "Univ." stands for "Universe of Discourse," an idea which will be discussed in the next chapter. For present purposes you need know only that "Univ." indicates a class of which all the terms of the sorites are subclasses or members. Thus in the dictionary for 1 below, "E" stands for "easy logic examples worked by me," "M" stands for "logic examples worked by me which make my head ache," and so on.

Carroll is also fond of using complicated exceptive forms, which make standardizing difficult. In some cases your only recourse is to take the two terms in a sentence and try them in various standard form statements, asking yourself if the standard form statement gives you the meaning of the original. However, to aid you I give below a few typical Carrollisms with corresponding standard forms. These cannot be applied mechanically, however, since context can alter meaning. Use your knowledge of English and your common sense. "Nothing except A is B" usually means "Every B is A." "No A fails to be B" is usually equivalent to "Every A is B." "Nothing is A unless it is B" usually means "Every A is B." Be careful also of Carroll's habits of inverting subject and predicate by using clauses and of the way in which the "univ." term is sometimes stressed, sometimes omitted.

Note: These exercises and others in this volume that are quoted directly from Carroll's *Symbolic Logic* preserve Carroll's spelling and punctuation.

1. When I work a Logic-example without grumbling, you may be sure it is one that I can understand;
   These soriteses are not arranged in regular order, like the examples I am used to;
   No easy example ever makes my head ache;
   I can't understand examples that are not arranged in regular order, like those I am used to;
   I never grumble at an example, unless it gives me a headache.

   Univ. "Logic-examples worked by me"; A # arranged in regular order, like the examples I am used to; E # easy; G # grumbled at by me; M # making my head ache; T # these Soriteses; U # understood by me.

2. Every idea of mine, that cannot be expressed as a Syllogism, is really ridiculous;
   None of my ideas about Bath-buns are worth writing down;
   No idea of mine, that fails to come true, can be expressed as a Syllogism;
   I never have any really ridiculous idea, that I do not at once refer to my solicitor;
   My dreams are all about Bath-buns;
   I never refer any idea of mine to my solicitor, unless it is worth writing down.

   Univ. "my ideas"; A # able to be expressed as a Syllogism; B # about Bath-buns; C # coming true; D # dreams; R # really ridiculous; S # referred to my solicitor; W # worth writing down.

3. None of the pictures here, except the battle-pieces, are valuable;
   None of the unframed ones are varnished;
   All the battle-pieces are painted in oils;
   All those that have been sold are valuable;
   All the English ones are varnished;
   All those in frames have been sold.

   Univ. "the pictures here"; B # battle-pieces; E # English; F # framed; O # oil-paintings; S # sold; V # valuable; D # varnished.

4. Animals, that do not kick, are always unexcitable;
   Donkeys have no horns;
   A buffalo can always toss one over a gate;
   No animals that kick are easy to swallow;
   No hornless animal can toss one over a gate;
   All animals are excitable, except buffaloes.

   Univ. "animals"; A # able to toss one over a gate; B # buffaloes;
   D # donkeys; E # easy to swallow; X # excitable; H # horned;
   K # kicking.

5. No one, who is going to a party, ever fails to brush his hair;
   No one looks fascinating, if he is untidy;
   Opium eaters have no self-command;
   Every one, who has brushed his hair, looks fascinating;
   No one wears white kid gloves, unless he is going to a party;
   A man is always untidy, if he has no self-command.

   Univ. "persons"; G # going to a party; H # having brushed
   one's hair; S # having self-command; L # looking fascinating; O #
   opiumeaters; T # tidy; W # wearing white kid gloves.

6. A plum-pudding, that is not really solid, is mere porridge;
   Every plum-pudding, served at my table, has been boiled in a cloth;
   A plum-pudding that is mere porridge is indistinguishable from soup;
   No plum-puddings are really solid, except what are served at *my*
   table.

   Univ. "plum-puddings"; B # boiled in a cloth; D # distinguishable from soup; M # mere porridge; R # really solid; S # served at my table.

7. No interesting poems are unpopular among people of real taste;
   No modern poetry is free from affectation;
   All *your* poems are on the subject of soap-bubbles;
   No affected poetry is popular among people of real taste;
   No ancient poem is on the subject of soap-bubbles.

   Univ. "poems"; A # affected; N # ancient; I # interesting; S #
   on the subject of soap-bubbles; P # popular among people of real
   taste; W # written by you.

8. All the fruit at this Show, that fails to get a prize, is the property of the
     Committee;
   None of my peaches have got prizes;
   None of the fruit, sold off in the evening, is unripe;
   None of the ripe fruit has been grown in a hot-house;
   All fruit, that belongs to the Committee, is sold off in the evening.

   Univ. "fruit at this Show"; B # belonging to the Committee; G #
   getting prizes; H # grown in a hot-house; P # my peaches;
   R # ripe; S # sold off in the evening.

9. Promise-breakers are untrustworthy;
   Wine-drinkers are very communicative;

A man who keeps his promises is honest;
No teetotalers are pawnbrokers;
One can always trust a very communicative person.

Univ. "persons"; H # honest; P # pawnbrokers; B # promise-breakers; T # trustworthy; V # very communicative; W # wine-drinkers.

10. No kitten, that loves fish, is unteachable;
No kitten without a tail will play with a gorilla;
Kittens with whiskers always love fish;
No teachable kitten has green eyes;
No kittens have tails unless they have whiskers.

Univ. "kittens"; G # green-eyed; L # loving fish; T # tailed; E # teachable; W # whiskered; P # willing to play with a gorilla.

C. Put the following enthymemes and soriteses into standard syllogistic form, supplying missing elements where necessary. Ignore phrases in parentheses. (Source: Duns Scotus, *Ordinatio*.)

1. [The Philosopher argues that] the First Being has infinite power because it moves with an endless movement.

2. [One can argue equally well that] the First Being has infinite power since it can cause endless motion.

3. [Now it is clear that] since the First Being exists in virtue of itself, it has the ability to cause endless motion.

4. The First Being has an infinite effect in its power, but whatever has an infinite effect in its power is infinite; therefore, etc.

5. Any being which possesses all causal power is infinite, but [Avicenna assumes] the First Being does possess all causal power; therefore, etc.

6. [Some argue that] the First Cause has infinite power, because any being which can bridge a gap between infinite extremes has infinite power. But a being which can create something from nothing can bridge a gap between infinite extremes [being and nothingness], and the First Cause can do this.

7. The First Being after God depends on Him totally and is made from no material; thus it is created from nothing.

8. The things that can be known are infinite in number, but they are all known by God. Therefore the mind of God is infinite.

9. We can always love and seek something greater than any finite being. We cannot love or seek anything greater than God, therefore, etc.

10. An absolutely perfect being cannot be excelled in perfection. But any finite being can be excelled in perfection. God is an absolutely perfect being, therefore, etc.

3.5 PHILOSOPHICAL APPLICATIONS

As was pointed out at the beginning of this chapter, medieval philosophers used syllogistic logic extensively. However this does not mean that they wrote in a series of neat formal syllogisms. Even where simple syllogisms are used, they are seldom stated formally, and in many cases one has to supply premises or reconstruct a seeming syllogism as a sorites. To show this, we will, in this section, take a fairly representative example of medieval philosophy and examine some syllogistic and near syllogistic arguments which occur in it.

Arguments from Duns Scotus

The work we have chosen is the Prologue to the *Ordinatio* of Johns Duns Scotus, one of the major medieval philosophers. The question considered in the Prologue is this: "Does Man in his present state need to be supernaturally inspired with some knowledge?" Duns Scotus carefully examines this question, proposing and criticizing arguments on both sides of the question before coming to a final conclusion. The organization of the work is quite complex, but for our purposes we can simply take some arguments, both pro and con, and examine their main structure, usually ignoring subsidiary arguments which Duns Scotus gives in support of the premises.

Duns' first argument is one (which he later refutes) to show that man does not need supernatural knowledge in his present state:

> That he needs none, I argue as follows—Every faculty which has something common as its primary object, is as competent by nature in regard to everything contained under this object as it is with regard to what is of itself the natural object. . . . The natural primary object of our intellect is being *qua* being. Therefore our intellect is able to know naturally any being whatsoever, and consequently any intelligible non-entity for "affirmation explains denial." Therefore, etc.* Proof of the minor. . . . Proof of the major. . . .

Now although Duns Scotus speaks airily of the major and minor, it is obvious that a single syllogism cannot express his argument. The argument in fact can partly be expressed as a rather complex sorites.

P 1   Every faculty which has being qua being as an object is a faculty which is naturally able to know any being whatever.

P 2   Man's intellect is a faculty which has being qua being as an object.

C 1   Man's intellect is a faculty which is naturally able to know any being whatever.

P 3   Every faculty naturally able to know any being whatever is a faculty able to know everything intelligible.

C 2   Man's intellect is a faculty able to know everything intelligible.

P 4   No faculty able to know everything intelligible needs to be supernaturally inspired with some knowledge.

C 3   Man's intellect is not a faculty which needs to be supernaturally inspired with some knowledge.

So far so good. We have reproduced at least part of Duns Scotus' argument as a series of syllogisms. All of the premises are derived from what Scotus

---

* This means "the conclusion is obvious, draw it yourself." It is often found in medieval writers.

says, and the conclusion is the one we were trying to reach. Although P 4 is not explicit in Duns Scotus, it is obviously the principle he uses to reach the desired conclusion, In P 3 we have a somewhat more convenient way of expressing what Duns Scotus says—strictly, there should be a subsidiary argument here. Obviously P 2 is explicit in the text. However, P 1 must be derived from Duns' first sentence with the aid of the premise "Every being whatever is contained in the common notion of being qua being." This transition, however, cannot be expressed syllogistically, and thus Duns' argument here cannot be completely expressed as a syllogism. We will, in due course, encounter logical techniques which can handle such transitions.

Thus we see that, when Duns Scotus calls the first sentence quoted the major and P 2 the minor, he is using these terms in a very extended way.

A similar argument for the same conclusion given by Duns is the following:

> Anyone capable by nature of knowing a principle can know naturally the conclusions included in that principle. . . . Now we know naturally the first principles in which all conclusions are virtually contained. Hence we can also know naturally all conclusions which can be known.

Again the argument cannot be completely reconstructed in syllogistic logic. The following is a valid syllogism.

P 1   Every creature which knows naturally the first principles can know naturally all conclusions which can be known.
P 2   Man knows naturally the first principles.
─────
C 1   Man can know naturally all conclusions which can be known.

As before we would have to supply a premise to get the final conclusion.

P 3   No creature which can know naturally all conclusions which can be known is a creature who needs to be inspired supernaturally with some knowledge.
─────
C 2   Man is not a creature which needs to be inspired supernaturally with some knowledge.

But also as before, P 1 is not Duns' major and cannot be derived from it syllogistically.

Some of Duns Scotus' "con" arguments also can be reconstructed syllogistically:

> Every agent who acts knowingly needs a distinct knowledge of his destiny or end. . . . But man can have no definite knowledge of his end from what is natural; therefore he needs some supernatural knowledge thereof.

This can be rendered as a syllogism but at the cost of making the premises rather complex:

P 1 Every agent who acts knowingly and has no natural knowledge of his destiny needs a supernatural knowledge of his destiny.
P 2 Man is an agent who acts knowingly and has no natural knowledge of his destiny.

C   Man needs a supernatural knowledge of his destiny.

A fairly simple argument is concealed by complicated terms in the following example:

Every person who knowingly acts for the sake of an end needs to know how and in what way such an end may be attained. In addition, he must know all that is necessary for this end. Thirdly, he must know that this is all that is required. . . .

But by natural reason one in this life is unable to know these three points. . . . Therefore, etc.

Scotus leaves the reader to draw the conclusion that supernatural argument is required. The reconstruction could be

P 1 Every creature which acts knowingly for the sake of an end and does not know 1, 2, 3 naturally is a creature which needs to know 1, 2, 3 supernaturally.
P 2 Man is a creature who acts knowingly for the sake of an end and does not know 1, 2, 3 naturally.

C   Man is a creature who needs to know 1, 2, 3 supernaturally.

In both these latter examples one should note that the ultimate conclusion "Man is a creature who needs to know *something* supernaturally" does not follow *syllogistically* from the actual conclusion unless a premise is supplied.

In conclusion, let me repeat that, although the medievals used the terminology and sometimes the machinery of syllogistic logic, a good many of their arguments can be reduced to syllogistic form only by first performing other inferences, inferences which are called obvious or intuitive but which cannot themselves be reduced to syllogistic arguments. Duns Scotus is an excellent example of this, but it is also true of other medieval philosophers.

A Modern Argument

Various examples of the use of syllogistic arguments may be found in modern philosophers. An interesting example is the following.

In his paper "Four Forms of Scepticism,"* G. E. Moore presents the following argument:

> Russell says to me: "You don't know for certain that you heard the sound 'Russell' a little while ago, not even that there *was* such a sound, *because* in dreams we often remember things that never happened." In what way could the alleged reason, if true, be a reason for the conclusion? . . . Suppose that I have had experiences which resembled this one in the respect that I felt as if I remembered hearing a certain sound a little while before while yet it is not true that a little while before I did hear the sound in question. Does that prove that I don't know for certain now that I did hear the sound "Russell" just now? It seems to me that the idea that it does is a mere fallacy, resting partly on a confusion between two different uses of the words "possible" or "may." . . . The argument seems to me to be precisely on a par with the following: It is possible for a human being to be of the female sex; (but) I am a human being; *therefore* it is possible that I am of the female sex. The two premises here are perfectly true, and yet obviously it does not follow from them that I do not know that I am not of the female sex. I do (in my view) happen to know this, in spite of the fact that the two premises are both true; but whether I know it or not the two premises certainly don't prove that I don't.

This argument is at least partially a refutation by logical analogy: it is alleged that a sceptical argument attributed to Russell (which we will call "the sceptic's argument") is precisely on a par with a case presented by Moore (which we will call "the parallel argument") which seems to be a clear case of an argument with true premises and a false conclusion. Is Moore correct in calling the parallel argument a fallacy, and is it a fallacy for the reasons given by Moore? And, is it true, as Moore alleges, that the sceptic's argument is "precisely on a par" with the parallel argument? Moore presents the following criticism of the parallel argument.

> The conclusion *seems* to follow from the premises because the premise "It is possible for a human being to be of the female sex" or "Human beings may be of the female sex" is so easily falsely taken to be of the same form as "Human beings are mortal," i.e., to mean "In the case of every human being it is possible that the human being in question is of the female sex" or "Every human being *may* be of the female sex." If, and only if, it did mean this then the combination of this with the minor premise "I am a human being" would the conclusion follow: It is possible that I am of the female sex; or I may be of the female sex. But in fact the premise "Human beings may be of the female sex" does not mean "Every human being *may* be," but only, "Some human beings *are*." "May" is being used in a totally different sense from any in which you would possibly assert of a particular human being "This human being *may* be so and so." And so soon as this is realized it is surely quite plain that from this, together with the premise "I am a human being," there does not follow, "I may be of the female sex." There may be something more in

* First printed in *Philosophical Papers* (George Allen and Unwin, Ltd., London, U.K.), 1956, pp. 193–222.

the argument . . . than this simple fallacy. But I cannot see that there is anything more in it.

Now what is the "simple fallacy" which Moore says has been committed? It seems to me that Moore is thinking in terms of syllogistic arguments. He first suggests the valid argument:

> Every human being (is a being which) may be of the female sex.
> I am a human being.
> _____
> (Therefore) I (am a being which) may be of the female sex.

He then alleges that the correct translation of the true statement, "It is possible for a human being to be of the female sex" is not "Every human being (is a being which) may be of the female sex," but, rather, "Some human beings are (beings) of the female sex." The argument then becomes:

> Some human beings are (beings) of the female sex.
> I am a human being.
> _____
> (Therefore) I (am a being which) may be of the female sex.

Since this argument commits the fallacy of four terms and that of undistributed middle, Moore is obviously justified in saying that the conclusion does not follow from the premises. If Moore is right, then the parallel argument is a glaring nonsequitor. Clearly the crucial point here is Moore's analysis of the premise, "It is possible for a human being to be of the female sex."

Is the sceptic's argument in fact "precisely on a par with" the parallel argument? Moore states that it is and gives a criticism of it on the same lines as his criticism of the parallel argument:

> What really does follow from this premise (that I have had experiences which resembled this one in the respect that I felt as if I remembered hearing the sound "Russell" a little while before, while yet it is not true that a little while before I did hear the sound "Russell") is this: That is it possible for an experience of a sort, of which my present experience is an example, i.e., one which resembles my present experience in a certain respect, *not* to have been preceded within a certain period by the sound "Russell." Whereas the conclusion which is alleged to follow is: It is possible that *this* experience was not preceded within that period by the sound "Russell." Now in the first of these sentences the meaning of "possible" is such that the whole sentence means merely: Some experiences of feeling as if one remembered a certain sound are not preceded by the sound in question. But in the conclusion: It is possible that this experience was not preceded by the word "Russell" or This experience *may* not have been preceded by the word "Russell"; "possible" and "may" are being used in an entirely different sense. Here the whole expression merely means the same as: "*It is not known* for certain that this experience was preceded by that sound." And how from "Some experiences of this kind were not

preceded" can we possibly be justified in inferring, "It is not known that this one was preceded?"

As before, if Moore is correct in saying that the crucial premise means merely that "Some experiences of seeming to remember a certain sound are not preceded," then he is surely right in calling the sceptic's argument a fallacy. The valid argument would be:

Every experience of seeming to remember a certain sound is possibly not preceded by the sound in question.
This is an experience of seeming to remember a certain sound.

(Therefore) this is possibly not preceded by the sound in question.

The invalid argument, which again commits the fallacies of four terms and undistributed middle, would be:

Some experiences of seeming to remember a certain sound are not preceded by the sound in question.
This is an experience of seeming to remember a certain sound.

(Therefore) this is possibly not preceded by the sound in question.

On examining arguments which occur in contemporary philosophers, it will often be found, as we found in this case, that, although syllogistic forms are not explicitly mentioned, it is both easy and natural to express the arguments in syllogistic forms.

DISCUSSION QUESTIONS

1. In the exercises in this chapter, is something lost when we translate from ordinary English to standard form statements?
2. What ideas or statements were difficult to express in standard form statements?
3. Compare propositional logic with syllogistic logic as a tool for analyzing philosophical arguments.
4. The notion of distribution is often puzzling to beginners. What difficulties, if any, did you have with this notion?
5. What difficulties did you find in translating Lewis Carroll. What difficulties in translating Duns Scotus? Were they similar difficulties or different ones?

Chapter 4
CLASS LOGIC

Syllogistic logic is both more powerful and more restricted than propositional logic. It can handle the "all-some" distinction, which propositional logic cannot, but it is restricted to standard form statements and their transformations and to arguments which are either syllogisms, incomplete syllogisms, or chains of syllogisms. It may have occurred to you that a logic which could make the distinction between all and some but which has the greater flexibility of propositional logic would be desirable. In fact, there are at least two such logics. One is predicate logic, discussed in Chapter 5, while the other is class logic, which we will examine in this chapter.

Class logic is interesting and useful in its own right and also throws light on certain philosophical problems which arise in connection with logic and mathematics. Class logic is a part or fragment of set theory, which is a fundamental part of mathematics. Class logic, as we use this term, is that part of set theory which can be used to analyze and test arguments in ordinary language.

4.1 NAMES OF CLASSES

The basic building blocks of class logic which correspond most closely to propositions and operators on propositions in propositional logic are *class names* and *operators on class names*. The notion of class is often said to be so basic or intuitive that efforts to explain or define it are useless. Whether or not this is true, we will take the same approach to class that we took to *true* and *false* in Chapter 1. We will assume that the reader understands this notion well enough to use it and will postpone any further discussion of the problems raised by it. However, just as we said in Chapter 1 that propositions, by definition, were true or false, so we will build certain restrictions into the meaning of *class*. Our restriction is that we will not call anything a class unless there is some workable way of saying whether any object does or does not belong to that class. This rules out not only certain groups or collections which are too vaguely defined to meet this condition, but also certain paradoxical classes which we will discuss in Section 4.5.

Classes can be composed of things which are not themselves classes, for example, teaspoons, philosophers, dreams. In addition, classes can be composed of other classes, for example, the class of all abstract classes, the class of all finite classes. We will reserve the small letters of the ordinary English alphabet, except *a*, for names of members of classes which are not themselves classes (we will call these *individuals* though the term is not always appropriate) and the capital letters of the ordinary English alphabet, except *X*, *Y* and *Z*, for names of classes. We will use the same symbol $\#$ (stands for) that we used in Chapters 1 to 3, thus:

$$p \ \# \ \text{Plato}$$
$$d \ \# \ \text{the dream Caesar had on March 14}$$
$$D \ \# \ \text{(the class of) dreams}$$
$$F \ \# \ \text{the class of finite classes}$$

When we need variables, in due course, we will use *X*, *Y*, *Z*, and *a*.

Operators and Class Connectives

Operators on class names will be expressions which, when added to the name of a class or classes, yield the name of a class. Operators on two or more classes will be called *class connectives*. A class whose name is formed from other class names by the use of class connectives is called a *compound class*. A *simple class* is defined negatively as a class whose name is not formed from other classes by the use of class connectives.

The class connectives with which we will be concerned have a property akin to the truth functionality of the connectives of propositional logic. This property is sometimes called *extensionality* and is described as follows: If we have an effective test for membership in the simple classes of which a compound class is formed, then this, together with the definition of the connectives, gives us an effective test for membership in the compound class. The question as to whether there are nonextensional class connectives is an interesting one which has been debated in philosophy of logic. It has no generally accepted solution.

Union

The main class connectives are closely parallel to the connectives of propositional logic and can be defined by a device akin to the matrices used in Section 1.1. Consider two arbitrary classes A and B. The compound class which is called the *union* of A and B is that class whose members are members of A *or* of B *or* of both. The symbol for union is ∪, and the name of the union of A and B is written as A ∪ B. This means that ∪ is a class connective since, when added to the names of two classes, it gives the name of another class. (In principle we could write ∪ AB or AB ∪, but, by convention connectives are written *between* the class names, as above.) The symbol ∪ represents an extensional connective since, if we know an effective test for membership in A and in B, we can discover whether an individual (or class, if A or B are classes of classes) is a member of A ∪ B by determining whether it is a member of either A or B.

Now consider some arbitrary class or individual which might be a member of A or B or both. (To avoid this cumbersome phrase we will use the word *element* as short for "class or individual which is a member of a class.") This element might be a member of A and also of B, of A but not of B, of B but not of A or of neither A nor B. We can write these possibilities as follows, using 1 and 0 for "is a member" and "is not a member," respectively, making the first class the vertical line and the second the horizontal (Matrix 4.1).

MATRIX 4.1

		Second Class	
		1	0
First	1		
Class	0		

We can now give a matrix definition of ∪ (Matrix 4.2). This means that,

MATRIX 4.2

∪	1	0
1	1	1
0	1	0

if any element is a member of one or the other or both of two classes, it is a member of their union and is not a member of their union only if it is a member of neither. If we substitute "yes" and "no" for "1" and "0" this may become clearer (Matrix 4.3). The parallel of ∪ with the v matrix of Chapter 1 is, of course, obvious.

MATRIX 4.3

| | | Member of second class? | |
		Yes	No
Member of	Yes	Yes	Yes
first class?	No	Yes	No
		Member of their union?	

Intersection

There is also a class connective intersection that is like "and." Its symbol is ∩, which is defined in Matrix 4.4. This means that an element is a member of the intersection of two classes only if it is a member of both classes.

MATRIX 4.4

∩	1	0
1	1	0
0	0	0

The union and intersection of two classes can be represented graphically. Let us draw the first class as a circle, the second as a square. Since they may possibly overlap, we will draw them as overlapping, but this does not mean that we know that any element is a member of both classes. In fact, we may not know whether either class has any members at all. We draw the diagram "without prejudice" (Figure 4.1).

Figure 4.1

Class A is composed of all those elements, if any, within its boundaries, and class B is composed of all those elements, if any, within its boundaries. The union of A and B (indicated by shading) is all those elements, if any, within either boundary (Figure 4.2), and the intersection of A and B is the

Figure 4.2

class composed of all those elements, if any, which are inside both boundaries (Figure 4.3).

Figure 4.3

Complement

Let us now introduce an operator on class names which is not a connective This operator gives the *complement* of a class. Its symbol is a bar written over the original class name, for example, $\bar{A}$, $\bar{B}$, $\overline{A \cup B}$, or $\overline{A \cap B}$. Note that this is a convention different from that for the symbol $\sim$ in propositional logic.

To negate a compound proposition in propositional logic we put $\sim$ in front of parentheses enclosing the whole expression; to complement a compound class in class logic we put the — *over* the entire expression. It is often clearer also to include the negated compound in parentheses, and we will do this from now on. The matrix definition of complementation is shown in Matrix 4.5. That is, if an element *is* a member of a class, it is *not* a member of its

MATRIX 4.5

$-$	
1	0
0	1

complement, whereas if an element is *not* a member of a class, it is a member of the complement of that class. In other words, the complement of a class is everything whatsoever which is not in that class.

Now consider the union of a class and its complement, $A \cup \bar{A}$. This must be a class which contains everything whatsoever, for everything will be either a member of the class or not a member of the class and therefore a member of its complement. Graphically, the complement of a class A could be partially represented as the shaded portion of Figure 4.4. I say partially because theoretically the shading should extend to infinity on every side!

Figure 4.4

127

Universal and Null Classes

The class composed of everything or the union of a class and its complement is called the *universe* or *universal class*. The universal class has a symbol, V, and also a complement, $\bar{V}$ or Λ, which is called the *empty* or *null class*. Since the universal class contains everything, the null class contains nothing. The null class can also be defined as the (of course, empty) intersection of a class and its complement, $A \cap \bar{A}$.

A universal class which contains everything whatsoever is sometimes too large for convenience, and, therefore, we sometimes confine ourselves to a given limited universe for the purposes of a particular discussion. This "universe of discourse" might be, for instance, "human beings" or "numbers." This should have an odd effect on the null class, but by convention the null class remains the perfectly empty class, which suggests that what we do when we use a universe of discourse is to pretend that only those things exist which are in that universe. The effect of using a universe of discourse is often to make complements out of terms which are not usually thought of as complements. If our universe is "people," "male" and "female" will be complementary classes: their union will include everything in the universe of discourse and, assuming that nothing is both male and female, their intersection is empty. In a larger universe "male" and "female" would not be complementary classes because, even assuming that they are mutually exclusive classes, their union does not include everything since, for example, chairs are *neither* male *nor* female.

If we are using a given limited universe of discourse, such as people, our universal class will be different from cases in which we use another such universe of discourse, for example, numbers. Within any given universe of discourse, however, there will be a number of different names for the universal class and also a number of different names of the null class. For example, take two classes, A and B, and some universe of discourse. We can test a compound class name to see if it is a name of the universal or the null classes in exactly the same way that we test compound propositions to see if they are tautologies or contradictions, using membership tables instead of truth tables. A name of the universal class has only 1's under its final connective, a name of the null class only 0's.

The following are names of the universal class (parentheses are used as in propositional logic).

$$A \cup \bar{A}$$
$$B \cup \bar{B}$$

$$\overline{(A \cap B)} \cup A$$
$$\overline{((\bar{A} \cup B) \cap A)} \cup B$$
$$(A \cup B) \cup \overline{(\bar{A} \cup \bar{B})} \qquad \text{etc.}$$

The following are names of the null class:

$$A \cap \bar{A}$$
$$B \cap \bar{B}$$
$$\overline{(A \cup B) \cap A}$$
$$(A \cup B) \cap A$$
$$(A \cup B) \cap (\bar{A} \cap \bar{B}) \qquad \text{etc.}$$

Some of these may remind you of tautologies and contradictions in propositional logic and there is, in fact, a close relation. It is this: if we write the tautologies and contradictions of propositional logic using only the symbols $\sim$, $\vee$, and $\cdot$ and then replace propositional variables with class names, $\sim$ with —, $\cdot$ with $\cap$, and $\vee$ with $\cup$, then every tautology thus transposed becomes a name of the universal class and every contradiction thus transposed becomes a name of the null class. The converse process, starting with names of the universal and null classes, also yields propositional logic tautologies and contradictions.

EXERCISES 4.1

A. Using the following dictionary describe the following classes in colloquial English.

A # Acorn-loving animals	F # Friendly animals
B # Bears	G # Gloomy animals
C # Condensed-milk-loving animals	H # Honey-loving animals
D # Donkeys	P # Piglets
E # Thistle-eating animals	T # Tiggers

1. $A \cap B$
2. $A \cup C$
3. $A \cap \bar{E}$
4. $B \cap H$
5. $(B \cap C) \cap \bar{E}$
6. $D \cap \overline{(H \cup C)}$
7. $D \cup (E \cup G)$
8. $\bar{E} \cap (F \cap T)$
9. $((E \cup H) \cup C) \cap P$
10. $\overline{(E \cup D)} \cap G$

B. Translate the following into names of classes using the following dictionary:

E # Animals who like Eeyore	G # Animals who growl
F # Fuzzy animals	H # Honey-loving animals

1. Fuzzy animals who like Eeyore
2. Animals who like honey and growl
3. Fuzzy, honey-loving animals who like Eeyore
4. Growling animals who like neither honey nor Eeyore
5. Fuzzy animals who like either Eeyore or honey
6. Animals who neither growl nor love honey but who like Eeyore
7. Animals who growl and are either fuzzy or honey-loving
8. Animals who are either fuzzy and growl or else are not fuzzy but like honey
9. Animals who either like Eeyore and are not fuzzy but do growl or else do growl but are neither fuzzy nor like Eeyore

10. Animals who are either not fuzzy and do not like Eeyore or else are not fuzzy or are honey-loving

C. Devise a dictionary which will enable you to express all of the descriptions below in terms of simple classes and class connectives. Then write out each description in symbols. (If you know the Pooh stories, suggest a character who is a member of the class so formed.)
1. Very small animals
2. Very small animals entirely surrounded by water
3. Animals with no brain at all who like honey
4. Brainy animals who like honey
5. Friends and relations of Rabbit
6. Friends of both Pooh and Rabbit
7. Very small friends and relations of Rabbit
8. Brainy friends of Pooh
9. Friends of Pooh entirely surrounded by water
10. Bouncy animals who don't like honey

4.2 STATEMENTS ABOUT CLASSES

You will have noticed that nothing was said in the last section about class connectives that are analogous to $\supset$ and $\equiv$. Such connectives could be formed, but they are not, in fact, used in class logic. Instead, we have certain operators which, when added to the names of classes, form *not* names of other classes but *statements* about classes. The operator analogous to $\supset$ is written $\subseteq$, and the operator analogous to $\equiv$ is written $=$.

There are two major sources of confusion here about which we have to be very careful. As we will see, the class statement most closely comparable to a propositional implication such as

$$A \supset B \quad \text{is class statement such as} \quad A \subseteq B$$

By a really staggering piece of ineptitude, the commonest symbol for implication and the commonest symbol for its closest analog in class logic *face opposite ways*, causing untold confusion to beginners. In addition, whereas $A \vee B$ and $A \supset B$ are both propositions, $A \cup B$ is a class *name* and $A \subseteq B$ is a statement about classes. Also besides $\subseteq$ and $=$ there is one other operator, $\in$, which forms statements. These three operators function as follows: The symbol $\in$ is a two-place operator which states that the individual *or* class written to the left of the $\in$ is a *member* of the *class* written to the right of the $\in$. Thus $i \in A$ says that the individual i is a member of the class A, while $A \in B$ says that the class A is a member of the class B, which, of course, must be a class at least some of whose members are classes. The statements $a \in b$ and $A \in b$ are both meaningless since individuals, by definition, don't have members. (Note that the symbols $\subseteq$, $=$, and $\in$ all form statements by putting names in certain relations to each other.)

Subclasses and Elements

The operator $\subseteq$ is a two-place operator which says that the *class* to the left of the $\subseteq$ is a subclass of the *class* to the right. A subclass A of a given class B is a class which contains no members which are not members of B. The subclass may contain all the members of B (thus B is a subclass of itself), some members of B, or no members at all. (The empty class is thus a subclass of every class.) A subclass is often said to be *included* in the class of which it is a subclass (called its *superclass*). A *proper* subclass A of a super-class B contains no members which are not members of B and does *not* contain all of the members of B. (Thus no class is a proper subclass of itself, but the empty class is a proper subclass of every class except itself). There is a special symbol, $\subset$, for indicating proper subclasses. So $A \subseteq B$ means "A is a subclass of B," and $A \subset B$ means "A is a *proper* subclass of B." Both symbols may be reversed: $A \supseteq B$ means "B is a subclass of A," and $A \supset B$ means "B is a proper subclass of A." One could also read $A \supseteq B$ as "A is the superclass of B" and $A \supset B$ as "A is the proper superclass of B." In this book we will usually use only the $\subseteq$ symbol, unreversed, but you should be aware of the meaning of the other symbols if you encounter them, for they are sometimes useful. Beware also of the occasional book which uses $\subset$ for $\subseteq$, ignoring the distinction between subclass and proper subclass.

It is easy to confuse $\in$ and $\subseteq$ in some cases, especially when $\in$ appears with two class names. One way to remember the difference is this: $\subseteq$ obeys a law analogous to Hypothetical Syllogism;

$$\text{if} \quad A \subseteq B \quad \text{and} \quad B \subseteq C, \quad \text{then} \quad A \subseteq C$$

Thus, if humans are a subclass of animals and animals a subclass of living things, humans must be a subclass of living things. But if $A \in B$ and $B \in C$, it does not at all follow that $A \in C$. For example, Texas is a member of the United States and the United States is a member of the United Nations. But this does not mean that Texas is a member of the United Nations. Remember that $A \subseteq B$ says that A is a class which contains at least some of the members of B, and only such members, whereas $A \in B$ says that A is a class which *itself* is a member of B, which must, therefore, be a class some of whose members are classes.

Equivalents

Turning to the symbol $=$ we will define $A = B$ (which we will read as "A is equivalent to B" not as "A is identical with B" or as "A is equal to B") to mean that every member of A is a member of B and that every member of B is a member of A. Thus A and B must both be classes: $a = B$, $A = b$ and $a = b$ are all meaningless statements in class logic. Of course, $A = B$ and $B = A$ mean the same. (Since every empty class no matter how defined

has the same members (none) as every other, we speak of *the* empty class.)
We will also use the symbol ≠ (which we will read as "is not equivalent
to"). We define A ≠ B to mean "not every member of A is a member of B
or not every member of B is a member of A."

Standard Form Statements

Now, given the machinery we have built up so far, we can write with
precision the standard form statements of syllogistic logic.

A	Every A is B	becomes	$A \subseteq B$
E	No A is B	becomes	$A \subseteq \bar{B}$
I	Some A is B	becomes	$A \cap B \neq \wedge$
O	Some A is not B	becomes	$A \cap \bar{B} \neq \wedge$
A'	i is B	becomes	$i \in B$
E'	i is not B	becomes	$i \in \bar{B}$

To understand the relation of these class statements to the standard form
statements, we will diagram them. First we will draw a square representing
the universe (or universe of discourse) and divide it into A and Ā (Figure
4.5). Remember that a class and its complement exhaust the universe.

Figure 4.5

We then divide the universe vertically to represent B and B̄ thus giving us a
division into four cells (Figure 4.6). Using a 0 to indicate that a class is

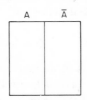

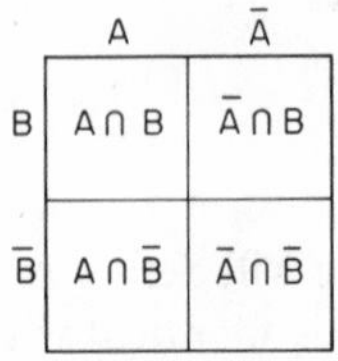

Figure 4.6

empty and a 1 to indicate that a class has at least one member, we can
diagram the first of the four standard form statements as in Figure 4.7.

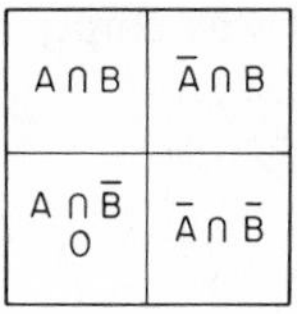

Figure 4.7   A ⊆ B

This is like the diagrams in Chapter 3 where we represented "Every A is B" by a diagram similar to that of Figure 4.8 where the small circle was the

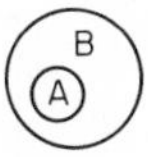

Figure 4.8

class A ∩ B, the large circle outside the small one Ā ∩ B, the area outside the large circle Ā ∩ B̄, and A ∩ B̄ was not represented at all.

In the present diagram (Figure 4.7) we have all four classes, but we eliminate A ∩ B̄ by showing with a zero that it is empty. Notice that we have not said that the other three cells have anything in them: A universal premise does not tell us this. All we know is that there are no A's which are not B's; therefore A ∩ B̄ is empty. The diagram for an E statement (Figure 4.9) is

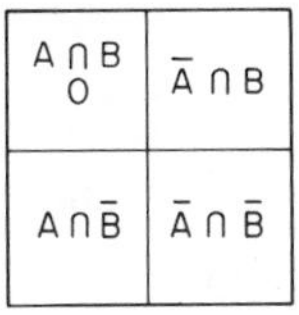

A ∩ B 0	Ā ∩ B
A ∩ B̄	Ā ∩ B̄

Figure 4.9   A ⊆ B

similar. For particular statements we know that one cell has at least one member (Figures 4.10 and 4.11). This doesn't necessarily mean that the others are empty.

We can see that with this new diagram to show that A was completely included in B, we simply showed that the A class outside of B was empty, as in Figure 4.7. To show that A was completely excluded from B we showed

Figure 4.10   A ∩ B ≠ ∧   **Figure 4.11   A ∩ B̄ ≠ ∧**

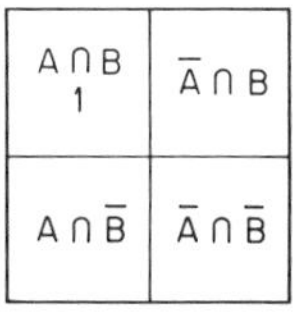

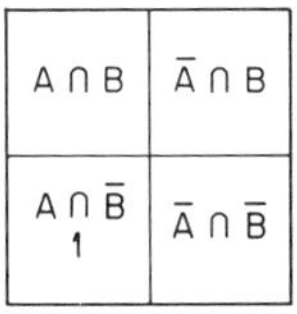

A ∩ B 1	Ā ∩ B
A ∩ B̄	Ā ∩ B̄

A ∩ B	Ā ∩ B
A ∩ B̄ 1	Ā ∩ B̄

that the class of both A and B was empty as in Figure 4.9. This suggests that we could also write

$$A \subseteq B \text{ as } A \cap \bar{B} = \Lambda \quad \text{and} \quad A \subseteq \bar{B} \text{ as } A \cap B = \Lambda$$

These are equally good ways of expressing "Every A is B" and "No A is B." To represent i ∈ B (Figure 4.12) and i ∈ B̄ (Figure 4.13), we need only class B and a heavy dot for i.

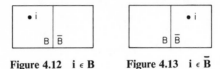

Figure 4.12   i ∈ B   **Figure 4.13   i ∈ B̄**

So far we have not gone beyond syllogistic logic. However, we can represent a good many other statements besides standard form syllogistic logic statements. Let

p ∦ Pooh   B ∦ Bears
e ∦ Eeyore   H ∦ Honey lovers
g ∦ Piglet   F ∦ Friends of Christopher Robin

We can say, for example:

p ∈ (B ∩ H) or "Pooh is a honey-loving bear"
g ∈ (F ∩ B̄) or "Piglet is a friend of Christopher Robin who is not a bear"
e ∈ (F ∩ $\overline{B \cup H}$) or "Eeyore is a friend of Christopher Robin who is neither a bear not a honey lover"

Notice that this is not a completely flexible symbolism. To say "Eeyore, Piglet, and Pooh are friends of Christopher Robin," we must say

$$e \in F \quad g \in F \quad p \in F$$

and nothing in *class* logic enables us to connect these separate statements.

Class logic as we have defined it does not include a systematic development of the theory of classes and their relations. We are concerned with classes only insofar as they enable us to symbolize and test arguments in ordinary language. However, there are certain rules which we can give which describe how certain compound classes must, in virtue of their form, have the same members as certain other compound classes. Also the rules describe certain permissible transformations involving $\subseteq$. We will use X, Y, and Z as class variables and a double bar to indicate a complement of a complement. Thus a statement form such as

$$X = \overline{\overline{X}}$$

has as substitution instances such statements as

$$A = \overline{\overline{A}}$$
$$(A \cap B) = \overline{\overline{(A \cap B)}}$$
$$A \cap (B \cup C) = \overline{\overline{A \cap (B \cap C)}} \qquad \text{etc.}$$

These statement forms will be logical truths, but proving them to be so is beyond the scope of this chapter. The class equivalences of Table 4.1 hold for any consistent substitution of class names for the variables.

TABLE 4.1

Name	Class Equivalences
Double Complementation (DC)	$X = \overline{\overline{X}}$
DeMorgan's rules for Classes (DeMC)	$\overline{(X \cup Y)} = \bar{X} \cap \bar{Y}$ $\overline{(X \cap Y)} = \bar{X} \cup \bar{Y}$
Commutation for Classes (ComC)	$(X \cap Y) = (Y \cap X)$ $(X \cup Y) = (Y \cup X)$
Distribution for Classes (DistC)	$(X \cap (Y \cup Z)) = ((X \cap Y) \cup (X \cap Z))$ $(X \cup (Y \cap Z)) = ((X \cup Y) \cap (X \cup Z))$
Association for Classes (AssocC)	$(X \cup (Y \cup Z)) = ((X \cup Y) \cup Z)$ $(X \cap (Y \cap Z)) = ((X \cap Y) \cap Z)$
Repetition for Classes (RepC)	$X = (X \cap X)$ $X = (X \cup X)$

In Table 4.2 inference patterns that hold for $\subseteq$ are the Hypothetical Syllogism for Classes and Contraposition. The Definition of Subclass is an inference pattern that holds for $\subseteq$ and $\in$, letting a stand for an element which is either an individual or a class. The Special Subclass Rule involves $\subseteq$ and $\neq$.

These inference patterns in Table 4.2 plus the class equivalences in Table

TABLE 4.2

Name	Inference Patterns
Hypothetical Syllogism for Classes (HSC)	$X \subseteq Y$ $Y \subseteq Z$ $\overline{}$ $X \subseteq Z$
Contraposition (Contrap)	$\dfrac{X \subseteq Y}{\bar{Y} \subseteq \bar{X}}$ or $\dfrac{\bar{X} \subseteq \bar{Y}}{Y \subseteq X}$
Definition of Subclass (DSC)	$\begin{array}{c} X \subseteq Y \\ a \in X \\ \hline a \in Y \end{array}$ or $\begin{array}{c} X \subseteq \bar{Y} \\ a \in \bar{Y} \\ \hline a \in \bar{X} \end{array}$
Special Subclass Rule (SSR)	$Y \subseteq Z$ $X \cap Y \neq \wedge$ $\overline{}$ $X \cup Z \neq \wedge$

4.1 will enable us to justify any syllogistic inference, immediate or mediate, as well as many other valid inferences, as we shall see in the following section.

EXERCISES 4.2

A. Using the following dictionary translate the following statements from symbols to colloquial English.

A # Acorn-loving animals   F # Friendly animals

B # Bears   G # Gloomy animals

C # Condensed-milk-loving animals   H # Honey-loving animals

D # Donkeys   P # Piglets

E # Thistle-eating animals   T # Tiggers

1. $B \subseteq (H \cap C)$
2. $B \subseteq \overline{(A \cup E)}$
3. $(B \cap F) \neq \wedge$
4. $B \cap \overline{(H \cup C)} = \wedge$
5. $B \cap (E \cup \bar{H}) = \wedge$
6. $D \cap G \neq \wedge$
7. $D \subseteq E$
8. $(D \cap G) \cap \overline{(C \cup H)} \neq \wedge$
9. $(D \cap B) \cap (H \cup E) \neq \wedge$
10. $(D \cap E) \cap \bar{G} = \wedge$
11. $P \subseteq (A \cap F)$
12. $P \cap (G \cup \bar{F}) = \wedge$
13. $(P \cap C) \cap F \neq \wedge$
14. $P \cap \overline{(E \cap \bar{A})} \neq \wedge$
15. $P = A$
16. $T \subseteq ((C \cup H) \cup T)$
17. $(T \cap F) \neq \wedge$
18. $T \cap (G \cup \bar{F}) = \wedge$
19. $T \neq B$
20. $(T \cap E) \subseteq (T \cap G)$

B. Express each of the following statements as a statement about classes. Give your own dictionary. (Source: Milne, *The House at Pooh Corner.**)

1. Tiggers like all foods except honey and haycorns.
2. Tiggers are extraordinary good flyers who can fly as well as Owl.

---

* Paraphrases from the book *The House at Pooh Corner* by A. A. Milne. Copyright 1928 by E. P. Dutton and Co., Inc. Renewal, 1956 by A. A. Milne. Used by permission of the publishers.

3. Jagulars hide in the branches of trees and drop on you as you go underneath.
4. Accidents are funny things; you never have them till you're having them.
5. What's all very well for jumping animals like Kangas is quite different for swimming animals like Tiggers.
6. A thing that Rabbit knows, that's what learning is.
7. All the animals in the Forest, except (of course) the spotted and herbaceous Backson, ... now know what Christopher Robin does in the mornings.
8. Either looking for Small or organizing an expedition is a reason for going to see everybody.
9. Rabbit is clever and has brains, but he never understands anything.
10. I want a thinnish piece of rope, or if there isn't any, bring a thickish piece of string.

4.3 SYLLOGISTIC LOGIC AS CLASS INFERENCE

In this section we will show that the immediate and syllogistic inferences of Chapter 3 can be justified by class logic. We will first examine immediate inference.

Conversion of E statements is justified by the principles of Contraposition and Double Complementation: We go from $S \subseteq \bar{P}$ to $\bar{P} \subseteq \bar{S}$ by Contraposition, and then use Double Complementation to get $P \subseteq \bar{S}$.

Conversion of I statements involves only Commutation for classes; to commute we go from $S \cap P \neq \Lambda$ to $P \cap S \neq \Lambda$.

Contraposition of A statements is simply Contraposition; to contrapose we go from $S \subseteq P$ to $\bar{P} \subseteq \bar{S}$.

Contraposition of O statements involves Commutation and Double Complementation. We first go from $S \cap \bar{P} \neq \Lambda$ to $\bar{P} \cap S \neq \Lambda$ then to $\bar{P} \cap \bar{S} \neq \Lambda$.

Obversion of A statements uses Double Complementation: We simply go from $S \subseteq P$ to $S \subseteq \bar{\bar{P}}$.

Obversion of E statements is trivial since the form we use for E statements, $S \subseteq \bar{P}$ can be read either as "No S is P" or as "Every S is non-P."

Obversion of I statements uses only Double Complementation, going from $S \cap P = \Lambda$ to $S \cap \bar{\bar{P}} = \Lambda$.

Finally obversion of O statements also is trivial since the form used, $S \cap \bar{P} \neq \Lambda$, can be read either as "Some S is not P" or as "Some S is non-P."

There are fifteen syllogisms which are valid by the rules given in Chapter 3. These fall into a few general types, and we will take one or two examples from each type. We will justify each of these both by the class logic inference patterns given in Section 4.2 and by a new kind of diagram, the *Carroll* diagram. This is a slight modification of a kind of logic diagram invented by Lewis Carroll.

Carroll and Venn Diagrams

To make a Carroll diagram we first make a square for our universe of discourse and then divide it into four areas representing the possible combinations of S, P, $\bar{S}$, and $\bar{P}$ (Figure 4.14). We then draw a circle in the middle

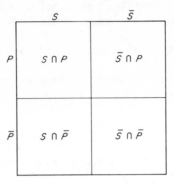

Figure 4.14

of the diagram for M and use the earlier convention that inside of the circle represents M and outside of it represents $\bar{M}$ (Figure 4.15).

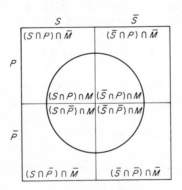

Figure 4.15

I myself find the Carroll diagram just described to be clearer and more convenient than any other type of diagram. However, some logicians prefer to use another type of diagram, the so-called Venn diagram (named for an English logician and mathematician, John Venn). This diagram (Figure 4.16) has three overlapping circles within a box representing the universal class. For the convenience of those who prefer this type of diagram, each time I use a Carroll diagram I will include the corresponding Venn diagram.

We thus have areas representing all the subclasses of a universe with respect to three classes S, P and M. As before, a 0 in a cell indicates that the

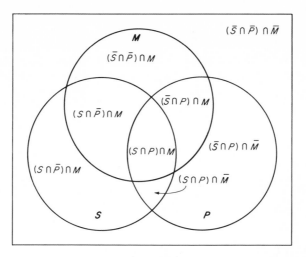

Figure 4.16

class which the cell represents has no members, a 1 in a cell indicates that the corresponding class has at least one member. If a 1 is placed on the line dividing two cells it indicates that one or the other of the subclasses represented by the cells has at least one member (or both), *but we are not sure which.*

Let us use a diagram to show why the Special Subclass Rule

$$A \subseteq B$$
$$\frac{C \cap A \neq \Lambda}{C \cap B \neq \Lambda}$$

is justified. First let us draw a diagram for any three arbitrary classes, A, B, and C (Figure 4.17). We then diagram the first premise, showing A ⊆ B.

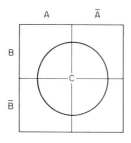 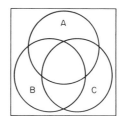

Figure 4.17

This is equivalent to A ∩ B̄ = Λ, as we have seen. Thus we wish to indicate as empty the class A ∩ B̄. But this is divided into two subclasses,

$$(A \cap \bar{B}) \cap C \quad \text{and} \quad (A \cap \bar{B}) \cap \bar{C}$$

139

so we must indicate both these as empty to indicate A ∩ B̄ as empty (Figure 4.18).

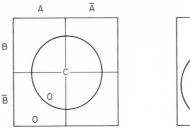
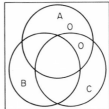

Figure 4.18

We can now diagram the second premise, C ∩ A ≠ Λ (Figure 4.19).

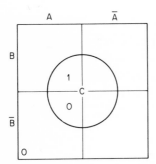
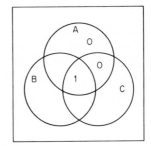

Figure 4.19

Since the only portion of A within C which is not empty is within B, the 1 must go in the indicated cell. As we can see, this means that there is at least one member in the class (A ∩ B) ∩ C, which means that there is at least one member in the class C ∩ B. This is what we set out to prove. Since A, B, and C were any arbitrarily chosen classes, this holds for any three classes that we may choose.

Syllogisms with HSC, SSR, and DSC

Let us now turn to syllogisms. The first type of valid syllogism has three universal affirmative premises. There is only one representative of this type,

Every *M* is *P*
Every *S* is *M*
Every *S* is *P*

which can be symbolized as either

$$
\begin{array}{c}
M \subseteq P \\
S \subseteq M \\
\hline
S \subseteq P
\end{array}
\qquad \text{or} \qquad
\begin{array}{c}
M \cap \bar{P} = \wedge \\
S \cap \bar{M} = \wedge \\
\hline
S \cap \bar{P} = \wedge
\end{array}
$$

In the first version, the conclusion obviously follows from the premises by Hypothetical Syllogism for Classes (HSC); the second version is handier for marking the diagram (Figure 4.20). Since the portion of M outside P is

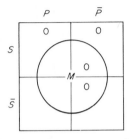 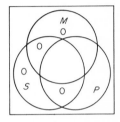

Figure 4.20

empty and the portion of S outside M is empty, the only remaining portion of S is inside P and $S \cap \bar{P}$ is empty, as we wished to show.

Another type of valid syllogism has one universal affirmative premise and one universal negative premise. The conclusion is, of course, universal negative. An example of this type is

$$
\begin{array}{c}
\text{No } M \text{ is } P \\
\text{Every } S \text{ is } M \\
\hline
\text{No } S \text{ is } P
\end{array}
$$

symbolized as either

$$
\begin{array}{c}
M \subseteq \bar{P} \\
S \subseteq M \\
\hline
S \subseteq \bar{P}
\end{array}
\qquad \text{or} \qquad
\begin{array}{c}
M \cap P = \wedge \\
S \cap \bar{M} = \wedge \\
\hline
S \cap P = \wedge
\end{array}
$$

In the first version, HSC obviously justifies the inference. Using the second version to mark the diagram we get Figure 4.21. The only remaining part

Figure 4.21

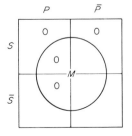 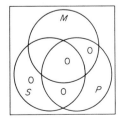

of S is outside P. So $S \subseteq \bar{P}$ or $S \cap P = \Lambda$. Another example of this type would be

$$\frac{\begin{array}{c}\text{No } P \text{ is } M \\ \text{Every } S \text{ is } M\end{array}}{\text{No } S \text{ is } P}$$

The diagram would be the same, but to justify

$$\frac{\begin{array}{c}P \subseteq \bar{M} \\ S \subseteq M\end{array}}{S \subseteq \bar{P}}$$

by HSC we would first have to transpose the first premise, giving us the first syllogism of this type. In other examples of this type it is necessary to use contraposition on the universal affirmative premise before we can use HSC.

A third type of valid syllogism has one universal affirmative premise, a particular affirmative premise, of course, a particular affirmative conclusion. An example:

$$\frac{\begin{array}{c}\text{Every } M \text{ is } P \\ \text{Some } S \text{ is } M\end{array}}{\text{Some } S \text{ is } P} \quad \text{symbolically} \quad \frac{\begin{array}{c}M \subseteq P \\ S \cap M \neq \Lambda\end{array}}{S \cap P \neq \Lambda} \quad \text{or} \quad \frac{\begin{array}{c}M \cap \bar{P} = \Lambda \\ S \cap M \neq \Lambda\end{array}}{S \cap P \neq \Lambda}$$

The first symbolic version is obviously an example of the Special Subclass Rule, and the diagram will be the same as for our demonstration of that rule. Another example of this type of valid syllogism has some different features:

$$\frac{\begin{array}{c}\text{Some } M \text{ is } P \\ \text{Every } M \text{ is } S\end{array}}{\text{Some } S \text{ is } P} \quad \text{becomes} \quad \frac{\begin{array}{c}M \cap P \neq \Lambda \\ M \subseteq S\end{array}}{S \cap P \neq \Lambda} \quad \text{or} \quad \frac{\begin{array}{c}M \cap \bar{S} = \Lambda \\ M \cap P \neq \Lambda\end{array}}{S \cap P \neq \Lambda}$$

To apply SSR to the first version we should commute $M \cap P \neq \Lambda$ to $P \cap M \neq \Lambda$. The diagraming goes like this: If we diagram the first premise first we have a 1 on the line between $(S \cap P) \cap M$ and $(\bar{S} \cap P) \cap M$ (Figure 4.22). When we diagram the second premise, we see that the 1 must

Figure 4.22

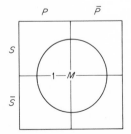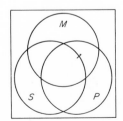

142

be in $(S \cap P) \cap M$ since $M \cap \bar{S}$ is empty (Figure 4.23). Thus, since the class $(S \cap P) \cap M$ has at least one member, so does $S \cap P$.

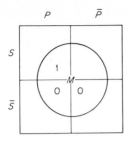
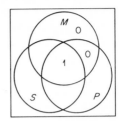

Figure 4.23

There are two remaining types of syllogisms having respectively E and I premises and O conclusions and A and O premises and O conclusions. They can all be justified by SSR with some use of immediate inferences. Neither the justifications nor the diagrams add anything new, so we will leave examples of these types for the exercises.

As we have gone some way towards showing, valid syllogisms with two universal premises can all be justified by using HSC, and valid syllogisms with mixed universal and particular premises can all be justified by the use of SSR. Syllogisms with an individual premise can be justified by the rule DSC (Definition of Subclass). For example, the syllogism

Every M is P		$M \subseteq P$		$M \cap \bar{P} = \wedge$
s is M	becomes	$s \in M$	or	$s \in M$
s is P		$s \in P$		$s \in P$

The first version can be seen to be a case of the rule DSC. To diagram the argument we can use a four-cell diagram and a solid dot for s (Figure 4.24).

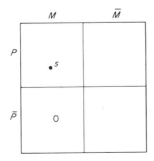
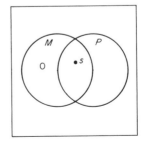

Figure 4.24

Since M outside of P is empty, if s is to be in M it must also be in P.

Any sorites turns out to be justifiable by repeated uses of HSC with no more than one use of SSR or DSC. (Of course, immediate inferences may be needed.)

Diagraming as Disproof

The Carroll diagrams can be used also as a disproof method: if the premises of a syllogism are correctly diagramed on a Carroll diagram, then, if the syllogism is valid, the conclusion has been diagramed. If the premises have been correctly diagramed and the conclusion does not appear, then the syllogism is not valid. For example, the following syllogism is invalid because of an undistributed middle.

Every P is M		$P \cap \bar{M} = \Lambda$
Every S is M	symbolized	$S \cap \bar{M} = \Lambda$
Every S is P		$S \cap \bar{P} = \Lambda$

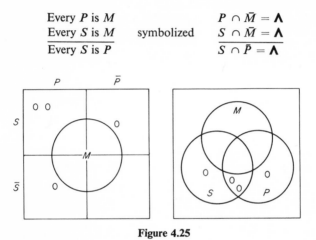

Figure 4.25

Notice (Figure 4.25) that the area $(S \cap \bar{P}) \cap M$ has not been emptied, so that the desired conclusion does not appear after the premises are diagramed. (The fact that $(S \cap P) \cap \bar{M}$ was marked empty by two premises does not by itself mean that the syllogism is invalid: This sometimes happens in valid arguments as in the example which follows.)

Finally, no inference that depends on the subalternation of I to A or O to E statements can be justified by class logic or by Carroll diagrams unless the fact is explicitly stated as an additional premise that the classes used are not empty. Class logic gives what is called a Boolean (after George Boole, a pioneer of symbolic logic) interpretation of syllogistic logic, which eliminates all those inferences which depend on subalternation. Thus, for example

$$S \subseteq P \quad \text{and} \quad S \subseteq \bar{P}$$

are not contraries since, if S is an empty class, it *can* be a subclass of both P and $\bar{P}$. This has some peculiar results: For example, the argument

Every bear is a creature fond of honey
Every bear is a furry creature
Some furry creature is fond of honey

seems intuitively satisfactory. It cannot be justified, however, either by class logic or by Carroll diagrams. In Chapter 3 we solved a similar problem by using subalternation if all the classes in question had members. Class logic, however, offers a more difficult problem. We have to express the statement that there are bears as an additional premise. Let

B $\#$ Bears   H $\#$ Honey-loving creatures   F $\#$ Fuzzy creatures

We symbolize the syllogism as:

$$B \cap \bar{H} = \Lambda$$
$$B \cap \bar{F} = \Lambda$$
$$\underline{B \neq \Lambda}$$
$$F \cap H \neq \Lambda$$

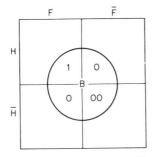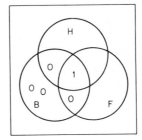

Figure 4.26

The diagram (Figure 4.26) gives us the desired conclusion. (Notice that $(B \cap \bar{H}) \cap F$ was emptied twice.) We could introduce also an additional rule for cases like this, calling it the Subalternation Rule (SR):

$$A \subseteq B$$
$$\underline{A \neq \Lambda}$$
$$A \cap B \neq \Lambda$$

The Subalternation Rule says, in effect, what we already know; that, provided the classes in question are not empty, A implies I and E implies O. This would simplify our justifications of syllogisms which break no rule except the one that two universals do not imply a particular, and which are intuitively valid since the classes in question have members. However, it turns out that in every case where we would want to use this rule what is actually needed in the proof is not the original A or E statement but its subalternate as derived by the Subalternation Rule. Furthermore, adding the extra, existential premise makes the argument no longer properly syllogistic. So in most cases it seems most convenient to use the Subalternation Rule on the appropriate premise *before* proceeding with the syllogistic argument, just as in many of the Lewis Carroll syllogisms and soriteses we had to perform such processes as to obvert or transpose before we could treat one of Carroll's examples as a syllogism or syllogism chain. Thus, once subalternation has been used (where justified, of course), we can proceed with the syllogistic argument using either the class logic rules we have established so far or Carroll diagrams.

EXERCISES 4.3

A. Test by Carroll diagram, putting in standard form where necessary.

1. No Don is honest.
    Some, who are not Dons, are
    _____
    rich.
    Some who are rich are dishonest.

2. No idler wins fame.
    Some painters are not idle.
    _____
    Some painters win fame.

3. No bird except the peacock is proud of its tail.
    Some birds that are proud of their tails cannot sing.
    _____
    Some peacocks cannot sing.

4. No muffin is wholesome.
    Every bun is unwholesome.
    _____
    No bun is a muffin.

5. Some pillows are soft.
    No poker is soft.
    _____
    Some pokers are not pillows.

B. Translate into statements about classes, and find and prove the conclusions of each of the following soriteses. (Source: Lewis Carroll, *Symbolic Logic*.)

1. No books sold here have gilt edges, except what are in the front shop;
    All the authorised editions have red labels;
    All the books with red labels are priced at 5s. and upwards;
    None but authorised editions are ever placed in the front shop.

    Univ. "books sold here"; A # authorised editions; G # gilt-edged; R # having red labels; F # in the front shop; P # priced at 5s. and upwards.

2. Remedies for bleeding, which fail to check it, are a mockery;
    Tincture of Calendula is not to be despised;
    Remedies, which will check the bleeding when you cut your finger, are useful;
    All mock remedies for bleeding are despicable.

    Univ. "remedies for bleeding"; A # able to check bleeding; D # despicable; M # mockeries; C # Tincture of Calendula; U # useful when you cut your finger.

3. None of the unnoticed things, met with at sea, are mermaids;
    Things entered in the log, as met with at sea, are sure to be worth remembering;

I have never met with anything worth remembering, when on a voyage;
Things met with at sea, that are noticed, are sure to be recorded in the log;
Univ. "things met with at sea"; E # entered in log; M # mermaids; W # met with by me; N # noticed; R # worth remembering.

4. The only books in this library, that I do *not* recommend for reading, are unhealthy in tone;
The bound books are all well-written;
All the romances are healthy in tone;
I do not recommend you to read any of the unbound books.

Univ. "books in this library"; B # bound; H # healthy in tone; R # recommended by me; O # romances; W # well-written.

5. No birds, except ostriches, are 9 feet high;
There are no birds in this aviary that belong to any one but *me*;
No ostrich lives on mince-pies;
I have no birds less than 9 feet high.

Univ. "birds"; A # in this aviary; L # living on mince-pies; M # my; N # 9 feet high; O # ostriches.

C. The following are Aristotle's description of some of the various syllogisms valid in his system of syllogistic logic. Symbolize each in class logic, and prove its validity. (Source: Aristotle, *Prior Analytics*.)
  1. If A is predicated of all B,* and B of all C, A must necessarily be predicated of all C.
  2. If A is predicated of none of B and B of all of C, it follows that A will apply to no C.
  3. Let A apply to all B and B to some C. Then A must apply to some C.
  4. If A applies to no B but B applies to some C, A must necessarily not apply to some C.
  5. Let M be predicated of no N but of all O, then N applies to no O.
  6. If M applies to all N but to no O, N will apply to no O.
  7. If M applies to no N but to some O, it must follow that N does not apply to some O.
  8. If M applies to all N but does not apply to some O, it must follow that N does not apply to some O.
  9. If R applies to all S and if P to some S, P must apply to some R.
  10. If R applies to some S and if P to all S, P must apply to some R.
  11. If R applies to all S and if P does not apply to some S, it necessarily follows that P does not apply to some R.
  12. If P applies to no S and if R applies to some S, P will not apply to some R.
  13. If B is predicated of none of A and of all of C, then A will apply to no C.
  14. If B applies to no A but to some C, then A will not apply to some C.
  15. If A applies to no B and C to some B, then A will not apply to some C.

* Note that "A is predicated of all B" is translated into our standard form statement "Every B is A." Look at other examples in the even-numbered exercises at the back of the book.

4.4 NONSYLLOGISTIC CLASS INFERENCES

If class logic merely gave us an alternative way of justifying syllogistic arguments, it would hardly be worth studying. However, class logic is considerably more flexible and considerably wider in scope than is syllogistic logic. To properly develop class logic would require a carefully selected group of inference rules, probably about as many as were needed for propositional logic. To give some idea of the scope and power of class logic, we will add to the inferences we already have to give the rules in Table 4.3, where X, Y, and Z are class variables, and a represents an element of a class which is either an individual or a class. To these rules, we will add the equivalences listed in Tables 4.1 and 4.2 of Section 4.2. Using these

TABLE 4.3

Definition of Subclass (DSC)	$\dfrac{\begin{array}{c}a \in X \\ X \subseteq Y\end{array}}{a \in Y}$	or	$\dfrac{\begin{array}{c}a \in \bar{Y} \\ X \subseteq Y\end{array}}{a \in \bar{X}}$
Hypothetical Syllogism for Classes (HSC)	$\dfrac{\begin{array}{c}X \subseteq Y \\ Y \subseteq Z\end{array}}{X \subseteq Z}$		
Contraposition (Contrap)	$\dfrac{X \subseteq Y}{\bar{Y} \subseteq \bar{X}}$	or	$\dfrac{\bar{X} \subseteq \bar{Y}}{Y \subseteq X}$
Class Disjunctive Syllogism (CDS)	$\dfrac{\begin{array}{c}a \in (X \cup Y) \\ a \in \bar{Y}\end{array}}{a \in X}$	or	$\dfrac{\begin{array}{c}X \subseteq (Y \cup Z) \\ X \subseteq \bar{Z}\end{array}}{X \subseteq Y}$
Conjunction for Classes (ConjC)	$\dfrac{\begin{array}{c}a \in X \\ a \in Y\end{array}}{a \in (X \cap Y)}$	or	$\dfrac{\begin{array}{c}X \subseteq Y \\ X \subseteq Z\end{array}}{X \subseteq (Y \cap Z)}$
Special Subclass Rule (SSR)	$\dfrac{\begin{array}{c}Y \subseteq Z \\ X \cap Y \neq \wedge\end{array}}{Y \cap Z \neq \wedge}$		
Generalization for Classes (GenC)	$\dfrac{a \in Y}{Y \neq \wedge}$	or	$\dfrac{Y = \wedge}{a \in \bar{Y}}$
Addition for Classes (AddC)	$\dfrac{a \in X}{a \in (X \cup Y)}$	or	$\dfrac{X \subseteq Y}{X \subseteq (Y \cup Z)}$
Simplification for Classes (SimpC)	$\dfrac{a \in (X \cap Y)}{a \in X}$	or	$\dfrac{X \subseteq (Y \cap Z)}{X \subseteq Y}$

rules, we can justify such inferences as the following (using the same form for proofs as in propositional logic).

No-one at Kanga's house or at Owl's house saw Christopher Robin today, but he was seen both in Eeyore's corner of the Forest and at Rabbit's hole.

Pooh saw Christopher Robin today, but he was not at Rabbit's hole. So Pooh must have been in Eeyore's corner of the Forest and not either at Kanga's house or Owl's.

Let p # Pooh
    C # those who saw
          Christopher Robin today
    K # those at Kanga's house
          today

O # those at Owl's house today
E # those at Eeyore's corner of
    the Forest today.
R # those at Rabbit's hole today

We can then symbolize:

$$
\begin{array}{ll}
1 & (K \cup O) \subseteq \bar{C} \\
2 & C \subseteq (E \cup R) \\
3 & p \in C \\
4 & p \in R
\end{array}
\left.\vphantom{\begin{array}{l}1\\2\\3\\4\end{array}}\right\} \quad p \in (E \cap \overline{(K \cup O)})
$$

and prove the conclusion as follows:

$$
\begin{array}{lll}
5 & \bar{\bar{C}} \subseteq \overline{(K \cup O)} & 1,\ \text{Contrap} \\
6 & C \subseteq \overline{(K \cup O)} & 2,\ \text{DC} \\
7 & p \in \overline{(K \cup O)} & 3,\ 6,\ \text{DSC} \\
8 & p \in (E \cup R) & 3,\ 2,\ \text{DSC} \\
9 & p \in E & 4,\ 8,\ \text{CDS} \\
10 & p \in (E \cap \overline{(K \cup O)}) & 7,\ 9,\ \text{ConjC} \qquad \text{Q.E.D.}
\end{array}
$$

A somewhat more complex argument is the following:

All of Christopher Robin's friends are peaceful animals. No peaceful animal is fierce, unless he has a good reason. Any animal whose child is stolen is fierce. Kanga's child was stolen. Therefore, Kanga has good reason to be fierce. [Understood: Kanga is a friend of Christopher Robin.]

Let: C # Friends of Christopher
       Robin
    A # Animals
    P # Peaceful creatures
    F # Fierce animals

R # Animals who have good
    reason to be fierce
S # Animals whose child is stolen
k # Kanga

We can symbolize and prove as follows:

$$
\begin{array}{ll}
1 & C \subseteq (A \cap P) \\
2 & ((A \cap P) \cap F) \subseteq R \\
3 & (A \cap S) \subseteq F \\
4 & k \in C \\
5 & k \in S
\end{array}
\left.\vphantom{\begin{array}{l}1\\2\\3\\4\\5\end{array}}\right\} \quad k \in R
$$

6	$k \in (A \cap P)$	4, 1, DSC
7	$k \in A$	6, CSimp
8	$k \in (A \cap S)$	5, 7, ConjC
9	$k \in F$	8, 3, DSC
10	$k \in ((A \cap P) \cap F)$	9, 6, ConjC
11	$k \in R$	2, 10, DSC Q.E.D.

Finally, an even more complex argument:

> Tigger will not chew or swallow any food any that is either prickly or sweet. All liquid foods are distasteful to Tigger except Roo's strengthening medicine. Tigger will swallow any food which is not distasteful to him. So Tigger will swallow some food that is not sweet.

Let: F # Foods   W # Sweet things
     C # Things Tigger will chew   L # Liquids
     S # Things Tigger will swallow D # Things distasteful to Tigger
     P # Prickly things   r # Roo's strengthening medicine

Symbolize and prove as follows:

1	$(F \cap (C \cup S)) \subseteq \overline{(P \cup W)}$	
2	$r \in ((L \cap F) \cap \bar{D})$	$S \cap (F \cap W) \neq M$
3	$\bar{D} \subseteq S$	
4	$r \in \bar{D}$	2, SimpC
5	$r \in S$	3, 4, DSC
6	$r \in (L \cap F)$	2, SimpC
7	$r \in F$	6, SimpC
8	$r \in (C \cup S)$	5, AddC
9	$r \in (F \cap (C \cup S))$	7, 8, ConjC
10	$r \in \overline{(P \cup W)}$	9, 1, DSC
11	$r \in (\bar{P} \cap \bar{W})$	10, DeMC
12	$r \in \bar{W}$	11, SimpC
13	$r \in (F \cap \bar{W})$	7, 12, ConjC
14	$r \in (S \cap (F \cap \bar{W})$	5, 14, ConjC
15	$S \cap (F \cap \bar{W}) \neq \Lambda$	13, GenC Q.E.D.

In general, a wide variety of arguments can be handled even with the simple equipment which we have so far. There is no simple way, however, to expand class logic to deal with certain arguments, for example, those which are concerned with *relations* between two or more things. The ability to formalize arguments dealing with relations is an important feature of the more powerful kind of logic which we examine in the next chapter. First, however, we will briefly examine certain philosophically interesting difficulties which arise in set theory, of which class logic is a part.

EXERCISES 4.4

A. Use the techniques described in this section to give proofs for the following.

1. $m \in (\bar{A} \cup B)$ $\left.\vphantom{\begin{array}{c}a\\a\end{array}}\right\}$ $\bar{A} \neq \wedge$

    $B = \wedge$

2. $n \in C$ $\left.\vphantom{\begin{array}{c}a\\a\end{array}}\right\}$ $n \in ((C \cup E) \cap D)$

    $n \in D$

3. $\bar{A} \subseteq B$
   $B \subseteq C$ $\left.\vphantom{\begin{array}{c}a\\a\\a\end{array}}\right\}$ $A \neq \wedge$
   $m \in \bar{C}$

4. $n \in ((G \cup H) \cup F)$
   $F = \wedge$ $\left.\vphantom{\begin{array}{c}a\\a\\a\end{array}}\right\}$ $n \in H$
   $G = \wedge$

5. $m \in (A \cap B)$
$\left.\vphantom{\begin{array}{c}a\\a\\a\end{array}}\right\}$ $m \in \bar{D}$
  $A \subseteq (C \cap \bar{D})$

B. Symbolize and prove using class logic. Give a dictionary. (Source: Leibnitz, *Abridgement of the Theodicy.*)
1. Whoever does not choose the best is lacking in power or in knowledge or in goodness.
    God does not choose the best in creating this world.
    Therefore God is lacking in power in knowledge or in goodness.
2. Whoever makes things in which there is evil, which could have been made without any evil, or the making of which could have been omitted, does not choose the best.
    God has made a world in which there is evil. A world which could have been made without any evil, or the making of which could have been omitted altogether.
    Therefore God has not chosen the best.
3. If there is more evil than good in intelligent creatures then there is more evil than good in the work of God.
    There is more evil than good in intelligent creatures.
    Therefore there is more evil than good in the work of God.
4. If it is always impossible not to sin, then it is always unjust to punish.
    Now it is always impossible not to sin, or in other words every sin is necessary.
    Therefore it is always unjust to punish.
5. All that is predetermined is necessary.
    Every event is predetermined.
    Therefore every event is necessary and consequently sin is necessary also.
6. That which is future, that which is foreseen, that which follows from its causes, is predetermined.
    Every event is such.
    Therefore every event is predetermined.
7. Whoever can prevent the sin of another and does not do so, but rather contributes to it, although he is well informed of it, is accessory to that sin.

God can prevent the sin of intelligent creatures, but he does not do so, and rather contributes to it by his concurrence and by the opportunities which he brings about, although he has a perfect knowledge of it.

Therefore God is an accessory to sin.

8. Whoever produces all that is real in a thing is its cause.

God produces all that is real in sin.

Therefore God is the cause of sin.

9. Whoever punishes those who have done as well as it was in his power to do is unjust.

God does so.

Therefore God is unjust.

10. Whoever gives only to some, and not to all, the means which produces in them effectively a good will and saving faith has not sufficient goodness.

God does this.

Therefore God has not sufficient goodness.

4.5 PHILOSOPHICAL DIFFICULTIES

Let us now return to the problem we postponed at the beginning of this chapter: the meaning of the concept of a class and the problems connected with the foundations of set theory.

Probably the first notions of a class or group came from small groups of material objects near each other in space and time, for example, a flock of sheep or a pile of stones. From this it is only a step to thinking of things as a group even when separated in space and time (for example, thinking of the sheep as a flock even when scattered or dispersed).

Defining Classes

Now there are two ways in which we can group or class things together. We can give some sort of list of things and think of the class simply as the things on this list or we can give a characteristic which the things have in common and think of all the things which have this characteristic as a class. One convention for defining classes by listing which is often used in set theory is to place names or designations of the members of the class between braces (often separated by commas). Thus:

$$\{ 1, 2, 3, 4 \}$$

is a way of naming the class composed of the listed numbers, and

$$\{ \text{Lincoln, Garfield, Kennedy} \}$$

would name the class composed of these three presidents, and so on.

A convention often used for the other way of forming a class is to give within braces the defining characteristic, often using the notation $``x \mid x$

is . . .," read as "the class of all things which are . . ." or "the class of all x such that x is. . . ." In this notation our previous classes would be:

$$\{x \mid x \text{ is an integer between 1 and 4 inclusive}\}$$

and

$$\{x \mid x \text{ is a President of the U.S. assassinated in office}\}$$

So long as we form classes by listing, no difficulties arise. All such classes are clearly defined, for example, since to see if any element is a member of the class we simply see if it is listed. However, for most interesting classes the listing procedure is plainly impossible. We can list all presidents of the United States but not all of such classes as numbers, sheep or stones. Some classes are known to be infinite, and thus listing them is impossible. Others are simply unmanageably large. Once we start defining classes by giving characteristics, however, we run into the following sort of difficulty.

Classes That Are Members of Themselves

It seems to be reasonable to say that some classes are members of themselves. The class of all abstract classes is surely an abstract class and thus a member of itself. The class of teaspoons, on the other hand, is obviously not a member of itself. Now consider the class of all classes which are not members of themselves. Is this class a member of itself or not? If it is a member of itself, then by the defining condition for the class it is not a member of itself. But if it is not a member of itself, then it falls under the defining condition and is a member of itself. Thus if it is possible to have such a class we have an irreconcilable paradox. Both the statement "this class is a member of itself" and its denial seem to be true. We know from propositional logic that, if a contradiction can be proved to be true, anything at all can be proved. Our only escape seems to be to deny the existence of this class so that both assertions about it are either false or meaningless, depending on what position we take on the somewhat controversial question as to how we should regard assertions about nonexistent things. (Neither answer causes trouble in propositional logic, since no statement which is not definitely true or definitely false is a proposition, as we defined proposition.)

It can be seen that the restriction adopted in Section 4.1 prevents this paradox from arising in class logic as we have defined it. There is at least one element such that we cannot say whether it is a member of the class of all classes which are not members of themselves (that is, the class itself). Therefore, it fails to meet the requirement set in Section 4.1 for all classes dealt with in class logic and is not a class at all in our sense!

This kind of solution has recommended itself to at least some able mathematicians. For example Paul Halmos in *Naive Set Theory* (Van Nostrand, New York, 1960, pp. 6–7) states the paradox above and seems (the passage is somewhat cryptic) to draw the conclusion that not every condition defines a class. But if not, why not? And what sort of conditions are those which form these pseudo classes? Do they have anything in common? Can we further justify the rather ad hoc exclusion of paradox-generating pseudo classes? I am, frankly, heretical on this point. I see nothing especially *ad hoc* in ruling out paradoxical classes just because they generate paradoxes. Some of the references at the end of this section give a more sympathetic examination of the paradoxes and the attempts to eliminate them from set theory in ways that lack the alleged failings of the ad hoc elimination.

A final word on this point: The late Bertrand Russell, who discovered the paradox above and brought the attendant problem to light, once restated it in the form of the Spanish Barber Paradox as follows:

"In a small Spanish town there is a barber, male, adult, and cleanshaven, who shaves everyone who does not shave himself, and shaves no one who does shave himself. Who shaves the barber?" The question is unanswerable. The only reasonable answer to the paradox is that no such barber can exist. Exactly the same answer seems to me to apply to the paradox in its class form. No such class can exist.

READING LIST

These two books of readings include many articles on philosophical problems connected with syllogistic logic:

Copi, I., and Gould, J. *Readings in Logic* (The Macmillan Company, New York), 1964, Part Three.

Jager, R. *Essays in Logic, from Aristotle to Russell* (Prentice-Hall Inc., Englewood Cliffs, N.J.), 1963.

The following parts of the history of logic mentioned earlier give the history of syllogistic and class logic:

Kneale, W., and Kneale, M. *The Development of Logic* (Oxford University Press, New York), 1962. *Syllogisms:* chapter 2, section 6; chapter 4, sections 1, 2, 3; chapter 5, sections 4 and 5. *Class logic:* chapter 5, sections 1 and 2; chapter 6, sections 3 and 4; chapter 7; chapter 10, section 4; chapter 11.

Chapter 5
PREDICATE
LOGIC

Syllogistic logic and class logic both have their advantages. The procedure for checking the validity of syllogistic arguments is simple, the arguments themselves seem close to ordinary patterns of reasoning, and a surprising number of arguments can be fitted into the patterns of syllogistic reasoning. Class logic offers still more power and flexibility and is closely related to mathematical concepts and procedures which are of philosophical interest. Neither system, however, is sufficiently powerful and flexible to serve as a general tool for the analysis of philosophically interesting arguments. As we have seen, the medievals attempted to use syllogistic logic for this purpose but were forced to use many non-syllogistic arguments. Class logic has never been used for the analysis of arguments by any large group of philosophers.

The system of logic that we are now about to consider is capable of being used as a basic philosopher's tool and has been so used by many modern philosophers. It is historically a comparatively recent development. Some of its basic notions were discovered in the last century by Gottlöb Frege and C. S. Peirce, but its greatest development has been in this century. Major contributions have been made by Russell and Whitehead, Gentzen, Quine, and others. Because it has tools for dealing adequately with both subjects and predicates it would be appropriately called subject-predicate logic but in fact is usually referred to as predicate logic.

In the system of predicate logic developed in this book an attempt is made to combine flexibility and ease of use with a certain degree of philosophical (not mathematical) sophistication as to what we are doing and how we are doing it.

5.1 SUBJECTS, PREDICATES, AND QUANTIFIERS

Class logic as we have developed it so far is a powerful and flexible tool, and even further developments are possible. However, the logical techniques which we are now about to consider are still more powerful and flexible. Yet the machinery of the system is basically simple, as we shall see. Part of it is already familiar to us; the propositional connectives of propositional logic. What we will connect with these connectives are expressions that are not unlike propositions in many respects. In fact, the simplest statements of predicate logic *are* propositions. However, instead of regarding the proposition as an unanalyzed unit and letting a single letter stand for it, we will use a symbolism that enables us to separate the subject and the predicate of a proposition and symbolize them separately.

Thus, to begin with, we will need two kinds of constants; constants which stand for subject terms* and constants which stand for predicate terms. We will use the small letters of roman type from "a" to "t" as stand-ins for specific subject terms and the capital letters of roman type from "A" to "W" as stand-ins for specific predicate terms. Thus if we wished to symbolize the proposition "Bilbo is a hobbit" we would give the following dictionary.

$$b \ \# \ Bilbo$$

$$H \underline{\hspace{1.5em}} \ \# \ \underline{\hspace{1.5em}} \text{ is a hobbit}$$

Note two things about the predicate stand-in. First it has a blank associated with it, both in the symbol and in the phrase for which it stands. Until this blank is filled in, a predicate expression makes no assertion and is neither true or false. If I say "_____ is a hobbit," I have said nothing until I fill in the blank. Since eventually we will have various blanks to keep track of, we will introduce subject variables, which are place-holders for any subject term, just as propositional variables are place-holders for any proposition. For subject

---

* The subject terms will be the names or designations of whatever we choose to regard as individuals. Initially these will be such things as persons or objects, but eventually we will extend the notion of individual to places, times, and even to propositions and actions.

variables we will use the small letters u to z, but we will usually begin with x and use u to w only after using up the letters x to z. Thus instead of

$$H \underline{} \# \underline{} \text{ is a hobbit}$$

we will write

$$Hx \# x \text{ is a hobbit}$$

Again, as in the case of the proposition with the blank, "x is a hobbit" says nothing true or false until the blank is filled in, that is, until we substitute a subject term for the variable. Because of a mathematical analogy, Hx or "x is a hobbit" is sometimes called a "propositional function." Just as a mathematical expression like x^2 has no numerical value until some x is specified, when it becomes equal to some specific number, so Hx says nothing until some x is specified, when it becomes a definite proposition with a definite truth value.

The second thing to notice about $H \underline{}$ or Hx is that the blank or variable is on the *right*-hand side. This is a rather silly and confusing convention which is, unfortunately, too deeply entrenched in modern logic to ignore. It would be much more natural to symbolize "Bilbo is a hobbit" by bH or even Bh (changing our conventions for constants) and I would prefer to do so. But it would make it difficult for the student who will be reading other works in which the conventional reversal is used; so, after this grumble, I will follow the standard procedure.

Eventually we will need predicate variables, but in this section we will use only constant predicates combined either with subject variables or with subject constant. If we had only subject and predicate constants, predicate logic would be of very little more use than propositional logic. We could symbolize the compound proposition "If Bilbo is a hobbit, then Bilbo is not an elf" as

$$Hb \supset \sim Eb$$

where

$$b \# \text{Bilbo}$$
$$Hx \# x \text{ is a hobbit}$$
$$Ex \# x \text{ is an elf}$$

Aside from making it obvious that both propositions have Bilbo as their subject, there is no advantage in this over a propositional logic proposition. In fact $Hb \supset \sim Eb$ *is* a proposition in propositional logic, with a somewhat different convention for symbolizing propositions than that used in Chapter 1. (This will become important in due course.)

Quantification

Now we might try to write a proposition using subject variables. For example, we might write $Hx \supset \sim Ex$ and try to read it as "If x is a hobbit, then x is not an elf." However, this would be to confuse subject variables, which are merely like blanks, which can be filled in with any subject term, and the quasi name which we will discuss later in this chapter. Remember that a letter such as x is just a convenient substitute for a blank, and the nearest sentence in ordinary English to $Hx \supset \sim Ex$ would be "If ____ is a hobbit, then ____ is not an elf."

It would, however, be very convenient to be able to symbolize the sort of thing we say in English with the help of words like "anyone" and "someone." For example, "if anyone is a hobbit, then he is not an elf" or "someone is an elf." Since $Hx \supset \sim Ex$ and Ex will not do the job, we must find something that will. The device we will use is called *quantification*. We will introduce two operators called *quantifiers* which can stand in front of propositional functions, somewhat as the symbol $\sim$ can stand in front of a simple proposition or compound proposition. Like $\sim$, these operators will have a range of application or *scope*, which is indicated by parentheses. The two quantifiers are: (1) a subject variable within parentheses, for example, (x), (y), (z), or (w); (2) a subject variable within parentheses with a backward E in front of it, for example, $(\exists x)$, $(\exists z)$, or $(\exists u)$. When a quantifier stands in front of a left parenthesis, its scope extends to the corresponding right parenthesis, just as in the case of $\sim$.

These operators have two important features. First, we can use them to express the key ideas of universality and particularity; and, second, we can use them to solve the problem which we could not solve in propositional logic, cross-reference between propositions. For example, consider the proposition

$$(x)\,(Hx \supset \sim Ex)$$

The quantifier (x), which is called the *universal quantifier*, can be read as "for anything whatsoever." But, most vital, the succeeding occurrences of x are related to this introductory phrase by the fact that they are x's and the quantifier is an (x). Thus, the whole proposition

$$(x)\,(Hx \supset \sim Ex)$$

will read "For anything whatsoever, if *that* thing is a hobbit, then *that* thing is not an elf." Notice that this is a *proposition* and *not* a propositional function. It makes an assertion, and that assertion is either true or false (presumably true, in this case). However, if we had two different propositional variables with one quantifier, for example,

$$(x)\,(Hx \supset \sim Ey)$$

then we again have a propositional function, for we are saying in effect "For anything whatsoever, if that thing is a hobbit, then _____ is not an elf." The y does not relate to the (x) and, therefore, remains a variable, a blank to be filled in. The technical terminology which logicians use to describe this situation is that in $(x) (Hx \supset \sim By)$ the x is a *bound* variable, bound by the quantifier (x), while the variable y is a *free* variable since there is no (y) or $(\exists y)$ quantifier. Bound variables are like such pronouns as "something, or anything," whereas free variables are like blanks. So an expression which contains free variables, contains, in effect, blanks and is a propositional function. But an expression which contains only bound variables is a proposition and is either true or false.

The other quantifier $(\exists x)$, $(\exists y)$, etc., is called the *existential quantifier*. It can be read as "for at least one thing"; for example,

$$(\exists x) (Hx \cdot \sim Ex)$$

can be read as "For at least one thing, that thing is a hobbit and not an elf." Several points can be made about the way of reading propositions with quantifiers or, as logicians call them, *quantified propositions*. First, if the brief forms "for anything whatsoever . . ." or "for at least one thing . . ." are unclear, these can be read as

"it is true of anything whatsoever that . . ."

and

"it is true of at least one thing that . . ."

or else as

"for anything whatsoever, it is true that . . ."
"for at least one thing it is true that . . ."

and therefore $(x) (Hx \supset \sim Ex)$ could be read

It is true of anything whatsoever that, if that thing is a hobbit, then that thing is not an elf.

or as

For anything whatsoever it is true that, if that thing is a hobbit, then that thing is not an elf.

Secondly, when we have several "anythings" or "somethings" to keep track of, as we will have, it is hard to keep them straight. So the following piece of logicians' jargon is useful:

$$(x) (Hx \supset \sim Ex)$$

is read as

For any x, if x is a hobbit, then x is not an elf

and

$$(\exists x) (Hx \cdot \sim Ex)$$

is read as

For some x, x is a hobbit and x is not an elf

Taken literally, these readings are not very meaningful; but, regarded as a short way of saying such things as "For any *thing* whatsoever, if *that* thing ...," they are a useful verbal shorthand. As the name existential quantifier suggests, there is one more way of reading ($\exists x$). We can read it as "*there is* at least one thing..." or "there *exists* at least one thing..." so that, for example, ($\exists x$) (Hx) becomes "There is at least one thing which is a hobbit" or "There exists at least one thing which is a hobbit" or, more colloquially, "At least one hobbit exists." The logicians' jargon for this is "There is an x such that" or "There exists an x such that"; so that ($\exists x$) (Hx) is read as "There is an x such that x is a hobbit" or "There exists an x such that x is a hobbit."

Multiple Subjects and Quantifiers

Some philosophical profit comes when we consider predicates with more than one subject and quantified propositions with more than one quantifier. First, consider predicates with more than one subject. Many expressions in English relate two or more objects or individuals; for example, "Bilbo met Gandalf" or "Bilbo introduced Frodo to Gandalf." In predicate logic we regard these predicates as having several blanks each of which needs to be filled with subject terms to make a proposition. Thus, we might give the dictionary

b ∦ Bilbo   Mxy ∦ x met y
f ∦ Frodo   Ixyz ∦ x introduced y to z
g ∦ Gandalf

and symbolize the two propositions as

Mbg (Bilbo met Gandalf)

and

Ibfg (Bilbo introduced Frodo to Gandalf)

Notice that the variables are arranged in alphabetical order to the right of the predicate letter; and, in the expression being symbolized, the variables occur also in alphabetical order, but at those points in the expression where a subject term needs to be inserted to make a proposition of the propositional function.

Again, Mbx would not symbolize a proposition since it would be the same as "Bilbo met _____." But, when we have two variables in a predicate of the kind which has more than one place for subject terms (we will call these *relational predicates*), we can use a quantifier for each variable to make a surprisingly large number of statements. Thus, if

$$Lxy \# x \text{ is as large as } y$$

we can write $(x)(y)(Lxy)$, which we can read as "For anything whatsoever and for any (other, possibly different) thing whatsoever, the first thing is as large as the second thing" or "Everything is as large as everything." We can write also $(x)(\exists y)(Lxy)$, which we read as "For anything whatsoever there is some (other) thing such that the first thing is as large as the second thing" or "Everything is as large as something."

However using two variables does not imply that we must fill in the blanks with two different subject terms. In fact $(x)(\exists y)(Lxy)$ is true because everything is as large as itself, so everything is as large as something.

When we combine relational predicates and multiple quantification with propositional connectives, we can symbolize an outstanding variety of complex statements in a clear and concise manner. Thus the statement "If anything is caused, then it is either self-caused or caused by something else" can be symbolized using only the dictionary

$$Cxy \# x \text{ causes } y \qquad Sxy \# x \text{ is the same as } y$$

as

$$(x)((\exists y)(Cyx) \supset (Cxx \lor (\exists z)(Czx \cdot {\sim}Szx)))$$

or the statement "Every cause is caused" can be symbolized as

$$(x)((\exists y)(Cxy) \supset (\exists z)(Czx))$$

Notice the scope of the quantifiers; in the first symbolization the scope of the $(\exists y)$ is only (Cyx) while the scope of the $(\exists z)$ is $(Czx \lor Szx)$, and the scope of (x) is the whole expression. Similarly, in the second symbolication the universal quantifier applies to the whole expression, while each of the existential quantifiers applies to only one predicate.

It seems to me less confusing to write $(\exists x)(Cxy)$, clearly marking off the scope of the quantifier, even though in the corresponding use of the symbol ${\sim}$ we would write ${\sim}Cxy$ rather than ${\sim}(Cxy)$. When a quantifier occurs with a ${\sim}$ or when two quantifiers occur at the beginning of an expression, we will omit some parenthesis when this can be done without confusion. For example, we will allow ourselves to write

$$(x){\sim}(Hx \supset x) \qquad \text{rather than} \qquad (x)({\sim}(Hx \supset Ex))$$

We will also write

$$\sim(x) \sim(Hx \supset Ex) \qquad \text{rather than} \qquad \sim((x) (\sim(Hx \supset Ex)))$$

and so on, using the convention that, when both a $\sim$ and a quantifier stand in front of a left-hand parenthesis, the scope of both of them extends to the corresponding right-hand parenthesis. We will use a similar convention with two or more quantifiers which stand before a left-hand parenthesis writing

$$(x) (y) (Cxy)$$
$$(\exists x) (\exists y) (Cxy) \qquad \text{and so on}$$

rather than

$$(x) ((y) (Cxy))$$
$$(\exists x) ((\exists y) (Cxy)) \qquad \text{and so on}$$

The two conventions combined give us

$$(x) \sim(\exists y) (Cxy) \qquad \text{rather than} \qquad (x) (\sim((\exists y) (Cxy)))$$

A further point which may cause possible confusion is a *vacuous* occurrence of a quantifier, an occurrence of a quantifier when there is no corresponding variable in the expression before which the quantifier stands, for example

$$(\exists x) (Hb) \qquad \text{or} \qquad (\exists x) (\exists y) (Cxb)$$

We will rule out such vacuous occurrences, regarding them as nonsensical. Thus neither of the expressions above are any more admissible than, for example,

$$\sim \vee pq$$

would be in propositional logic.

Finally, two occurrences of the same letter in a quantifier will not be allowed within the same proposition. Thus

$$(x) (x) (Cxx)$$
$$(x) (\exists x) (Cxx)$$
$$(x) (Hx \supset (\exists x) (\sim Dx))$$
$$(x) (Hx \supset (\exists y) (\exists x) (Cyx))$$

are all ruled out. The first two expressions are plainly confusing: it looks as if one quantifier must occur vacuously. But someone might want to allow the use of the third and fourth expressions, arguing that there is no chance of confusion. We will save ourselves trouble of various kinds by not allowing such expressions and, instead, by insisting that each new quantifier in an expression use a new letter. If in some very complex statement we needed more letters than u through z, we could employ some device such as listing in the dictionary certain letters which normally serve as constants but which, for a certain problem, would serve as extra variables.

EXERCISES 5.1

A.   Translate from symbols to English using the following dictionary:

      Axy ⧣ x asks questions of y Ex ⧣ x is an elf

      Bxy ⧣ x believes y f ⧣ Frodo

      Cxy ⧣ x communicates (tells) something to y g ⧣ Gandalf

      Dx ⧣ x is a dwarf

      1. $\sim$D$f \cdot \sim$Ef 2.   A$fg \cdot$ (C$gf \supset$ Bfg)

      3. (x) (D$x \supset$ (C$gx \supset$ Bxg))

      4. (x) (y) ((E$x \cdot$ Dy) $\supset$ ($\sim$B$xy \cdot \sim$Byx))

      5. $(\exists x)$ $(\exists y)$ ((E$x \cdot$ Dy) $\cdot$ Cxy)   6. $(\exists x)$ (E$x \cdot$ Cxf)

      7. (x) (E$x \supset$ (C$gx \supset$ Bxg))   8. $(\exists x)$ (y) ((D$x \cdot$ Ey) $\cdot$ Axy)

      9.   E$f \supset$ (x) (D$x \supset \sim$Bxf)   10.   D$f \supset$ (x) (B$xf \supset \sim$ Ex)

B.   Translate into symbols, giving your own dictionary. (Source: J. R. R. Tolkein, *Fellowship of the Ring.**)

    1.   Each year the Bagginses had given very lively combined birthday parties at Bag End.

    2.   No one had a more attentive audience than old Ham Gamgee.

    3.   In Hobbiton and Bywater, every day in the year was somebody's birthday.

    4.   Many young hobbits were included and present by parental permission.

    5.   Hobbits were easygoing with their children in the matter of sitting up late.

    6.   Bilbo was never seen by any hobbit in Hobbiton again.

    7.   Bilbo had usually given new presents.

    8.   Every one of the various parting gifts had labels written out personally by Bilbo.

    9.   There was plenty of everything left for Frodo.

    10.   There was no sign or mention of money or jewelry

5.2 QUANTIFIER EQUIVALENCES AND IMPLICATIONS

Let us go back for a while to talking about predicates with a single subject and propositions with a single quantifier. Since the things we are about to say concern quantifiers and subject terms and are true no matter what predicate we use, it will be useful to introduce letters which are dummies or stand-ins for any predicate. For this we will use X, Y, and Z.

---

* Quotes from J. R. R. Tolkien, *The Fellowship of the Ring* (Boston, Houghton Mifflin Co.), 1965. Used by permission of the publishers.

However, first consider some quantified propositions with an ordinary predicate. Let

$$Bx \,\#\, x \text{ is blue}$$

Now consider the following propositions:

1.	$(x)\,(Bx)$	2.	$(x) \sim (Bx)$
3.	$(\exists x)\,(Bx)$	4.	$(\exists x) \sim (Bx)$

Proposition (1) says that everything is blue while (4) says that something is not blue. These statements cannot both be true, and they seem to divide the possibilities between them. If everything without exception is blue, (1) will be true and (4) false while, if this is false and at least one thing is not blue, (4) will be true and (1) will be false. Since (1) and (4) cannot both be true and yet one of them must be true, they are of course, contradictories. The same is true of (2) and (3); they also are contradictories.

Now consider (1) and (3). It would seem at first glance that, if everything were blue, then something would have to be blue and that (3) is the subaltern of (1). However, consider the following very peculiar possibilities. Suppose that there was nothing at all in the universe. Then *every* existential statement would be false. If every existential statement were false, both (4) and (3) would be false, and their contradictories (1) and (2) would have to be true. So if the universe were empty (1) would be true, and (3) would be false so that (3) would not be true if (1) was true and could, therefore, not be the subaltern of (1). So again we have subalternation dependent on a condition, although a very minimal sort of condition: that the universe not be empty.

However, on this condition, (3) will be the subaltern of (1) and (4) will be the subaltern of (2), and therefore (1) and (2) will be contraries and (3) and (4) will be subcontraries. The reasoning is the same as in Chapter 3: (1) and (2) cannot both be true because, if (1) were true, its subaltern (3) would be true and, if (3) were true, *its* contradictory (2) would be false.

The same applies if we start with (2): (1) must be false if (2) is true since if (2) is true, its subaltern (4) is true and, if (4) is true, then *its* contradictory (1) must be false. Also, as before, (3) and (4) cannot both be false for, if (3) is false, its contradictory (2) must be true and, if (2) is true, its subaltern (4) must be true.

The same argument applies if we start with (4). However, nothing prevents (3) and (4) from both being true and (1) and (2) from both being false. Thus, if at least one individual exists, we have a full square of opposition for (1), (2), (3), and (4). Since this holds true for any predicate, not just for "x is blue," we will write the square with one of our dummy predicates, Z (Figure 5.1).

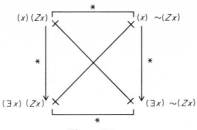

Figure 5.1

The asterisks indicate, as in Chapter 2, that the starred relations hold only subject to a condition. We can write out these relations with propositional connectives.

$$\sim(x)\,(Zx) \equiv (\exists x)\sim(Zx)$$
$$\sim(x)\sim(Zx) \equiv (\exists x)\,(Zx)$$
$$*(x)\,(Zx) \supset (\exists x)\,(Zx)$$
$$*(x)\sim(Zx) \supset (\exists x)\sim(Zx)$$
$$*\sim((x)\,(Zx)\,\cdot\,(x)\sim(Zx))$$
$$*(\exists x)\,(Zx)\,\text{v}\,(\exists x)\sim(Zx)$$

Quantifier Exchange

Again, beginning with Bx, we can see in two ways that

    5. $(x)\,(Bx)$ and   6. $\sim(\exists x)\sim(Bx)$

are equivalent. First "everything is blue" and "it is false that there is something that is not blue" seem to say the same thing. If you doubt this, consider that (6) is the denial of the contradictory of (5) and, by the principle of double negation, must be equivalent to (5). The same is true of

    7. $(\exists x)\,(Bx)$ and   8. $\sim(x)\sim(Bx)$

We can write also, with dummy predicates, the following quantifier equivalences:

    $(x)\,(Zx) \equiv \sim(\exists x)\sim(Zx)$ and $(\exists x)\,(Zx) \equiv \sim(x)\sim(Zx)$

These equivalences will be called Quantifier Exchange (QE) and can be used with the replacement Rule to manipulate quantified expressions. By use of QE and Double Negation, together with other familiar propositional logic rules, a number of other manipulations are possible (Table 5.1). For the sake of convenience we will justify the use of any of the equivalences of Table 5.1 by simply referring to QE.

TABLE 5.1

$$\sim(x)(Zx) \equiv \; \sim\sim(\exists x)\sim(Zx)$$
$$\equiv (\exists x)\sim(Zx)$$
$$(x)\sim(Zx) \equiv \; \sim(\exists x)\sim\sim(Zx)$$
$$\equiv \; \sim(\exists x)(Zx)$$
$$\sim(\exists x)(Zx) \equiv \; \sim\sim(x)\sim(Zx)$$
$$\equiv (x)\sim(Zx)$$
$$(\exists x)\sim(Zx) \equiv \; \sim(x)\sim\sim(Zx)$$
$$\equiv \; \sim(x)(Zx)$$

Quantifier Distribution

Some other manipulations which are possible with quantified statements cannot be completely justified until later, but we give in Table 5.2 the logically true equivalences and implications which enable us to manipulate quantified propositions.

TABLE 5.2

$$(x)(Zx \cdot Yx) \equiv ((x)(Zx) \cdot (x)(Yx))$$
$$(\exists x)(Zx \vee Yx) \equiv ((\exists x)(Zx) \vee (\exists x)(Yx))$$
$$((x)(Zx) \vee (x)(Yx)) \supset (x)(Zx \vee Yx)$$
$$(\exists x)(Zx \cdot Yx) \equiv ((\exists x)(Zx) \cdot (\exists x)(Yx))$$

In Table 5.2 the converses of the two implications are *not* logical truths. This can be made reasonably convincing if the propositions are written out with specific predicates. For example, let

$$Bx \;\#\; x \text{ is blue} \qquad \text{and} \qquad Cx \;\#\; x \text{ is circular}$$

Now if "everything is both blue and circular" is true, then "everything is blue" and "everything is circular" is true, and vice versa. Similarly, if something is either blue or circular then either something is blue, or something is circular, and vice versa. If everything is blue or everything is circular, then everything is either blue or circular. But the converse, that if everything is either blue or circular then either everything is blue or everything is circular, does not follow since, if half the things were blue and half were circular, the antecedent would be true and the consequent false. Similarly, if something is blue and circular, then something is blue and something is circular. But the converse does not follow since, if something was blue and something *else* was circular, it would not follow that something was *both* blue and circular.

The two equivalences and two implications of Table 5.2 will be called collectively Quantifier Distribution (QD) and can be used together with the Replacement Rule and the Inference Rule to manipulate quantified propositions. When propositions to which we wish to apply QD have negation signs, we must use QE plus equivalences such as DeM or DN to ensure that negation signs appear only before predicates. Thus to apply QD to

$$1 \quad \sim(x)(\sim Bx \lor \sim Cx)$$

we would have to go through the following steps:

2	$\sim\sim(\exists x) \sim(\sim Bx \lor \sim Cx)$	1, QE, RR
3	$(\exists x) \sim(\sim Bx \sim Cx)$	2, DN, RR
4	$(\exists x)(\sim\sim Bx \cdot \sim\sim Cx)$	3, DeM, RR
5	$(\exists x)(Bx \cdot Cx)$	4, DN, RR
6	$(\exists x)(Bx) \cdot (\exists x)(Cx)$	5, QD, IR

Thus from "it is not true that everything is either not blue or not circular, we have derived "something is blue and something is circular."

Here is an interesting philosophical application of QE: Suppose we wish to deny that "every cause is caused by something else." If we let

$$Cxy \mathrel{\#} x \text{ causes } y \quad\text{ and }\quad Sxy \mathrel{\#} x \text{ is the same as } y$$

then we will first write

$$(x)((\exists y)(Cxy) \supset (\exists z)(Czx \cdot \sim Szx))$$

"For anything whatsoever, if that thing causes something, then there is something which causes the first thing and which is not the same as the first thing." We then deny the whole thing

$$1 \quad \sim(x)((\exists y)(Cxy) \supset (\exists z)(Czx \cdot \sim Szx))$$

and use Quantifier Exchange.

$$2 \quad (\exists x) \sim (\exists y)(Cxy \supset (\exists z)(Czx \cdot \sim Szx))$$

Negation of Material Implication gives

$$3 \quad (\exists x)((\exists y)(Cxy) \cdot \sim(\exists z)(Czx \cdot \sim Szx))$$

Quantifier Exchange again gives

$$4 \quad (\exists x)((\exists y)(Cxy) \cdot (z) \sim(Czx \cdot \sim Szx))$$

Finally De Morgan and Double Negation give

$$5 \qquad (\exists x) ((\exists y) (Cxy) \cdot (z) (\sim Czx \lor Szx))$$

This can be read: "There is something, x, such that it causes something else, y, and, for anything whatsoever, z, either that thing, z, does not cause the first thing, x, or else that thing, z, is the same as the first thing, x." In other words the denial of the statement "everything is caused by something else" is equivalent (since we have used only equivalences in getting from (1) to (5) to the assertion "Something exists which is either uncaused (not caused by anything) or self-caused (caused by something which is the same as itself)." As we will see later, this is an essential step in an historically important argument for the existence of God.

An interesting example of QD is the following: Suppose that an atheist wishes to deny that God is all-powerful. He might try to do this by denying the following statement made by a believer

$$(x) (Gx \supset Ax)$$

where $Gx \# x$ is God and $Ax \# x$ is all-powerful. But the simple denial leads to the following embarrassing consequence:

1	$\sim(x) (Gx \supset Ax)$	Premise
2	$(\exists x) \sim(Gx \sim Ax)$	1, QE, RR
3	$(\exists x) (Gx \cdot \sim Ax)$	2, NMI, RR
4	$(\exists x) (Gx) \cdot (\exists x) (\sim Ax)$	3, QD, IR
5	$(\exists x) (Gx)$	4, Simp, IR

Thus by denying the believer's statement the atheist implies that God exists! This is not so surprising if we realize that the same inadvertent implication can occur in ordinary language:

Believer: God is all-powerful.
Atheist: God is *not* all-powerful.
B: You admit then that there is a God!
A: No, what I really meant is that there is no God, all powerful or not.

Similarly in the symbolic argument the atheist should assert $\sim(\exists x) (Gx)$, which is what he really wishes to say, instead of simply denying $(x) (Gx \supset Ax)$ which leads to the consequence described.

This is a consequence of the fact that predicate logic, like the Boolean class logic makes no existential assumptions for universal statements. The four standard form statements of traditional logic are symbolized in predicate logic as follows.

A	All S is P	is symbolized as	$(x) (Sx \supset Px)$
E	No S is P	is symbolized as	$(x) (Sx \supset \sim Px)$

I   Some S is P is symbolized as $(\exists x)\,(Sx \cdot Px)$

O   Some S is not P is symbolized as $(\exists x)\,(Sx \cdot \sim Px)$

Since we have S and P available as predicate variables, we have used them in our predicate logic versions of A, E, I, and O statements. But notice that whereas S was once introduced as shorthand for "subject." S here is a *predicate* variable. Just as in class logic the subject term and the predicate term of the traditional statement forms became class names, so in predicate logic, both became propositional functions composed of a predicate with a variable in the subject position. Just as in class logic we could distinguish universal statements from statements about individuals, so we can in predicate logic. "All Greeks are mortal" would be

$$(x)\,(Gx \supset Mx)$$

but "Socrates is mortal" would be Ms, where

Gx $\#$ x is Greek   Mx $\#$ x is mortal   s $\#$ Socrates

Why do we have a Boolean interpretation of the existential import of universal statements? Primarily because particular statements are written with existential quantifiers. If

Gx $\#$ x is a griffon   and   Bx $\#$ x is blue

then $(\exists x)\,(Gx \cdot Bx)$ is false; there are no blue griffons since there are no griffons of any kind. But if $(\exists x)\,(Gx \cdot Bx)$ is false, then its contradictory $(x)\,(Gx \supset \sim Bx)$ must be true. However, if there are no griffons $(\exists x)\,(Gx \cdot \sim Bx)$ is also false, and $(x)\,(Gx \supset Bx)$, its contradictory, is also true. Thus if there are no griffons, particular statements about them are always false and universal statements about them are always true. So I and O cannot be the subalterns of A and E since in some cases A and E will be true and I and O will be false.

Thus, without subalternation, we have only a partial square of opposition: contradiction holds between A and O and between E and I, but no other relations hold. If there is any doubt that A and O, for example, *are* contradictories, we can show by QE and NMI that O is equivalent to the denial of A:

1     $(x)\,(Sx \supset Px)$
2     $(\exists x)\,{\sim}(Sx \supset Px)$ 1, QE, RR
3     $(\exists x)\,(Sx \cdot \sim Px)$ 2, NMI, RR

The same holds for E and I.

$$
\begin{array}{lll}
1 & \sim(x)\,(Sx \supset \sim Px) & \\
2 & (\exists x)\,\sim(Sx \supset \sim Px) & \text{1, QE, RR} \\
3 & (\exists x)\,(Sx \cdot \sim\sim Px) & \text{2, DMI, RR} \\
4 & (\exists x)\,(Sx \cdot Px) & \text{3, DN, RR}
\end{array}
$$

By the use of the rules we have so far, we can justify all of the traditional immediate inferences which are valid on a Boolean interpretation.

Manipulations with Multiple Qualifiers

Let us now return to multiple quantification and the manipulations that are possible with propositions which have more than one quantifier. The simplest cases are those in which two quantifiers occur unnegated at the beginning of an expression. If

$$Cxy \ \# \ x \text{ causes } y$$

we can write

1.	$(x)\,(y)\,(Cxy)$		2.	$(y)\,(x)\,(Cxy)$
3.	$(\exists x)\,(\exists y)\,(Cxy)$		4.	$(\exists y)\,(\exists x)\,(Cxy)$
5.	$(x)\,(\exists y)\,(Cxy)$		6.	$(\exists x)\,(y)\,(Cxy)$
7.	$(y)\,(\exists x)\,(Cxy)$		8.	$(\exists y)\,(x)\,(Cxy)$

The first proposition, "for any x and for any y, x causes y," is plainly "everything causes everything." But what is proposition (2)? How does "for any y and for any x, x causes y" differ from "for any x and for any y, x causes y." A good rule of thumb is the following: if the quantifiers and the occurrence of the bound variables are in the same order, interpret the verb as being in the active voice; if they are in reverse order, interpret the verb as being in the passive voice. (If, in the dictionary for the proposition the verb is passive, this rule must be reversed.) Thus (2) is "everything is caused by everything." However, if both quantifiers are universal or both are existential, then order doesn't matter. "Everything causes everything," comes to the same as "everything is caused by everything," and "something causes something" comes to the same as "something is caused by something."

If the quantifiers are mixed, universal and existential, the order can be crucial. Thus (5), which is "for any x there is at least one y such that x causes y" or "everything causes something," is quite different from (6), "there is an x such that, for any y, x causes y" or "something causes everything." Furthermore both are different from (7), "for any y there is an x such that x causes y" or "everything is caused by something" and (8), "there is a y such that, for any x, x causes y," or "something is caused by everything."

There are some interesting relations between those of the group (1)–(8) which are not equivalent. Thus (8) implies (5) since, if something is caused by everything, everything must cause something. Also (6) implies (7) since, if something causes everything, then everything is caused by something. On the assumption that there is at least one individual in the universe, (1) implies (3), (5), and (6), and (2) implies (4), (7), and (8).

With three or more quantifiers or with more complicated expressions in the scope of the quantifiers, some rules could be laid down for equivalences and inferences involving multiple quantifiers. (Notice, for example, that the inference from (8) to (5) and from (6) to (7) have the same pattern: "existential-universal" implies "universal-existential.") But the more general proof techniques which will be given in the next section will enable us to do everything which we might do with such a set of rules, and do it more simply. The quantifier exchange and quantifier distribution rules, on the other hand, enable us to perform certain manipulations more simply then they could be performed in any other way.

We will also find, in the chapter on modal logic, that there are analogues to the quantifier exchange and quantifier distribution rules for modal operators. Thus the familiarity gained with such operations in this chapter can be carried over to similar operations in Chapter 7. But the rules are useful in their own right, as we will see.

EXERCISES 5.2

A. (1) Translate from symbols to English, where $Sxyz \# x$ causes y to change z.
(2) For each statement, state which of the others implies or is implied by that statement.
(3) For each statement, state and support an opinion as to its truth.

1. $(x)(y)(z)(Sxyz)$	2. $(x)(y)(\exists z)(Sxyz)$
3. $(x)(\exists y)(z)(Sxyz)$	4. $(\exists x)(y)(z)(Sxyz)$
5. $(x)(\exists y)(\exists z)(Sxyz)$	6. $(\exists x)(y)(\exists z)(Sxyz)$
7. $(\exists x)(\exists y)(z)(Sxyz)$	8. $(\exists x)(\exists y)(\exists z)(Sxyz)$
9. $(z)(\acute{y})(\exists x)(Sxyz)$	10. $(z)(\exists y)(x)(Sxyz)$
11. $(\exists z)(y)(x)(Sxyz)$	12. $(\exists z)(\exists y)(x)(Sxyz)$
13. $(\exists z)(y)(\exists x)(Sxyz)$	14. $(z)(\exists y)(\exists x)(Sxyz)$
15. $(\exists x)(y)(z)(\sim Sxyz)$	16. $(x)(\exists y)(z)(\sim Sxyz)$
17. $(x)(y)(\exists z)(\sim Sxyz)$	18. $(\exists x)(\exists y)(z)(\sim Sxyz)$
19. $(\exists x)(y)(\exists z)(\sim Sxyz)$	20. $(x)(\exists y)(\exists z)(\sim Sxyz)$

B. For each of the following groups of statements, prove which are true and which are false if the starred statement above the group is true. (Source: J. R. R. Tolkein, *The Hobbit*.)
*Some hobbits have adventures.
1. Hobbits exist.
2. No one has adventures.
3. Hobbits do not exist.
4. There are some adventurers.
5. No hobbits have adventures.

*Hobbits dress in bright colors and wear no shoes.
6. Hobbits neither dress in bright colors nor wear shoes.
7. Some hobbits do not dress in bright colors, but wear shoes.
8. There is nothing which is a hobbit and which neither dresses in bright color nor fails to wear shoes.
9. Everything which does not dress in bright colors, but wears shoes, is not a hobbit.
10. Either someone dresses in bright colors and does not wear shoes, or he is not a hobbit.

5.3 PROOFS IN PREDICATE LOGIC

By the introduction of one simple rule we can extend our system in such a way that it can handle syllogistic inferences which involve subject terms which are names of individuals. To state this rule in the simplest way we will use the *boldface* capital $\mathbf{Z}$ and the boldface small $\mathbf{w}$ and $\mathbf{o}$ in the following way. Consider expressions such as

$$\mathbf{B}x \qquad \mathbf{G}x \supset \mathbf{M}x \qquad (y)\,((\mathbf{B}x \cdot \mathbf{C}y) \supset \mathbf{M}xy) \qquad \mathbf{T}a \supset (\mathbf{B}x \vee \mathbf{C}x)$$

What all of these expressions have in common is that they have one or more occurrences of a predicate with a free variable. Where there is more than one such occurrence, the free variable is the same in each case. Now in stating the rules we will let $\mathbf{Zw}$ serve as a shorthand way of referring to any expression of this general kind. The $\mathbf{Z}$ will be a way of talking about any propositional function which contains a certain free variable, which we call $\mathbf{w}$, and the boldface $\mathbf{w}$ will be a way of talking about *every* occurrence of $\mathbf{w}$ in $\mathbf{Z}$. We can use $(\mathbf{w})\,(\mathbf{Zw})$ as a way of talking about the result of binding every occurrence of $\mathbf{w}$ by the appropriate quantifier $(\mathbf{w})$. Thus $(\mathbf{w})\,(\mathbf{Zw})$ is a way of talking about propositions, whereas $\mathbf{Zw}$ is a way of talking about propositional functions. We will use $\mathbf{Zo}$ as a way of talking about the proposition which results from replacing every occurrence of $\mathbf{w}$ in $\mathbf{Zw}$ by some constant $\mathbf{o}$.

Several things may need clarification here. First $\mathbf{Zw}$, $(\mathbf{w})\,(\mathbf{Zw})$, and $\mathbf{Zo}$ are not expressions *in* predicate logic. They are a convenient device for talking about a variety of expressions in predicate logic. The boldface $\mathbf{w}$ and $\mathbf{o}$ are a device for talking about what may be only one occurrence (but may be many) of a subject variable and a subject constant. They may be any subject variable and subject constant, but they must be tied together in the way described. The expression $\mathbf{Zo}$ is not just any expression with occurrences of a constant, but one which results from replacing every occurrence of $\mathbf{w}$ in $\mathbf{Zw}$ by $\mathbf{o}$. In stating later rules, we will use this notation in reverse. Starting with some expression $\mathbf{Zo}$, which has at least one occurrence of a subject constant, $\mathbf{o}$, we will use $\mathbf{Zw}$ to talk about the propositional function which results from replacing every occurrence of $\mathbf{o}$ in $\mathbf{Zo}$ by some subject variable,

w. Finally, the formulas we are talking about by using **(w) (Zw)** are not necessarily only those which *begin* with a quantifier. Such expressions as

$$Ta \supset (x)\,(Fx) \qquad (Ta \lor Pa) \supset (y)\,(Gy \supset Fy)$$

are among the expressions which we wish to talk about by using **(w) (Zw)**. However, the scope of the quantifier must extend to the end of the expression, and there must not be another quantifier or a $\sim$ before the quantifier. Thus

$$(x)\,(Fx) \supset Ty \qquad (\exists x)\,(y)\,(Fxy) \qquad \sim(x)\,(Fx)$$

are not among the expressions we are talking about by using **(w) (Zw)**.

Universal Instantiation

We can now state part of the inference pattern called Universal Instantiation (UI) as follows:

$$\frac{\textbf{(w) (Zw)}}{\textbf{Zo}}$$

Warning: The **(w)** must not be within the scope of a $\sim$ or another quantifier; and its scope must extend to the end of the expression.

The statement of universal instantiation means that, for any universally quantified statement, we can drop the quantifier and replace all the variables bound by that quantifier with a given subject constant. Thus if

$$\begin{array}{ll} a \quad \# \text{ Aristotle} & Gx \# x \text{ is a Greek} \\ Mx \# x \text{ is mortal} & Ix \ \# x \text{ is imperfect} \end{array}$$

then we could go from

$$(x)\,(Ix) \qquad \text{to} \qquad Ia$$

from

$$(x)\,(Gx \supset Mx) \qquad \text{to} \qquad Ga \supset Ma$$

from

$$Ma \supset (x)\,(Gx \supset Ix) \qquad \text{to} \qquad Ma \supset (Ga \supset Ia)$$

and so on, citing in each case UI as our justification.

Various simple syllogisms such as

> All mortals are imperfect.
> Aristotle is mortal.
> ——————————————
> Aristotle is imperfect.

173

can be symbolized and proved in predicate logic.

1	$(x) (Mx \supset Ix)$ ⎫	
2	Ma ⎭ Ia	
3	Ma $\supset$ Ia	1, UI
4	Ia	2, 3, MP, IR Q.E.D.

Also some more complex arguments can already be handled, for example,

> All Greeks are mortal.
> All mortals are imperfect.
> Aristotle is a Greek.
> ___
> Aristotle is imperfect.

(which is a sorites) can be symbolized and proved as

1	$(x) (Gx \supset Mx)$ ⎫	
2	$(x) (Mx \supset Ix)$ ⎬ Ia	
3	Ga ⎭	
4	Ga $\supset$ Ma	1, UI
5	Ma $\supset$ Ia	2, UI
6	Ga $\supset$ Ia	4, 5, HS, IR
7	Ia	3, 6, MP, IR Q.E.D.

The nonsyllogistic argument

> All Greeks and all imperfect things are mortal.
> Aristotle is a Greek.
> ___
> Aristotle is mortal.

can be symbolized and proved

1	$(x) ((Gx \lor Ix) \supset Mx)$ ⎫	
2	Ga ⎭ Ma	
3	(Ga $\lor$ Ia) $\supset$ Ma	1, UI
4	Ga $\lor$ Ia	2, Add, IR
5	Ma	4, 3, MP, IR Q.E.D.

The presence of other quantifiers *inside* the one that is being dropped does not prevent us from applying UI, but we must always begin with the outermost (leftmost) quantifier. For example, consider the argument

> Any Greek bearing gifts would be feared by all men of Ilium.
> Aristotle is a Greek.
> ___
> Aristotle bearing gifts would be feared by all men of Ilium.

If

$$Bx \ \# \ x \text{ is bearing gifts} \qquad Ix \ \# \ x \text{ is a man of Ilium}$$
$$Fxy \ \# \ x \text{ would be feared by } y$$

(in addition to the symbols we have been using), then we can symbolize and prove as follows:

1	$(x) ((Gx \cdot Bx) \supset (y) (Iy \supset Fyx))$	
2	Ga	
3	$(Ga \cdot Ba) \supset (y) (Iy \supset Fya)$	1, UI
4	$Ga \supset (Ba \supset (y) (Iy \supset Fya))$	3, Exp, RR
5	$Ba \supset (y) (Iy \supset Fya)$	2, 4, MP, IR Q.E.D.

with lines 1 and 2 grouped giving $Ba \supset (y) (Iy \supset Fya)$

Notice that applying UI to line (1) "picked out" *all* occurrences of x, including that which was inside the quantified statement $(y) (Iy \supset Fyx)$. We can also apply UI successively with different quantifiers. If we add to the symbols we have

$$h \ \# \ \text{Hector}$$

then we can take the argument

> Any Greek bearing gifts would be feared by all men of Ilium.
> Aristotle is a Greek.
> Hector is a man of Ilium.
> _____
> If Aristotle bore gifts, Hector would fear him.

We symbolize and prove as follows:

1	$(x) ((Gx \cdot Bx) \supset (y) (Iy \supset Fyx))$	
2	Ga	
3	Ih	
4	$(Ga \cdot Ba) \supset (y) (Iy \supset Fya)$	1, UI
5	$(Ga \cdot Ba) \supset (Ih \supset Fha)$	4, UI
6	$Ga \supset (Ba \supset (Ih \supset Fha))$	5, Exp, RR
7	$Ba \supset (Ih \supset Fha)$	2, 6, MP, IR
8	$(Ba \cdot Ih) \supset Fha$	7, Exp, RR
9	$(Ih \cdot Ba) \supset Fha$	8, Com, RR
10	$Ih \supset (Ba \supset Fha)$	9, Exp. RR
11	$Ba \supset Fha$	10, 3, MP, IR Q.E.D.

with lines 1 and 2 grouped giving $Ba \supset Fha$

Existential Generalization

We are already doing proofs that could not be done in class logic. If we add a further rule we extend our system still further. This rule is called Existential Generalization (EG) and can be partially stated as follows:

$$\frac{\textbf{Zo}}{(\exists \textbf{w})\,(\textbf{Zw})}$$

(Remember **Zw** is the result of replacing every **o** in **Zo** by the same variable **w**).

That is, from a statement about a given individual we can get to a quantified statement about *some* individual. Applying this to the conclusions of our arguments so far we could get from

$$\text{Ia} \qquad \text{to} \qquad (\exists x)\,(Ix)$$

from

$$\text{Ma} \qquad \text{to} \qquad (\exists x)\,(Mx)$$

from

$$\text{Ba} \supset (y)\,(Iy \supset Fya) \qquad \text{to} \qquad (\exists x)\,(Bx \supset (y)\,(Ix \supset Fyx))$$

and from

$$\text{Ba} \supset \text{Fha} \qquad \text{to} \qquad (\exists x)\,(Bx \supset Fhx)$$

or, by a double application of EG, to $(\exists y)\,(\exists x)\,(Bx \supset Fyx)$.

As we have stated them so far, UI and EG are relatively easy to understand and apply and give rise to no special problems. However, our next two inference patterns are somewhat more complex, and this complexity will eventually involve more complex versions of UI and EG.

To state them at all, we need a new kind of symbol for what we will call a *quasi name*. Legal textbooks and casebooks sometimes use a somewhat similar device. A textbook on the law of contracts might say, "If John Doe and Richard Roe form a partnership and John Doe dies, the obligations of Richard Roe are. . . ." The names "John Doe" and "Richard Roe" are, of course, not names of actual individuals but a device for saying more clearly and conveniently, "If any two individuals form a partnership and one or the other dies, the obligations of the surviving partner are. . . ." In other words, they are not real names but pseudo names or quasi names which enable us *to express generality without quantification*.

In principle, it might have been possible to develop a predicate logic in which quasi names served many of the purposes of variables bound by quantifiers. Because of the manner which predicate logic actually developed, quasi names are used as an auxiliary for certain limited purposes. A good deal of confusion surrounds their use, and they are often confused with variables of some kind. But this confusion arises from ignoring the fact that, if quasi names are understood as lawyers, for example, understand them, then "If John Doe and Richard Roe are partners, then they are jointly responsible for debts incurred by the partnership" is a proposition and is either true or false. If John Doe and Richard Roe were variables of any ordinary kind, the statement would contain blanks and would not be either true or false.

The reason that we need quasi names is that we need to be able to apply the *implications* of propositional logic to quantified statements. The equivalences of propositional logic can be applied inside quantified statements, as we have seen, and with the aid of QE and QD we can do a great deal with equivalences in predicate logic. However, implications are much more difficult to handle. "All mortals are imperfect; all Greeks are mortals; therefore all Greeks are imperfect" is an obviously valid inference that can be handled by syllogistic or class logic. But, so far, we have no rule which enables us to get from

$$(x)\,(Mx \supset Ix) \quad \text{and} \quad (x)\,(Gx \supset Mx) \quad \text{to} \quad (x)\,(Gx \supset Ix)$$

The quantifiers, as it were, stand in the way of applying HS, which is what we need to use. We get around this by using a different version of UI, where we instantiate not to a real name but to a quasi name. Since a quasi name is a device for expressing universality without quantification, once we have instantiated and used propositional logic implications such as HS, we can *restore* the quantifiers, which is impossible if we instantiate to a real name. As our symbols for these quasi names, we will use the small letters from à to ż with a grave accent over the letter. (We will read à as "a grave," ò as "o grave," and so on.) Thus "a" is a symbol for a name and can appear in a dictionary. Also x is a variable and can be quantified over. But à and x́ are neither names nor variables and can *neither* appear in a dictionary *nor* be bound by a quantifier. The expression Ga $\supset$ Ma is a proposition about an individual; its meaning depends on the meaning given Gx, Mx, and a in a dictionary, and it is true or false given those meanings. Now Gx $\supset$ Mx is a propositional function; its meaning can be given only partially, using blanks or similar devices, and it is neither true nor false. But Gà $\supset$ Mà is a *general* proposition, a way of expressing $(x)\,(Gx \supset Mx)$ without quantifiers.

We can now give a second version of Universal Instantiation, where ò represents any quasi name of this sort and (w) is not in the scope of a $\sim$ or another quantifier, and the scope of (w) extends to the end of the expression.

$$\frac{(w)\,(Zw)}{Zò}$$

Universal Generalization

We can now give also a new rule, *Universal Generalization* (UG) as follows:

$$\frac{\text{Z}\grave{\text{o}}}{(\text{w})\,(\text{Zw})}$$

That is, for any statement with this sort of quasi name, we can replace all quasi names with variables and bind them with a universal quantifier. This can be done even when **Zò** is an expression in which variables are bound by other quantifiers or is an expression containing other quasi names.

Restrictions and Conditions

However, certain restrictions are necessary to avoid fallacious arguments in these more complex cases. The first thing to observe is that UG must be applied in such a way that the scope of the quantifier added extends to the end of the expression **Zò**. (This is true also for all forms of EG.) Thus, while it is in general true that from

$$(x)\,(Fx \supset (Hx \vee (\exists y)\,(Gy)))$$

we can instantiate to

$$F\dot{x} \supset (H\dot{x} \vee (\exists y)\,(Gy))$$

obviously we cannot derive from this by UG the line

$$(x)\,(Fx \supset (H\dot{x} \vee (\exists y)\,(Gy)))$$

where only one occurrence of $\dot{x}$ was changed to a variable and bound by a quantifier. But neither can we derive the line

$$(x)\,(Fx \supset Hx) \vee (\exists y)\,(Gy)$$

in which the scope of the universal quantifier is only the first disjunct.

Another sort of problem arises when we find it convenient to have an expression with a universal quasi-name as an assumption for conditional proof. If we simply introduced an arbitrary expression containing a universal quasi name, we could get the following fallacious derivation.

*1	$F\dot{x}$	ACP
*2	$(x)\,(Fx)$	1, UG
3	$F\dot{x} \supset (x)\,(Fx)$	1–2, RCP
4	$(y)\,(Fy \supset (x)\,(Fx))$	

It turns out that the easiest way to bar this and other fallacious derivations without forbidding certain valid arguments is to put the following restriction on Universal Generalization: UG cannot be applied within a conditional proof to a universal quasi name introduced as an assumption in that proof. This allows the valid argument

1	$(x)(Fx \supset Gx)$		
2	$(x)(Fx \supset Hx)$	$(x)(Fx \supset (Gx \cdot Hx))$	
3	$F\grave{x} \supset G\grave{x}$	1, UJ	
4	$F\grave{x} \supset H\grave{x}$	2, UI	
*5	$F\grave{x}$	ACP	
*6	$G\grave{x}$	5, 3, MP, IR	
*7	$H\grave{x}$	5, 4, MP, IR	
*8	$G\grave{x} \cdot H\grave{x}$	6, 7, Conj, IR	
9	$F\grave{x} \supset (G\grave{x} \cdot H\grave{x})$	5–8, RCP	
10	$(x)(Fx \supset (Gx \cdot Hx))$	9, UG	Q.E.D.

At the same time, this restriction forbids further fallacious arguments which cannot be stated until we have developed some further machinery. One further restriction on UG must also wait until we have developed this machinery.

Existential Instantiation

The necessary development involves a rule for *Existential Instantiation*. Frequently we wish to talk about someone without knowing who that person is or even if there is more than one, for example, in a mystery story we may talk about "the individual or individuals who committed the crime." Sometimes we talk of such people as "the murderer" or "the thief," but notice how often detective story writers use that useful letter x. There are colloquial terms which serve the same purpose: we may talk of "that man I met at the convention—what was his name? Anyway Whoosis and I had a great time." Names like x or whoosis are not real names, yet they are not the same sort of quasi names as is John Doe. However they can be used to form propositions. If the detective says "After firing three shots, x's gun jammed" or if the conventioneer says "Whoosis and I had a great time," both are saying something which is true or false. In other words this kind of quasi name does some of the work of *existential quantification*.

The detective could say, "Some individual fired three shots, after which his gun jammed." The conventioneer can say, "Some individual and I had a great time." We must thus distinguish between universal quasi-names and existential quasi names, and it would be fatal to confuse them. For existential quasi names we will use the same letters as for universal quasi names, using an *acute* accent. (We will read á as "a acute," ó as "o acute," and so on.) Thus "a" is a name, à is a universal quasi name, and á is an existential quasi name. Using ó as we did ò, we can state a third version of UI (where, as before, (w) must not be within the scope of a ~ or another quantifier):

$$\frac{(w)\,(Zw)}{Z\acute{o}}$$

and a new rule, Existential Instantiation (EI) as follows:

$$\frac{(\exists w)\,(Zw)}{Z\acute{o}}$$

Warning: (∃w) must not be within the scope of a ~ or of another quantifier, and the scope of (∃w) must extend to the end of the expression. Existential Instantiation has one important restriction: Each time we use EI in a given proof we must use a *new* existential quasi name. The reason for this will be explained presently. Finally, we can give two additional versions of Existential Generalization.

$$\frac{Z\grave{o}}{(\exists w)\,(Zw)} \quad \text{and} \quad \frac{Z\acute{o}}{(\exists w)\,(Zw)}$$

We will now state why the restriction on EI is necessary. Lacking it, we could easily prove a contradiction, for example, "something is a Greek and not a Greek" from true premises. Since it is certainly true that something is a Greek and that something is not a Greek, we could proceed as follows if EI was not restricted and thus prove a contradiction from true premises:

	1	$(\exists x)\,(Gx)$	⎫ $(\exists x)\,(Gx \cdot \sim Gx)$
	2	$(\exists x)\,(\sim Gx)$	⎭
	3	$G\acute{a}$	1, EI
Forbidden →	4	$\sim G\acute{a}$	2, EI
	5	$G\acute{a} \cdot \sim G\acute{a}$	3, 4, Conj, IR
	6	$(\exists x)\,(Gx \cdot \sim Gx)$	5, EG, IR Q.E.D.

We can now give an example of a rather ingenious fallacious derivation forbidden by our restriction on UG:

	1	$(\exists x)\,(y)\,(Fxy)$ ⎱	$(x)\,(Fxx)$
	*2	$(y)\,(F\grave{x}y)$	ACP
	*3	$F\grave{x}\grave{x}$	2, UI
Forbidden →	*4	$(x)\,(Fxx)$	3, UG
	5	$(y)\,(F\grave{x}y) \supset (Fxx)$	2–4, RCP
	6	$(x)\,((y)\,(Fxy) \supset (x)\,(Fxx))$	5, UG
	7	$(y)\,(F\acute{x}y)$	1, EI
	8	$(y)\,(F\acute{x}y) \supset (x)\,(Fxx)$	6, UI
	9	$(x)\,(Fxx)$	7, 8, MP, IR Q.E.D.

Notice that, although all of the steps using other rules are perfectly acceptable by our rules, the derivation is blocked by our restriction on UG.

A final restriction is needed to prevent the fallacious interchange of quantifiers which occurs in the following argument:

1	$(x)(\exists y)(Fx \supset \sim Fy)$ }	$(\exists y)(x)(Fx \supset \sim Fy)$
2	$(\exists y)(F\dot{x} \supset \sim Fy)$	1, UI
3	$F\dot{x} \supset \sim F\acute{y}$	2, EI
4	$(x)(Fx \supset \sim F\acute{y})$	3, UG
5	$(\exists y)(x)(Fx \supset \sim Fy)$	4, EG

The problem is that, where in the premise the second quantifier is within the scope of the first, the instantiated form fails to show this since we have no way of showing such subordination with quasi names. One way to

TABLE 5.3

Rule		Formula
Universal Instantiation (UI) Restrictions: Every **w** in **Zw** must be replaced by **o**, **ò**, or **ó** as the case may be; (**w**) must not be within the scope of a $\sim$ or of another quantifier; and the scope of (**w**) must extend to the end of the expression.	(a)	$\dfrac{(w)(Zw)}{Zo}$
	(b)	$\dfrac{(w)(Zw)}{Z\grave{o}}$
	(c)	$\dfrac{(w)(Zw)}{Z\acute{o}}$
Existential Instantiation (EI) Restriction: A new existential quasi name must be used for each application of EI; (∃**w**) must not be within the scope of a $\sim$ or another quantifier; and the scope of (∃**w**) must extend to the end of the expression.		$\dfrac{(\exists w)(Zw)}{Z\acute{o}}$
Universal Generalization (UG) Restrictions: Every **ò** must be replaced by **w**, and the scope of (**w**) must extend to the end of the expression; UG must not be used within a conditional proof on a universal quasi name which occurs in an assumption for that conditional proof; UG must not be applied to an expression which contains an existential quasi name introduced by EI.		$\dfrac{Z\grave{o}}{(w)(Zw)}$
Existential Generalization (EG) Restrictions: Every **o**, **ò**, or **ó** as the case may be must be replaced by a **w**, and the scope of (∃**w**) must extend to the end of the expression.	(a)	$\dfrac{Zo}{(\exists w)(Zw)}$
	(b)	$\dfrac{Z\grave{o}}{(\exists w)(Zw)}$
	(c)	$\dfrac{Z\acute{o}}{(\exists w)(Zw)}$

prevent such fallacious derivations as that above would be some way of showing in our quasi name notation the sort of subordination of one statement to another that is shown by parentheses before we drop quantifiers.

There are, in fact, ways of doing this but they are intolerably complicated in practice. It seems to be sufficient for present purposes to bar by the following device such fallacious derivations as the one mentioned: We forbid the application of UG to *any* expression containing an existential quasi name introduced by EI. This is somewhat restrictive, but will serve. We can now state all the instantiation and generalization rules, with their exceptions (Table 5.3).

EXERCISES 5.3

A. Using the techniques of this section, provide a proof for each of the following.

1. $(x) \sim (Fx \cdot Gx)$
    Fa
    $\Big\}$ $\sim Ga$

2. $\sim (\exists x)(Fx \cdot Gx)$
    $(x)(Hx) \supset (Fx \supset Gx))$
    $\Big\}$ $\sim (\exists x)(Hx \cdot Fx)$

3. $(x)((Fx \supset Gx) \vee (Hx \supset Jx))$
    $(\exists x)(Fx \cdot Hx)$
    $\Big\}$ $(\exists x)(Gx \vee Jx)$

4. $(x)(Fx \supset Gx)$
    $(x)(Gx \supset \sim Hx)$
    $(x)(Jx \supset Hx)$
    $\Big\}$ $(x)((Jx \cdot Fx) \supset Hx)$

5. $(x)(Fx \supset Gx) \vee (\exists x)(Fx \cdot Hx)$
    $(x)((Fx \cdot Jx) \supset \sim Hx)$
    $(\exists x)(Fx \cdot \sim Gx)$
    $\Big\}$ $(\exists x)(Fx \cdot \sim Jx)$

6. $(x)(Gx \supset Fx)$
    $(x)(Fx \supset Hx)$
    $(\exists x)(Fx \cdot \sim Gx)$
    $\Big\}$ $(\exists x)(Hx \cdot \sim Gx)$

7. $(x)((Fx \supset Gx) \supset (Hx \supset \sim Fx))$
    $(x)(Hx \supset Jx)$
    $(x)(Jx \supset Fx)$
    $(\exists x)(Gx \cdot Jx)$
    $\Big\}$ $(\exists x)(\sim Hx)$

8. $(x)(Fx \supset Gx)$
    $\sim (x)(Gx \supset Fx)$
    $\Big\}$ $(\sim x)(Fx \equiv Gx)$

9. $(x)(Fx) \supset \sim (Gx \cdot Hx))$
    $\sim (x)(Fx \supset (Gx \equiv \sim Hx))$
    $\Big\}$ $(\exists x)(Fx \cdot (\sim Gx \cdot \sim Hx))$

10. $(\exists x)(Fx \cdot \sim Gx) \supset (\exists x)((Hx \cdot Jx) \cdot Lx))$
    $(x)(Jx \supset Lx)$
    $(x)((Lx \cdot Hx) \supset Kx)$
    $\sim (\exists x)(Lx \cdot Kx)$
    $\Big\}$ $(x)(Fx \supset Gx)$

B. Symbolize and prove the conclusion of each of the following, using predicate logic. (Source: Lewis Carroll, *Symbolic Logic*.)

1. No husband, who is always giving his wife new dresses, can be a cross-grained man;
    A methodical husband always comes home for his tea;
    No one, who hangs up his hat on the gas-jet, can be a man that is kept in proper order by his wife;

A good husband is always giving his wife new dresses;

No husband can fail to be cross-grained, if his wife does not keep him in proper order;

An unmethodical husband always hangs up his hat on the gas-jet.

A good husband always comes home for his tea.

Univ. "husbands"; A # always coming home for his tea; D # always giving his wife new dresses; C # cross-grained; G # good; H # hanging up his hat on the gas-jet; K # kept in proper order; M # methodical.

2. Everything, not absolutely ugly, may be kept in a drawing-room;
    Nothing, that is encrusted with salt, is ever quite dry;
    Nothing should be kept in a drawing-room, unless it is free from damp;
    Bathing-machines are always kept near the sea;
    Nothing, that is made of mother-of-pearl, can be absolutely ugly;
    Whatever is kept near the sea gets encrusted with salt.

    Bathing-machines are never made of mother-of-pearl.

    Univ. "things"; U # absolutely ugly; B # bathing-machines; E # encrusted with salt; K # kept near the sea; M # made of mother-of-pearl; Q # quite dry; D # things that may be kept in a drawing-room.

3. I call no day "unlucky", when Robinson is civil to me;
    Wednesdays are always cloudy;
    When people take umbrellas, the day never turns out fine;
    The only days when Robinson is uncivil to me are Wednesdays;
    Everybody takes his umbrella with him when it is raining;
    My "lucky" days always turn out fine.

    Rainy days are always cloudy.

    Univ. "days"; L # called by me "lucky"; C # cloudy; U # days when people take umbrellas; R # days when Robinson is civil to me; Y # rainy; T # turning out fine; W # Wednesdays.

4. I trust every animal that belongs to me;
    Dogs gnaw bones;
    I admit no animals into my study, unless they will beg when told to do so;
    All the animals in the yard are mine;
    I admit every animal, that I trust, into my study;
    The only animals, that are really willing to beg when told to do so, are dogs.

    All the animals in the yard gnaw bones.

    Univ. "animals"; A # admitted to my study; T # animals that I trust; D # dogs; G # gnawing bones; Y # in the yard; M # my; W # willing to beg when told.

5. All the human race, except my footmen, have a certain amount of common-sense;
    No one, who lives on barley-sugar, can be anything but a mere baby;

None but a hop-scotch player knows what real happiness is;
No mere baby has a grain of common sense;
No engine-driver ever plays hop-scotch;
No footman of mine is ignorant of what true happiness is.

No engine-driver lives on barley-sugar.

Univ. "human beings"; E # engine-drivers; C # having common-sense; H # hop-scotch players; K # knowing what real happiness is; L # living on barley-sugar; M # mere babies; F # my footmen.

6. No shark ever doubts that it is well fitted out;
A fish, that cannot dance a minuet, is contemptible;
No fish is quite certain that it is well fitted out, unless it has three rows of teeth;
All fishes, except sharks, are kind to children;
No heavy fish can dance a minuet;
A fish with three rows of teeth is not to be despised.

No heavy fish is unkind to children.

Univ. "fishes"; M # able to dance a minuet; F # certain that he is well fitted out; C # contemptible; T # having 3 rows of teeth; H # heavy; K # kind to children; S # sharks.

7. All the dated letters in this room are written on blue paper;
None of them are in black ink, except those that are written in the third person;
I have not filed any of them that I can read;
None of them, that are written on one sheet, are undated;
All of them, that are not crossed, are in black ink;
All of them, written by Brown, begin with "Dear Sir";
None of them, written on more than one sheet, are crossed;
All of them, written on blue paper, are filed;
None of them, that begin with "Dear Sir," are written in the third person.

I cannot read any of Brown's letters.

Univ. "letters in this room"; B # beginning with "Dear Sir"; C # Crossed; D # dated; F # filed; I # in black ink; T # in third person; R # letters that I can read; P # on blue paper; O # on one sheet; W # written by Brown.

8. Animals are always mortally offended if I fail to notice them;
The only animals that belong to *me* are in that field;
No animal can guess a conundrum, unless it has been properly trained in a Board-School;
None of the animals in that field are badgers;
When an animal is mortally offended, it always rushes about wildly and howls;
I never notice any animal, unless it belongs to me;
No animal, that has been properly trained in a Board-School, ever rushes about wildly and howls.

No badger can guess a conundrum.

Univ. "animals"; C ⌗ able to guess a conundrum; B ⌗ badgers; F ⌗ in that field; M ⌗ mortally offended; Y ⌗ my; N ⌗ noticed by me; P ⌗ properly trained in a Board-School; R ⌗ rushing about wildly and howling.

9. The only animals in this house are cats;
   Every animal is suitable for a pet, that loves to gaze at the moon;
   When I detest an animal, I avoid it;
   No animals are carnivorous, unless they prowl at night;
   No cat fails to kill mice;
   No animals ever take to me, except what are in this house;
   Kangaroos are not suitable for pets;
   None but carnivora kill mice;
   I detest animals that do not take to me;
   Animals, that prowl at night, always love to gaze at the moon.

   I always avoid a kangaroo.

   Univ. "animals"; A ⌗ avoided by me; C ⌗ carnivora; T ⌗ cats; D ⌗ detested by me; H ⌗ in this house; K ⌗ kangaroos; M ⌗ killing mice; L ⌗ loving to gaze at the moon; P ⌗ prowling at night; S ⌗ suitable for pets; I ⌗ taking to me.

10. I never put a cheque, received by me, on that file, unless I am anxious about it;
    All the cheques received by me, that are not marked with a cross, are payable to bearer;
    None of them are ever brought back to me, unless they have been dishonoured at the Bank;
    All of them, that are marked with a cross, are for amounts of over £100;
    All of them, that are not on that file, are marked "not negotiable";
    No cheque of yours, received by me, has ever been dishonoured;
    I am never anxious about a cheque, received by me, unless it should happen to be brought back to me;
    None of the cheques received by me, that are marked "not negotiable," are for amounts of over £100.

    No cheque of yours received by me is payable to bearer.

    Univ. "cheques received by me"; B ⌗ brought back to me; C ⌗ cheques that I am anxious about; H ⌗ honoured; M ⌗ marked with a cross; N ⌗ marked "not negotiable"; O ⌗ on that file; R ⌗ over £100; P ⌗ payable to bearer; Y ⌗ your.

C. Symbolize the following arguments using the machinery of predicate logic, and prove their validity. (Source: Leibnitz, *The Monadology*.)
   1. There must be simple substances since there are composites, and a composite is a collection of simple substances.
   2. Where there are no parts, divisibility is not possible. Simple substances have no parts. Therefore, it is not possible to divide them.
   3. Simple substances can neither begin by being formed out of parts nor end by being divided into parts. Since the only other way in which they

can begin is by creation and the only other way in which they can end is by being annihilated, then, if they begin, they are created and, if they end, they are annihilated.

4. Simple substances cannot be changed by being added to or by having their parts rearranged. External causes of change must either add something or rearrange parts. Therefore, the causes of change in simple substances must be internal.

5. To change, something must either have parts or have many properties and relations. Simple substances change, but have no parts. Therefore, they must have many properties and relations.

6. Since the soul is a simple substance and has many properties and relations, it is a mistake to say that no simple substance has many properties.

7. A soul in the wider sense is anything which has perceptions and desires. Simple substances have perceptions and desires and are therefore souls in the wider sense.

8. A soul in the narrower sense has clear perception and memory. Since simple substances have unclear perception and no memory, they are not souls in the stricter sense.

9. A soul in the narrower sense, which is unconscious, has desire and perception but not clear perception and does not have memory. Therefore, since a soul in the wider sense is what has unclear perception and desire but not memory, an unconscious soul in the narrow sense is the same as a soul in the wider sense.

10. No simple substance can be totally without perception. Since a soul is a simple substance, an unconscious soul is not totally without perception.

5.4 DISPROOFS IN PREDICATE LOGIC

There is no mechanical and universally applicable disproof procedure for predicate logic, that is, no standard procedure which, if applied to any given invalid argument, will show that it is invalid. There is, however, a procedure which will show the invalidity of *some* arguments and a shortcut method which makes the basic method less cumbersome. (Mechanical disproof methods exist for some parts of predicate logic but are not as generally useful as the techniques described here.)

Small Worlds

The basic procedure depends on what I will call small worlds, that is, hypothetical universes with a severely limited number of things in them. We will be chiefly interested in universes with no members, that is, empty universes, and in universes with one, two, or three members. (The term member is borrowed from class logic to do duty for more cumbersome phrases such as "thing, object, in a universe"). We have already discussed empty universes in Section 5.1. Remember that in an empty universe all existential statements are false and therefore all universal statements are true. Consider now a one-member universe. In a one-member universe any universal statement would be equal to an existential statement. Call the single member of the universe "Tom." Saying "everything is blue" would be the same as saying "Tom is blue," since Tom is everything in that universe. But saying "something is blue" is also the same as saying "Tom is blue" since Tom is the only thing in the universe. So "everything is blue" is equivalent to "something is blue," and the same holds for more complex statements.

In a two-member universe we find a different situation. Call the two members "Tom" and "Dick." Then "everything is blue" would be the same as "Tom is blue and Dick is blue" and "something is blue" would be the same as "either Tom is blue or Dick is blue." In general, no matter how large the universe or how complex the statement, a universal statement can be regarded as making a statement about one member of the universe *and* another and another and so on.

Consider a three-member universe, containing Tom, Dick, and Harry. If

$$t \# \text{Tom} \qquad Bx \# x \text{ is blue}$$
$$d \# \text{Dick} \qquad Cx \# x \text{ is circular}$$
$$h \# \text{Harry} \qquad Ox \# x \text{ is oblong}$$

then

$$(x)(Bx) \equiv (Bt \cdot Bd) \cdot Bh$$

and

$$(x)(Bx \supset Cy) \equiv (((Bt \supset Ct) \cdot (Bd \supset Cd)) \cdot (Bh \supset Ch))$$

and

$$(x)(Bx \supset (Cx \lor Ox)) \equiv (((Bt \supset (Ct \lor Ot)) \cdot (Bd \supset (Cd \lor Od)) \cdot (Bh \supset (Ch \lor Oh)))$$

and so on. As for a two-member universe, existentially quantified statements would be equivalent to disjunctions. Thus

$$(\exists x)(Bx) \equiv ((Bt \lor Bd) \lor Bh)$$

and

$$(\exists x)(Bx \cdot Cx) \equiv (((Bt \cdot Ct) \lor (Bd \cdot Cd)) \lor (Bh \cdot Ch))$$

and so on. Mixed universal and existential quantifications can also be translated

$$((x)(Bx) \supset (\exists y)(Cy)) \equiv (((Bt \lor Bd) \lor Bh) \supset ((Ct \lor Cd) \lor Ch))$$

while

$$(\exists x)\,(Bx \supset (y)\,(Cy)) \equiv (((Bt \supset ((Ct \cdot Cd) \cdot Ch)) \vee (Bd \supset ((Ct \cdot Cd) \cdot Ch)))$$
$$\vee\,(Bn \supset ((Ct \cdot Cd) \cdot Ch)))$$

With complex statements and mixed quantifiers, translations can be extremely complex for even quite small universes. We will eventually see a way of avoiding a good deal of such complexity so far as our purposes are concerned.

The point of such translation is that quantified statements are translated into statements which are ordinary propositions which can be dealt with in propositional logic. Specifically they can be tested by truth table, and arguments with quantified premises can be translated into ordinary propositional logic arguments and tested by truth-table shortcut. It may at first seem unimportant to be able to do this, for the whole procedure seems to rest on the odd hypothesis that the universe has only such a small number as two or three members. However, it can be proved in mathematical logic that any argument which is invalid for a universe with *n* members is invalid for any *larger* universe. Thus if a given argument with quantified premises is invalid for a universe with two members, it is invalid for our universe.

This technique is severely limited, for we could keep on checking an argument by this technique until we ran out of patience, always finding it valid and still not be sure that it might not be invalid for some larger universe that we have not tried. Therefore this technique can definitely establish invalidity for some arguments, but failure to prove invalidity does not mean that the argument is valid since it may be invalid for some larger universe.

First let us examine the working of the technique for certain arguments which can be shown to be invalid for any universe with two members, and so for any larger universe. Take the invalid syllogism:

> Some circular thing is blue.
> Some blue thing is oblong.
> ——————————————
> Some circular thing is oblong.

We symbolize as follows:

$$(\exists x)\,(Cx \cdot Bx)$$
$$(\exists x)\,(Bx \cdot Ox)$$
$$\overline{(\exists x)\,(Cx \cdot Ox)}$$

Translate it for a universe of two members, and show its invalidity by truth-table shortcut (Truth Table 5.1). We will do the same for one more complex

TRUTH TABLE 5.1

$$
\begin{array}{ccc}
\text{T} & \text{T} & \text{F} \\
\checkmark & & \checkmark \\
\text{T T} & & \text{F T} \\
\checkmark\ \checkmark & \checkmark & \checkmark\ \checkmark \\
(\text{Ct} \cdot \text{Bt}) & \text{v} & (\text{Cd} \cdot \text{Bd}) \\
\text{F} & \text{T} & \text{T} \\
\checkmark & & \checkmark \\
\text{T F} & & \text{T T} \\
\checkmark\ \checkmark & & \\
(\text{Bt} \cdot \text{Ot}) & \text{v} & (\text{Bd} \cdot \text{Od}) \\
\text{F} & \text{F} & \text{F} \\
\checkmark & & \checkmark \\
\text{T F} & & \text{F T} \\
\checkmark\ \checkmark & & \checkmark\ \checkmark \\
(\text{Ct} \cdot \text{Ot}) & \text{v} & (\text{Cd} \cdot \text{Od}) \\
\end{array}
$$

argument before going on to our shortcut method. Consider the argument:

> All blue things are either circular or oblong.
> Something is not circular.
> Something is not blue.
>
> Something is not oblong.

We symbolize as follows

$$(x)\ (Bx \supset (Cx \lor Ox))$$
$$(\exists x)\ (\sim Cx)$$
$$(\exists x)\ (\sim Bx)$$
$$\overline{(\exists x)\ (\sim Ox)}$$

and show invalidity as in Truth Table 5.2.

TRUTH TABLE 5.2

$$
\begin{array}{cccccc}
\text{T} & \text{F} & & \text{T} & \text{T} & \\
& \checkmark & & & \checkmark & \\
\text{F} & \text{F} & \text{F} & \text{T} & \text{T} & \text{F} \\
\checkmark & \checkmark & \checkmark & \checkmark & \checkmark & \checkmark \\
\end{array}
$$

$$(Bt \supset (Ct \lor Ot)) \cdot (Bd \supset (Cd \lor Od))$$
$$\text{T}$$

$$
\begin{array}{cc}
\text{T F} & \text{F T} \\
\checkmark\ \checkmark & \checkmark\ \checkmark \\
\end{array}
$$
$$\sim Ct \lor \sim Cd$$
$$\text{T}$$

$$
\begin{array}{cc}
\text{T F} & \text{F T} \\
\checkmark\ \checkmark & \checkmark\ \checkmark \\
\end{array}
$$
$$\sim Bt \lor \sim Bd$$
$$\overline{\text{F}}$$

$$
\begin{array}{cc}
\text{F T} & \text{F T} \\
\checkmark\ \checkmark & \checkmark\ \checkmark \\
\end{array}
$$
$$\sim Ot \lor \sim Od$$

Trying to test any reasonably complex argument by this cumbersome method is time consuming and annoying.

The Shortcut

Fortunately, a shortcut is possible. What we do is this: we start out with premises in quantified form and instantiate the premises as if we intended to proceed with the proof. We then *reinterpret* the quasi names we have used in instantiating *as if* they were names of the members of a small world. The size of the small world is determined by the number of different quasi names we have used in instantiating. We then translate the quantified conclusion into the equivalent statement for a universe of that size, using the reinterpreted quasi names.

We can now attempt a truth-table shortcut. If the argument is invalid, this technique will show its invalidity unless some mistake has been made in instantiating. Because of this possibility, the shortcut technique is not quite as reliable as the longer one, but it is very much less cumbersome. Furthermore it can be done as a quick check before going on to attempt a proof. If the argument does not seem to be invalid, one can proceed with the proof. Let us redo our previous two examples with this technique. The first will be as shown in Truth Table 5.3.

TRUTH TABLE 5.3

$$
\begin{array}{ll}
1 & (\exists x)\,(Cx \cdot Bx) \\
2 & (\exists x)\,(Bx \cdot Ox)
\end{array} \Bigg\} \quad (\exists x)\,(Cx \cdot Ox)
$$

$$
\begin{array}{c}
\text{F} \\[2pt]
\text{F} \qquad\qquad \text{F} \\
\surd \qquad\qquad\; \surd \\
\text{T} \quad \text{F} \qquad \text{F} \quad \text{T} \\
\surd \quad \surd \qquad \surd \quad \surd \\
(C\acute{a} \cdot O\acute{a}) \; \text{v} \; (C\acute{c} \cdot O\acute{c})
\end{array}
$$

$$
\begin{array}{lll}
 & \text{T} & \\
 & \text{T} \quad \text{T} & \\
 & \surd \quad \surd & \\
3 & C\acute{a} \cdot B\acute{a} & \text{1, EI} \\
 & \text{T} & \\
 & \text{T} \quad \text{T} & \\
 & \surd \quad \surd & \\
4 & B\acute{c} \cdot O\acute{c} & \text{2, EI}
\end{array}
$$

Comparison of this with the longer disproof made earlier will show the similarities which make the shortcut method possible. Note that the disjuncts whose truth made the long form of the premises true, while the conclusion was false, are parallel to those which appear as instantiated lines in the shortcut method. This will, in fact, always be the case: What the shortcut method does in effect is ignore unnecessary elements of the longer method. If assigning truth values to statements with quasi names bothers you (it should, strictly), leave off the accents until you go on with the proof (if you do). The second disproof can be done as shown in Truth Table 5.4.

TRUTH TABLE 5.4

1	$(x)(Bx \supset Cx \vee (Ox))$		
2	$(\exists x)(\sim Cx))$		$(\exists x)(\sim Ox)$
3	$(\exists x)(\sim Bx)$		

$$\begin{array}{cc} \text{T} & \text{F} \\ & \surd \end{array} \qquad \text{F}$$

$$\begin{array}{ccc} \text{F} & \text{F} & \text{F} \\ \surd & \surd & \surd \end{array} \qquad \begin{array}{cc} \text{F} & \text{F} \\ \surd & \surd \end{array}$$

4   Bá $\supset$ (Cá v Oá)   1, UI $\sim$Oá v Oć

     T

5    $\sim$Cá   2, EI

     T

6    $\sim$Bć   3, EI

For the existential premises the shortcut method picks out the true disjuncts. Notice that for the universal premise we have only one conjunct, but if we instantiated to the other quasi name, that line would be true also:

$$\begin{array}{cc} \text{T} & \text{T} \\ & \surd \end{array}$$

$$\begin{array}{ccc} \text{F} & \text{F} & \text{F} \\ \surd & \surd & \surd \end{array}$$

$$\text{Bć} \supset (\text{Cć} \vee \text{Oć})$$

Now consider an argument which would be intolerably complex to disprove by the longer technique.

> All Greeks and men of Ilium are mortal and imperfect.
> Some Greeks are courageous.
> All men of Ilium are brash.
> Some men of Ilium are obstinate.
> No Greeks are brash.
> Some mortals are neither obstinate or courageous.
> _____
> Therefore: Some imperfect beings are neither Greeks or men of Ilium.

If we give the following dictionary, then we can symbolize as in Truth Table 5.5.

Bx $\#$ x is brash   Cx $\#$ x is courageous   Gx $\#$ x is Greek
Ix $\#$ x is a man of Ilium   Mx $\#$ x is mortal   Ox $\#$ x is obstinate
              Px $\#$ x is imperfect

TRUTH TABLE 5.5

$$(\exists x)\,(Px \cdot (\sim Gx \cdot \sim Ix))$$
$$\quad\quad\ \ F \quad\ F \quad\quad\ F$$
$$\quad\quad\ \sqrt{} \quad \sqrt{} \quad\quad \sqrt{}$$
$$\quad\quad\ T \quad\ F \quad\quad\ T$$
$$\quad\quad\ \sqrt{} \quad \sqrt{} \quad\quad \sqrt{}$$

1	$(x)\,((Gx \vee Ix) \supset (Mx \cdot Px))$
2	$(\exists x)\,(Gx \cdot Cx)$
3	$(x)\,(Ix \supset Bx)$
4	$(\exists x)\,(Ix \cdot Bx)$
5	$(x)\,(Gx \supset \sim Bx)$
6	$(\exists x)\,(Mx \cdot (\sim Ox \cdot \sim Cx))$

$$((((Pá \cdot (Gá \cdot \sim Iá)) \vee$$
$$\quad\quad F \quad\ F \quad\quad F$$
$$\quad\quad \sqrt{} \quad \sqrt{} \quad\quad \sqrt{}$$
$$\quad\quad T \quad\ F \quad\quad T$$
$$\quad\quad \sqrt{} \quad \sqrt{} \quad\quad \sqrt{}$$
$$(Pć \cdot (Gć \cdot \sim Ić))) \vee$$
$$\quad\quad F \quad\ T$$
$$\quad\quad \sqrt{} \quad \sqrt{}$$
$$\quad F \quad\ T \quad\quad T$$
$$\quad \sqrt{} \quad \sqrt{} \quad\quad \sqrt{}$$
$$(Pé \cdot (Gé \cdot \sim Ié)))$$

$$\quad\quad T \quad\ T \quad\quad\ T$$
$$\quad\quad \sqrt{} \quad\quad\quad\ \sqrt{}$$
$$\quad\ T \quad T \quad\ T \quad\ T$$
$$\quad\ \sqrt{} \quad \sqrt{} \quad \sqrt{} \quad \sqrt{}$$

| 7 | $(Gá \vee Ia) \supset (Má \cdot Pá)$ | 1, UI |

$$\quad T$$
$$\quad\ T \quad\ T$$
$$\quad\ \sqrt{} \quad \sqrt{}$$

| 8 | $Gá \cdot Cá$ | 2, EI |

$$\quad T$$
$$\ T \supset T$$
$$\ \sqrt{} \quad \sqrt{}$$

| 9 | $Ić \supset Bć$ | 3, UI |

$$\quad T$$
$$\ T \quad\ T$$
$$\ \sqrt{} \quad \sqrt{}$$

| 10 | $Ić \cdot Oć$ | 4, EI |

$$\quad\ T$$
$$\ T \quad\quad\ T$$
$$\ \sqrt{} \quad\quad \sqrt{}$$

| 11 | $Gá \supset \sim Bá$ | 5, UI |

$$\quad\ T \quad\ T$$
$$\quad\quad\quad\ \sqrt{}$$
$$\ T \quad\ T \quad\ T$$
$$\ \sqrt{} \quad \sqrt{} \quad \sqrt{}$$

| 12 | $Mé \cdot (\sim Oé \cdot \sim Cé)$ | 6, EI |

Notice that the restriction on EI forces us to use three quasi names here. In fact this argument is valid for a two-member universe and can be proved invalid only for universes with three or more members. Even if one wishes to use the longer method to avoid possible errors in applying the shortcut, it is a useful rule of thumb that, if an argument is invalid at all, it is often invalid for a universe with k members, where k is either one or the number of existential premises in the argument, whichever is larger.*

These disproof techniques have some interesting features, but our interest in them is purely practical. We are interested in presenting philosophically interesting arguments as formally valid. For quantified premises we can do this only by means of a proof. The disproof techniques are valuable because they save us from wasting our time trying to do proofs of invalid arguments.

EXERCISES 5.4

A. Symbolize the following arguments and attempt to do a shortcut disproof to check for validity. (Most are invalid.) Give a dictionary. (Source: Lewis Carroll, *Symbolic Logic*.)

1. Pain is wearisome;
    No pain is eagerly wished for.
    _____
    No eagerly wished for thing is wearisome.

2. No bald person needs a hair-brush;
    No lizards have hair.
    _____
    No lizard needs a hair-brush.

3. All thoughtless people do mischief;
    No thoughtful person forgets a promise.
    _____
    All thoughtful people do mischief.

4. I do not like John;
    Some of my friends like John.
    _____
    There is at least one person I like and my friends don't.

5. No potatoes are pine-apples;
    All pine-apples are nice.
    _____
    No potatoes are nice.

6. Babies are illogical;
    Nobody is despised who can manage a crocodile;
    Illogical persons are despised.
    _____
    Babies cannot manage crocodiles.

7. My saucepans are the only things I have that are made of tin;
    I find all your presents very useful;
    None of my saucepans are of the slightest use.
    _____
    Your presents to me are made of tin.

8. No potatoes of mine, that are new, have been boiled;
    All my potatoes in this dish are fit to eat;
    No unboiled potatoes of mine are fit to eat.
    _____
    My potatoes in this dish are new.

* It can be proved in mathematical logic that arguments of a certain class are *always* invalid for a universe of 2^m members where m is the number of predicates in the argument.

9. There are no Dons in the kitchen;
    Everyone who teaches Logic is a Don;
    My servants are all in the kitchen.

    My servants do not teach logic.

10. No ducks waltz;
    No officers ever decline to waltz;
    All my poultry are ducks.

    My poultry are not officers.

11. Every one who is sane can do Logic;
    No lunatics are fit to serve on a jury;
    None of your sons can do Logic.

    Everyone of your sons are fit to serve on a jury.

12. There are no pencils of mine in this box;
    No sugar-plums of mine are cigars;
    The whole of my property, that is not in this box, consists of cigars.

    No sugar-plums are in this box.

13. No experienced person is incompetent;
    Jenkins is always blundering;
    No competent person is always blundering.

    Jenkins is experienced.

14. No terriers wander among the signs of the zodiac;
    Nothing, that does not wander among the signs of the zodiac, is a comet;
    Nothing but a terrier has a curly tail.

    Everything, that is a terrier, has a curly tail.

15. No one takes in the *Times* unless he is well-educated;
    No hedge-hogs can read;
    Those who cannot read are not well-educated.

    Some hedge-hogs take the *Times*.

B. The following are taken from Aristotle's description of some of the syllogisms invalid in his system of syllogistic logic. Symbolize each in predicate logic and prove its invalidity. Give your own dictionary. (Source: Aristotle, *Prior Analytics*.)

1. A applies to some B;* B applies to all C;* therefore A applies to some C.
2. A does not apply to some B; B applies to all C; therefore A does not apply to some C.
3. B applies to no C; A applies to some B; therefore A does not apply to some C.
4. B applies to no C; A does not apply to some B; therefore A does not apply to some C.
5. A applies to all B; B does not apply to some C; therefore A does not apply to some C.

* As in Chapter 4, "B applies to all C" is read as "every C is B."

6. A applies to no B; C does not apply to some B; therefore A does not apply to some C.
7. M is predicated of all N and all O; therefore N is predicated of all O.
8. M is predicated of no N and no O; therefore N is predicated of no O.
9. M is predicated of all O but not of all N; therefore N is not predicated of all O.
10. M is predicated of no O but of some N; therefore N is not predicated of some O.

5.5 PHILOSOPHICAL APPLICATIONS

Predicate logic enables us to symbolize and test for validity a great number of philosophically interesting arguments.

Aquinas' Causal Argument

One interesting and historically important argument which we can now deal with is Aquinas' causal argument for the existence of God. The argument is as follows:

The existence of God can be proved from the nature of the efficient cause. In the world of sense we find there is an order of efficient causes. There is no case known (neither is it, indeed, possible) in which a thing is found to be the efficient cause of itself; for so it would be prior to itself, which is impossible. Now in efficient causes it is not possible to go on to infinity because, in all efficient causes following in order, the first is the cause of the intermediate cause, and the intermediate is the cause of the ultimate cause, whether the intermediate cause be several or one only. Now to take away the cause is to take away the effect. Therefore, if there be no first cause among efficient causes, there will be no ultimate nor any intermediate cause. But if in efficient causes it is possible to go on to infinity, there will be no first efficient cause, neither will there be an ultimate effect nor any intermediate efficient causes; all of which is plainly false. Therefore it is necessary to admit a first efficient cause, to which everyone gives the name of God.

The only dictionary we would actually need to deal with this argument is the following.

$$Cxy \# x \text{ causes } y \qquad Sxy \# x \text{ is the same as } y$$

However, we will simplify the argument by using the additional predicates

$$Ex \# x \text{ is a cause} \qquad Dx \# x \text{ is caused}$$

These two predicates can actually be defined in terms of our first two.

$$Ex = \text{def } (\exists y)(Cxy) \qquad Dx = \text{def } (\exists y)(Cyx)$$

To simplify the argument, we will use Ex and Dx, even though they could be eliminated.

The first premise we will symbolize is, "There is no case ... in which a thing is found to be the efficient cause of itself. ...." (We will regard the rest of this sentence as a supporting argument which is outside of our present scope.) This premise can be symbolized as

$$(x) \, (\sim Cxx)$$

Another premise we will need is "in efficient causes it is not possible to go on to infinity." We can approach the symbolization of this argument indirectly by asking what an infinite regress in causes would mean. Evidently to assert an infinite regress in causes is to say that every cause is caused by something other than itself, or

$$(x) \, (Ex \supset (\exists y) \, (Cyx \cdot \sim Syx))$$

To get Aquinas' premise, we simply deny this, to get,

$$\sim (x) \, (Ex \supset (\exists y) \, (Cyx \cdot \sim Syx))$$

We need also to add a premise which was too obvious to be stated in Aquinas' argument: "if something is caused it is caused by itself or by something else," which is

$$(x) \, (Dx \supset (Cxx \vee (\exists y) \, (Cyx \cdot \sim Syx)))$$

With these three premises we can prove Aquinas' conclusions that a "first" or, uncaused, cause exists: $(\exists x) \, (Ex \cdot \sim Dx)$. The proof then proceeds as follows.

1	$(x) \, (\sim Cxx)$	
2	$\sim (x) \, (Ex \supset (\exists y) \, (Cyx \cdot \sim Syx))$	$(\exists x) \, (Ex \cdot \sim Dx)$
3	$(x) \, (Dx \supset (Cxx \vee (\exists y) \, (Cyx \cdot \sim Syx)))$	
4	$(\exists x) \sim (Ex \supset (\exists y) \, (Cyx \cdot \sim Syx))$	3, QE, RR
5	$(\exists x) \, (Ex \cdot \sim (\exists y) \, (Cyx \cdot \sim Syx))$	4, NMI, RR
6	E$á \cdot \sim (\exists y) \, (Cya \cdot \sim Syá)$	5, EI
7	D$á \supset (Cáá \vee (\exists y) \, (Cyá \cdot \sim Syá))$	3, UI
8	$\sim Cáá$	1, UI
9	$\sim (\exists y) \, (Cyá \cdot \sim Syá)$	6, Simp, IR
10	$\sim Cáá \cdot \sim (\exists y) \, (Cyá \cdot \sim Syá)$	8, 9, Conj, IR
11	$\sim (Cáá \vee (\exists y) \, (Cyá \cdot \sim Syá))$	10, DeM, RR
12	$\sim Dá$	11, 7, MT, IR
13	E$á$	6, Simp, IR
14	E$á \cdot \sim Dá$	12, 13, Conj, IR
15	$(\exists x) \, (Ex \cdot \sim Dx)$	14, EG Q.E.D.

Notice several things about the argument. From the purely technical point of view, it has several points of interest. It combines transformations by Quantifier Exchange with inferences and equivalences first met with in propositional logic. The relative simplicity of the proof is obtained by leaving two quantified statements uninstantiated; otherwise further transformations and reshufflings would have been necessary. What we are doing in the proof is fairly clear, but it is not at all easy to reproduce each step of the proof in ordinary language.

From the philosophical point of view, the proof makes it clear that anyone who wishes to deny Aquinas' conclusion must deny one of his premises. Premise 3 is hardly disputable—if a thing is caused at all it must either be self-caused or caused by something else. Therefore the objector has to deny Premise 1 or Premise 2 (or both) or else admit Aquinas' conclusion.

Denying Premise 1 does not eliminate a "first cause"; if Premise 1 is left out we can derive the conclusion

$$(\exists x) (Ex \cdot (Cxx \lor \sim Dx))$$

That is, there is either a self-caused or an uncaused cause. However, Aquinas objects to the idea of a self-caused cause. In terms of our symbolization, he supports Premise 1 by a subargument: "If a thing caused itself, it would be prior to itself, which is impossible. Therefore there is no case in which a thing is the cause of itself." If we add to our dictionary $Pxy \neq x$ is prior to y, this subargument can be symbolized and proved as follows.

1	$(x) (Cxx \supset Pxx)$	$(x) (\sim Cxx)$
2	$(x) (\sim Pxx)$	
3	$Càà \supset Pàà$	1, UI
4	$\sim Pàà$	2, UI
5	$\sim Càà$	3, 4, MT, IR
6	$(x) (\sim Cxx)$	5, UG Q.E.D.

Since the argument is valid, the objector again has two choices: deny one or both of the premises or admit the conclusion. Thus the objector must assert that something can be prior to itself (exactly what this means would need clarification) or deny that self-causation involves something being prior to itself.

Infinite Regress

The objector who wishes to avoid any sort of first cause must deny Aquinas' denial of the possibility of infinite regress, that is, he must assert the possibility of infinite regress. This is clearly the crucial premise: if infinite regression is granted, a first cause must exist, either as uncaused or as self-caused. Aquinas' supporting argument for this premise is much harder to symbolize, and a complete analysis of it would involve philosophical problems of great importance. Without going too far afield, we can note that Aquinas' argument is that, if there were no first cause in either sense (self-caused or uncaused), there would be no causal order at all, "which is plainly false." In our symbolism this argument would be roughly as follows:

1	$\sim (\exists x) ((Ex \cdot (Cxx \vee \sim Dx)) \supset$ $\sim ((\exists y) (Ey) \vee (\exists z) (Dz)))$	$(x) (Ex \cdot (Cxx \cdot \sim Dx))$	
2	$(\exists y) (Ey) \cdot (\exists z) (Dz)$		
3	$((\exists y) (Ey) \vee (\exists z) (Dz)) \supset$ $(\exists x) (Ex \cdot (Cxx \cdot \sim Dx))$	1, Transp, RR	
4	$(\exists y) (Ey)$	2, Simp, IR	
5	$(\exists y) (Ey) \vee (\exists z) (Dz)$	4, Add, IR	
6	$(\exists x) (Ex \cdot (Cxx \vee \sim Dx))$	3, 5, MP, IR	Q.E.D.

Since Premise 2 is plainly true, the objector would need to deny Premise 1 to deny the conclusion. The argument on this point involves questions which are philosophical rather than logical: supporters of Aquinas argue that a "vicious" regress (where each member of a series depends on a previous member in some way) requires a first member if there are to be subsequent members and that a causal regress is vicious. Again, objectors may deny one contention or both, but there is no obvious way in which formal logic can solve this disagreement.

So we see, as we have seen before, that logic while it cannot itself settle philosophical disputes can nevertheless assist in clarifying the points on which disagreements hinge and in showing the consequences of taking certain positions.

One final remark about this argument: there is still a good deal that our symbolization has not taken into account or that we have not commented on. For example the words "impossible" and "possible" may play an important part in the argument, but we have as yet no way of dealing with them. On the other hand, the conclusion must, like any existentially quantified conclusion, be read as there is *at least* one uncaused cause. This is not a defect in our symbolism: The argument given by Aquinas, even if completely satisfactory, proves only that the existence of at least one uncaused cause, leaving for further discussion the question of whether there is *only* one uncaused cause.

DISCUSSION QUESTIONS

1. You should be able to symbolize and prove or disprove in predicate logic any argument which you could symbolize and prove or disprove in propositional logic, syllogistic logic, or class logic. Discuss any cases in which you would have difficulty doing this or not know how to do it.

2. What statements or ideas have you had difficulty expressing in predicate logic? Discuss any translation difficulties in the exercises in this section.

3. Do any proofs in this section seem odd or intuitively invalid? Discuss any such cases.
4. What are the limitations of predicate logic? How might we add to it to make it more powerful?
5. If an argument cannot be symbolized or proved in predicate logic, what does this tell us about the argument? Compare this with your answer to Question 5 in Discussion Questions 2.5.

Part II
ADVANCED LOGIC

Chapter 6
EXTENDED PREDICATE LOGIC

The logical techniques discussed in this section are largely twentieth century developments. However, the problems to which they are applicable are perennial problems of philosophy. Properties and properties of properties, the identity of one thing with another, uniqueness and unique description—these are all matters which have interested philosophers since the beginnings of philosophy in fifth-century Greece. The logical techniques which we are about to study will not answer the long-standing philosophical questions, but they will help us to state them more clearly and argue more cogently toward their solution.

Because the developments in this chapter are recent, it is harder to see clearly which are most important and who among contemporary philosophers have contributed most to their understanding. However, credit for the first research into much of the material in this chapter ought to go to Bertrand Russell and Alfred North Whitehead, both in their joint work *Principia Mathematica* and in other works, for example, Russell's important paper "On Denoting," first printed in *Mind*, 1905, and often reprinted. Other logicians who should be mentioned in connection with these developments are W. V. O. Quine, Alonzo Church, and my own teacher, Rudolf Carnap.

6.1 PREDICATE VARIABLES AND QUANTIFIERS

So far in subject-predicate logic we have had subject constants, subject variables, and predicate constants. But, except for the special variables used in stating the instantiation and generalization rules and some of the quantifier equivalences, we have not used predicate variables. We will now introduce predicate variables and discuss some of their uses and their attendant problems. A predicate variable is, of course, like a blank into which any predicate may be inserted. A sentence which contains a free variable is neither true nor false: It contains a blank and, until the blank is filled, makes no assertion.

Symbols for Predicate Variables

For predicate variables we will use all of the script capitals except $\mathscr{A}$, $\mathscr{B}$, and $\mathscr{C}$. We will generally use the letters $\mathscr{F}$, $\mathscr{G}$, $\mathscr{H}$, and so on, first and others as needed. Predicate variables may be one place, two place, or many placed. Thus if

$$f \# \text{Frodo} \qquad g \# \text{Gandalf} \qquad b \# \text{Bilbo}$$

then

$\mathscr{F}$f means "Frodo _____"
$\mathscr{G}$bf means "Bilbo _____ Frodo"
$\mathscr{H}$bfg means "Bilbo _____ Frodo _____ Gandalf"

where the gaps must be filled with predicates, either simple or relational. So substitution instances of these three propositional functions might be

Frodo is a hobbit
Bilbo is the uncle of Frodo
Bilbo was brought to Frodo by Gandalf

A propositional function with predicate variables *and* subject variables is, of course, a complete blank: it has nothing but gaps. Thus, $\mathscr{F}xy$ is a mere dummy: Any statement which states any relation between any two individuals is a substitution instance of it.

We can quantify over predicate variables by using predicate quantifiers. The universal quantifier is a predicate variable between parentheses $(\mathscr{F}) \ldots$, $(\mathscr{G}) \ldots, (\mathscr{H}) \ldots$; the existential quantifier is a predicate variable preceded by a $\exists$ between parentheses: $(\exists \mathscr{F}) \ldots, (\exists \mathscr{G}) \ldots, (\exists \mathscr{H}) \ldots$, and so forth. As with subject variables, the scope of the quantifier is indicated by parentheses. Using the dictionary above we can now say such things as

$(\exists\mathscr{F})\,(\mathscr{F}b)$ Bilbo has at least one property

$(\exists\mathscr{G})\,(\mathscr{G}bf)$ Bilbo has at least one relation to Frodo

$(\mathscr{H})\,(\mathscr{H}bg \supset \mathscr{H}fg)$ Any relation Bilbo has to Gandalf, Frodo has to Gandalf

As before, there are convenient ways of reading these expressions:

There is an F such that Bilbo has F
There is a G such that Bilbo has G to Frodo
For any H, if Bilbo has H to Gandalf, then Frodo has it to Gandalf

These are bits of logicians' jargon and are only short ways of saying such things as

There is at least one property such that Bilbo has that property
There is at least one relation such that Bilbo has it to Frodo

There seems to be no difficulty in mixing subject and predicate quantifiers, thus we can say

$$(\exists x)\,(\exists\mathscr{F})\,(\mathscr{F}x)$$

which means "something has some property." (This might be called the most general empirical statement one can make: It is not logically true but is true if there is any universe at all.) In fact, with a two-place predicate variable and two subject variables, we can symbolize a number of interesting statements, for example,

$(\mathscr{F})\,(x)\,(y)\,(\mathscr{F}xy)$ Everything has every relation to everything

$(x)\,(y)\,(\exists\mathscr{F})\,(\mathscr{F}xy)$ Everything has some relation to everything (else)

$(\exists x)\,(y)\,(\exists\mathscr{F})\,(\mathscr{F}xy)$ Something has some relation to everything

So far, there seem to be no difficulties in this widening of predicate logic. The statements we are able to make by the use of our symbolism seem clear enough, and they are plainly statements which it is useful to be able to symbolize.

Predicates of Predicates

However, we may be tempted to extend our symbolism in a way which leads to certain problems. Consider the following simple argument:

Frodo has all of Bilbo's good qualities. Bilbo is courageous.
Courage is a good quality. So Frodo is courageous.

The argument is certainly valid, and we would like to be able to symbolize it and give a proof. But to symbolize it we need a predicate, "is a good quality," which seems to name a quality of *qualities*, not of *individuals*. Suppose that we expand our symbolism, at least temporarily, to include "predicates of predicates" or "qualities of qualities." We will temporarily use outsized roman capitals for predicates of predicates.

$$f \# Frodo \qquad Cx \# x \text{ is courageous}$$
$$b \# Bilbo \qquad \mathbf{G}\mathscr{F} \# \mathscr{F} \text{ is a good quality}$$

(Note that $\mathscr{F}$ is used to indicate a blank, like x in "x is courageous.") Symbolize as follows:

$$
\left.
\begin{array}{ll}
1 & (\mathscr{F})((\mathscr{F}b \cdot \mathbf{G}\mathscr{F}) \supset \mathscr{F}f) \\
2 & Cb \\
3 & \mathbf{G}c
\end{array}
\right\} \ Cf
$$

This is a natural way to symbolize the English statements but it gives rise to some curious problems. Notice, for example, that "C" appears in Premise 2 as a predicate with its subject gap filled by a subject term. On the other hand, in Premise 3 it appears as if to symbolize an abstract noun, "courage." But no such meaning of C appears in the dictionary, and, in fact,

$$\mathbf{G}c$$

is an ill-formed proposition which reads, "is courageous is a good quality," which is nonsense. If we enter in the dictionary, C # (the quality of) courage then C will be ambiguous in its several occurrences, being sometimes a predicate which takes a subject or a subject blank and sometimes an abstract noun that *is* a subject and *fills* a subject blank. The argument in English is convincing precisely because we recognize the connection between "is courageous" and "courage." If we are to rely on this connection in the symbolized argument, however, we must have some formal rule which enables us to make such connections.

Predicates of Individuals

In Section 6.4 we will consider the *lambda operator*, which represents one solution to this problem. A simpler but more restrictive solution, which we will follow for the time being, is to eliminate for now all predicates of predicates and express everything in terms of predicates of individuals. To symbolize our sample argument we add to the dictionary

$$Gx \# x \text{ has a good quality}$$

and resymbolize:

$$
\begin{array}{ll}
1 & (\mathscr{F})\,((\mathscr{F}b \cdot (x)\,(\mathscr{F}x \supset Gx)) \supset \mathscr{F}f) \\
2 & Cb \\
3 & (x)\,(Cx \supset Gx)
\end{array} \left.\vphantom{\begin{array}{l}1\\2\\3\end{array}}\right\} \quad Cf
$$

To prove "Cf" we must instantiate. We must, therefore, add to our instantiation rules at least the rule

$$
\text{UI (e)} \quad \frac{(\mathscr{A})\,(\mathscr{A}\mathbf{a})}{\mathbf{Pa}}
$$

where **a** is a bound variable or a subject constant, **P** is some definite predicate, and $\mathscr{A}$ refers to one or more occurrences of the same predicate variable (like **o** for individual variables). Given this rule we can proceed as follows:

$$
\begin{array}{lll}
4 & (Cb \cdot (x)\,(Cx \supset Gx)) \supset Cf & \text{1, UI} \\
5 & Cb \cdot (x)\,(Cx \supset Gx) & \text{2, 3, Conj, IR} \\
6 & Cf & \text{4, 5, MP, IR} \qquad \text{Q.E.D.}
\end{array}
$$

We will also have the rule

$$
\text{EG (d)} \quad \frac{\mathbf{Pa}}{(\exists\mathscr{A})\,(\mathscr{A}\mathbf{a})}
$$

There seems no reason not to allow universal quasi predicates and existential quasi predicates, which provide the additional rules with, of course, analogues of the usual restrictions.

$$
\text{UI (f)} \;\; \frac{(\mathscr{A})\,(\mathscr{A}\mathbf{a})}{\mathscr{A}\mathbf{a}} \qquad
\text{UI (g)} \;\; \frac{(\mathscr{A})\,(\mathscr{A}\mathbf{a})}{\mathscr{A}\mathbf{a}} \qquad
\text{UG (b)} \;\; \frac{\mathscr{A}\,\mathbf{a}}{(\mathscr{A})\,(\mathscr{A}\mathbf{a})}
$$

$$
\text{EG (c)} \;\; \frac{\mathscr{A}\mathbf{a}}{(\exists\mathscr{A})\,(\mathscr{A}\mathbf{a})} \qquad
\text{EG (f)} \;\; \frac{\mathscr{A}\mathbf{a}}{(\exists\mathscr{A})\,(\mathscr{A}\mathbf{a})} \qquad
\text{EI (b)} \;\; \frac{(\exists\mathscr{A})\,(\mathscr{A}\mathbf{a})}{\mathscr{A}\mathbf{a}}
$$

Of course $\mathscr{A}$ and $\mathscr{A}$ stand for the appropriate universal and existential quasi predicates, replacing each occurrence of $\mathscr{A}$ in the original expression.

Using these rules we can symbolize and prove a wide variety of interesting arguments. Although there are a number of theoretical difficulties connected with this extension of predicate logic, it can hardly be doubted that the increased scope and flexibility provided by the extension is worth having and is a valuable tool in the logical analysis of philosophical arguments.

EXERCISES 6.1

A. (1) Translate from symbols to English.
(2) State which statements imply which others.
(3) Give and support an opinion as to the truth of each.

1. $(x)(y)(\mathscr{F})(\mathscr{F}xy)$ 2. $(x)(y)(\exists\mathscr{F})(\mathscr{F}xy)$
3. $(x)(\exists y)(\mathscr{F})(\mathscr{F}xy)$ 4. $(\exists x)(y)(\mathscr{F})(\mathscr{F}xy)$
5. $(\exists x)(\exists y)(\mathscr{F})(\mathscr{F}xy)$ 6. $(\exists x)(y)(\exists\mathscr{F})(\mathscr{F}xy)$
7. $(x)(\exists y)(\exists\mathscr{F})(\mathscr{F}xy)$ 8. $(\exists x)(\exists y)(\exists\mathscr{F})(\mathscr{F}xy)$
9. $(x)(y)(\exists\mathscr{F})(\mathscr{F}yx)$ 10. $(x)(\exists y)(\mathscr{F})(\mathscr{F}yx)$
11. $(\exists x)(y)(\mathscr{F})(\mathscr{F}yx)$ 12. $(\exists x)(\exists y)(\mathscr{F})(\mathscr{F}xy)$
13. $(\exists x)(y)(\exists\mathscr{F})(\mathscr{F}yx)$ 14. $(x)(\exists y)(\exists\mathscr{F})(\mathscr{F}yx)$
15. $(\exists x)(\exists y)(\exists\mathscr{F})(\mathscr{F}yx)$

B. Translate Exercises 1–5 from English to symbols. Let $Ixy \not\equiv x$ is identical with y.

1. If a thing has any property, it will have the property of being identical with itself.
2. If anything had every property, it would have the property of not being identical with itself.
3. If a thing had every property, it would have the property of being identical with itself and also the property of not being identical with itself.
4. Nothing has every property.
5. Something is identical with itself.

Using these symbolizations, do the following:

6. Show that 5 follows from 1 and 4.
7. Show that 3 follows from 1 and 2.
8. Comment on the ambiguity of "any property" in 1 and "every property" in 2.
9. Show that 4 follows from 3.
10. In the light of your answer to 8, comment on the truth or falsity of 1 and 2.

C. Translate Exercises 1–5 below into symbols, using both individual and predicate variables. (Treat substances as individuals.) (Source: Spinoza, *Ethics*.)

1. Every property is a property of some substance.
2. Two substances which have no (nonrelational) properties in common have no relation to each other.
3. Things which have no relation to each other cannot be causes or effects of one another.
4. If two things are not the same, then they have no properties in common.
5. Nothing causes or is caused by anything other than itself.

Using these symbolizations, do the following:

6. Show that 3 is logically true.
7. Comment on the truth or falsity of 2.
8. Comment on the truth or falsity of 4.
9. Show that 5 follows logically from 1–4.
10. In the light of your answers to 7 and 8, comment on the soundness of Spinoza's argument.

6.2 IDENTITY

We will now expand subject-predicate logic once more, by the introduction of an additional connective, identity symbolized by a $=$ sign. The identity symbol can appear *only* between individual constants or individual variables. Identity thus differs in a crucial respect from class equivalence for which we also used the symbol $=$. I would prefer to use two different symbols for these very different connectives, but established usage is against me. Since class equality can never occur with individual constants or variables, as identity always does (so far as we treat it in this book, at any rate), it is to be hoped that no confusion will occur. We will use a $\neq$ b as short for $\sim(a = b)$, as in class logic.

In one sense the introduction of identity is not an expansion of predicate logic since identity can be explained in terms of quantified predicate variables:

$$(x)\,(y)\,((x = y) \equiv (\mathscr{F})\,(\mathscr{F}x \equiv \mathscr{F}y))$$

In words this is: Two things are identical if and only if any property of one is a property of the other. Notice that this is a very strong sense of identity. I am not in this sense identical with myself last year or even myself five minutes ago, for I do not have all the same properties now which I had last year or minutes ago. Therefore, for most purposes it is preferable to use a somewhat wider sense of identity. To state it we will need a convention for dating predicates. Let $\mathscr{F}x^T$ be read as "$\mathscr{F}$ is a property of x at time T" or "x has property $\mathscr{F}$ at T." Every occurrence of T is understood to refer to the *same* time. We can now write

$$(x)\,(y)\,((x = y) \equiv (\mathscr{F})\,(\mathscr{F}x^T \equiv \mathscr{F}y^T))$$

In words, this is: "For any x and any y, x is identical with y if and only if, for every property, that property is a property of x at a given time if and only if it is a property of y at that time."

This explanation eliminates one difficulty in the earlier notion of identity. In this second sense of identity a thing can change but still be identical with its earlier self. However, in some cases a thing may change so drastically as to raise some doubt as to its identity with its earlier self. One famous case is that of a ship whose parts are replaced plank by plank, nail by nail, sail by sail, and so on, until every part of the original ship has been replaced. At any given time a unique description of the ship can be given which distinguishes it from any other ship. Our first definition of identity says that we have a different ship as soon as one nail is replaced, which seems unreasonable. Our second explanation of identity, however, will allow us to identify the ship whose every part has been replaced with the original ship. This is because predicates are stratified chronologically, so to speak. Consider two individuals, a and b. If they have different properties at the *same*

209

time they *cannot* be identical, but if they have different properties at different times this does not in itself prevent them from being identical.

You may feel that this notion of identity is too liberal. Certain major changes may destroy identity: Even a minor change repeated often enough may do so. For example, remove one cell from my body, and I may be the same. But remove another, and another. . . . At some point there will not be enough left of me to call me the same person as at the beginning.

Essential Properties

These considerations have led some philosophers to talk of essential properties and define identity in such a way that a is identical with b if and only if every *essential* property of a is an essential property of b. However, the notion of essential property is not sufficiently clear to enable us to incorporate this suggestion into our formal machinery.

There is, however, one further complication. According to the two explanations proposed so far, if a and b are identical, then, if a has a property at T, so does b. But suppose that a is in fact identical with b but I neither know nor believe this. Now suppose I have a certain belief about a, say, for example, that I believe a exists. It does not at all follow that I have the same belief about b. Now if being believed to exist by me is a property, then it is a property that a has but which b lacks. But since by hypothesis a is identical with b, we seem to have a contradiction.

Intensional Properties

The sorts of properties which raise this problem are those which are sometimes called *intensional* properties; properties having to do with mental states such as belief, knowledge, or doubt, linguistic acts, such as saying, asking, or ordering, and properties related to these in various ways. This class of properties is difficult to delimit, but the concept of an intensional property is sufficiently clear to be usable in formal logic. An *extensional* property is definable negatively as a nonintensional property,* and, using this terminology, we will define the identity symbol as follows

$$(x)\,(y)\,((x = y) \equiv (\mathscr{E})\,(\mathscr{E}x^T \equiv \mathscr{E}y^T))$$

where the variable $\mathscr{E}$ is restricted to extensional properties.

While by no means the simplest notion of identity, this seems the most flexible and generally satisfactory one for most philosophical purposes. No two numerically distinct things can be identical in this sense for there will be at least one property (for instance, spatial or temporal position) which

---

* For a careful attempt at dealing with the problems connected with these notions, see Rudolf Carnap's *Meaning and Necessity* (University of Chicago Press, Chicago), 1947.

they do not have in common. In fact, we can really write the identity sign only between two designations of the same thing if we wish to make a true statement. However, as restricted as this notion is, it is still useful for many purposes.

Identity and Nonidentity Inference Patterns

Certain useful patterns of inference are based on this basic notion of identity. For example, if we find that **a** is identical with **b** and that **a** has a certain property or group of properties, we seem to be justified in concluding that **b** has that property or those properties. Conversely, if we find that **a** has a property which **b** lacks, then we seem justified in concluding that **a** is not identical with **b**. Of course, if any of the properties are intensional ones or if questions of time are relevant, then these inferences become questionable. To state these rules formally, let us use **Z** as we did in Chapter 5, but let **a**, **b**, and **c** refer to either subject variables or to proper names. We can then state two inference patterns, Identity (Id) and Nonidentity (NId).

$$
\begin{array}{ll}
\text{Identity} & \dfrac{\begin{array}{l}\mathbf{Za}\\ \mathbf{a = b}\end{array}}{\mathbf{Zb}} \\
\text{(Id)} &
\end{array}
\qquad
\begin{array}{ll}
\text{Nonidentity} & \dfrac{\begin{array}{l}\mathbf{Za}\\ \sim \mathbf{Zb}\end{array}}{\sim(\mathbf{a = b})} \quad \text{or} \quad (\mathbf{a \neq b}) \\
\text{(NId)} &
\end{array}
$$

These are independent rules, like UI or EG, and do not involve an appeal to the Inference Rule. Two other inference patterns involving identity are

$$
\dfrac{\mathbf{a = b}}{\mathbf{b = a}} \qquad \text{and} \qquad \dfrac{\begin{array}{l}\mathbf{a = b}\\ \mathbf{b = c}\end{array}}{\mathbf{a = c}}
$$

which might be called Commutativity of Identity and Transitivity of Identity, respectively. However, a full development of the logic of identity is beyond the scope of this section. Naturally all of the rules involving identity have to be qualified or restricted if questions of time or intensionality are involved.

However we can deal with some simple arguments by the use of the rule Identity. We can, for example, symbolize and validate arguments such as this one: "Bilbo is the author of *There and Back Again*. Bilbo and Mr. Baggins of Underhill are the same. So Mr. Baggins of Underhill is the author of *There and Back Again*." Let

$$b \mathbin{\#} \text{Bilbo} \qquad m \mathbin{\#} \text{Mr. Baggins of Underhill}$$
$$Ax \mathbin{\#} x \text{ is the author of } \textit{There and Back Again}$$

and symbolize and prove as follows:

1	Ab	} Am
2	b = m	
3	Am	1, 2, Id

Numbers

We can do other things also with identity, even express cardinal numbers in a very indirect and cumbersome fashion. To do this we must first see how to say "at least" and "at most." To say, for example, "At least two hobbits have been in Rivendell," we use two existential quantifiers, then deny that the things designated by the two quantifiers are the same. Let

$Hx \#$ x is a Hobbit $Rx \#$ x has been in Rivendell

We can then symbolize:

$$(\exists x)\,(\exists y)\,(((Hx \cdot Rx) \cdot (Hy \cdot Ry)) \cdot \sim(x = y))$$

We have thus said "at least two" since we have said there are two which are not the same. It is useful to use $(x \neq y)$ for $\sim(x = y)$, and we will do this from now on.

To say "some and at most two" we can proceed as follows; we use two existential quantifiers and then state that any third thing which meets the conditions must really be the same as one of the first two. So "At most two Hobbits have been to Rivendell," can be symbolized.

$$(\exists x)\,(\exists y)\,(((Hx \cdot Rx) \cdot (Hy \cdot Ry)) \cdot (z)\,((Hz \cdot Rz) \supset ((z = x) \vee (z = y))))$$

Since "at least two" does not exclude "more than two" and "at most two" does not exclude "less than two," to say "exactly two" we must say both. So "Two Hobbits have been to Rivendell" can be symbolized as

$$(\exists x)\,(\exists y)\,((((Hx \cdot Rx) \cdot (Hy \cdot Ry)) \cdot (x \neq y)) \cdot (z)\,((Hz \cdot Rz) \supset ((z = x) \vee (z = y))))$$

This is a somewhat cumbersome way of saying "two," and of course the cumbersomeness increases as the numbers go up, so that things soon become unmanageable.

A number of exceptives and other complex ideas can be expressed using identity. For example "No one but Gandalf could have done it" can be symbolized as follows. Let

$g \#$ Gandalf $Cx \#$ x could have done it

and symbolize as

$$Cg \cdot (x) ((x \neq g) \supset {\sim} Cx)$$

That is, "Gandalf could have done it, and anyone other than Gandalf could not have done it."

EXERCISES 6.2

A. Provide proofs for the following, using the rules Identity and Nonidentity.

1. $(x) (Ax \supset Bx)$
   Aj
   $j = k$
   } Bk

2. $(x) (Cx \supset {\sim} Dx)$
   Dm
   $m = n$
   } ${\sim} Cn$

3. Ej
   Fk
   $j = k$
   $(x) (Fx \supset Gx)$
   } $(\exists x) (Ex \cdot Gx)$

4. $(x) ((Hx \cdot Jx) \supset Lx)$
   Hm
   Jn
   $n = m$
   ${\sim} Lo$
   } $o \neq n$

5. $(x) Mx \supset (Nx \supset Lx))$
   Mj
   ${\sim} Lk$
   $j = k$
   } $(\exists x) ({\sim} Nx)$

B. Symbolize the following, using the identity symbol.
   1. Sam and Frodo were the only hobbits on the last stage of the journey.
   2. Two hobbits started out, but only one finished the journey.
   3. Only Frodo could destroy the Ring.
   4. There was one creature besides Frodo in the cave.
   5. As the two struggled, a third figure appeared.

C. Symbolize the following statements, using quantifiers with predicate constants, subject constants, and subject variables and the identity symbol. Give a dictionary. (Source: Plato, *Ion.*)
   1. If several people are talking about number, and one speaks better than the rest, then somebody will be able to pick out the good speaker.
   2. If a number of people are discussing which foods are healthy and one is speaking much the best, then either the same person will recognize that the best speaker speaks best and the worst speaker speaks worst, or one person will recognize the best speaker and another the worst.

3. In general the same person will always know who speaks well and who speaks badly when a number of people are speaking about the same thing, or else, if he does not know the bad speaker, he will not know the good speaker either.

4. If you recognize the one who speaks well, you will recognize the ones who speak worse.

5. There are some things about which both Homer and Hesiod speak, and what Homer says is the same as what Hesiod says.

6. When Hesiod says the same as Homer, then Ion can explain what Hesiod says as well as he can explain what Homer says.

7. If Ion were a diviner and if two poets said the same thing about divination and he was able to explain the one as well as the other, then, if the two poets said different things about divination, he would be able to explain the one as well as the other.

8. Some poets other than Homer spoke of the same things as Homer.

9. If poets other than Homer spoke of the same things as Homer, then Homer spoke of those things better than they did.

10. If a person can pick out the good speaker, he can also pick out the bad speakers.

6.3 DEFINITE DESCRIPTIONS AND THE IOTA OPERATOR

Suppose that I say, "The author of *The Hobbit* lives in Oxford." There are several ways in which I might be mistaken in asserting this sentence. The simplest way that I could be mistaken has to do with the predicate of my statement: The author of *The Hobbit* might live in London, for example. But some rather interesting possibilities of mistake have to do with the subject of the statement. Suppose that I discover that there is no *single* person who is the author of *The Hobbit* because the book was the result of a collaboration between several authors. I would make this sort of mistake, for example, in speaking of *the* author of *Principia Mathematica*, which was the result of a collaboration between Russell and Whitehead. Or suppose I discover that no one was the author of *The Hobbit* because, for example, no such book really existed. I would make this mistake if I seriously asserted something about the author of the *Book of Mazarbul*, for no such book ever really existed.

Making Implications Explicit

It seems, then, that if I assert something in the present tense about *the* author of such and such a work, I seem to imply or indicate or suggest that there is at least one and at most one author of that work. Ordinarily, although I may in fact imply or indicate or suggest this, I do not in fact *state* it. It is convenient and sometimes philosophically interesting, nevertheless, to make such implications explicit when we symbolize statements containing expressions which include the word "the." The symbolization will make use of what we learned in the last section about symbolizing "at least" and "at most." So, to symbolize "The author of *The Hobbit* lives in Oxford," we would understand this as, "At least and at most one person wrote *The Hobbit*, and this person lives in Oxford." If we let

$Ax \# x$ wrote *The Hobbit* $Ox \# x$ lives in Oxford

then we can symbolize as follows

$$(\exists x) ((Ax \cdot (y) (Ay \supset (y = x))) \cdot Ox)$$

or somewhat more conveniently

$$(\exists x) ((Ax \cdot Ox) \cdot (y) (Ay \supset (y = x)))$$

In general, any statement containing "the" can be symbolized in a similar fashion. The "the" may appear as part of the predicate or as part of both subject and predicate. For example, if we let

$t \# $ J. R. R. Tolkien $Lx \# x$ wrote *The Lord of the Rings*

then we can symbolize "J. R. R. Tolkien wrote *The Hobbit*" as

$$(\exists x) ((Ax \cdot (y) (Ay \supset (y = x))) \cdot (x = t))$$

or

$$(\exists x) ((Ax \cdot (x = t)) \cdot (y) (Ay \cdot (y = x)))$$

Of course, unless we wish to emphasize the "at least one and at most one" aspect of the statement, it would be sufficient to symbolize the statement as

$$At$$

We can also symbolize "The author of *The Hobbit* is the author of *The Lord of the Rings*" as

$$(\exists x) ((Ax \cdot (y) (Ay \supset (y = x))) \cdot (\exists z) (Lz \cdot (w) (Lw \supset (w = z))) \cdot (x = z))$$

or more simply as

$$(\exists x) ((Ax \cdot Lx) \cdot (y) ((Ay \vee Ly) \supset (y = x)))$$

Other statements involving individuals, where the individual is described as "*the* such and such," can be dealt with along similar lines. Such descriptions using "the" are referred to generally as "definite descriptions." This expression is contrasted with "indefinite descriptions," which usually, although not always, use the indefinite article "a" or "an," such as "an author" or "an author of *Principia Mathematica*" or "one of the authors of *Principia Mathematica*." Such indefinite descriptions need only an existential quantifier for their symbolization. For example, if

$$Px \# x \text{ wrote } Principia\ Mathematica$$

"An author of *Principia Mathematica* lives in Oxford," can be symbolized as

$$(\exists x)\,(Px \cdot Ox)$$

Similar translations suffice for other indefinite descriptions.

The way of symbolizing definite descriptions given above was originally introduced by Bertrand Russell as an analysis of the use of "the" phrases in ordinary language.* As such, it would seem to be incorrect for, if we treat "the" phrases in the suggested way, statements containing definite descriptions will assert the existence of the individual referred to and will thus be false if no such individual exists. However, if I use a definite description which does not refer to an existing individual, it has been argued† that I say something which is neither true nor false but rather "nonsensical" in some sense or "logically odd." If this contention is correct, then in symbolizing definite descriptions in the way suggested above we change the meaning of the English sentence which we are symbolizing.

In a good many cases this change in meaning is not objectionable and can be regarded as part of the inevitable distortion involved in translating from a rich and flexible natural language to a clear but relatively poor and limited symbolic language. However, eventually we will wish to turn our attention to the sense in which we imply or suggest or indicate certain statements by making other statements or by using certain expressions. In Chapter 9 we will examine this question, as well as the question of the sense in which certain expressions can be said to be "nonsensical" or "logically odd." In the meantime we will use the Russellian method of symbolizing statements containing definite descriptions, remembering that there are dangers in applying it in misleading ways.

Contextual Definition

As you may have noticed, the Russell method of translating statements containing definite descriptions does not give us a way of translating the definite description in isolation, but gives us a way of going from a statement

---

* "On Denoting," reprinted in *Logic and Knowledge*, edited by R. C. Marsh (Allen and Unwin, London, U.K.), 1956.
† P. R. Strawson, "On Referring" in *Essays in Conceptual Analysis*, edited by A. Flew (St. Martin's Press, New York), 1956.

which contains a definite description to a similar statement (Russell would have said an equivalent statement) which does not contain a definite description. This process Russell called *contextual definition*, and it has certain points of interest. Moreover the process is also useful if we are to be able to give an expression equivalent in some sense to a definite description taken in isolation. The difficulty is that a definite description is like a name, rather than like a statement. So what we need is an operator which forms names (in a broad sense) from the materials which we normally use to form statements, that is, from subject variables and predicates. This will be a new sort of operator. We have previously seen operators which would

1. Form statements from statements, for example, $\sim$
2. Form statements from propositional functions, for example (x), $(\exists x)$, $(\mathscr{F})$, $(\exists \mathscr{F})$
3. Form statements from names, for example, $\subseteq$, the two kinds of $=$, $\equiv$
4. Form names from names, for example, $\cap$, $\cup$, the overbar such as $\bar{A}$
   Our new operators will
5. Form names from propositional functions

This operator consists of a Greek lowercase letter ι (iota), *upside down* ($\imath$) placed in front of a subject variable within a parentheses, thus $(\imath x)$, $(\imath y)$, or $(\imath z)$. This *iota operator* stands in front of a proposition function, its scope being indicated in the usual way by parentheses. Its effect is to form a namelike expression. Thus, using the dictionaries from the last section: $(\imath x)$ (Ax) would symbolize "the author of *The Hobbit*," $(\imath x)$ (Lx) would symbolize "the author of *The Lord of The Rings*," and so on. We could also read $(\imath x)$ (Ax) as "the unique individual x such that x wrote *The Hobbit*" $(\imath x)$ (Lx) as "the unique individual x such that x wrote *The Lord of The Rings*."

Restrictions on the Iota Operator

An interesting complication arises from this notation. Since it is a designation of an individual it can presumably stand in the subject gap of a predicate to form a statement. Thus O $(\imath x)$ (Ax) would symbolize "the author of *The Lord of The Rings* lives in Oxford." Now suppose I write O $(\imath x)$ (Px), which means "the unique individual x such that x wrote *Principia Mathematica* lives in Oxford." Since there is no such unique individual the statement must be false or nonsensical. For Russell such a statement would be simply false, since

$$O\ (\imath x)\ (Px) \equiv (\exists x)\ ((Px \cdot Ox) \cdot (y)\ (Py \supset (y = x)))$$

on his analysis. On the whole, it seems best to regard such an equivalence as true by definition in predicate logic, in other words, to define the iota operator as follows:

$$Z(\imath x)\,(Yx) = \text{def}\,(\exists x)\,((Yx \cdot Zx) \cdot (y)\,(Yy \supset (y = x)))$$

We must also have a special rule that we can never introduce an expression with an iota operator unless we are sure that there is a unique individual corresponding to the description. If this seems restrictive or cumbersome, reflect that we have already accepted such a rule for individual names.

If we do not restrict our use of iota expressions, (expressions formed by the use of iota operators) in this way, we will not be able to use Existential Generalization with iota expressions, for example, to reason from "the first man to climb Mt. Everest is a hero" to "someone is a hero."

There will also be problems with Universal Instantiation: if I form the nonreferring iota expression $(\imath x)\,(Mx)$ where $Mx \;\#\; x$ is the first man to reach Mars, then I could reason from the true statement

$$(x)\,(Hx \supset Ix)$$

where $Hx \;\#\; x$ is human and $Ix \;\#\; x$ is imperfect, to

$$H(\imath x)\,(Mx) \supset I(\imath x)\,(Mx)$$

by Universal Instantiation. I could then derive

$$(\exists x)\,((Mx \cdot (Hx \supset Ix)) \cdot (y)\,(My \supset (y = x)))$$

by the equivalence mentioned above, and then by QD and Simp derive $(\exists x)\,(Mx)$.

Therefore, if we are to avoid troubles with EG and UI and at the same time allow obviously valid inferences such as "the first man to climb Mt. Everest is a hero, therefore, there is at least one hero," we must use iota expressions only where we know that there is a unique individual corresponding to the definite description. For the moment, then, we will introduce the rules

$$\frac{\mathscr{A}\,(\imath w)\,(\mathscr{B} w)}{(\exists w)\,((\mathscr{A} w \cdot \mathscr{B} w) \cdot (u)\,(\mathscr{B} u \supset (u = w)))} \qquad \frac{(\exists w)\,((\mathscr{A} w \cdot \mathscr{B} w) \cdot (u)\,(\mathscr{B} u \supset u = w))}{\mathscr{A}\,(\imath w)\,(\mathscr{B} w)}$$

both of which we will call Definition of Iota Operator (DIO). At present we lack any way of indicating a useful weaker connection between the use of a definition description and assertion of existence and uniqueness.

Finally, since iota expressions are in many ways like proper names, we will allow the use of iota expressions with the identity symbol. In other words, an expression like $(\imath x)\,(Fx) = a$ or $(\imath x)\,(Fx) = (\imath x)\,(Gx)$ will be allowable.

EXERCISES 6.3

A. Give proofs for the following, using the rule DIO

1. $A(\imath x)(Bx)$ } $(x)(Bx \supset Ax)$ 2. $C(\imath x)(Dx)$
   $\sim Cj$ } $\sim Dj$

3. $E(\imath x)(Fx)$
   $(\exists x)(Gx)$
   $(x)(Ex \supset Gx)$

4. $H(\imath x)(Jx)$
   $(x)(\sim Kx \supset \sim Hx)$ } $\sim Jm$
   $\sim Km$

5. $L(\imath x)(Mx)$
   $(x)(Lx \equiv Nx)$ } Nj
   Mj

B. Translate from English to symbols, using the dictionary:
   b # Bilbo   f # Frodo   Hx # x is a hobbit   Rxy # x destroyed y
   r # the ring   Fxy # x first wore y
   1. Bilbo is not the hobbit who destroyed the Ring.
   2. Frodo is the hobbit who destroyed the Ring.
   3. The one who destroyed the Ring was a hobbit.
   4. The hobbit who first wore the Ring is not the hobbit who destroyed it.
   5. Frodo is not the hobbit who first wore the Ring, but is the hobbit who destroyed it.

C. Translate the following into symbols, using iota operators. (Source: Plato, *Phaedo*.)
   1. The servant of the eleven told Socrates it was time to take the cup of hemlock.
   2. Criton nodded to the boy, who went out and came back with the man who was to give the poison.
   3. Socrates asked the man who brought the poison whether or not a libation was permitted.
   4. The man who brought the poison told Socrates to lie down when his legs became heavy.
   5. The man who brought the poison showed us that Socrates was growing cold and stiff.
   6–10. Rewrite 1–5 eliminating iota expressions by DIO.

6.4 THE LAMBDA OPERATOR

Another operator which forms names in the broad sense from propositional functions is the *lambda operator*, which consists of the lowercase Greek letter λ standing before an individual variable, enclosed in parentheses thus, (λx), (λy), or (λz).

This stands before a propositional function composed of a predicate constant and a variable, for example, $(\lambda x)(Ax)$, $(\lambda \mathscr{F})(L\mathscr{F})$, or $(\lambda \mathscr{F})(P\mathscr{F})$. The usual conventions hold for parentheses to indicate scope.

The effect of the lambda operator is to make a property name or designation out of a propositional function. Thus, using the same dictionaries as previously,

$(\lambda x)(Ax)$ the property of having written *The Hobbit*
$(\lambda x)(Lx)$ the property of having written *The Lord of The Rings*

As a predicate name or designation, an expression with a lambda operator may appear in the subject gap of a predicate of properties, thus solving the problem postponed in Section 6.1. The philosophical problems raised by this are dealt with in Section 6.5, but there are also some technical problems involved in fitting lambda expressions (expressions formed by the use of lambda operators) into predicate logic.

Problems with Lambda Expressions

One of these is a trivial typographical problem of symbolizing predicates of properties, predicates of properties of properties, and so on, without spreading out all over the page by using larger and larger letters. We solve this by leaving predicates of individuals as they are, and putting *super*scripts for higher predicate letters. Thus,

> G is a predicate of an individual
> G^2 is a predicate of a property
> G^3 is a predicate of a property of a property   and so on.

More vital is the problem of how lambda expressions are to fit into the rules we already have. We have a rule, DIO, which enables us to eliminate any iota expression and replace the statement containing it with an equivalent expression containing no iota expression. We can do the same for $=$. Can we do the same for lambda expressions? Consider the following case. Let

$$Cx \# x \text{ is courageous} \qquad G^2\mathcal{F} \# \mathcal{F} \text{ is a good property}$$

Then we can symbolize "courage is a good property" as

$$G^2 (\lambda x)(Cx)$$

In Section 6.1 we treated G as a property of an individual and translated "courage is a good property" as

$$(x)(Cx \supset Gx)$$

But with G^2, which is a property of properties, this will not work. In fact, there seems to be no way of eliminating lambda expressions when they occur with second-level predicates.

This shows something important about the lambda notation. Whereas the iota operator is merely a convenience which enables us to say something which we could say without it so that even = can be eliminated if we have predicate variables, the introduction of the lambda operator and the idea of predicates of properties introduce a genuinely new element into predicate logic.

Some very able logicians have argued that extending predicate logic in this way is questionable or even illegitimate. Whether or not this is true, we take one kind of step by extending predicate logic with predicate variables and quantifying over these variables and another and perhaps more questionable step in introducing predicates of properties and lambda expressions. The two steps are often together, but they are quite separate and distinct. The first can be taken without committing us to the second. I have argued that predicate variables and quantifiers are a valuable extension of predicate logic: whether this further extension, involving predicates of properties and lambda expression, is necessary or even valuable, I leave to further philosophical discussion. At any rate, this is the further extension of logic in this direction which will be discussed in this book. At the end of the next section, some references will be found to discussions of this topic by philosophers of logic.

Predicates of Properties

However, one sort of problem has to be discussed before we leave this subject. This problem arises if we allow predicates of properties. If properties can have predicates then it would seem that some properties can be predicated of themselves. For example, the property of being abstract seems to be an abstract property. Also it seems to be true that some properties are not predicable of themselves: The property of being blue is not blue.

Let us call a property *impredicable* if it is not predicable of itself. Now is the property of being impredicable predicable or not? If it is predicable of itself, then it is impredicable and is not predicable of itself by definition. However, if it is not predicable of itself then this means that it is impredicable. So if it is, it isn't, and if it isn't, it is. This, of course, is a full-blown two-sided paradox, like that of the class of all classes which are not members of themselves.

This paradox can be expressed in symbols, though not very easily. Ignoring our superscripts for higher level predicates for the moment, we can express the paradox as follows: By definition an impredicable predicate is not predicable of itself. So it is logically true that

$$(\mathscr{F}) \, (\mathrm{I} \, (\lambda x) \, (\mathscr{F} x) \equiv \sim \mathscr{F} \, (\lambda x) \, (\mathscr{F} x))$$

Since this is a universal generalization it seems plausible to universally instantiate to I itself

$$\mathrm{I} \, (\lambda x) \, (\mathrm{I} x) \equiv \sim \mathrm{I} \, (\lambda x) \, (\mathrm{I} x)$$

which is an explicit contradiction. However, let us now restore the super-scripts. If "impredicable" is a predicate of properties, can we have it appear twice, once as a predicate of properties and a second time as an expression which can fit in the subject position in a predicate of properties? Doesn't the second occurrence make it a predicate of individuals? Can any substitution instance of the form

$$\mathscr{F}^n \, (\lambda x) \, (\mathscr{F}^n x)$$

be meaningful where n is the same number in the two occurrences of $\mathscr{F}^n$?

One solution to the apparent paradox is to answer this question in the negative; to make it a rule that any expression involving predicates of predicates must have the general form

$$\mathscr{F}^{n+1} \, (\lambda x) \, (\mathscr{F}^n x)$$

In other words, the rule would state that a predicate of the same level cannot appear meaningfully in the subject gap of a predicate of properties.

However, this solution has some drawbacks. When fully worked out it has the effect of stratifying predicates and eventually creates problems about references to all predicates. We must superscript not only occurrences of variables within the scope of quantifiers but also the quantifiers them-selves. Furthermore there seem to be certain properties such as "can be expressed in English," which apply to predicates of individuals, predicates of properties, predicates of properties of properties, and so on. It has been suggested that predicates of this kind be superscripted in some special way, for example, with an omega, ω, so that, although Fx is a predicate of an individual and $F^2\mathscr{F}$ a predicate of a property (and so on), the expression $F^\omega\mathscr{F}$ would be a predicate which would apply to any property, thus

$$E^\omega \, \mathscr{F} \, \# \, \mathscr{F} \text{ is a property expressible in English}$$

Certainly, it would sometimes be useful to have such superpredicates available. However, some paradox-generating predicates might turn out to be predi-cates of this kind, and we would find ourselves faced with paradoxes once again.

A simple solution, and one in line with solutions which we have already adopted for propositional logic and class logic, is simply to bar self-referring properties. Just as classes which are alleged to be members of themselves must be barred from class logic and propositions which are alleged to refer to themselves must be barred from propositional logic, so properties which are alleged to refer to themselves must be barred from predicate logic. The reason is the same in all three cases: permitting self-reference gives rise to paradox. The simplest way of eliminating the paradox is to eliminate self-reference. The objection that this solution is ad hoc fails to move me.

Formally, this solution can be expressed as a prohibition of any expression of the form

$$\mathscr{F}\,(\lambda x)\,(\mathscr{F} x)$$

where the two occurrences of $\mathscr{F}$ are occurrences of the *same* predicate (or to be cautious, of two predicates with the same meaning). This rule may be unnecessarily restrictive, since some weak forms of self-reference are nonparadoxical. For example, if

$$E^{\omega}\mathscr{F} \neq \mathscr{F} \text{ is a property expressible in English}$$

then

$$E^{\omega}\,(\lambda\mathscr{F})\,(E^{\omega}\mathscr{F})$$

would seem to be true and nonparadoxical. However, since a more selective rule would be more difficult to state and since the harmless self-references are usually trivial, we will adopt the restriction above as a restriction on the lambda notation. That is, just as the iota notation could not be used unless there was a unique individual satisfying the description, the lambda notation cannot be used if the predicate which is used to form a name by the lambda notation is the predicate in whose subject gap the lambda expression is inserted. For example, for given predicates $\mathscr{F}^{\omega}$ and $\mathscr{G}^{\omega}$, the expressions

$$\mathscr{F}^{\omega}\,(\lambda x)\,(\mathscr{G}^{\omega}x) \qquad \text{and} \qquad \mathscr{G}^{\omega}\,(\lambda x)\,\mathscr{F}^{\omega}x)$$

are unobjectionable, but the expressions

$$\mathscr{F}^{\omega}\,(\lambda x)\,(\mathscr{F}^{\omega}x) \qquad \text{and} \qquad \mathscr{G}^{\omega}\,(\lambda x)\,(\mathscr{G}^{\omega}x)$$

are both illegitimate.

Properties of Relations

Some rather interesting examples of properties of properties can be found in certain properties of relations. In order to talk about these it will be necessary to expand the lambda notation somewhat so that we can distinguish between relations and other properties. To do this, we consider

$$(\lambda x)\,(\mathscr{F} x)$$

the form of names of qualities of single individuals,

$$(\lambda xy)\,(\mathscr{F} xy)$$

the form of names of relational qualities which link two individuals, and so on. We can then define the properties of relations called *transitivity, symmetry*, and *reflexivity*, using the following dictionary

$$T^2 \mathscr{F} \,\#\, \mathscr{F} \text{ is transitive}$$
$$S^2 \mathscr{F} \,\#\, \mathscr{F} \text{ is symmetrical}$$
$$R^2 \mathscr{F} \,\#\, \mathscr{F} \text{ is reflexive}$$

and the following definitions for any relation, R

$$T^2 \,(\lambda xy)\,(Rxy) \,=\, \text{def}\,(x)\,(y)\,(z)\,((Rxy \cdot Ryz) \supset Rxz)$$
$$S^2 \,(\lambda xy)\,(Rxy) \,=\, \text{def}\,(x)\,(y)\,(Rxy \supset Ryx)$$
$$R^2 \,(\lambda xy)\,(Rxy \,=\, \text{def}\,(x)\,(Rxx)$$

This is to say, a relation is transitive if it is such that, if one thing has it to another and that thing has it to a third, then the first thing has it to the third. "Is larger than" is a transitive relation, but "in love with" is not.

A relation is symmetrical if it is such that, whenever one thing has it to another, the second also has it to the first. "Is a sibling of" is symmetrical, but "is a sister of" is not (a could be the sister of b and b the brother of a).

Relations which have the property of being reflexive are rare and usually carry some notion of identity or sameness such as "is the same weight as" or "is identical with."

To say that a relation is *nontransitive, nonsymmetrical* or *nonreflexive* we need merely deny that it has the positive quality. However, there are also interesting properties called *intransitivity, asymmetry*, and *irreflexivity* which are defined as follows. Let

$$N^2 \mathscr{F} \,\#\, \mathscr{F} \text{ is intransitive}$$
$$A^2 \mathscr{F} \,\#\, \mathscr{F} \text{ is asymmetrical}$$
$$I^2 \mathscr{F} \,\#\, \mathscr{F} \text{ is irreflexive}$$

then for any relation, R,

$$N^2 \,(\lambda xy)\,(Rxy) \,=\, \text{def}\,(x)\,(y)\,(z)\,((Rxy \cdot Ryz) \supset {\sim} Rxz)$$

(thus "is the mother of" is intransitive)

$$A^2 \,(\lambda xy)\,(Rxy) \,=\, \text{def}\,(x)\,(y)\,(Rxy) \supset {\sim} Ryx$$

(thus "is the wife of" is asymmetrical)

$$I^2 \,(\lambda xy)\,(Rxy) \,=\, \text{def}\,(x)\,({\sim} Rxx)$$

(thus, "is larger than" is irreflexive).

Whether or not a given relation has these properties can often be determined by a little thought, although in some cases it can be quite difficult to determine. Professor Irving Copi* has pointed out that some arguments about relations in everyday life are enthymatic: For example, if I say that a is larger than b, I conclude that b is not larger than a without needing to explicitly mention that the relation "is larger than" is asymmetrical.

EXERCISES 6.4

A. Translate from symbols to English, using the following dictionary:

Fxy ⧧ x is the father of y Axy ⧧ x is the ancestor of y
Bxy ⧧ x is a brother or sister of y $T^2 \mathscr{F}$ ⧧ $\mathscr{F}$ is transitive
$S^2\mathscr{F}$ ⧧ $\mathscr{F}$ is symmetrical

1. $\sim T^2 (\lambda xy) (Fxy)$
2. $T^2 (\lambda xy) (Axy)$
3. $T^2 (\lambda xy) (Bxy)$
4. $\sim S^2 (\lambda xy) (Fxy)$
5. $\sim S^2 (\lambda xy) (Axy)$
6. $S^2 (\lambda xy) (Bxy)$
7. $S^2 (\lambda xy) (Bxy) \sim T^2 (\lambda xy) (Bxy)$
8. $\sim T^2 (\lambda xy) (Axy) \supset \sim S^2 (\lambda xy) (Axy)$
9. $(\mathscr{F}) (T^2 (\lambda xy) (\mathscr{F}xy) \supset S^2 (\lambda xy) (\mathscr{F}xy))$
10. $(\mathscr{F}) (\sim T^2 (\lambda xy) (\mathscr{F}xy) \supset \sim S^2 (\lambda xy) (\mathscr{F}xy))$

B. Using the same dictionary as for the last exercise, translate Exercises 1–5 below from English to symbols.
1. The relation of not being a father is not transitive.
2. The relation of not being an ancestor is not transitive.
3. The relation of being a brother or sister is symmetrical but not transitive.
4. The relation of not being an ancestor is not transitive, but it is symmetrical.
5. If a two-place relation is symmetrical, it is transitive.

Using these symbolizations in 1–5, answer the following questions:
6. Which of 1–5 are true?
7. Show that if 3 is true then 5 is false.
8. Show that if 4 is true then 3 is false.
9. What is the relation between 4 and 5?
10. At most, how many of 1–5 could be true?

C. Translate the following into symbols, using the lambda operator to symbolize abstract qualities. Ignore phrases in parentheses. (Source: Plato, *Republic*.)
1. [Thrasymachus claims that] justice is serving the interest of the stronger.
2. [He also claims that] justice is obedience to the rulers of the state.
3. [But Socrates shows that] if rulers make mistakes, some who obey the rulers of the state do not serve the interest of the stronger and (therefore) justice cannot be both serving the interest of the stronger and obeying the rulers of the state.

---

* I. Copi, *Symbolic Logic*, third edition (The Macmillan Company, New York), 1967, chap. 5.

4. [Thrasymachus replies that] being strong is incompatible with making mistakes.
5. [To this Socrates replies that] being a ruler and being the stronger are not the same.
6–10. Attempt to rewrite 1–5 without lambda operators. Comment on any difficulties.

6.5 PHILOSOPHICAL DIFFICULTIES

Predicate logic is the most powerful and flexible variety of logic we have developed so far, but it abounds in philosophical difficulties. In this section I will choose three typical problems for discussion—to try to consider all of the problems associated with predicate logic would be impractical.

Operators in Quantified Statements

The first goes back to Section 5.1 where we introduced subject variables and quantifiers and used them in connection with propositional logic connectives. Our discussion at that point ignored a problem which is a serious one that is usually passed over too lightly. It will be recalled that in propositional logic all operators and connectives were defined by truth tables and were completely truth functional. This creates no difficulties where we have constant predicates and constant subjects. The operators and connectives in

$$\sim\!At \qquad At \cdot Lt \qquad At \supset Pt \qquad Ot \vee \sim\!Ot$$

and so forth, can be interpreted as truth functional. However, when operator or connective appears in a propositional function, one kind of problem arises, and if it appears in a quantified statement another and more serious problem appears. The operators and connectives in such expressions as

$$\sim\!Ax \qquad Ax \cdot Lx \qquad Ax \supset Px \qquad Ox \vee \sim\!Ox$$

can be interpreted conditionally. That is, if the x in $\sim\!Ax$ is replaced in such a way that Ax becomes a true proposition, then $\sim\!Ax$ will become false; if the x in $Ax \cdot Lx$ is replaced in such a way that Ax and Lx both become true then $Ax \cdot Lx$ will become true; otherwise it will become false; and so on. But now consider a proposition such as

$$(x)\,(Ax \supset Px) \qquad \text{or} \qquad (\exists x)\,(Ax \cdot \sim\!Lx)$$

The expressions which appear on either side of the connectives are expressions with *bound* variables; we cannot speak of them as true in the way in which At or Ht · Lt are true. Therefore, it may be said that we have changed the meaning of the connectives when we use them in quantified expressions: They are no longer truth functional in any simple way.

One solution to this difficulty is to recall the method we used for disproofs in predicate logic, the small-world technique. We saw then that, for a two-member universe with members a and b,

$$(x)(Ax \supset Px) \equiv ((Aa \supset Pa) \cdot (Ab \supset Pb))$$
$$(\exists x)(Ax \cdot \sim Lx) \equiv ((Aa \cdot \sim La) \vee (Ab \cdot \sim Lb))$$

and so on. Now, since the right-hand expressions create no problems about the meaning of the connectives and operators, neither do the left-hand ones. In an unrestricted universe which may have an infinite number of members, the conjunctions and disjunctions corresponding to quantified statements will be infinite in length. But there seems no reason why this should destroy the truth-functional nature of the connectives. In some cases it may be impossible in practice to prove the truth or falsity of a quantified statement, but in principle the question could be settled by truth-table methods. (We know what to do, but can't finish the job because of the infinite size of the universe.) So the first difficulty seems to be overcome.

Notice that we have not in any strict sense *reduced* expressions with universal quantifiers to conjunctions or expressions with existential quantifiers to disjunctions. The number of individuals in a given universe is not a matter of logic. If we know as a matter of extralogical fact that a universe has *n* elements, then we know that universally quantified statements are equivalent to conjunctions with *n* conjuncts and existentially quantified statements are equivalent to disjunctions with *n* disjuncts. This equivalence is not a matter of logic but depends on facts about the universe.

Furthermore, a universally quantified statement has more content than the materially equivalent conjunction for a universe of given size for the universally quantified statement says something about *all* individuals. The conjunction is equivalent because we know that the *n* individuals *are* all the individuals there are. But the conjunction does not assert this fact.

This does not destroy our point about the basic similarity of the connectives in propositional logic and predicate logic. We know that, for a universe of any given size, a quantified expression is equivalent to one in which the connectives are purely truth functional. Whether or not we know the size of a given universe, whether or not we could ascertain the truth value of the conjuncts or disjuncts equivalent to a quantified statement, we know that a truth-functional equivalent exists and that, therefore, the connectives are basically the same.

The Existential Quantifier

This leads us into our second problem, which is the meaning of the two quantifiers, especially the existential quantifier. What do we mean when we say "there is . . ." or "there exists . . ."? Do we mean the same thing by "is" when we say "there is an individual . . ." and when we say "there is a property . . ."? Do we even mean the same thing by "is" when we say "there is at least one thing such that that thing is a person . . ." and when we say "there is at least one thing such that that thing is a time . . ." or "there is at least one thing such that that thing is a place . . ."? We might put these questions in another way by asking such questions as

Is "existence" ambiguous as used in predicate logic?
Does it mean different things when it is applied to different sorts of objects?
Should we perhaps restrict the types of things to which we apply quantifiers?

It seems quite likely that such questions are inspired by the lurking notion that only material objects, things we can kick or draw a circle around, *really* exist. But whether or not this sort of existence is in some sense primary, it seems clear that we ordinarily use "existence" with regard to things other than material objects. Such questions as "Is there such a color as mauve iridescent?" or "Does blindness exist among reptiles?" are perfectly sensible and understandable. Furthermore, they can be answered in the affirmative: a color called mauve iridescent *does* exist and there *is* blindness among reptiles. So unless we wish to legislate a certain philosophical attitude into our logical machinery, we would be well advised to allow the varied expressions of existence which occur in ordinary language to be expressible in predicate logic. Of course, some philosophers have wished to make certain kinds of statements impossible to express with their formal logical machinery. This seems to me to be a mistake: If a statement can be made in ordinary language, we may wish to symbolize it in the course of dealing with some philosophical argument. We should have ways of dealing with statements which we wish to reject as well as those which we wish to accept.

The question remains, however, as to whether "existence" as applied to these various things is ambiguous. Granted that we may wish to speak of different senses, or different levels, or different kinds of existence, do these different senses have anything in common?

An interesting and illuminating attempt to deal with this question was made by Aristotle and further developed by the medievals. They distinguished three main senses of existence: (1) the sense in which "substances" (for example, material objects and—for Aristotle and the medievals—God and disembodied spirits) exist; (2) the sense in which qualities of substance exist; and (3) the sense in which the subject of any true affirmative statement exists. (As we mentioned in Chapter 3, Aristotle counted negative statements about nonexistent things as true.) Of the things we have mentioned earlier in this discussion, persons and material objects would exist in sense (1), colors and other properties of persons and material objects would exist in sense (2), and such things as blindness would exist only in sense (3). Times and places represent a problem on this view: They do not seem to be substances, but are they qualities of substances or do they exist only in sense (3)?

It is evident that, unless we modify the practice of quantifying over variables which refer to times and places, the three senses of existence distinguished by Aristotle and the medievals do not correspond in any systematic fashion to the quantifiers of predicate logic. Quantifiers over individual variables for instance, do not correspond to existence in sense (1) since times and places are not substances, and, though many statements about the existence of properties might be conveniently symbolized by quantifiers over predicate variables, the cases marked out by Aristotle's sense (2) do not seem to be the same in every case as those in which we would use quantifiers over predicate variables. Aristotle's type (3) cases seem mostly ones in which we would use individual variables and rephrase the sentence. For example "blindness exists among reptiles" might be symbolized as

$$(\exists x) \, (\mathrm{R}x \cdot \mathrm{B}x)$$

where $\mathrm{R}x \# x$ is a reptile and $\mathrm{B}x \# x$ is blind.

An interesting theory about existence put forward by W. V. O. Quine, a major American logician, is that "to exist is to be a value of a variable." Thus, the sense in which both persons and times exist is that some statements of the forms $\mathrm{T}x$ and $\mathrm{P}x$ are true where $\mathrm{T}x \# x$ is a time and $\mathrm{P}x \# x$ is a person.

In effect, this amounts to making Aristotle's sense (3) the primary sense of existence. To say that persons exist is to say $(\exists x) \, (\mathrm{P}x)$, which is to say that at least one statement of the form "x is a person" is true. Suppose that "J. R. R. Tolkien is a person" is a true substitution instance of the form "x is a person." Then at least one person exists, J. R. R. Tolkien.

To say that "blue" exists raises some difficulties on this view. It seems natural to say that blue exists if at least one thing is blue, that is $(\exists x) \, (\mathrm{B}x)$, where $\mathrm{B}x \# x$ is blue. This is essentially Aristotle's sense (2). But "blue" is a constant in $(\exists x) \, (\mathrm{B}x)$, and, to make it a value of a variable, we have to consider statements which have forms such as "my new suit is _____" or, letting $m \# my$ new suit, $\mathscr{F}m$. If "my new suit is blue" is a true substitution instance of $\mathscr{F}m$, then blue exists, since it is the value of a variable. This is, however, a rather awkward approach to the existence of properties. A similarly awkward approach would have to be taken to "blindness exists." Quine would probably do better to separate two senses of existence: one for those things which are values of individual variables and another for qualities which appear in true statements.

On either Aristotle's view or Quine's, the problems of existence seem to be intimately related to problems of what we can say truly, and the relation of the different senses of existence seems to be a problem in philosophy of logic and in metaphysics.

READING LIST

Further material on some of the topics in this chapter and the previous one may be found in:

Quine, W. V. O. *Methods of Logic*, revised edition (Henry Holt and Co., New York), 1959.

Carnap, Rudolf *Introduction to Symbolic Logic and its Applications* (Dover Publications, Inc., New York), 1958.

Copi, Irving *Symbolic Logic*, third edition (The Macmillan Company, New York), 1967.

Kneale, W., and Kneale, M. *Development of Logic* (Oxford University Press, New York), 1962.

Copi, I., and Gould, J. *Contemporary Readings in Logical Theory* (The Macmillan Company, New York), 1967.

Chapter 7
PROPOSI-
TIONAL
MODAL
LOGIC

Modal logic, which we are now about to consider, was considered an important part of logic by the Greeks and medievals. It then suffered a period of neglect, which lasted until comparatively recent times. It is still regarded with suspicion by some able logicians but has recently been gaining acceptance by mathematical logicians as a legitimate area for technical investigation and by philosophers as a useful tool for the analysis of philosophical arguments.

In modal logic we attempt to deal formally with the logical behavior of such notions as necessity, possibility, logical implication, and the like. When such notions are added to the machinery of propositional logic, we have propositional modal logic, the subject of this chapter. Propositional modal logic is the least controversial variety of modal logic and is accepted by many logicians who look askance at some of the extensions of modal logic that are discussed in the next chapter.

The first author to discuss the logic of modalities was Aristotle, who discovered some of the basic behavior of modal terms. The subject was further advanced by several able medieval logicians, including St. Anselm and a writer whose works were attributed (whether correctly or not is in dispute) to Duns Scotus. The major figures in the modern renaissance of modal logic have been C. I. Lewis, Rudolf Carnap, Jaakko Hintikka and G. H. Von Wright; the major critic of these developments has been W. V. O. Quine.

7.1 IMPLICATIONS IN PROPOSITIONAL MODAL LOGIC

The kind of logic which we will consider in this section adds one basic operator that is not truth functional to propositional logic. The operator is "it is possible that . . . ," and its symbol is $\Diamond$. This operator can stand in front of a simple proposition or in front of an expression in parentheses, very much as $\sim$ can. However, $\sim$ can stand in front of $\Diamond$, or $\Diamond$ can stand in front of $\sim$ or both, so that if A $\#$ Aristotle is wise, we can write

$\Diamond$ A   It is possible that Aristotle is wise
$\Diamond$ $\sim$A   It is possible that Aristotle is not wise
$\sim\Diamond$ A   It is not possible that Aristotle is wise *or*
    It is impossible that Aristotle is wise
$\sim\Diamond$ $\sim$A   It is not possible that Aristotle is not wise

The last statement might be expressed in English also by saying "It is necessary that Aristotle is wise" or "It is necessarily true that Aristotle is wise." It will be useful to have a separate symbol for "it is necessary that . . . ," and this is $\Box$. This symbol can be defined as

$$\Box \ p = \text{def} \sim \Diamond \sim p$$

and we can thus, by the Definition Rule mentioned in Section 2.4, set down the equivalence

$$\Box \ p \equiv \sim \Diamond \sim p$$

From this it follows, by the Substitution Rule mentioned in Section 2.4, that

$$\Box \ \sim p \equiv \sim \Diamond \sim \sim p$$

which by Double Negation* becomes

$$\Box \ \sim p \equiv \sim \Diamond \ p$$

---

* In general it is permissible to use listed logical equivalences on formulas within the scope of a modal operator, just as it was permissible to use such equivalences within the scope of a quantifier.

Relations Between Necessity and Possibility

This equivalence is interesting in itself for it asserts the equivalence of the form "it is necessary that not p" and the form "it is impossible that p." Furthermore, using the equivalence Complementarity,

$$(p \equiv q) \equiv (\sim p \equiv \sim q)$$

we can transform our last new equivalence into $\sim \square \sim p \equiv \sim \sim \lozenge p$, which by double negation becomes

$$\sim \square \sim p \equiv \lozenge p$$

This means that we can always replace an expression containing $\lozenge$ with one containing $\sim \square \sim$ in the same position, just as our original definition showed that we can always replace an expression containing $\square$ by one containing $\sim \lozenge \sim$ in the same position. These two equivalences plus Double Negation, and other standard propositional logic rules, enable us to give the following sets of equivalences,

$$\lozenge p \equiv \sim \square \sim p \qquad \sim \lozenge p \equiv \square \sim p$$
$$\lozenge \sim p \equiv \sim \square p \qquad \sim \lozenge \sim p \equiv \square p$$

which of course correspond exactly to the quantifier exchange equivalences with $\square$ playing the part of (x) and $\lozenge$ the part of $(\exists x)$. The expressions $\lozenge p$ and $\sim \lozenge p$ are of course contradictories, as are $\square p$ and $\sim \square p$. So we can begin to set up a modal square of opposition (Figure 7.1).

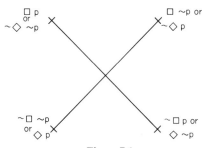

Figure 7.1

In connection with our new operators, we can give also two new valid inferences:

$$\text{SI 1} \quad \frac{\square p}{p} \qquad \text{and} \qquad \text{SI 2} \quad \frac{p}{\lozenge p}$$

Since the modal operators are not truth functional, these are not based on truth-table tautologies, but they seem to be obviously true. SI 1 says that, if a proposition is necessarily true, it is true, and SI 2 says that, if a proposition is true, it is possible that it is true. By using these two inferences, one after the other, we can easily show that any proposition which is necessarily true is possibly true. Thus in the modal square of opposition $\diamond$ p is implied by $\square$ p and is therefore its subaltern. The same is true for $\diamond$ ~p and $\square$ ~p, so that subalternation holds for the modal square of opposition. This, in turn, means that subcontriety holds between $\diamond$ p and $\diamond$ ~p (by the same argument by which subcontriety was established for I and O statements in Section 3.2) and that $\square$ p and $\square$ ~p are contraries (by the same argument by which contriety was shown for A and E statements in Section 3.2). Thus we have (Figure 7.2) a full square of opposition for modal operators. This makes possible the usual set of immediate inferences. There are no starred inferences since the subalternation of $\diamond$ p to $\square$ p holds unconditionally.

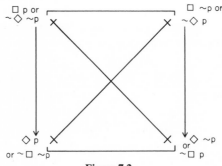

Figure 7.2

The modal square of opposition, which is extremely easy to set up and justify with modern methods, was discovered by Aristotle by an astounding feat of unaided analysis. Aristotle made two mistakes in his first statement of the square, at least one of which he corrected. It is not clear that Aristotle knew that he had a full square of opposition for modal propositions, but he had discovered most of the equivalences and rules we have discussed so far and at least realized that he had a partial square. His two mistakes apparently arose from a hesitation over whether to take "it is possible that" as his basic modal notion or to take as basic the more complex notion of "possibly and possibly not."

Aristotle was also the discoverer of the two inferences mentioned above, SI 1 and SI 2. These were well known to the later Greeks and to the medieval logicians, who gave them Latin names, *a necesse ad esse* for SI 1 and *ab esse ad posse* for SI 2. We will use these names and abbreviate them as NE and EP, respectively.

The rediscovery of modal logic by the American philosopher C. I. Lewis in this century, after its Greek and medieval developments had largely been forgotten, was prompted largely by a desire to get a more satisfactory equivalent for our ordinary language "if . . . , then" than is provided by $\supset$.

Strict Implication

Because of the weaknesses of $\supset$ for symbolizing "if . . ., then" in ordinary usage, which were discussed in Section 1.1 and because of the paradoxes of material* implication discussed in Section 1.5, Lewis felt that a stronger connective than $\supset$ should be used in propositional logic. He suggested that an "if . . ., then" operator which expressed a logical connection between the antecedent and the consequent would be preferable to $\supset$ for many purposes. He argued that a logical connection was a necessary connection and that if we had modal operators we could express this "logical implication" or, as Lewis called it, "strict implication" by means of these modal operators. He thus reinvented modal logic in a symbolic version.

Lewis's symbol for strict implication was $\dashv 3$. His own definition of strict implication was

$$p \dashv 3\ q = def \sim \diamondsuit\ (p \cdot \sim q)$$

But $\sim \diamondsuit\ (p \cdot \sim q)$ is easily transformed to $\square \sim (p \cdot \sim q)$ by one of the equivalences mentioned above, then to $\square\ (p \supset q)$ by DMI.

TABLE 7.1

Name	Symbolization
Modus Ponens	$((p \supset q) \cdot p) \dashv 3\ q$
Modus Tollens	$(p \supset q) \cdot \sim q) \dashv 3\ \sim p$
Disjunctive Syllogism	$((p \vee q) \cdot \sim p) \dashv 3\ q$
Hypothetical Syllogism	$((p \supset q) \cdot (q \supset r)) \dashv 3\ (p \supset r)$
Constructive Dilemma	$(((p \supset q) \cdot (r \supset s)) \cdot (p \vee r)) \dashv 3\ (q \vee s)$
Destructive Dilemma	$(((p \supset q) \cdot (r \supset s)) \cdot (\sim q \vee \sim s)) \dashv 3\ (\sim p \vee r)$
Addition	$p \dashv 3\ (p \vee q)$
Simplification	$(p \cdot q) \dashv 3\ p$
	$(p \cdot q) \dashv 3\ q$
Conjunction	$((p) \cdot (q)) \dashv 3\ (p \cdot q)$

* The symbols $\supset$ and $\equiv$ are sometimes called "material implication" and "material equivalence" to distinguish them from other kinds of implication and equivalence, as we noted in Section 1.2.

We can do two sorts of things with this new connective. First, since truth-table tautologies are logical truths, we can rewrite all the tautologous inferences of Chapter 1 with the new symbol as shown in Table 7.1.

We can also ask what similar inferences hold with ⊰ itself substituted for ⊃ in the premises of arguments. It turns out that for strict implication the argument forms of Table 7.2 are valid within the system of modal logic considered in this section.

TABLE 7.2

	Argument Form	Symbolization
SI 3	Strict Modus Ponens (SMP)	p ⊰ q
		p
		q
SI 4	Strict Modus Tollens (SMT)	p ⊰ q
		~q
		~p
SI 5	Strict Hypothetical Syllogism (SHS)	p ⊰ q
		q ⊰ r
		p ⊰ r
SI 6	Strict Constructive Dilemma (SCD)	p ⊰ q
		r ⊰ s
		p ∨ q
		r ∨ s
SI 7	Strict Destructive Dilemma (SDD)	p ⊰ q
		r ⊰ s
		~q ∨ ~s
		~p ∨ ~r

Other interesting logical truths involving strict implication are the following:

$$\text{SI 8} \quad (\Box \, p \lor \Box \, q) \dashv \Box \, (p \lor q)$$
$$\text{SI 9} \quad \Diamond \, (p \cdot q) \dashv (\Diamond \, p \cdot \Diamond \, q)$$

These, along with two equivalences discussed below, will be called Modal Operator Distribution (MOD). Another interesting implication is

$$\text{SI 10} \quad (p \dashv q) \dashv (\Diamond \, p \dashv \Diamond \, q)$$

This will be called Strict Implication of Possibles (SIP). The ten strict implications discussed so far are shown in Table 7.3.

TABLE 7.3

Strict Implication	Symbolization
SI 1 *a necesse ad esse* (NE)	$\square$ p ⥽ p
SI 2 *ab esse ad posse* (EP)	p ⥽ $\lozenge$ p
SI 3 Strict Modus Ponens (SMP)	((p ⥽ q) · p) ⥽ q
SI 4 Strict Modus Tollens (SMT)	((p ⥽ q) · ~q) ⥽ ~p
SI 5 Strict Hypothetical Syllogism (SHS)	((p ⥽ q) · (q ⥽ r)) ⥽ (p ⥽ r)
SI 6 Strict Constructive Dilemma (SCD)	(((p ⥽ q) · (r ⥽ s)) · (p ∨ r)) ⥽ (q ∨ s)
SI 7 Strict Destructive Dilemma (SDD)	(((p ⥽ q) · (r ⥽ s)) · (~q ∨ ~s)) ⥽ (~p · ~r)
SI 8 Modal Operator Distribution (MOD)	($\square$ p ∨ $\square$ q) ⥽ $\square$ (p ∨ q) and $\lozenge$ (p · q) ⥽ ($\lozenge$ p · $\lozenge$ q)
SI 10 Strict Implication of Possibles (SIP)	(p ⥽ q) ⥽ ($\lozenge$ p ⥽ $\lozenge$ q)

EXERCISES 7.1

A. Determine by using SI 1 through SI 10 and propositional logic rules whether the following are logically true:

1. (p · q) ⥽ ($\lozenge$ p · p)
2. (p · q) ⥽ ($\lozenge$ p · $\lozenge$ p)
3. (p · q) ⥽ ($\lozenge$ p · $\square$ p)
4. (p · q) ⥽ ($\lozenge$ p · ~q)
5. (p · q) ⥽ ($\lozenge$ p · q)
6. (p · q) ⥽ ($\lozenge$ p · $\lozenge$ q)
7. (p · q) ⥽ ($\lozenge$ p · $\square$ q)
8. (p · q) ⥽ (p · $\lozenge$ p)
9. (p · q) ⥽ (p · $\square$ p)
10. (p · q) ⥽ (p · ~p)
11. (p · q) ⥽ (p · q)
12. (p · q) ⥽ (p · $\lozenge$ q)
13. (p · q) ⥽ (p · $\square$ q)
14. (p · q) ⥽ (p · ~q)
15. (p · q) ⥽ ($\square$ p ∨ $\lozenge$ p)
16. (p · q) ⥽ ($\square$ p ∨ $\square$ p)
17. (p · q) ⥽ ($\square$ p ∨ ~p)
18. (p · q) ⥽ ($\square$ p ∨ q)
19. (p · q) ⥽ ($\square$ p ∨ $\lozenge$ q)
20. (p · q) ⥽ ($\square$ p ∨ $\square$ q)

B. (1) Translate the following statements into the symbolism of propositional modal logic. Give your own dictionary.

(2) Check the truth of each statement. (Source: Aristotle, *On Interpretation*.)

1. If it is not possible for a thing not to happen, it is impossible for it not to happen.

2. If it is impossible for a thing not to happen, then it is necessary that it should happen.

3. If a thing could either happen or not happen, it would not happen necessarily.
4. It is not possible that a certain event neither will nor will not happen.
5. This coat may be cut in two halves, or it may happen that it is not cut in two halves.
6. What is needs must be when it is.
7. What is not cannot be when it is not.
8. *What is needs must be when it is* is not the same as *if it is, then it necessarily is.*
9. That a statement is necessarily true or false does not imply that it is necessarily true or necessarily false.
10. A sea fight must either take place tomorrow or not take place tomorrow, but this does not mean that it necessarily takes place tomorrow or necessarily does not take place tomorrow.

7.2 EQUIVALENCES IN PROPOSITIONAL MODAL LOGIC

The strict equivalence connective $\equiv$ can be defined by

$$p \equiv q = \text{def} \; \Box \, (p \equiv q)$$

Just as with strict implication, our whole group of tautologous equivalences for propositional logic could be rewritten with strict equivalence as the main connective. We can also give a revised replacement rule which will read as follows:

Any form or part of a compound form may be replaced by a strictly equivalent form and any proposition or part of a compound proposition may be replaced by a strictly equivalent proposition.

It is interesting to examine the strict equivalences which hold for strict equivalence itself.

The strict implication variants of Consequentia Mirabilis and Negative Consequentia Mirabilis are

SE 1	$\Box \, p \equiv (\sim p \dashv 3 \; p)$	Strict Consequentia Mirabilis (SCM)
SE 2	$\Box \sim p \equiv (p \dashv 3 \sim p)$	Strict Negative Consequentia Mirabilis (SNCM)

These equivalences show several things:

(a) Strict implication could have been the basic modal operator, and $\Box$ could have been defined in terms of $\dashv 3$.

(b) A necessarily true proposition is *logically* implied by its own negation: If a proposition is necessarily true, then its negation is necessarily false, and a necessarily false proposition implies anything.

(c) Similarly, a necessarily false proposition implies its own negation; but of course its negation is a logical truth, and a logical truth is implied by any proposition.

Some interesting philosophical applications of the SNCM are the following:

(a) The proposition "All statements are false" is logically false for if it were true it would logically imply that it itself was false.

(b) The proposition "Epimenides, the Cretan, truly said that all Cretans always lie" is necessarily false, for if it were true it would logically imply its own falsity.

In both these cases no true paradox arises since both are universal statements, and, if they are false, only the particular statements are true, "some statements are true" or "some Cretans don't always lie." But consider a full-fledged paradox such as

(c) "This statement is false."

Here SNCM and SCM aggravate the situation. If (c) is true, it follows logically that it is false; so (c) is necessarily false by SNCM. However, if (c) is false, then it follows logically that it is true, so that (c) is necessarily true by SCM. Therefore, if we allow self-reference, this paradox gives us a statement which is *necessarily* true and *necessarily* false.

There are some interesting strict equivalences involving strict implication. The definitions of strict implication mentioned above (Lewis's original definition and our definition) can both be given as strict equivalences:

$$\text{SE 3} \quad (p \prec q) \equiv \Box (p \supset q) \qquad \left.\right\} \quad \text{Definition of Strict}$$
$$\text{SE 4} \quad (p \prec q) \equiv \mathord{\sim}\Diamond (p \cdot \mathord{\sim} q) \qquad \text{Implication (DSI)}$$

The negation of strict implication resembles that of material implication, except that possibility is involved.

$$\text{SE 5} \quad \mathord{\sim}(p \prec q) \equiv \Diamond (p \cdot \mathord{\sim} q) \qquad \text{Negation of Strict}$$
$$\text{Implication (NSI)}$$

We also find that transposition holds for strict implication:

$$\text{SE 6} \quad (p \prec q) \equiv (\mathord{\sim} q \prec \mathord{\sim} p) \qquad \text{Strict Transposition}$$
$$\text{(STransp)}$$

Also, commutation holds for strict equivalence:

$$\text{SE 7} \quad (p \equiv q) \equiv (q \equiv p) \qquad \text{Strict Commutation}$$
$$\text{(SCom)}$$

Complementarity also holds for $\equiv$:

SE 8 $(p \equiv q) \equiv (\sim p \equiv \sim q)$ Strict Complementarity (SComp)

The negation of a strict equivalence is related to that of a material equivalence:

SE 9 $\sim(p \equiv q) \equiv \Diamond (\sim p \equiv q)$ $\Big\}$ Negation of Strict
SE 10 $\sim(p \equiv q) \equiv \Diamond (p \equiv \sim q)$ Equivalence (NSE)

Strict equivalence may be defined as necessary material equivalence:

SE 11 $(p \equiv q) \equiv \Box (p \equiv q)$

Strict equivalence may also be defined in terms of strict implication:

SE 12 $(p \equiv q) \equiv ((p \dashv 3 q) \cdot (q \dashv 3 p))$ Definition of Strict Equivalence (DSE)

However, if we define it in terms of $\cdot$ and v, we must take care to distinguish it from material equivalence:

SE 13 $(p \equiv q) \equiv \Box ((p \cdot q) v (\sim p \cdot \sim q))$

If the $\Box$ were left out before the disjunction, this strict equivalence would not be a logical truth.

All of the modal operator exchanges can also be written as strict equivalences:

SE 14 $\Diamond p \equiv \sim\Box \sim p$
SE 15 $\Diamond \sim p \equiv \sim\Box p$
SE 16 $\sim\Diamond p \equiv \Box \sim p$
SE 17 $\sim\Diamond \sim p \equiv \Box p$

These will be collectively referred to as Modal Operator Exchange (MOE) and can be seen to be precisely parallel to similar exchange rules for existential and universal quantifiers.

Also similar to quantifier rules are the remaining rules involving Modal Operator Distribution (MOD). (The first two were implications SI 8 and SI 7.)

SE 18 $\Box (p \cdot q) \equiv (\Box p \cdot \Box q)$
SE 19 $\Diamond (p v q) \equiv (\Diamond p v \Diamond q)$

Just as with quantifiers, the patterns strong operator with strong connective and weak operator with weak connective lead to equivalences rather than to implications. Also, just as with quantifiers, the distribution rules cannot be used if the operator to be distributed is within the scope of a ~ or of another modal operator.

We may summarize our results so far by the list of modal equivalences given in Table 7.4.

TABLE 7.4

		Modal Equivalence	Symbolization
SE	1	Strict Consequentia Mirabilis (SCM)	$\Box\, p \equiv (\sim p \mathrel{\prec} p)$
SE	2	Strict Negative Consequentia (SNCM)	$\Box \sim p \equiv (p \mathrel{\prec} \sim p)$
SE	3	Definition of Strict Implication (DSI)	$(p \mathrel{\prec} q) \equiv \Box\,(p \supset q)$
SE	4	Definition of Strict Implication (DSI)	$(p \mathrel{\prec} q) \equiv\ \sim \Diamond\,(p \cdot \sim q)$
SE	5	Negation of Strict Implication (NSI)	$\sim(p \mathrel{\prec})q \equiv \Diamond\,(p \cdot \sim q)$
SE	6	Strict Transposition (STransp)	$(p \mathrel{\prec} q) \equiv (\sim q \mathrel{\prec} \sim p)$
SE	7	Strict Commutation (SCom)	$(p \equiv q) \equiv (q \equiv p)$
SE	8	Strict Complementarity (SComp)	$(p \equiv q) \equiv (\sim p \equiv \sim q)$
SE	9	Negation of Strict Equivalence (NSE)	$\sim(p \equiv q) \equiv \Diamond\,(\sim p \equiv q)$
SE	10	Negation of Strict Equivalence (NSE)	$\sim(p \equiv q) \equiv \Diamond\,(p \equiv \sim q)$
SE	11	Definition of Strict Equivalence (DSE)	$(p \equiv q) \equiv \Box\,(p \equiv q)$
SE	12	Definition of Strict Equivalence (DSE)	$(p \equiv q) \equiv \Box\,((p \cdot q) \vee (\sim p \cdot \sim q))$
SE	13	Definition of Strict Equivalence (DSE)	$(p \equiv q) \equiv ((p \mathrel{\prec} q) \cdot (q \mathrel{\prec} p))$
SE	14	Modal Operator Exchange (MOE)	$\Box\, p \equiv\ \sim \Diamond \sim p$
SE	15	Modal Operator Exchange (MOE)	$\sim \Box\, p \equiv \Diamond \sim p$
SE	16	Modal Operator Exchange (MOE)	$\Box \sim p \equiv\ \sim \Diamond\, p$
SE	17	Modal Operator Exchange (MOE)	$\sim \Box \sim p \equiv \Diamond\, p$
SE	18	Modal Operator Distribution (MOD)	$\Box\,(p \cdot q) \equiv (\Box\, p \cdot \Box\, q)$
SE	19	Modal Operator Distribution (MOD)	$\Diamond\,(p \vee q) \equiv (\Diamond\, p \vee \Diamond\, q)$

EXERCISES 7.2

A. For the following list determine for each item: (1) which, if any, of the other items it is equivalent to, and (2) which, if any, of the others it implies or is implied by.

1. $E \cdot \square E$	2. $E \cdot \lozenge E$	3. $E \cdot \lozenge \sim E$
4. $E \cdot \square \sim E$	5. $\sim E \cdot \square E$	6. $\sim E \cdot \lozenge E$
7. $\sim E \cdot \lozenge \sim E$	8. $\sim E \cdot \square \sim E$	9. E
10. $\sim E$	11. $\square E$	12. $\square \sim E$
13. $\lozenge E$	14. $\lozenge \sim E$	15. $\lozenge E \cdot \lozenge \sim E$

B. Translate the following statements into the symbolism of propositional modal logic, and check the truth of the starred assertions that appear before each group. (Source: Aristotle, *On Interpretation*.)

*A The following pairs must be considered as five contradictory pairs.

1. It may be   It cannot be
2. It is possible   It is not possible
3. It is impossible   It is not impossible
4. It is necessary   It is not necessary
5. It is true   It is not true

*B From the statements on the left, those on the right follow.

6. It may be   It is possible
                       It is not impossible
                       It is not necessary

7. It is possible   It may be

8. It may not be   It is not necessary that it should not be
                       It is not impossible that it should not be

9. It is not possible It is necessary that it should not be
                        It is impossible that it should be

10. It cannot not be   It is necessary that it should be
                        It is impossible that it should not be

*C The expressions in the following group are all equivalent.
11. It may be
12. It is possible
13. It is not impossible that it should be
14. It is not necessary that it should be

*D The expressions in the following group are all equivalent.
15. It cannot be
16. It is not possible
17. It is impossible that it should be
18. It is necessary that it should not be

*E The following group are all equivalent.
19. It may not be
20. It is possible that it should not be
21. It is not impossible that it should be
22. It is not necessary that it should not be

*F The following group are all equivalent.
23. It cannot not be

24. It is not possible that it should not be
25. It is impossible that it should not be
26. It is necessary that it should be

*G   The statements on the left are contradictories of those on the right.
27. It is impossible   It may be
                                               It is possible

28. It is not impossible that it should be   It cannot be
                                               It is not possible

*H   The following pair are contraries.
29. It is necessary   It is impossible

*I   The following pair are subcontraries.
30. It may be   It may not be

7.3   THE LEWIS SYSTEMS S.3, S.4, and S.5

There is nothing in propositional modal logic which parallels the use of truth tables to establish that certain propositions are logical truths.

Four-Valued Quasi Truth Tables

However there is a technique which enables us to show that certain statements are *not* logical truths. This technique involves the use of quasi truth tables which have four values rather than two. Such tables have 4^n lines, where n is the number of variables. We fill the rightmost column with sets of 1, 2, 3, 4; the next column with four 1's, four 2's, and so on; the next, if necessary, with sixteen 1's, sixteen 2's, and so on. For two variables we need $4^2 = 16$ rows. The reference columns of such a table look like Table 7.5.

TABLE 7.5

p	q
1	1
1	2
1	3
1	4
2	1
2	2
2	3
2	4
3	1
3	2
3	3
3	4
4	1
4	2
4	3
4	4

A table such as Table 7.5 is not actually analogous to a truth table since we will see that it is not possible to make a really satisfactory interpretation of the numbers as extended truth values. However, we can give definitions of modal operators and connectives using such tables and use them to reach a decision as to whether a given modal proposition is not a logical truth. In terms of a four-valued matrix for one variable, we can define the modal operators and negation as in Matrices 7.1, 7.2, and 7.3.

MATRIX 7.1			MATRIX 7.2			MATRIX 7.3	
~			◇			□	
1	4		1	1		1	2
2	3		2	1		2	4
3	2		3	1		3	4
4	1		4	3		4	4

It can be seen that the value of the negation of a proposition is always 5 minus the value of that proposition (that is, the value of a proposition added to that of its negation equals 5).

We can define the connectives as shown in Table 7.6. To see whether a

TABLE 7.6

⊼	1	2	3	4
1	2	4	4	4
2	2	2	4	4
3	2	4	2	4
4	2	2	2	2

•	1	2	3	4
1	1	2	3	4
2	2	2	4	4
3	3	4	3	4
4	4	4	4	4

v	1	2	3	4
1	1	1	1	1
2	1	2	1	2
3	1	1	3	3
4	1	2	3	4

⊃	1	2	3	4
1	1	2	3	4
2	1	1	3	3
3	1	2	1	2
4	1	1	1	1

≡	1	2	3	4
1	1	2	3	4
2	2	1	4	3
3	3	4	1	2
4	4	3	2	1

≡	1	2	3	4
1	2	4	4	4
2	4	2	4	4
3	4	4	2	4
4	4	4	4	2

proposition may be logically true, we proceed just as with truth functional operators, setting down a table and figuring the value of a compound expression from the values of the variables for that line and the matrix definitions for the operators involved. Unless all of the values under the main connective are 1's or 2's, the compound proposition is not a logical truth.

Thus, for example we can show (Table 7.7) that NE and EP can be logical truths, but their converses cannot.

Let us now explore the meaning of the four values. It may have occurred to you already that 1 could stand for "logically true," 2 for "true but not logically true," 3 for "false but not logically false," and 4 for "logically

TABLE 7.7

p	□ p ⊰ p	p ⊰ ◇ p	p ⊰ □ p	◇ p ⊰ p
1	2 1 2 1	1 2 1 1	1 4 2 1	1 1 2 1
2	4 2 2 2	2 2 1 2	2 4 4 2	1 2 4 2
3	4 3 2 3	3 2 1 3	3 2 4 3	1 3 4 3
4	4 4 2 4	4 2 3 4	4 2 4 4	3 4 4 4
	√ √ √	√ √ √	√ √ √	√ √ √

false." This interpretation can be carried through to a very large extent, but there are certain problems.

For operators on one proposition the interpretation shown in Table 7.8

TABLE 7.8

p	◇ p	□ p	(p · ◇ ~p)
1	1 1	2 1	1 3 3 4 1
2	1 2	4 2	2 2 1 3 2
3	1 3	4 3	3 3 1 2 3
4	3 4	4 4	4 4 1 1 4
	√	√	√ √ √ √

is plausible. Notice that, on this interpretation of the number for a given proposition A, the value ◇ A is true in every case except the case where A is logically false. (The kind of truth or falsity attributed to modal statements will be considered later, for example, the question "why is ◇ A logically true when true and factually false when false?") Also □ A is true only if A is logically true and false otherwise. The statement A · ◇ ~A is true if A is factually true, false otherwise. All this is as it should be. However, consider Matrices 7.4, 7.5, and 7.6 for ⊰, ·, and v. On the analogy of the operator of · in

MATRIX 7.4

⊰	1	2	3	4
1	2	4	4	4
2	2	2	4	4
3	2	4	2	4
4	2	2	2	2

MATRIX 7.5

·	1	2	3	4
1	1	2	3	4
2	2	2	4	4
3	3	4	3	4
4	4	4	4	4

MATRIX 7.6

v	1	2	3	4
1	1	1	1	1
2	1	2	1	2
3	1	1	3	3
4	1	2	3	4

propositional logic, one would expect the value of p · q to be the "weakest" value of the two variables. Thus if A and B are both logically true, then A · B should be logically true, but, if A is logically true and B is factually true, A · B should be only factually true, and so on. This works out in propositional logic; for example, if a contingent is joined by · to a tautology, the resulting compound is a contingent.

For statements joined with v, the value of the compound should be that of the "strongest" disjunct. For example, a tautology joined with v to a contingent statement is a tautology, and so forth.

Examination of the four-valued table for · and v (Matrices 7.5 and 7.6) shows that these expectations hold in all cases except two. If A is factually true and B is factually false or vice versa, then A · B has the value 4, which we have interpreted as *logically* false and A v B has the value 1, which we have interpreted as *logically* true. This cannot be avoided without either destroying the relation of p ─3 q to such values as □ (p ⊃ q) or else changing the values for p ─3 q at two points to correspond to the changes we would have to make in · and v. If we do change the definition of p ─3 q, it turns out that both

$$p\!\dashv\!3\ (p \cdot p) \qquad \text{and} \qquad (p \cdot q)\!\dashv\!3\ p$$

cease to be logical truths!

How severe is the difficulty? Notice that we don't have a true value where we should have a false, or vice versa, in the tables for · and v. We merely have in two cases a "stronger" value than seems justified. If we ignore this, we have a workable and reasonably convenient technique for deciding which modal expressions are logical truths. Except for these two cases the values derived are reasonable on the interpretation of 1 as logical truth, 2 as factual truth, and so on.

Proof and Disproof Procedures

It turns out that, although the four-valued tables are an effective disproof procedure (rather like the disproof procedure which we had for predicate logic), they cannot function as a proof procedure, as two-valued truth tables can. There are certain formulas of modal logic which according to the tables can be logical truths but which are not provable in modal logic and which, are in fact counterintuitive. These all depend in some way on the four-valued character of the tables. In fact, we find on further investigation into modal logic* that an adequate modal logic must be free to consider an infinite range of possibilities (or "possible worlds" if you like). This is not possible with only four values. Specifically, we can think of a four-valued system as allowing only one alternate possibility, or possible world. Let us call this the "Other World." We can then read the four values as follows:

    1 = true both in this actual world and in the Other World
    2 = true in this world and false in the Other World
    3 = false in this world and true in the Other World
    4 = false in both worlds

---

* Those interested in the problems involved may consult A. N. Prior, *Time and Modality* (Oxford University Press, New York), 1957 and my paper "Four-Valued Tables for Modal Logic" in *Notre Dame Journal of Formal Logic*, Vol. XI, No. 4, October, 1970.

On this interpretation, all the anomalous values can be seen to be precisely what is to be expected. However, it is equally obvious that this system is not sufficiently rich for many purposes.

We are forced in the direction of an infinite-valued system for modal logic, but we can recognize that a great many truths of modal logic do not depend on the infinite-valued aspect of an adequate modal logic. For such truths four-valued tables are an adequate test. In addition the four-valued system has a certain independent interest.

So far we have not discussed the possibility of applying more than one modal operator to the same proposition. In the system we have been using so far, some peculiar things happen if we do so apply them (Table 7.9).

TABLE 7.9

p	◇p	□p	◇◇p	□□p	◇◇~p
1	1 1	2 1	1 1 1	4 2 1	1 3 4 1
2	1 2	4 2	1 1 2	4 4 2	1 1 3 2
3	1 3	4 3	1 1 3	4 4 3	1 1 2 3
4	3 4	4 4	1 3 4	4 4 4	1 1 1 4
	√	√	√ √	√ √	√ √ √

p	□□~p	◇□p	□◇p
1	4 4 4 1	1 2 1	2 1 1
2	4 4 3 2	3 4 2	2 1 2
3	4 4 2 3	3 4 3	2 1 3
4	4 2 1 4	3 4 4	4 3 4
	√ √ √	√ √	√ √

Notice that doubling ◇ gives a logical truth, while doubling □ gives the exact opposite. Mixing the operators produces new patterns. But consider (Table 7.10) the relations of these mixed operators to single operators. As one

TABLE 7.10

p	□◇p ⋺ ◇p	◇□p ⋺ □p	◇□p ⋺ ◇p
1	2 1 12 1 1	3 2 14 2 1	1 2 12 1 1
2	2 1 22 1 2	1 4 24 4 2	3 4 22 1 2
3	2 1 32 1 3	1 4 34 4 3	3 4 32 1 3
4	4 3 42 3 4	1 4 44 4 4	3 4 42 3 4
	√ √ √ √ √	√ √ √ √ √	√ √ √ √ √

might expect, $\square \diamond$ p strictly implies $\diamond$ p since this is merely an instance of the valid argument form

$$\frac{\square\ p}{p}$$

with $\diamond$ p substituted for p. However $\diamond \square p \dashv3 \square$ p is not a logical truth although $\diamond \square p \dashv3 \diamond$ p may be a logical truth.

Now stated verbally all this has a certain plausibility. It amounts to saying that

1. Any proposition is possibly possible.
2. No proposition is necessarily necessary.
3. If a proposition is possibly necessary, it doesn't follow that it is necessary.
4. If a proposition is possibly necessary it follows that it is possible.

Different Systems of Propositional Modal Logic

However, systems of propositional modal logic have been devised that are different than the one we have been working with. They are stronger than the system we have been using in the sense that all the logical truths which we have considered can be proved in these systems, but also additional propositions which are not logical truths in the earlier systems are logical truths in these other systems.

The system which we have been using is called an S.3 system since it is the third of five possible modal logic systems discussed by Lewis.* The next strongest system is S.4, in which the following propositions are logical truths. (The asterisk, as usual, indicates the inference is based on a challengeable assumption.)

$$\begin{aligned} &\text{*SI 11} \quad \diamond \diamond p \dashv3 \diamond p \\ &\text{*SI 12} \quad \square p \dashv3 \square \square p \end{aligned}$$

The strongest system of all is S.5 in which the following propositions are logical truths. (The double asterisk indicates a further assumption.)

$$\begin{aligned} &\text{**SI 13} \quad \diamond p \dashv3 \square \diamond p \\ &\text{**SI 14} \quad \diamond \square p \dashv3 \square p \end{aligned}$$

We will not consider the S.4 system in detail, but a few comments about it are in order. First, *SI 11 and *SI 12 could have been written as equivalences;

---

* See C. I. Lewis and C. H. Langford, *Symbolic Logic*, second edition (Dover Publications, Inc., New York), 1952. SI 10, Strict Implication of Possibles, is true in S.3 but not in weaker systems. Most of our other rules hold for even weaker systems than S.3.

248

their converses are true even in an S.3 system. Second, they can be seen to amount to a decision to regard iterated modalities as simply the same as uniterated ones: "possibly possible" will just mean "possible," and "necessarily necessary" will just mean "necessary." Since this has a certain appeal, an S.4 system might well be regarded as desirably simpler than an S.3 one. Finally, although I know of no arguments of great philosophical interest which depend on using an S.4 system rather than an S.3 system, there are some rather interesting effects of adopting such a system, for example, the effect on distribution of modal operators. In an S.4 system, for example, from the assertion of

$$\Diamond (p \cdot \Diamond \sim p) \qquad \text{it follows that} \qquad \Diamond p \cdot \Diamond \sim p$$

which is not true in an S.3 system.

Of course both S.4 and S.5 systems require matrix definitions different from those of an S.3 system. The matrices are shown in Table 7.11. The matrices for $\sim$ and $\cdot$, v, $\supset$, and $\equiv$ remain the same.

TABLE 7.11

S.4	$\dashv$	1	2	3	4		$\Diamond$			$\Box$	
	1	1	4	3	4		1	1		1	1
	2	1	1	3	3		2	2		2	4
	3	1	4	1	4		3	1		3	3
	4	1	1	1	1		4	4		4	4

S.5	$\dashv$	1	2	3	4		$\Diamond$			$\Box$	
	1	1	4	4	4		1	1		1	1
	2	1	1	4	4		2	1		2	4
	3	1	4	1	4		3	1		3	4
	4	1	1	1	1		4	4		4	4

The S.4 proposition, *SI 12 is sometimes called the Weak Reduction Principle (WRP); as we have seen, its effect is to reduce doubled modal operators to single ones. The S.5 proposition, **SI 14 is sometimes called the Strong Reduction Principle (SRP). The effect of **SI 14 (and **SI 13, which can be proved from it) is to state that any true modal proposition is necessarily true.

This can be seen if we put **SI 13 and **SI 14 together with *SI 11 and *SI 12, which are also provable in an S.5 system. We can then see that:

1. If a proposition is necessarily true, it is necessarily necessarily true (by *SI 12).
2. If a proposition is possibly true, it is necessarily possibly true (by **SI 13).
3. If a proposition is possibly possibly true, it is possibly true (by *SI 11) and hence necessarily possibly true (by **SI 13).

4. If a proposition is possibly necessarily true, it is necessarily true (by **SI 14) and hence necessarily necessarily true (by *SI 12).

The four-valued tables for S.5 and S.4 systems reflect these features. Consider Table 7.12, which presents S.3 and S.5 tables for ◇ p, □ p, and

TABLE 7.12

S.3	p	◇p	□p	□p -3 p		S.5	p	◇p	□p	□p -3 p
	1	1	2	2			1	1	1	1
	2	1	4	2			2	1	4	1
	3	1	4	2			3	1	4	1
	4	3	4	2			4	4	4	1

□ p -3 p. Notice that in S.3, if ◇ p is false, it is factually false, and, if □ p is true, it is factually true, and, if a proposition is logically true, it is factually true, for all values of p. The 1 for the cases where ◇ p is true reflects the fact that ◇ ◇ p is logically true in S.3. Any statement *may* be possible, but as a matter of *fact* some are logically false. Similarly □ p is factually true if it is true, and □ p -3 is factually true since it is the same as □ □ (p ⊃ q), and necessity is factually true if it is true. The 4's under □ p reflect the fact that □ □ p is a logical falsehood in S.3.

In the S.5 tables, on the other hand, we have only 1's and 4's, which reflects the idea that "modal status is always necessary." The tables for an S.4 system similarly reflect the assumptions of the system, but in a somewhat more complicated way.

EXERCISES 7.3

A. Determine by four-valued tables which of the following could be logical truths and which could not be in: (1) an S.3 system, (2) an S.4 system, and (3) an S.5 system.

1. □ p -3 □ □ □ p
2. □ p -3 □ □ ◇ p
3. □ p -3 □ ◇ □ p
4. □ p -3 ◇ □ □ p
5. □ p -3 ◇ ◇ □ p
6. □ p -3 ◇ □ ◇ p
7. □ p -3 □ ◇ ◇ p
8. □ p -3 ◇ ◇ ◇ p
9. □ p -3 □ □ □ ◇ p
10. □ p -3 □ □ ◇ □ p
11. □ p -3 □ ◇ □ □ p
12. □ p -3 ◇ □ □ □ p
13. □ p -3 □ □ ◇ ◇ p
14. □ p -3 □ ◇ □ ◇ p
15. □ p -3 ◇ □ ◇ □ p
16. □ p -3 ◇ ◇ □ □ p
17. □ p -3 ◇ ◇ ◇ □ p
18. □ p -3 ◇ ◇ □ ◇ p
19. □ p -3 ◇ □ ◇ ◇ p
20. □ p -3 □ ◇ ◇ ◇ p

B. These exercises are intended to give practice in the use of repeated modal operators and do not bear directly on the differences between the Lewis systems. Translate from English to symbols, using the dictionary

    G ╫ God exists   E ╫ Evil exists   F ╫ Freedom exists
Use ⊃ unless -3 is clearly indicated by the context.

1.   It is possible that it is necessary that God exists.
2.   If it is possible that freedom exists, then it is necessary that it is possible that evil exists.
3.   If God exists, then, if it is possible that evil exists, it is necessary that it is necessary that evil exists.
4.   If it is possible that it is necessary that God exists, then it is necessary that it is possible that evil exists.
5.   If it is necessary that God exists, then it is necessary that it be possible that freedom exists.
6.   If it is necessary that freedom exists, then it is possible that it is necessary that God exists.
7.   If it is necessary that evil exists, then it is not necessary that it is necessary that God exists.
8.   If it is possible that it is necessary that evil exists or possible that it is necessary that freedom exists, then it is possible that it is not necessary that God exists.
9.   If it is possible that, if God exists, then freedom exists, then it is possible that it is necessary that evil exists.
10.   If it is necessary that, if God exists, then freedom exists, then it is necessary that it is possible that it is necessary that evil exists.

7.4 PROOFS IN MODAL LOGIC

Proofs in propositional modal logic resemble those in ordinary propositional logic with some important exceptions. For any inference involving $\dashv$ or $\equiv$ we must, of course, list the corresponding *strict* inference or equivalence, for example, SMP rather than MP or STransp rather than Transp. We will also have some implications and equivalences for which there are no parallels in ordinary propositional logic, such as NE, EP, MOE, or MOD.

Rule of Conditional Proof

The most important difference, however, is that the rule of conditional proof does not permit the inference of conclusions of the form p $\dashv$ q. An example may make it clear why this is so. The two statements "All the books on my shelf are blue" and "This is a book on my shelf" certainly logically imply "This book is blue." So we have an antecedent of the form $((p \cdot q) \dashv r)$. However, if we allow this to imply $(p \dashv (q \dashv r)$, we would be in the position of saying that the fact that all the books on my shelf are blue logically implies that this book's being on my shelf *logically* implies that it is blue. Now this is plainly false.

If a statement logically implies another, we should be able to use some acceptable principle of inference to infer the second from the first. But no acceptable principle of inference justifies the passage from "This is a book on my shelf" to "This book is blue." Thus, if we allowed a strict implication form of conditional proof we would admit plainly invalid arguments. We have three ways out of this difficulty.

1. We can give a Restricted Rule of Conditional Proof as follows: If a proposition Q can be proved solely from another proposition P with no other premises, the strict implication P ⥽ Q can be asserted. (The citation will be RRCP).

2. In many cases it is sufficient to show that one modal proposition is *materially* implied by another: In these cases the unrestricted Rule of Conditional Proof will be applicable.

3. In some cases we can use Reductio proof; however, this becomes very complicated since the negation of any reasonably complicated modal statement is almost sure to lead to iterated modalities. Of course in an S.4 or S.5 system this is fairly easily taken care of.

The following example shows how the Restricted Rule of Conditional Proof works. Consider the two strict implications:

$$\text{SI 15} \quad (p ⥽ q) ⥽ (\Diamond\, p ⥽ \Diamond\, q)$$
$$\text{SI 16} \quad (p ⥽ q) ⥽ (\Box\, {\sim}q ⥽ \Box\, {\sim}p)$$

They are both logical truths in an S.3 system. In fact, SI 15 is the characteristic principle by which an S.3 system differs from weaker systems. For lack of a better name we will dub it Strict Implication of Possibles (SIP). A philosopher* who used it in an interesting proof has given to SI 16 the name "Modal Modus Tollens" (MMT). We will retain this name, hoping that no confusion occurs with SMT. The two propositions mutually imply each other, and we will derive each from the other using the Restricted Rule of Conditional Proof.

SI 16 from SI 15

*1	$(p ⥽ q) ⥽ (\Diamond\, p ⥽ \Diamond\, q)$	ARCP
*2	$(p ⥽ q) ⥽ ({\sim}\Diamond\, q ⥽ {\sim}\Diamond\, p)$	1, STransp, RR
*3	$(p ⥽ q) ⥽ (\Box\, {\sim}q ⥽ \Box\, {\sim}p)$	2, MOE, RR
4	$((p ⥽ q) ⥽ (\Diamond\, p ⥽ \Diamond\, q)) ⥽ ((p ⥽ q)$ $⥽ (\Box\, {\sim}q ⥽ \Box\, {\sim}p))$	1–3, RRCP

SI 15 from SI 16

*1	$(p ⥽ q) ⥽ (\Box\, {\sim}q ⥽ \Box\, {\sim}p)$	ARCP
*2	$(p ⥽ q) ⥽ ({\sim}\Box\, {\sim}p ⥽ {\sim}\Box\, {\sim}q)$	1, 5, STransp, RR
*3	$(p ⥽ q) ⥽ (\Diamond\, p ⥽ \Diamond\, q)$	2, MOE, RR
4	$((p ⥽ q) ⥽ (\Box\, {\sim}q ⥽ \Box\, {\sim}p)) ⥽ ((p ⥽ q) ⥽ (\Diamond\, p ⥽ \Diamond\, q))$	1–3, RRCP

Notice that we used the Replacement Rule on *part* of an expression, which is quite legitimate. If we had tried to assume (p ⥽ q) in order to work

* Charles Hartshorne in *The Logic of Perfection* (Open Court Publishing Co., LaSalle, Ill.), 1962, chap. 2.

on ◇ p ⊰ ◇ q alone, we would have violated the restriction on the Restricted Rule of Conditional Proof.

*1	(p ⊰ q) ⊰ (◇ p ⊰ ◇ q)	ARCP
**2	(p ⊰ q)	ARCP
**3	(◇ p ⊰ ◇ q)	1, 2, SMP, IR
**4	(~◇ q ⊰ ◇ ~p)	3, STransp, RR
**5	(□ ~q ⊰ □ ~p)	4, MOE, RR
Forbidden: *6	(p ⊰ q) ⊰ (□ ~q ⊰ □ ~p)	2, 5, RRCP
7	(p ⊰ q) ⊰ ((◇ p ⊰ ◇ q) ⊰ ((p ⊰ q)	1–6, RCP
	⊰ (□ ~q ⊰ □ ~p))	Q.E.D.

This supposed justification for line 6 cannot be used since line 5 does not follow from line 2 alone but needs an additional premise, line 1.

Reductio Proof

We will give a short Reductio proof of NE to show how such a proof works in a strong modal system.

*1	~ (□ p ⊰ p)	ACP
*2	◇ (□ p · ~p)	1, NST, RR
*3	◇ □ p · ◇ ~p	2, MOD, RR
*4	◇ □ p	3, Simp, IR
*5	□ p	4, SRP, IR
*6	~◇ ~p	5, MOE, RR
*7	◇ ~p	6, Simp, IR
*8	~◇ ~p · ◇ ~p	4, 7, Conj, IR
9	~ (□ p ⊰ p) ⊰ (~◇ ~p · ◇ ~p)	1–8, RRCP
10	□ p ⊰ p	5, Red, RR Q.E.D.

Note that without the distinctive S.5 thesis, the strong reduction principle (SRP) at line 6, our Reductio proof would have been seriously embarrassed since in an S.3 system we have no rules dealing with iterated modalities and in an S.4 system none that would be useful at this point.

EXERCISES 7.4

A. Provide proofs for the following, using the techniques of this chapter:

1. ~F ⊰ ~P
   ◇ ~F   } ~ □ P
   (◇ ~F · ~◇ ~P) ⊰ ~(~F ⊰ ~P)

2. ~F ⊰ ~P
   ◇ ~F   } ~((◇ ~F · ~◇ ~P) ⊰ ~(~F ⊰ ~P))
   □ P

253

3. ~F ⊰ ~P
    (◇ ~F • ~◇ ~P) ⊰ ~(~F ⊰ ~P)   ⎫
    □ P   ⎬ ~◇ ~F
                                      ⎭
4. E ⊰ □ E }   ~◇(E • ◇ ~E)
5. ~E • ◇ E }   ◇(E • ◇ ~E)

B. Symbolize and provide proofs for the following, using the techniques of this chapter.

1. A perfect being exists and exists necessarily or does not exist and does not exist necessarily. A perfect being is possible. Therefore it exists.
2. A perfect being exists necessarily or does not exist necessarily. A perfect being possibly may not exist. Therefore it does not exist.
3. A perfect being, if it exists at all, exists necessarily. A perfect being possibly may not exist; therefore it does not exist.
4. A perfect being exists necessarily if it exists at all, and such a being is possible. If it is true that, if a perfect being exists at all, it exists necessarily, then, if it is possible that it should exist, it exists. Therefore, a perfect being exists.
5. A perfect being either exists and exists necessarily or exists and possibly may not exist or does not exist and does not exist necessarily or does not exist and may exist. If such a being exists at all, it exists necessarily. Such a being is possible. Therefore it exists. (Hint: Use the results of Exercises 7.4A, numbers 4 and 5.)

7.5 PHILOSOPHICAL APPLICATIONS

Since possibility, necessity, and related notions often enter into philosophical discussions, modal logic can often be useful in examining statements and arguments taken from actual philosophical sources, especially when the statements or arguments are fairly complex. But even fairly simple statements and arguments can profitably be subjected to such analysis.

Modal Distribution

Various modal implications have been used and misused in the history of philosophy. One persistent confusion is illustrated by the following argument:

Since you necessarily do a thing or do not do it, you necessarily do it or necessarily do not do it. Let D ⫫ You do a certain thing. Then the argument can be symbolized as follows:

$$\frac{\Box\,(D \vee \sim D)}{\Box\,D \vee \Box\,\sim D}$$

But although the implication

$$(\Box\,p \vee \Box\,q) \dashv3 \Box\,(p \vee q)$$

254

is valid, the reverse implication

$$\Box\,(p \lor q) \,\dashv\, (\Box\,p \lor \Box\,q)$$

does not hold. So even though the premise $\Box\,(D \lor \sim D)$ is true (since $D \lor \sim D$ is a logical truth and hence necessarily true), the argument is not valid and the conclusion does not follow.

A similar fallacy of modal distribution may occur in the argument:

> If God wills a thing, then it necessarily occurs.
> If a thing happens, then God wills it.
> _____
> If a thing happens, then it necessarily occurs.

If $G \,\#\,$ God wills x and $H \,\#\, x$ happens, then the argument can be symbolized as follows. (In general we will use $\supset$ for "if ..., then" unless $\dashv$ is clearly indicated.)

$$\frac{\begin{array}{c}\Box\,(G \supset H) \\ H \supset G\end{array}}{\Box\,(H \supset H)}$$

This argument is trivially valid since the conclusion is trivially true ($H \supset H$ is a logical truth, hence necessary). The second premise seems to be what was intended, and causes no problems. It might be argued that the conclusion should be $H \supset \Box\,H$. But, if the premises are as we have them, this does not follow. If the first premise were $G \supset \Box\,H$, the conclusion *would* follow, but $G \supset \Box\,H$ is highly disputable, even to those who would grant $\Box\,(G \supset H)$. In fact, the verbal argument is probably convincing because these two are confused.

An argument which is never stated explicitly but may have contributed to the confusion surrounding the concept of knowledge is the following:

> If a statement is not true, then necessarily you do not know it.
> Therefore, if you know a statement is true, it is necessarily true.

Let $T \,\#\, P$ is true and $K \,\#\,$ you know P to be true. Then the argument is either

$$\frac{\Box\,(\sim T \supset \sim K)}{\Box\,(K \supset T)}$$

which is valid but causes no particular problems, or else it is one of the two following, neither of which is valid:

$$\frac{\sim T \supset \Box \sim K}{K \supset \Box\,T} \qquad \text{or} \qquad \frac{\Box\,(\sim T \supset \sim K)}{K \supset \Box\,T}$$

Clarification by Modal Operators

An example of clarification of a statement by means of modal operators is the following. Consider the statement "You are able to write while you are not writing." If we let Y $\#$ you are writing at a certain time, then this can either be $\Diamond\,(\sim Y \cdot Y)$, which is false, since it states that a contradiction is possibly true, or $\sim Y \cdot \Diamond\, Y$, which is true, since it simply says that, although you are in fact writing, it is possible for you not to be writing.

In fact, for any proposition, "A," it is enlightening to distinguish these cases:

1. A (A is true.)
2. $\Box$ A (A is necessarily true.)
3. $\Diamond$ A (A is possibly true.)
4. A $\cdot \Diamond \sim$A (A is true, but might possibly not be true.)
5. $\Diamond$ A $\cdot \Diamond \sim$A (A may or may not be true.)

Statement 2 is incompatible with either 4 or 5, since they both contain its contradictory as a conjunct. Statement 4 is a useful way of stating that A is *factually* true, as opposed to being necessarily true, while 5 is at least one thing that we might mean by saying that A is *contingent*.

Modalized Version of the Ontological Argument

Since a fully developed propositional modal logic is of fairly recent date extended arguments or proofs using modal logic are not often found in the philosophical literature. An interesting and important exception to this rule is a modalized version of St. Anselm's famous Ontological Argument given by Professor Charles Hartshorne.* The following is my own version of Professor Hartshorne's argument. We begin by proving that in an S.5 system the following is a logical truth:

$$(p \dashv \Box\, p) \supset (\Diamond\, p \dashv p)$$

The proof is as follows. (The three premises, of course, are NE, SI13, and MMT.)

1	$\Box\, p \dashv p$	
2	$\Diamond\, p \dashv \Box\, \Diamond\, p$	$(p \dashv \Box\, p) \supset (\Diamond\, p \dashv p)$
3	$(p \dashv q) \dashv (\Box \sim q \dashv \Box \sim p)$	
4	$\sim\Box \sim p \dashv \Box \sim\Box \sim p$	2, MOE, RR
5	$\sim\Box\, p \dashv \Box \sim\Box\, p$	4, Subst $\sim p/p$, DN, RR
6	$(p \dashv \Box\, p) \dashv (\Box \sim\Box\, p \dashv \Box \sim p)$	3, Subst $\Box\, p/q$

* In *The Logic of Perfection* (Open Court Publishing Co., LaSalle, Ill.), 1962, chap. 2.

*7	$p \dashv3 \Box p$	ACP
*8	$\Box \sim\Box p \dashv3 \Box \sim p$	7, 6, SMP, IR
*9	$\sim\Box p \dashv3 \Box \sim p$	5, 8, SHS, IR
*10	$\sim\Box \sim p \dashv3 \Box p$	9, STransp, DN, RR
*11	$\Diamond p \dashv3 \Box p$	10, MOE, RR
*12	$\Diamond p \dashv3 p$	11, 1, SHS, IR
13	$(p \dashv3 \Box p) \supset (\Diamond p \dashv3 p)$	7–12, RCP

So far we are on purely logical ground. What we may call the ontological proof proper takes the theorem just proved

1     $(p \dashv3 \Box p) \supset (\Diamond p \dashv3 p)$

and adds to it two assumptions: "if the statement 'an absolutely perfect being exists' is true at all, it is necessarily true," or symbolically

2     $(\exists x) (Px) \dashv3 \Box (\exists x) (Px)$

and "It is possible that the statement 'an absolutely perfect being exists' is true":

3     $\Diamond (\exists x) (Px)$

We then substitute $(\exists x) (Px)$ for p in our theorem

4     $((\exists x) (Px) \dashv3 \Box (\exists x) (Px)) \supset (\Diamond (\exists x) (Px) \dashv3 (\exists x) (Px))$

Apply *modus ponens* to obtain

5     $\Diamond (\exists x) (Px) \dashv3 (\exists x) (Px)$

from 2 and 4, apply strict *modus ponens* again with 3 and 5 and obtain

6     $(\exists x) (Px)$

or "an absolutely perfect being exists."

The argument is valid, so that anyone who wishes to deny its conclusion must

(I) Deny the theorem, which will involve denying one or more of the three modal principles (or some other principle of logic used in the derivations).

(II) Deny the possibility of the existence of an absolutely perfect being, which amounts to asserting:

$$\sim\Diamond (\exists x) (Px)$$

(III) Deny that, if the statement "an absolutely perfect being exists" is true, then it is necessarily true. To deny an assertion of the form

$$p \dashv3 \Box p$$

it is convenient to replace the strict implication symbol by its definition:

$$\sim\Diamond\,(p\cdot\sim\Box\,p)$$

We can then deny the statement to obtain

$$\sim\sim\Diamond\,(p\cdot\sim\Box\,p)$$

and apply double negation to obtain

$$\Diamond\,(p\cdot\sim\Box\,p)$$

Substituting the proposition in question, it is clear that whoever *denies* that, if the statement "an absolutely perfect being exists" is true at all, then it is necessarily true thereby *asserts* that it is possible that the statement "an absolutely perfect being exists" is true, but not necessarily true. That is, to deny

$$(\exists x)\,(Px) \dashv3 \Box\,(\exists x)\,(Px)$$

is to assert

$$\Diamond\,((\exists x)\,(Px)\cdot\sim\Box\,(\exists x)\,(Px))$$

or the equivalent statement

$$\Diamond\,((\exists x)\,(Px)\cdot\Diamond\sim(\exists x)\,(Px))$$

which amounts to saying that possibly it is *factually* true that an absolutely perfect being exists. This, of course, is incompatible with (II), the second way of evading the conclusion of the argument by denial of the possibility of an absolutely perfect being. The assertion of

$$\Diamond\,((\exists x)\,(Px)\cdot\Diamond\sim(\exists x)\,(Px))$$

is compatible with the denial of some of the principles of modal logic mentioned earlier. Interestingly enough, if the strong reduction principle is accepted, this assertion is equivalent to the assertion

$$\Diamond\,(\exists x)\,(Px)\cdot\Diamond\sim(\exists x)\,(Px)$$

That is, "the existence of an absolutely perfect being and its nonexistence are both possible." (The principles involved are

$$\Diamond \, (p \cdot q) \dashv (\Diamond \, p \cdot \Diamond \, q)$$

which is provable in systems of medium strength, and the weak reduction principle,

$$\Diamond \, \Diamond \, p \dashv \Diamond \, p$$

which is, of course, provable in systems with the strong reduction principle.)

The argument used by supporters of the ontological argument from Anselm to Malcolm may be summarized as follows: The being under consideration is, by definition, absolutely perfect. But, if it were possible that this being did not exist, it would not be absolutely perfect. Therefore the supposition that it is true that such a being exists, but possible that it does not, leads to a contradiction. Therefore if such a being exists at all, it exists necessarily.

The contention that if it were possible that the being in question did not exist it would not be absolutely perfect has often been challenged. However, it does not seem unreasonable, at least *prima facie*, to make this part of the definition of "absolutely perfect," so what is meant by "absolutely perfect being" is a being such that, if it exists at all, then the statement that it exists is necessarily true. Consider the parallel case of a being such that, if it exists at all, the statement that it exists is universally disbelieved. I might call such a being, for obvious reasons, an "absolutely unknowable being." Whatever the problems raised by the existence of such a being, they are raised not by the form of the definition but by the qualification imposed in the consequent. There seems to be no objection in principle to defining a predicate by saying that, if x exists at all, then the statement that it exists is subject to certain qualifications (. . . is disbelieved, . . . is funny, and so on). So our definition is not, on the face of it nonsensical or self-contradictory.

But, unless possession of the property P involves nonsense or self-contradiction, how can it be true that it is impossible that the statement $(\exists x) \, (Px)$ be true? Therefore, as the conclusion of this line of argument, we seem to be faced with the following situation:

1. We seem to be free to define "absolutely perfect being" in the required way.

2. If we do so define this term, then the two required assumptions,

$$(\exists x) \, Px \dashv \Box \, (\exists x) \, (Px) \qquad \text{and} \qquad \Diamond \, (\exists x) \, (Px)$$

seem to follow directly from the definition.

3. In combination with the modal theorem proved previously, these two

assumptions are sufficient to prove (∃x) (Px). This, then, seems to be the strength of the modalized Ontological Argument.

So far formal logic can take us: the argument is unquestionably valid and the premises are plausible. The full meaning of the premises and their truth or falsity are matters for further philosophical discussion. Objections based on the fact that the strong reduction principle is used in Hartshorne's proof seemed to be met by a simpler proof (devised by me after discussing the earlier proof with Professor Hartshorne*) which did not use either the strong or the weak reduction principle. Unfortunately, this proof contained a simple logical error, which I only discovered later. Thus, I have discussed the earlier, valid, proof in this section. Portions of the unsuccessful proof are used in the exercises for Section 7.4.

DISCUSSION QUESTIONS

1. Do any of the truths of propositional modal logic discussed in this chapter seem to you to be doubtful or puzzling?

2. Are there any arguments, or steps in arguments, which are valid by the rules of propositional modal logic which you would want to challenge?

3. Are iterated modal operators ever found in ordinary speaking and writing? Is a statement like "It may be possible for me to come" an instance of the form ◇ ◇ p?

4. List some senses of "possible" other than "logically possible."

5. Do the rules of propositional modal logic seem to hold for those other senses?

---

* R. L. Purtill, "Ontological Modalities" in *Review of Metaphysics*, Vol. XXI, No. 2, December, 1967.

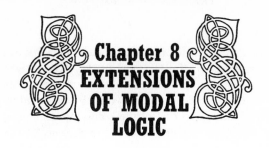

Chapter 8
EXTENSIONS
OF MODAL
LOGIC

The logical systems considered in this chapter lie on the frontiers of present-day logic. The questions about relations between modal operators and quantifiers discussed in Section 8.1 could not have been formulated before the development of predicate logic, which has taken place largely in the last hundred years. Also of comparatively recent date are the attempts to state systematically the logical relations between such terms as "knowledge" and "belief" or between "obligation" and "permissibility" which occupy us in the later sections. Logicians are still discussing and investigating these problems and, as in the case of second-order predicate logic, there are still many disagreements and uncertainties. I have tried to present some basic ideas in this area as clearly and simply as possible and to show how such systems of logic may be applicable to past and present philosophical problems.

Since the logic of such concepts as knowledge, or obligation has close parallels with modal logic, I have entitled this chapter "Extensions of Modal Logic." Some of the most interesting work in these areas has been done by

logicians who are also interested in modal logic. The work of two Scandina-
vian philosophers, Jaakko Hintikka and G. H. Von Wright, is especially
interesting, and the student interested in learning more about the subject
matter of this chapter is referred to the works by these authors cited in the
reading list. The outstanding critic of these developments is again W. V. O.
Quine. Some of his objections are discussed in Section 8.5.

8.1 QUANTIFIERS AND MODAL LOGIC

So long as quantified statements are mixed with modal operators in such
a way that no modal operator is within the scope of a quantifier, we have
not really left propositional modal logic. For example

$$\Box \; (x) \, (y) \, ((x = y) \supset (y = x))$$

is simply a substitution instance of $\Box$ p, and

$$\Diamond \; (\exists x) \, (\exists y) \, (x \neq y)$$

is simply a substitution instance of $\Diamond$ p, and so on.

Modal Operators within the Scope of Quantifiers

However, if we put a modal operator within the scope of a quantifier,
we have an extension of modal logic which in all probability cannot be
reduced to propositional modal logic. For example, if $Hx \# x$ is a human
and $Fx \# x$ is a female, then we can write

$$(x) \, (Hx \supset \Diamond \, Fx) \qquad \text{and} \qquad (\exists x) \, (Hx \cdot \Box \, Fx)$$

The first statement: "Any human may be a female" is very likely true,
while the second, "Some human is necessarily female," is quite possibly
false.* But we might want to say either of these things and to symbolize
them as part of an argument. Neither seems to be reducible in any way to
a statement in which the modal operator appears outside the quantifier.

To start with a simpler case, consider the possible shufflings of quantifiers
and modal operators possible with the propositional form Fx. The following
combinations are possible:

1.	$(x) \Box \, (Fx)$	2.	$\Box \, (x) \, (Fx)$
3.	$(x) \Diamond \, (Fx)$	4.	$\Diamond \, (x) \, (Fx)$
5.	$(\exists x) \Box \, (Fx)$	6.	$\Box \, (\exists x) \, (Fx)$
7.	$(\exists x) \Diamond \, (Fx)$	8.	$\Diamond \, (\exists x) \, (Fx)$

* In this section, where we often have to appeal to the intuitive feel for what makes sense in
English sentences, we will use "possibly" and "necessarily" in a somewhat wider sense than in
Chapter 7.

The even-numbered propositions are instances of the forms $\Box$ p and $\Diamond$ p and offer no problems. Of the odd-numbered statements, 1 implies 3, and 5 implies 7 by the modal square of opposition; 1 implies 5, and 3 implies 7 by the predicate logic square of opposition. (Similarly 2 implies 4 and 6, and also 4 and 6 imply 8.) Somewhat more controversial are the two equivalences and two implications:

$$\text{QME 1} \quad (x)\,\Box\,(Fx) \equiv \Box\,(x)\,(Fx)$$
$$\text{QME 2} \quad (\exists x)\,\Diamond\,(Fx \equiv \Diamond\,(\exists x)\,(Fx)$$
$$\text{QMI 1} \quad (\exists x)\,\Box\,(Fx) \dashv\!\!\!3\; \Box\,(\exists x)\,(Fx)$$
$$\text{QMI 2} \quad \Diamond\,(x)\,(Fx) \dashv\!\!\!3\;(x)\,\Diamond\,(Fx)$$

The case for these four depends on certain analogies with the equivalences and inferences

$$(x)\,(y)\,(Fxy) \equiv (y)\,(x)\,(Fxy)$$
$$(\exists x)\,(\exists y)\,(Fxy) \equiv (\exists y)\,(\exists x)\,(Fxy)$$
$$(\exists x)\,(y)\,(Fxy) \supset (y)\,(\exists x)\,Fxy$$

which are truths of predicate logic. However, all four quantifier–modal-operator statements are controversial. Consider an instance of QME 2 where $Fx \mathbin{\#} x$ is on fire. In this case

$$(\exists x)\,\Diamond\,(Fx) \equiv \Diamond\,(\exists x)\,Fx$$

would seem to say that "There is something which may be on fire" is equivalent to "There may be something on fire." As William Kneale points out,* "The first can be used to state that something is inflammable, and the second to say that our information does not rule out the possibility of a fire."

A similar difficulty arises with QM E1 if we let $Tx \mathbin{\#} x$ is a triangle and $Ax \mathbin{\#} x$ has three angles.

$$\Box\,(x)\,(Tx \supset Ax) \quad \text{and} \quad (x)\,\Box\,(Tx \supset Ax)$$

are both true, but do they mean the same? The second, of course, is equivalent to

$$(x)\,(Tx \dashv\!\!\!3\; Ax)$$

Does this mean the same as $\Box\,(x)\,(Tx \supset Ax)$ or not?

* *The Development of Logic* (Oxford University Press, New York), 1962, p. 615.

Despite intuitive difficulties, there are good reasons for thinking that all four of these questionable statements are true. Consider a universe with two individuals, a and b. As we saw in Chapter 5, in such a universe

$$(x)\,(Fx) \equiv (Fa \cdot Fb) \qquad (\exists x)\,(Fx) \equiv (Fa \lor Fb)$$

Now if we add modal operators, then $\square\,(x)\,(Fx) \equiv \square\,(Fa \cdot Fb)$ and, by modal operator distribution,

$$\square\,(Fa \cdot Fb) \equiv (\square Fa \cdot \square Fb) \qquad \text{therefore} \qquad \square\,(x)\,(Fx) \equiv (\square\,Fa \cdot \square\,Fb)$$

If, on the other hand, we start with $(x)\,\square\,(Fx)$, we can treat $\square\,Fx$ as a compound predicate and thereby show that

$$(x)\,\square\,(Fx) \equiv (x)\,(\square\,Fx) \qquad \text{and} \qquad (x)\,(\square\,Fx) \equiv (\square\,Fa \cdot \square Fb)$$

for a two-member universe. But since in general,

$$((p \equiv q) \cdot (q \equiv r)) \dashv 3 \ (p \equiv r)$$

we have shown $\square\,(x)\,(Fx) \equiv (x)\,\square\,(Fx)$ for a two-member universe. Presumably the process can be repeated for any sized universe, and thus in general

$$\square\,(x)\,(Fx) \equiv (x)\,\square\,(Fx)$$

Exactly parallel arguments hold for

$$\lozenge\,(\exists x)\,(Fx) \equiv (\exists x)\,\lozenge\,(Fx)$$
$$(\exists x)\,\square\,(Fx) \dashv 3\ \square\,(\exists x)\,(Fx)$$
$$\lozenge\,(x)\,(Fx) \dashv 3\ (x)\,\lozenge\,(Fx)$$

so that it would seem that all four can be justified.

The only thing which would prevent such justification would be some restriction on the distribution rules, and the only reason for such a restriction would seem to be certain intuitive counterexamples, such as Kneale's. However, there may be errors involved in these.

For example, we might challenge Kneale's assertion that $(\exists x)\,\lozenge\,(Fx)$ "can be used to state that something is inflammable." Surely "something is inflammable but not burning" would be better symbolized as

$$(\exists x)\,(\lozenge\,Fx \cdot {\sim}Fx)$$

and "something is inflammable and may be burning" would be better symbolized as

$$(\exists x)\,(\lozenge\,Fx \cdot \lozenge\,{\sim}Fx)$$

Neither of these is the same as $(\exists x) \Diamond (Fx)$. In fact, it can be plausibly maintained that "there is something which may be burning" and "there may be something which is burning" both say the same thing, namely, that a fire burning somewhere is a possibility. If we make the predicate $Fx \# x$ is *now* burning, this is even more plausible. "There is something which may now be burning" and "It may be that there is something burning now" seem to be equivalent and can be symbolized by

$$(\exists x) \Diamond (Fx) \quad \text{and} \quad \Diamond (\exists x) (Fx)$$

So far we have seen that two expressions with modal operators in the scope of quantifiers

$$(x) \Box (Fx) \quad \text{and} \quad (\exists x) \Diamond (Fx)$$

can be replaced by expressions with modal operators outside of quantifiers. But since the reverse of the expressions

$$(\exists x) \Box (Fx) \dashv \Box (\exists x) (Fx) \quad \text{and} \quad \Diamond (x) (Fx) \dashv (x) \Diamond (Fx)$$

do not hold,

$$(\exists x) \Box (Fx) \quad \text{and} \quad (x) \Diamond (Fx)$$

are not obviously equivalent to expressions without modal operators in the scope of quantifiers.

There seem to be other expressions also with modal operators within the scope of quantifiers which cannot be replaced by expressions without modal operators within the scope of quantifiers. For example, to replace

$$(x) (Hx \supset \Diamond Fx)$$

with an expression of the required kind we would presumably have to retain the predicates Hx and Fx along with some connective(s) and quantifier(s) and modal operator(s) outside the quantifier(s). But none of the following

1.	$\Diamond (x) (Fx \supset Hx)$	2.	$\Diamond (\exists x) (Fx \cdot Hx)$
3.	$\Box (x) (Fx \supset Hx)$	4.	$\Box (\exists x) (Fx \cdot Hx)$

seem satisfactory; (1) says that possibly every human is female, (2) that possibly some human is female, and so on.

The Parallel Argument

But, if we could not symbolize statements of this form, we could not analyze some very interesting arguments. For example, we might recall the argument from G. E. Moore discussed in Section 3.5. Remember that the key premise of this argument was "It is possible for a human being to be of the female sex" or "Any human being may be of the female sex." Is there any analysis of this premise, different from Moore's, which would save the validity of the parallel argument? I wish to consider a suggestion for such an alternative analysis.

The suggestion I wish to consider is the following: By "It is possible for a human being to be of the female sex" is meant "For any human being, it is *logically* possible that that human being be of the female sex." Or in symbols

$$(x)\,(Hx \supset \Diamond\, Fx)$$

where $Hx \not\equiv x$ is a human being and $Fx \not\equiv x$ is of the female sex. This is surely true, for to deny it is to assert that there is some human being who cannot possibly be of the female sex, that is,

$$(\exists x)\,(Hy) \cdot \sim\!\Diamond\, Fx)$$

which is the same as saying that there is some human being who is necessarily not of the female sex:

$$(\exists x)\,(Hx \cdot \Box \sim\! Fx)$$

But surely the sex of any individual is always a matter of contingent fact and never a matter of logical necessity. The parallel argument itself can now be symbolized as

$$(x)\,(Hx \supset \Diamond\, Fx)$$
$$\underline{\hspace{1em} Hm \hspace{3em}}$$
$$\Diamond\, Fm$$

The conclusion can be validly inferred from the premises by universal instantiation and modus ponens. Thus we have again a valid argument and in fact, the translation into symbolic form of Moore's valid syllogism, Since the premises are true, the conclusion must necessarily be true. However, this is not at all an embarrassing consequence if by $\Diamond\, Fm$ we mean only that it is logically possible that Moore is of the female sex. For example, it is quite compatible with the assertion that Moore is in fact a male and not of the female sex. In fact $\sim\! Fm \cdot \Diamond\, Fm$ would normally be understood simply as asserting that it was factually (and not logically) true that Moore was not of the female sex.

There might seem to be an air of paradox in asserting that Moore, a male, might be a female since this might be taken as implying that some male could be a female. This is to confuse the legitimate inference of

$$(\exists x)\,(\sim\! Fx \cdot \Diamond\, Fx) \qquad \text{from} \qquad \sim\! Fm \cdot \Diamond\, Fm$$

(by existential generalization) and the illegitimate passage from

$$\sim Fm \cdot \Diamond Fm \qquad to \qquad \Diamond \, (\exists x) \, (\sim Fx \cdot Fx)$$

or

$$(\exists x) \, \Diamond \, (\sim Fx \cdot Fx)$$

which, being contravalid modal propositions, cannot in fact be the conclusion of any valid inference.

Thus the alternative analysis of the crucial premise does not produce a version of the parallel argument which is a good argument and at the same time leads to the conclusion that, in any interesting sense, Moore may be of the female sex.

The Sceptic's Argument

A similar analysis may be applied to the second argument from Moore considered in Section 3.5, the one which we called the Sceptic's Argument. The crucial premise in the Sceptic's Argument might be interpreted as meaning: "For any experience of seeming to remember hearing the sound 'Russell' it is possible that that experience was not preceded by the sound 'Russell.'" Or, in symbols,

$$(x) \, (Sx \supset \Diamond \sim Px)$$

where $Sx \,\#\, x$ is an experience of seeming to remember a certain sound and $Px \,\#\, x$ is preceded by the sound in question. This premise must be considered true unless we wish to assert its contradictory,

$$(\exists x) \, (Sx \cdot \sim \Diamond \sim Px) \qquad \text{which is the same as} \qquad (\exists x) \, (Sx \cdot \Box \, Px)$$

That is, at least some experiences of this kind are necessarily preceded by the sound in question.

Would anyone wish to maintain this position? It might seem so, for someone might wish to claim that it is logically impossible that *all* experiences of seeming to remember a certain sound should not be preceded by the sound in question and that, therefore, some experiences of seeming to remember a certain sound must necessarily be preceded by the sound in question. Whatever the virtues of this claim, however, it does not lead to the conclusion that $(\exists x) \, (Sx \cdot \Box \, Px)$.

The original claim, that it is impossible that all experiences of seeming to remember should not be preceded, can be symbolized

$$\sim \Diamond \, (x) \, (Sx \supset \sim Px) \qquad \text{which is equivalent to} \qquad \Box \sim (x) \, (Sx \supset \sim Px)$$

which in turn is equivalent to

$$\square \, (\exists x) \sim (Sx \supset \sim Px) \qquad \text{and finally to} \qquad \square \, (\exists x) \, (Sx \cdot Px)$$

But this is neither equivalent to, nor does it imply $(\exists x) \, (Sx \cdot \square \, Px)$. Thus the assertion of

$$\sim \Diamond \, (x) \, (Sx \supset \sim Px)$$

gives no grounds for the assertion of

$$(\exists x) \, (Sx \cdot \square Px)$$

and indeed it would seem that it is always a matter of fact and never a matter of *logical* necessity whether or not a given sound precedes an experience of seeming to remember.

If we grant this and allow the premise $(x) \, (Sx \supset \Diamond \sim Px)$ being as true, then the argument will proceed as in the case of the parallel argument. It will be true in specific instances, and in those cases the argument

$$(x) \, (Sx \supset \Diamond \sim Px)$$
$$\underline{\qquad St \qquad}$$
$$\Diamond \sim Pt$$

(where t $\#$ this experience) will be a valid argument with true premises and prove the truth of the conclusion $\Diamond \sim Pt$.

But again, quite unembarrassingly, $\Diamond \sim Pt$ is quite compatible with Pt and indeed

$$Pt \cdot \Diamond \sim Pt$$

would be the standard way of saying that it was factually (and not logically) true that this experience was preceded by the sound in question. Nor need this have embarrassing consequences with regard to knowledge or certainty, since both knowledge or certainty are commonly claimed concerning factually true propositions.

Thus, the Sceptic's Argument may very well be valid and have true premises and therefore show that it is logically possible that an experience of seeming to remember was not preceded by the sound in question, without causing us any uneasiness about knowledge or certainty.

EXERCISES 8.1

A. Translate from symbols to English using the following dictionary:

Ax # x is an author   Bx # x has broad interests

1. $\Diamond (x)(Ax \supset Bx)$
2. $(x) \Diamond (Ax \supset Bx)$
3. $(x)(\Diamond Ax \supset Bx)$
4. $(x)(Ax \supset \Diamond Bx)$
5. $\Box (x)(Ax \supset Bx)$
6. $(x) \Box (Ax \supset Bx)$
7. $(x)(\Box Ax \supset Bx)$
8. $(x)(Ax \supset \Box Bx)$
9. $\Diamond (\exists x)(Ax \cdot Bx)$
10. $(\exists x) \Diamond (Ax \cdot Bx)$
11. $(\exists x)(\Diamond Ax \cdot Bx)$
12. $(\exists x)(Ax \cdot \Diamond Bx)$
13. $\Box (\exists x)(Ax \cdot Bx)$
14. $(\exists x) \Box (Ax \cdot Bx)$
15. $(\exists x)(\Box Ax \cdot Bx)$
16. $(\exists x)(Ax \cdot \Box Bx)$

B. Translate from English to symbols. Give your own dictionary. (Source: Aristotle, *Rhetoric*.)
1. If a man can be cured, he can also fall ill.
2. If of two similar things one is possible, so is the other.
3. If the harder of two things is possible, so is the easier.
4. If it is possible to have a beautiful house, it is possible to have a house.
5. Nothing impossible occurs or begins to occur.
6. If the end of a process is possible, so is the beginning.
7. Those things are possible of which the love or desire is natural.
8. No one loves or desires impossibilities.
9. Anything is possible, the first step in whose production depends on men or things which we can compel or persuade to produce it.
10. If anything is possible to inferior, weak, or stupid people, it is possible to their opposites.

8.2 EPISTEMIC LOGIC*

Let us now consider systems of logic which have a "knowledge" operator instead of a "necessity" operator as the strongest modal (more correctly, quasi-modal) operator. "Knows" can be considered as a two-place predicate, "＿＿ knows ＿＿," which asserts a relation between a person and a proposition. It could be written more strictly as "The person ＿＿ knows the proposition ＿＿." If we consider "knows" in this way, it will not be an operator which forms propositions out of propositions but will, rather, form propositions out of names, like all predicates. What appears in the second blank will be the name of a proposition, rather than a proposition. If we form a one-place predicate,

$$Kn \underline{\quad} \# \underline{\quad} \text{ is known by n}$$

where n is a given individual, the situation is in some respects the same: The gap should be filled with the name of a proposition. However, this

---

* Those familiar with the system of epistemic logic developed by Jaakko Hintikka in *Knowledge and Belief* (Cornell University Press, Ithaca, New York), 1962, should be warned that the quasi-modal system developed in this chapter is not Hintikka's system and that, although there are many parallels between the two systems, some apparent parallels are deceptive.

one-place predicate is much more like an operator, and it may be recalled that some logicians feel that $\Box$ and $\Diamond$ are predicates rather than true operators. Therefore, we will treat Kn as a quasi operator which we apply to propositions: The purist can understand it as containing understood quotation marks or some similar device to turn the propositions it is applied to into names of propositions. We will not further specify n, so long as it is always the same individual it does not matter for present purposes which individual it is.

Now Kn sounds promising as a quasi-modal operator (or quasi-modal quasi operator), for one of the basic implications of any modal system

$$\Box\, p \dashv 3\, p$$

seems to have a parallel in

$$EI\, 1 \qquad Knp \dashv 3\, p$$

that is, "if n knows p, then p is true," which is generally accepted as an epistemological truism.

However, when we look for a weak quasi-modal operator, we run into difficulties. The first candidate we think of is "n believes ——." But the quasi operator Bn does not work in either of the formulas parallel to the modal logic formulas

$$p \dashv 3 \Diamond\, p \qquad \text{or} \qquad \Diamond\, p \equiv\, \sim\Box \sim p$$

Neither of the two formulas

$$p \dashv 3\, Bnp \qquad \text{or} \qquad Bnp \equiv\, \sim Kn \sim p$$

is true or even plausible. The case is worse than this: No simple word or phrase in English seems to be substitutable for the weak operator in a quasi modal epistemic system.

The best we seem able to do is a phrase such as "for all n knows ——," which we will symbolize as Fn. By this quasi operator we shall mean precisely a phrase such that it is true to assert the two propositions

$$EI\, 2 \qquad p \dashv 3\, Fnp$$
$$EE\, 1 \qquad Fnp \equiv\, \sim Kn \sim p$$

The Square of Opposition for Knowledge

The equivalence tells us that by asserting "For all n knows p" we assert just "It is false that n knows it is false that p," and the implication reminds us that "if p is true, n cannot know $\sim p$" where $\sim p \dashv 3\, \sim Knp$ is the contrapositive of Knp $\dashv$ p, so "if p is true, then for all n knows p is true." The meaning of Fnp does not exclude Knp; it is, in fact, its subaltern, and we can draw a full or Aristotelian square of opposition for Knp and Fnp (Figure 8.1).

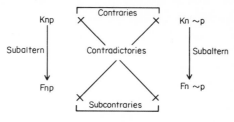

Figure 8.1

We also have a parallel to the equivalence $\square$ p $\equiv$ $\sim\diamond$ $\sim$p, which is

$$\text{EE 2} \qquad Knp \equiv \sim Fn \sim p$$

which follows directly from the definition of Fn.

Epistemic Implication and Equivalence

We can now define epistemic implication and epistemic equivalence symbolized as $\mathbf{E}^n$ and $\mathbf{\exists E}^n$ respectively and defined by the following equivalences:

$$\text{EE 3} \qquad (p \ \mathbf{E}^n \ q) \equiv Kn \ (p \supset q)$$
$$\text{EE 4} \qquad (p \ \mathbf{\exists E}^n \ q) \equiv Kn \ (p \equiv q)$$

Given these definitions, it is extremely plausible to assert that there is a parallel in epistemic logic to the characteristic S.3 implication, SI 10:

$$(p \dashv q) \dashv (\diamond \ p \dashv \diamond \ q)$$

The parallel implication for epistemic logic would presumably be

$$\text{EI 3} \qquad (p \ \mathbf{E}^n \ q) \dashv (Fnp \ \mathbf{E}^n \ Fnq)$$

This can be read as follows: "If n knows that if p is true then q is true, then this logically implies that n knows that if it is true that for all he knows p is true then it is true that for all he knows q is true." It might be objected that an abnormally stupid person might know the antecedent of this conditional without knowing the consequent. However, replacing Fnp by $\sim Kn \sim p$, we can see that what he would fail to know by failing to know the consequent would be "if it is false that n knows p is false, then it is false

271

that n knows q is false." To know that p ⊃ q and to fail to know this would be to know that p ⊃ q was true and fail to know that ~q ⊃ ~p was true.

Still, it might be argued that some persons fail to see the relation between p ⊃ q and ~q ⊃ ~p. So that perhaps not every person could be substituted for n. The person n in Knp, and Fnp must be a rational or logical or intelligent sort of person. This is not necessarily a weakness in epistemic logic: Any attempt to create an epistemic logic which will apply equally to all persons may be doomed.

More controversial yet is the possibility of a parallel to the characteristic S.4 proposition:

$$\Box\, p \dashv 3 \,\Box\, \Box\, p$$

The parallel for epistemic logic would be

*EI 4   Knp ⊣3 KnKnp

Or "if n knows p he knows that he knows p." (The asterisk as usual, indicates a questionable assumption.) This is a matter of current debate among epistemologists and cannot be settled without examination of the philosophical arguments on both sides.

Finally, we can ask whether there is a plausible parallel to the characteristic S.5 proposition,

$$\Diamond\, \Box\, p \dashv 3 \,\Box\, p$$

The parallel would presumably be

**EI 5   FnKnp ⊣3 Knp

This can be read "if for all n knows he knows p, then he does know p" (where the double asterisk indicates an additional questionable assumption). This sounds extremely implausible at first, but if we accept Knp ⊣3 KnKnp, a case can be made for EI 5. If we never know without knowing we know, presumably n can always give a yes or no answer to questions of the form "Do you know p?" If the answer is "no," then n doesn't know p, since he can't know p without knowing he knows it (~ KnKnp ⊣3 ~ Knp transposes to Knp⊣3 KnKnp). But if the answer is "yes," then it is false that he knows that it is false that he knows p, which is equivalent to saying that, for all he knows, he knows p. In other words, the only conditions which make FnKnp true also make Knp true. Again, however, this is a question which can be threshed out only by philosophical discussion.

Doxastic Logic

Earlier we dropped Bn out of contention as a weak quasi-modal operator with Kn. But Bn may well be a strong quasi-modal operator in a different kind of epistemic (or doxastic) logic. The chief problem is a parallel to the modal proposition:

$$\Box \, p \dashv 3 \, p$$

The apparent parallel to this, Bnp $\dashv 3$ p, is plainly false; believing something is no guarantee of its truth. However, it might be claimed that if anyone believes something he *acts* as if it were true. If we let Anp symbolize "n acts as if p were true," then the proposition

$$\text{DI 1} \qquad \text{Bnp} \dashv 3 \text{ Anp}$$

is at least plausible. (It could be claimed, however, that what we ought to examine in epistemic logic is certain logical relations, which hold regardless of how people behave.)

Square of Opposition for Belief

We now need a weak operator to fit into the formulas

$$\underline{\quad\quad}np \equiv \; \sim Bn \sim p$$
$$Anp \dashv 3 \underline{\quad\quad}np$$

Again there seems no word or phrase in common use which expresses the needed idea. So let us use the phrase "n doesn't disbelieve_____" symbolized as Dn, which means just what it needs to mean to make true the two propositions:

$$\text{DE 1} \qquad \text{Dnp} \equiv \; \sim Bn \sim p$$
$$\text{DI 2} \qquad \text{Anp} \dashv 3 \text{ Dnp}$$

Figure 8.2

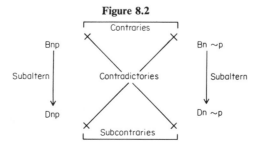

We can see (Figure 8.2) that a full square of opposition holds for Bnp and Dnp and that

DE 2   Bnp ≡ ~Dn ~p   holds if   DE 1   Dnp ≡ ~Bn ~p

does. Furthermore, we can define two connectives as follows: *doxastic implication* symbolized as $\rhd^n$ and *doxastic equivalence* symbolized as $\lhd \rhd^n$;

$$\text{DE 2} \quad (p \rhd^n q) \equiv Bn (p \supset q)$$
$$\text{DE 3} \quad (p \lhd \rhd^n q) \equiv Bn (p \equiv q)$$

The proposition parallel to the characteristic S.3 proposition will be

$$\text{DI 3} \quad (p \rhd^n q) \dashv 3 (Dnp \rhd^n Dnq)$$

which is plausibly true. The parallel to the characteristic S.4 proposition will be

$$\text{*DI 4} \quad Bnp \dashv 3 BnBnp$$

which is at least plausible. The parallel to the characteristic S.5 proposition will be

$$\text{**DI 5} \quad DnBnp \dashv 3 Bnp$$

which is more controversial. At any rate, we can see that there is some possibility of building up a variant of epistemic logic in which Bn is the strong quasi-modal operator.

Epistemic and Doxastic Relations

Supposing that our epistemic and doxastic systems are both workable, there seems to be a connection between them via the following proposition:

$$\text{KB 1} \quad Knp \dashv 3 Bnp$$

This proposition is especially plausible for those who define knowledge as true belief together with adequate grounds or conclusive grounds for the belief, but epistemologists with other views of belief may also find it acceptable.

We can fairly conclude, I think, that our version of epistemic logic has considerable plausibility, considered as a systematic account of the relations of belief and knowledge for a (perhaps somewhat idealized) rational or reasonable man. In fact, we might look at epistemic logic in a somewhat different way. If we let

$$Rx \# x \text{ is a rational person} \qquad Px \# x \text{ is a proposition}$$

then any of our implications could be stated in the same general form as the example:

$$(x)\,(y)\,((\mathrm{R}x \cdot \mathrm{P}y) \supset (\mathrm{K}xy \supset \mathrm{B}xy))$$

From this would follow

$$(x)\,(y)\,(\mathrm{P}y \supset (\sim(\mathrm{K}xy \supset \mathrm{B}xy) \supset \sim \mathrm{R}x))$$

In fact, our various implications and equivalences, stated in this way, might be regarded as a statement of the necessary conditions of rationality in knowledge and belief, a sort of indirect definition of "rational person."

One final note—by way of implication,

$$\text{DI 1} \qquad \mathrm{Bnp} \dashv 3 \text{ Anp}$$

and its contrapositive,

$$\sim \mathrm{Anp} \dashv 3 \sim \mathrm{Bnp} \qquad \text{we can derive} \qquad \sim \mathrm{Anp} \dashv 3 \sim \mathrm{Knp}$$

That is, if one does not act as if a statement is true, he does not know that it is true. It is first necessary to note what a wide variety of behavior "acting as if p were true" can cover. If a diner knows that the salt shaker is filled with arsenic, he normally would act as if this were true by not shaking the arsenic on his food. But consider such cases as where he plans suicide or where he is a spy trying to deceive hidden observers. Still, if the diner wishes to live, does not wish to eat food sprinkled with arsenic, and so on, and nevertheless sprinkles the stuff on his food and eat its with gusto, then it would seem that he did not really believe, and therefore did not really know, that the shaker was filled with arsenic. If this is not the case, then it seems safe to say that he is not rational. For it would seem that a characteristic of the rational man is that his actions as well as his beliefs conform to the world as it is.

Hintikka's Epistemic and Doxastic System

It may be worthwhile, in conclusion, to discuss the parallels of our system with that developed by Jaakko Hintikka in *Knowledge and Belief* (Cornell University Press, Ithaca, New York), 1962. Hintikka's strong epistemic operator and strong doxastic operator are supposed to be merely Kn_____ and Bn_____ respectively. However his weak epistemic operator is the complex idea "it is consistent with everything n knows that . . ." which can be symbolized as Pn_____. However, unlike our Fnp, it is not the case that Pnp is equivalent to $\sim \mathrm{Kn} \sim \mathrm{p}$. Rather, the meaning of Pnp has to be gathered from certain rules of Hintikka's system. One of these might be expressed in our notation as follows:

$$(\mathrm{Knp} \cdot \mathrm{Pnq}) \dashv 3 \Diamond (\mathrm{Knp} \cdot \mathrm{q})$$

for any two propositions p and q. As can be seen, this amounts to a requirement that, if it is possible, for all n knows, that p, then p must be consistent
not only with each proposition n knows, but also consistent with his knowing
that proposition.

Similarly, in his doxastic logic Hintikka's weak doxastic operator is the
complex notion "it is consistent with everything that n believe that . . ."
which can be symbolized as Cn____. Thus, unlike Dnp, Cnp is not equivalent
to $\sim$ Bn $\sim$p, and Hintikka's doxastic logic has a rule which can be expressed
as

$$(\text{Bn}p \cdot \text{Cn}q) \dashv 3 \Diamond (\text{Bn}p \cdot q)$$

One interesting consequence of this rule is that, if a proposition is consistent
with everything that some person believes, it must be logically possible. This,
in conjunction with a rule which can be expressed as

$$\sim \text{Cn}p \dashv 3 \sim \text{Bn}p$$

has the consequence that

$$\sim \Diamond \; p \dashv 3 \; \sim \text{Bn}p$$

for any n and p; that is, no one can believe impossible things. This in itself
might be plausible, but Leonard Linsky has shown* that these same rules can
be used to show that it is provable in Hintikka's system that one person
cannot believe that another person believes an impossible proposition, even
where neither of them knows it is impossible! This seems to be strongly
counterintuitive, and it is currently debated whether this difficulty is a serious
defect in Hintikka's doxastic logic.†

Hintikka's epistemic logic does not suffer from a parallel weakness since
of course it is completely acceptable to say that impossible (that is, necessarily
false) statements cannot be known or known to be known. However, there
are other difficulties in Hintikka's epistemic logic. It turns out that, given
Hintikka's approach to epistemic logic, we must be regarded as knowing, in
a certain sense, all the logical consequences of what we know. We have discussed the difficulties involved in such a position already. It also turns out
that, although

$$\text{Ka}p \dashv 3 \text{KaKa}p$$

does not have the position of a rule or axiom in Hintikka's system, it is
provable in that system. Thus Hintikka's epistemic logic is necessarily a
system like S.4, although it can be shown that it is not a system like S.5.

---

* "Interpreting Doxastic Logic," *Journal of Philosophy*, Vol. LXV, No. 17, 1968.

† Those who wish to pursue the question further may consult my paper "Believing the Impossible" in *Ajatus*, Spring 1970, and Professor Hintikka's paper in the same issue of *Ajatus*.

Our system of epistemic and doxastic logic on the other hand, is weaker than Hintikka's unless we choose to add EI 4 or EI 5 and DI 4 or DI 5 to it, but it is also free from some of the difficulties of Hintikka's epistemic and doxastic logics. So, while Hintikka's pioneering work made it possible to develop my system and most other systems of epistemic logic currently being discussed, it may not be the most convenient or natural system. The system described in this book is original to the extent that it is the only one known to me which takes seriously the parallel between modal and epistemic logic and the resemblance between both of these and doxastic logic.

EXERCISES 8.2

A. (a) Translate from symbols to English, where n is any individual and p and q are any statements.

(b) Comment briefly on the truth or falsity of each statement.

(c) Give an instance of each formula, in which n, p, and q are replaced by given persons and propositions, for example, "If I know snow is white, then I know snow is white or red."

(d) Use these instances from part (c) to support your answers to part (b).

1. $Knp \prec Kn(p \lor q)$ 2. $Knp \prec Kn(q \supset p)$
3. $(Knp \cdot Knq) \prec Kn(p \cdot q)$ 4. $(Kn(p \supset q) \cdot Knp) \prec Knq$
5. $(Kn(p \supset q) \cdot Kn(q \supset r)) \prec Kn(p \supset r)$

B. Translate Exercises 1–5, following, from English to symbols, using the dictionary:

   $g \,\#\, God$ $Px \,\#\, x$ is a person $Ox \,\#\, x$ is an object of knowledge

1. God knows everything.
2. No one but God knows everything.
3. If any person knew everything, that person would be God.
4. If any person does not know something, then that person is not God.
5. If any person is not God, then there is something that person does not know.

Using these symbolizations, answer the following questions:

6. How are 1 and 4 related?
7. How are 2 and 5 related?
8. Prove that 3 follows from 1 and 2.
9. Do both 4 and 5 follow from 3?

C. In a recent book on epistemic logic, the author uses sentences 1–5 below as examples. His a is like our n, an arbitrary individual, and p is an arbitrary proposition. Translate 1–5 into our symbolism. (Source: J. Hintikka, *Knowledge and Belief*, Cornell University Press, 1962.)

1. a knows whether p.
2. a does not know that p.
3. a does not know whether p.
4. It is possible, for all a knows, that p.
5. It is compatible with everything that a believes that p.

Using these symbolizations, decide whether the following statements by this author are true for our symbolism.

6. Statement 4 means the same as "It does not follow from what a knows that not-p."
7. The negation of 4 is not "It is impossible, for all a knows, that p."
8. The negation of 4 is "From what a knows, it follows that not-p."
9. The form of 1 is a disjunction, that of 3, a conjunction.
10. It is not correct to translate 2 as ~Kap.

8.3 DEONTIC LOGIC

The basic problem of deontic logic—the logic of ethical terms such as "obligatory" and "permissible"—is that it is *actions* to which ethical terms seem to apply, whereas the rest of logic is designed to deal with *statements*.

Restrictions

In order to explore some analogies between deontic logic, epistemic logic, and modal logic, we must somehow make the operators of deontic logic apply to statements. But we must be very careful as to which statements we choose. They must be statements descriptive of actions by human beings; for it makes sense to say "It is obligatory that n supports his wife," but it makes no sense to say, for example, "It is obligatory that it rain for 15 minutes today." We do not think of the factors that cause rain as moral agents nor as the sort of things which can have obligations. (If we did think this, such a statement would make sense. An ancient Roman might say "The priest of Jupiter Pluvius, who speaks for the god, promised me 15 minutes of rain today. So it is obligatory that it rain for 15 minutes today.")

Furthermore, the human being must be capable of acting as a moral agent: If n is in a coma or in prison he cannot be obliged to support his wife. In fact it is plausible to make the subjects of obligations to be choices rather than actions. We shall use the usual terminology and speak of agents being obliged to *do* certain things rather than being obliged to choose to do those things, but this is merely a shorter form used for convenience.

Thus, we will make our chief quasi-modal operator for deontic logic out of the predicate "it is obligatory for ____ that ____," where the first gap must be filled by the name of a person and the second by the name of one of a certain restricted class of propositions, those which describe a deliberate or intentional action to be performed by the person named. Let this predicate be symbolized by O. Then if j ≠ Jones and S ≠ Jones chooses to support his wife, we could write

$$OjS$$

which would be read "it is obligatory for Jones that Jones choose to support his wife" or, more simply though more misleadingly, "Jones is obliged to support his wife."

Throughout most of what follows we will use an arbitrary individual, as we did for epistemic logic. Initially we will put no restriction on the sort of individual to speak of, but in due course we will consider the effect of requiring n to be a "moral" individual, just as we required a rational individual for epistemic logic.

Implications and Equivalences

We can now state certain equivalences and implications for an arbitrary individual n and any proposition p which meets the conditions given above. The first equivalence defines a weak operator "it is permissible for ____ that ____" symbolized as Pnp

$$Onp \equiv \sim Pn \sim p$$

This is to say that, if it is obligatory for n that he choose to perform the action described by p, then it is not permissible for n that he not choose to perform the action described by p, and vice versa. "Not choosing to" includes two sorts of actions: deliberately choosing some incompatible action and not making any choice. Thus, if one has an obligation, it is not permissible *either* to choose to do something incompatible with one's obligation *or* to simply "let it slide."

The parallel equivalence

$$Pnp \equiv \sim On \sim p$$

says that, if it is permissible that n choose to perform the action described by p, then it is not obligatory for him not to choose to perform the action described by p, and vice versa. That is, if it is permissible for him to choose the action in question he is *neither* obliged to choose an incompatible action *nor* obliged to make no choice.

It would seem plausible to define two connectives, obligational implication and obligational equivalence, as follows:

$$(p \looparrowright^n q) \equiv (Onp \multimap Onq)*$$
$$(p \looparrowright^n q) \equiv (Onp \equiv Onq)$$

The superscript n in the $\looparrowright^n$ and $\looparrowright^n$ symbols remind us that obligations apply to assignable individuals.

The two symbols can be read as follows: $p \looparrowright^n q$ can be translated "that n does what is described by p *obliges* n to do what is described by q" and $p \looparrowright^n q$ can be read as "that n does what is described by p obliges n to do what

---

* The difference between this equivalence and its parallels in epistemic and doxastic logic is due to a doubt about the meaningfulness of such expressions as On $(p \supset q)$.

is described by q, and vice versa." Notice that our somewhat restricted notation has no way of saying that an action by someone else creates an obligation for n. This is a defect which perhaps should be remedied.

Square of Opposition for Deontic Logic

Provided that everything that is obligatory is permissible, which seems reasonable, then we can write the implications

$$Onp \dashv 3\ Pnp \quad \text{and} \quad On \sim p \dashv 3\ Pn \sim p$$

From the two equivalences above we can show that

$$Onp \quad \text{and} \quad Pn \sim p$$

as well as

$$On \sim p \quad \text{and} \quad Pnp$$

are contradictories. We thus have a full square of opposition for deontic operators (Figure 8.3).

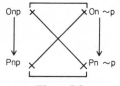

Figure 8.3

So far, you will note, we have had no parallels to the modal implications

$$\square\ p \dashv 3\ p \quad \text{and} \quad p \dashv 3 \lozenge\ p$$

Now obviously

$$Onp \dashv 3\ p \quad \text{and} \quad p \dashv 3\ Pnp$$

do not hold for all persons whose names might be substituted for n. People fail to perform actions which are obligatory and do perform actions which are not permissible. However, we might explore the possibility of speaking of a "moral individual" or "morally responsible person." If M ⧣ is a morally responsible individual, A ⧣ is an action, and D ⧣ deliberately chooses to do _____, then it might seem plausible to require that

$$(x)\ (y)\ ((Mx \cdot Ay) \supset (OxDxy \supset Dxy))$$

and

$$(x)\,(y)\,((Mx \cdot Ay) \supset (Dxy \supset PxDxy))$$

and these would be parallel to the modal statements

$$\Box\, p \prec p \quad\text{and}\quad p \prec \Diamond\, p$$

We could also ask about parallels to the modal statements

$$(p \prec q) \prec (\Diamond\, p \prec \Diamond\, p) \quad\text{and}\quad (p \prec q) \prec (\Box \sim q \prec \Box \sim p)$$

The following two statements seem to be parallel in some respects:

$$(p \circ\!\!\to^n q) \prec (Pnp \prec Pnq) \quad\text{and}\quad (p \circ\!\!\to^n q) \prec (On \sim q \prec On \sim p)$$

In words these are: "If doing p obliges n to do q, then, if it is permissible that n do p, it is permissible that n do q" and "If doing p obliges n to do q, then, if it is obligatory for n not to do q, it is obligatory for n not to do p." Both seem intuitively satisfactory. I have written the two statements in this way rather than as

$$(p \circ\!\!\to^n q) \prec (Pnp \circ\!\!\to^n Pnp) \quad\text{and}\quad (p \circ\!\!\to^n q) \prec (On \sim q \circ\!\!\to^n On \sim p)$$

since the two consequents are equivalent to

$$OnPnp \prec OnPnq \quad\text{and}\quad OnOn \sim q \prec OnOn \sim p$$

and it does not seem that the propositions Pnp, On $\sim$ q, and so on, belong to that very restricted class of statements to which it makes sense to apply the quasi operators On and Pn. The same criticism applies to

$$Onp \prec OnOnp \quad\text{and}\quad PnOnp \prec Onp$$

since statements that an obligation exists do not seem to be the sort of statements to which the quasi operators On and Pn can meaningfully be applied.

In sum then, the difficulties of making a quasi-modal system out of deontic logic seem even more formidable than those of making a quasi-modal system out of epistemic logic. In both cases, however, the possible rewards for success are great: Arguments of great interest in epistemology and ethics might be clarified and tested. It seems, then, that logicians should continue their efforts to formalize deontic and epistemic logic, despite the formidable difficulties.

EXERCISES 8.3

A. (a) Translate from symbols to English, where n is any individual and p and q are any statements which meet the appropriate conditions.

(b) Comment briefly on the truth or falsity of each statement.

(c) Give an instance of each formula in which n, p, and q are replaced by given persons and propositions for example, "If I am obliged to mail this letter, I am obliged to mail it or burn it."

(d) Use these instances to support your answers to part (b).

1. Onp $\prec$ On (p v q)   2. Onp $\prec$ (Onq $\supset$ Onp)
3. (Onp $\cdot$ Onq) $\prec$ On (p $\cdot$ q)   4. (Onp $\cdot$ (p $\circ\!\!\rightarrow^n$ q)) $\prec$ Onq
5. ((p $\circ\!\!\rightarrow^n$ q) $\cdot$ (q $\circ\!\!\rightarrow^n$ r) $\prec$ (p $\circ\!\!\rightarrow^n$ r)

B. Translate from English to symbols, where

F $\#$ n flies now   L $\#$ n pays later

1. If flying now obliges n to pay later, then, if it is permissible for n to fly now, it is permissible for n to pay later.
2. If flying now obliges n to pay later, then, if it is obligatory for n to fly now, it is not permissible for n not to pay later.
3. If flying now obliges n to pay later, then, if it is not permissible for n to pay later, he is obliged not to fly now.
4. If flying now is permissible for n but paying later is not permissible for him, then it cannot be that flying now obliges n to pay later.
5. If flying now is obligatory for n but it is permissible for n not to pay later, then it cannot be true that not paying later obliges n to not fly now.

C. In a discussion of deontic logic a contemporary logician uses Exercises 1–5, following, as examples. (a) Translate them into our symbolism; (b) comment on their truth or falsity. (Source: A. N. Prior, *Formal Logic*, Oxford University Press, New York, 1962.)

1. If we are obliged to do A then, if our doing A implies that we are obliged to do B, we are obliged to do B.
2. We ought to do what we ought to do.
3. If the doing of A and B jointly necessitates (that is, strictly implies) the doing of C, then, if we do A and are obliged to do B, we are obliged to do C.
4. If doing both C and not C necessitates doing C, then if we do C but ought not to do C, we ought to do C.
5. If loving God and our neighbour necessitates riding a bicycle, then, if we ought to love God and our neighbor, we ought to ride a bicycle.

8.4 MIXED MODALITIES

In this section we will take a brief look at some of the possibilities for clarification and argumentation which result from the availability of modal, epistemic, and deontic logic. We will treat the epistemic and deontic quasi operators more or less as ordinary predicates, remembering their peculiarities. Thus the epistemic quasi operators

Kxy $\#$ x knows y   Bxy $\#$ x believes y
Fxy $\#$ for all x knows, y   Dxy $\#$ x doesn't disbelieve y

all state relations between persons and propositions. Thus we will allow the subject variables of predicate logic to range over propositions as well as over persons, places, times, and so forth, and, where it is obvious that we are talking of propositions, we will not bother to make this explicit.

Also, where we are using epistemic and deontic predicates when it is obvious that we are talking of persons, we will not bother to state *this* explicitly. Thus,

$$(x)\ (y)\ (Kxy \supset Bxy)$$

is a short form of

$$(x)\ (y)\ ((Hx \cdot Py) \supset (Kxy \supset Bxy))$$

where Hx $\#$ x is a person and Px $\#$ x is a proposition. We shall also sometimes insert propositions of predicate logic into the blank reserved for propositions in epistemic and deontic predicates, for example,

$$(\exists x)\ (Hx \cdot KxHx)$$

(That is, "Some human knows he is human.") Here Hx occupies the proposition blank in Kx _____, and its variable is bound by the same quantifier as the x in Kx _____.

The deontic quasi operators

Oxy $\#$ x is obliged to choose what is described by y
Pxy $\#$ x is permitted to choose what is described by y

have the restriction described in Section 8.2: The second blank is occupied by a proposition but can only sensibly be occupied by a proposition describing something which can be chosen. In some cases this restriction does not come to the fore. A statement which would be asserted by many moralists is that, if an action is obligatory, it must be logically possible to do what is chosen. This might be symbolized as follows: Dxy $\#$ person x does what is described by proposition y.

$$(x)\ (y)\ (Oxy \supset \Diamond Dxy)$$

Literally this is "For any person x and any proposition y, if x is obliged to choose what is described by y, then it must be logically possible that y be done." Thus we can show that, if a proposition describes an action which cannot possibly be done, it cannot possibly describe something one is obliged to choose. No further investigation is needed: This holds simply by contraposing the statement above.

$$(x)\ (y)\ (\sim\!\Diamond Dxy \supset \sim Oxy)$$

However, the seemingly plausible statement

$$(x)\,(y)\,(\diamond\ \mathrm{D}xy \supset \diamond\ \mathrm{O}xy)$$

(that is, "if a proposition describes an action which can possibly be done, then it is possible that one may be obliged to choose what is described by it") cannot be true without qualification. Otherwise we could argue as follows: Let m represent a proposition describing some forbidden but possible action such as murder.

1	$(x)\,(y)\,(\diamond\ \mathrm{D}xy \supset \diamond\ \mathrm{O}x)$	$(x)\,(\diamond\ \mathrm{O}xm)$
2	$(x)\,(\diamond\ \mathrm{D}xm)$	
3	$(y)\,(\diamond\ \mathrm{D}\dot{x}y \supset \diamond\ \mathrm{O}\dot{x}y)$	1, UI
4	$\diamond\ \mathrm{D}\dot{y}m \supset \diamond\ \mathrm{O}\dot{x}m$	1, UI
5	$\diamond\ \mathrm{D}\dot{x}m$	2, UI
6	$\diamond\ \mathrm{O}\dot{x}m$	4, 5, MP
7	$(x)\,(\diamond\ \mathrm{O}xm)$	6, UG Q.E.D.

But murder is not the sort of thing which we could possibly be morally obliged to choose. However, if we let $\mathrm{M}x \not\equiv x$ is a proposition which describes an action which one might permissibly make the subject of a moral choice, then

$$(x)\,(y)\,((\mathrm{M}y \cdot \diamond\ \mathrm{D}xy) \supset \diamond\ \mathrm{O}xy)$$

may indeed be true.

Obligation and Necessity

Let us now consider some statements and arguments which can be clarified by the use of mixed modalities. Some moralists have claimed that, if anyone believes that he is obliged to do something, then he is obliged to do it.

1    $(x)\,(y)\,(\mathrm{B}x\mathrm{O}xy \supset \mathrm{O}xy)$

Now plainly some persons do believe that they have obligations

2    $(\exists x)\,(\exists y)\,(\mathrm{B}x\mathrm{O}xy)$

and by the following series of steps we can show that someone is obliged to do something, or in other words, that some obligations exist:

3	$\mathrm{B}\dot{x}\mathrm{O}\dot{x}\dot{y} \supset \mathrm{O}\dot{x}\dot{y}$	1, UI
4	$\mathrm{B}\dot{x}\mathrm{O}\dot{x}\dot{y}$	2, UI
5	$\mathrm{O}\dot{x}\dot{y}$	3, 4, MP, IR
6	$(\exists x)\,(\exists y)\,(\mathrm{O}xy)$	5, EG

Descartes' Scepticism

Another interesting argument can be found in a book by H. A. Prichard.*
In examining Descartes' scepticism, Prichard argues as follows:

1. We are certain of certain things, for example, that we are wondering
what is going to happen next . . . , that a three-sided figure is three angled . . . ,
and so on.

2. To be certain of something is to know it.

3. To know something is one thing, to believe something is another.

4. When we know something we either do or can directly know that we
are knowing it, and when we believe something we can know that we are
believing it and not knowing it.

From these premises Prichard concludes that "we know that in certain
instances of its use our intelligence is not defective, so that Descartes' difficulties fall to the ground." For present purposes we can say that "Descartes'
difficulties" amounted to the following statement: "We can never know the
truth of any statement except the statement 'I think; therefore, I exist.'"
Prichard's conclusion, then, will be the denial of this statement. Using the
following dictionary

$$Cxy \; \# \; x \text{ is certain of } y$$
$$c \; \# \text{ the proposition "I think, therefore, I exist"}$$

we can symbolize as follows:

1     $(x)\,(\exists y)\,(Cxy \cdot (y \neq c))$
2     $(x)\,(y)\,(Cxy \dashv 3\; Kxy)$
3     $(x)\,(y)\, \sim(Kxy \equiv Bxy)$
4     $(x)\,(y)\,(Kxy \dashv 3\; (KxKxy \vee \Diamond\, KxKxy))$
5     $(x)\,(y)\,(Bxy \dashv 3\; (KxBxy \vee \Diamond\, KxBxy))$

and reason to the conclusion

$$\sim(x)\,(y)\,((y \neq c) \dashv 3\; \sim\Diamond\, Kxy)$$

by the following steps:

6	$C\dot{x}\dot{y} \cdot (\dot{y} \neq c)$	1, VI, EI
7	$C\dot{x}\dot{y} \dashv 3\; K\dot{x}\dot{y}$	2, UI, EI
8	$K\dot{x}\dot{y} \dashv 3\; (K\dot{x}K\dot{x}\dot{y} \vee \Diamond\, K\dot{x}K\dot{x}\dot{y})$	4, VI, EI
9	$C\dot{x}\dot{y}$	6, Simp, IR
10	$K\dot{x}\dot{y}$	9, 7, SMP, IR
11	$K\dot{x}K\dot{x}\dot{y} \vee \Diamond\, K\dot{x}K\dot{x}\dot{y}$	8, 10, SMP, IR

* *Knowledge and Perception* (Oxford University Press, New York), 1950.

We must now introduce two steps which we will prove as subproofs (see below):

12	$K\dot{x}K\dot{x}\dot{y} \dashv3 \diamond K\dot{x}\dot{y}$	} subproofs
13	$\diamond K\dot{x}K\dot{x}\dot{y} \dashv3 \diamond K\dot{x}\dot{y}$	

We can then proceed:

14	$\diamond K\dot{x}\dot{y} \vee \diamond K\dot{x}\dot{y}$	11, 12, 13, SCD, IR
15	$\diamond K\dot{x}\dot{y}$	14, Rep, IR
16	$(\dot{y} \neq c)$	6, Simp, IR
17	$(\dot{y} \neq c) \cdot \diamond K\dot{x}\dot{y}$	15, 16, Conj
18	$\diamond ((\dot{y} \neq c) \cdot \diamond K\dot{x}\dot{y})$	17, EP, IR
19	$(\exists x)(\exists y) \diamond ((y \neq c) \cdot \diamond Kxy)$	18, EG, EG
20	$(\exists x)(\exists y) \sim ((y \neq c) \dashv3 \sim\diamond Kxy)$	19, NSI, IR
21	$\sim(x)(y) ((y \neq c) \dashv3 \sim\diamond Kxy)$	20, QE, RR Q.E.D.

The subproof for line 12 is easy enough:

*1	$K\dot{x}K\dot{x}\dot{y}$	ARCP
*2	$K\dot{x}\dot{y}$	1, By the principle
		$Knp \dashv3 p$
*3	$\diamond K\dot{x}\dot{y}$	2, EP, IR
4	$K\dot{x}K\dot{x}\dot{y} \dashv3 \diamond K\dot{x}\dot{y}$	1–3, RRCP

The subproof for line 13 goes as follows:

*1	$\diamond K\dot{x}K\dot{x}\dot{y}$	ARCP
**2	$K\dot{x}K\dot{x}\dot{y}$	ARCP
**3	$K\dot{x}\dot{y}$	2, by $Knp \dashv3 p$
*4	$K\dot{x}K\dot{x}\dot{y} \dashv3 K\dot{x}\dot{y}$	2–3, RRCP
*5	$\diamond K\dot{x}K\dot{x}\dot{y} \dashv3 \diamond K\dot{x}\dot{y}$	4, SIP, IR
*6	$\diamond K\dot{x}\dot{y}$	1, 5, SMP, IR
7	$\diamond K\dot{x}K\dot{x}\dot{y} \dashv3 \diamond K\dot{x}\dot{y}$	1–6, RRCP

The proof is extremely roundabout in order to preserve the restrictions on the rule of conditional proof described in Chapter 7.

Thus, in our somewhat simplified version of Prichard's argument, the conclusion follows from Premises 1, 2, and 4, and Premises 3 and 5 are unnecessary. But, although the argument is perfectly valid, Descartes might easily challenge either Premise 1 or 2. Premise 4 is a weaker version of the S.4-like statement

$$Kxp \dashv3 KxKxp$$

which, as we noted in an earlier section, is a matter of dispute among philosophers. Some who challenge the above principle might accept Prichard's weaker statement, but some clearly would not.*

The above arguments give some notion of the scope and power of arguments in which modal logic, epistemic logic, and deontic logic are combined with predicate logic.

EXERCISES 8.4

A. Translate from symbols to English.
1. KnOnp ⫤ BnOnp
2. Kn ~◇p⫤ Bn ~Onp
3. BnOnp ⫤ ~Bn □ ~p
4. KnOnp ⫤ Kn ◇p
5. OnBnp ⫤ ◇Bnp

B. Translate from English to symbols, where

a ⧣ Andrew   Dxy ⧣ x pays y's debts   b ⧣ Barbara
Mxy ⧣ x is married to y

1. If Andrew is obliged to pay his debts, then it is possible for Andrew to pay his debts.
2. If Barbara believes that Andrew is obliged to pay his debts, then she believes that it is possible for Andrew to pay his debts.
3. If Andrew is married to Barbara, then Andrew is obliged to pay Barbara's debts.
4. If Barbara is married to Andrew and if it is not possible for Andrew to pay his debts, then, if it is possible for Barbara to pay his debts, she is obliged to do so.
5. If Andrew knows that if Barbara believes that it is impossible for him to pay his debts then she is obliged to pay his debts, then, if it is possible for him to pay his debts, he is obliged to pay his own debts.

8.5 PHILOSOPHICAL DIFFICULTIES

If the reader looks back over the previous sections on philosophical difficulties he will notice that two kinds of difficulties have persistently arisen: difficulties about whether we know what we mean (for instance, by truth-functional connectives in the scope of quantifiers) and difficulties about seeming paradoxes or inconsistencies (for instance, the paradoxes of set theory). Both kinds of difficulties arise in modal logic and will be discussed in this section. Since neither deontic or epistemic logic are fully developed systems of logic, we will let suffice the discussion of their difficulties which has already been given.

---

* See E. J. Lemmon, "If I Know, Do I Know That I Know?" in *Epistemology*, edited by Avrum Stoll (Harper and Row, New York), 1967. Lemmon's objections to Kxp ⫤ KxKxp would apply to Prichard's principle also.

Meaning in Modal Logic

The meaning problem of modal logic is, of course, what we mean by necessity or possibility or strict implication. (Once any one of these notions is clear, the other two can be defined in terms of it.) Various interpretations of necessity can be given, each having its problems.

However, for particular logical systems we know fairly clearly what is meant by necessity, possibility, and strict implication. For example, for propositional logic "p is necessary" seems to be the same as "p is a tautology." Also "p is possible" seems to be the same as "p is not a contradiction," and "p strictly implies q" seems to be the same as "p ⊃ q is a tautology." Tautology and contradiction can, of course, be defined in terms of truth tables.

Again, for predicate logic "p is necessary" seems to mean "p is a tautology," and "p is possible" seems to mean "p is not a contradiction" where tautology and contradiction can be defined in terms of "proofs without premises." Further, "p strictly implies q" seems to mean "q can be proved from p by the rules of predicate logic."

Two difficulties now arise. The first concerns systems which are not as clear-cut or as well developed as are propositional logic or predicate logic. Can we be sure what is meant by such terms as necessity in such systems (for example, in deontic logic)? The answer to this seems to be that we can know what such terms as necessity mean in a system only if we have some way of telling what counts as logically true and what counts as logically false and if we can tell when one statement follows from another by the rules of the system. As we will see in Chapters 9 and 10, this raises certain problems when we try to systematize in ordinary language certain intuitions which we have about such terms as logical truth.

The second problem is a familiar one in a new guise: To what extent does a term such as necessary change its meaning as we move, for example, from propositional logic to predicate logic? Again the answer seems to depend on how much, if at all, such notions as "logical truth" or "tautology" or "logical falsehood" or "being implied by" change from system to system. At any rate, the difficuties which arise do not seem to be specific to modal logic but seem to be general difficulties about understanding and comparing various systems of logic. In a clearly defined system, such terms as necessity are clear; in two clearly defined systems the similarities and differences of such terms as necessity in the two systems are clear.

Paradoxes in Modal Logic

Do any paradoxes or similar difficulties arise in modal logic? In propositional modal logic we have already discussed the major sorts of difficulties (for example, interpreting the four-valued tables). But in modal logic with quantifiers certain difficulties arise.* To state these difficulties we need to remember rules which we have been using:

Universal Instantiation $\dfrac{(w)\,(Zw)}{Zo}$

where **o** is any proper name or definite description which designates an individual. Now the following two statements seem to be true:

$$1 \qquad (x)\,((x = 12) \supset \Box\,(x < 13))$$
$$2 \qquad a = 12$$

where a $\#$ the number of Apostles. But by universal instantiation we can seemingly go from 1 to

$$3 \qquad (a = 12) \supset \Box\,(a < 13) \qquad 1,\ UI$$

and by *modus ponens* to

$$4 \qquad \Box\,(a < 13) \qquad\qquad\qquad 2,\ 3,\ MP,\ IR$$

But surely it is not a matter of necessity that the number of Apostles was fewer than 13; surely Christ could have chosen 14 or 20 Apostles. Thus, it seems that from true premises we have got to a false conclusion, using only accepted rules of logic.

We could, in fact, quibble over the truth of the premises, but it seems better to make certain alterations in our rules. The required change is this: In any attempted use of UI where a variable to be replaced by a name or definite description is within the scope of a necessity operator, the instantiation is allowable only if the bearer of the name or subject of the definite description *necessarily* has the property in question. More formally, we place a new restriction on UI:

$$\dfrac{(x)\,(Zx)}{Zo}$$

Restriction: x in $(x)\,(Zx)$ must not be within the scope of a necessity operator unless $\Box$ **Zo**. This would allow the following inference.

---

* The two difficulties cited below are both objections to modal logic by W. V. O. Quine; cf. his *From a Logical Point of View* (Harvard University Press, Cambridge, Mass.), 1953. Another way of dealing with the difficulties is suggested by Saul Kripke in "Semantical Considerations in Modal Logic," *Acta Philosophica Fennica*, 1965.

$$\left.\begin{array}{ll} 1 & (x)\,((x = 12) \supset \square\,(x < 13))) \\ 2 & (7 + 5) = 12 \end{array}\right\} \qquad \square\,((7 + 5) < 13)$$

since $(7 + 5)$ necessarily has the properties of being equal to 12 and of being less than 13. Remember that **Z** in the Universal Instantiation formula is a short way of referring to *every* predicate with which the variable to be instantiated appears, so it must be true that

$$\square\,((7 + 5) = 12) \qquad \text{as well as that} \qquad \square\,((7 + 5) < 13)$$

Now, in our original problem, it is not true either that a is necessarily equal to 12 or that a is necessarily fewer than 13. So our new restriction forbids the use of UI in the case which gave rise to the difficulty. The same sort of restriction must be put on the identity rule:

$$\frac{\begin{array}{c} Ox \\ x = y \end{array}}{Oy}$$

Restriction: the x in Ox must not be within the scope of a necessity operator *unless* $\square\,(x = y)$. If this restriction were not adopted, we could make the following illegitimate inference. Let p $\#$ the number of planets; then

$$\left.\begin{array}{ll} 1 & \square\,(9 < 10) \\ 2 & p = 9 \\ 3 & \square\,(p < 10) \end{array}\right. \qquad \begin{array}{l} \square\,(p < 10) \\[1em] 1,\,2,\,\text{Identity} \end{array}$$

Our new restriction rules this out but, since $\square\,(3^2 = 9)$ permits

$$\left.\begin{array}{ll} 1 & \square\,(9 < 10) \\ 2 & 3^2 = 9 \\ 3 & \square\,(3^2 < 10) \end{array}\right. \qquad \begin{array}{l} (3^2 < 10) \\[1em] 1,\,2,\,\text{Identity} \end{array}$$

A similar restriction might have to be placed on other rules, but I can think of no plausible case which would make this necessary for any other rule.

To leave modal logic for a moment, there would seem to be a need for similar restrictions in epistemic and deontic contexts. For example, let

$$\begin{array}{ll} \text{m } \# \text{ the morning star} & \text{g } \# \text{ Gottlöb} \\ \text{v } \# \text{ Venus} & \text{S}xy \; \# \; x \text{ sees } y \end{array}$$

It might very well be true that

$$1 \qquad \text{KgSgm} \qquad \text{and} \qquad 2 \qquad \text{m} = \text{v}$$

but false that

$$3 \qquad \text{KgSgv}$$

even though 3 might seem to follow by the identity rule. A similar difficulty could be created using the epistemic operator K and UI.

Contexts in which names or variables are within the scope of modal or quasi-modal operators are one variety of what philosophers of logic have have called *opaque contexts.** It is often recognized that UI and Identity can lead to trouble in opaque contexts. The advantage of the restrictions on UI and Identity suggested above is that we can see when such trouble will occur, but also when it will not (so far as modal and quasi-modal operators are concerned).

READING LIST

The following books are still basic sources for propositional modal logic.

Lewis, C. I., and Langford, C. H. *Symbolic Logic* (Century, New York), 1932; 2nd edition revised (Dover Publications, Ihc.), 1952.

Carnap, R. *Meaning and Necessity* (University of Chicago Press, Chicago, Ill.), 1947.

Also worth special mention are Von Wright's book, which contains material on deontic and epistemic logic, and Hintikka's work, which is one of the most interesting and important in epistemic logic yet published. The Kneales's text contains material on modal logic, and Prior's book offers much valuable material on both modal and deontic logic.

Von Wright, H. G. *An Essay in Modal Logic* (North Holland Publishing Co., Amsterdam), 1951.

Hintikka, J. *Knowledge and Belief* (Cornell University Press, Ithaca, New York), 1962.

Kneale, W., and Kneale, M. *Development of Logic* (Oxford University Press, New York), 1962.

Prior, A. N. *Formal Logic* (Oxford University Press, New York,) 1962.

The following book contains a good introduction to modal logic from the point of view of mathematical logic:

Hughs, G. E., and Creswell, M. J. *Introduction to Modal Logic* (Methuen & Co. Ltd., London, U.K.), 1968.

---

* Verbs such as "know," "say," or "write" create opaque contexts. One short definition of "opaque context" is simply "a context in which substitution of identicals may cause trouble."

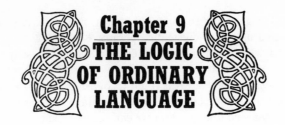

Chapter 9
THE LOGIC
OF ORDINARY
LANGUAGE

In recent years philosophers have been paying a great deal of attention to "ordinary language." Ordinary language here is not necessarily being contrasted with specialized or technical languages. Rather it is taken as the way in which people normally and unselfconsciously use words when they are going about their ordinary concerns, as opposed to the way in which philosophers or those influenced by philosophers may use those terms. Thus we may contrast the ordinary use of a term such as "knowledge" with the use some philosophers have made of it, but we may equally contrast the scientists' ordinary use of the term "explanation" with the things some philosophers have said about explanation. The philosophers' reasons for being interested in ordinary language were masterfully stated by J. L. Austin in his paper "A Plea for Excuses."*

* *Proceedings of the Aristotelian Society*, Vol. LVII, n.s., 1956–7.

First, words are our tools, and, as a minimum, we should use clean tools: we should know what we mean and what we do not, and we must forearm ourselves against the traps that language sets us. Secondly, words are not (except in their own little corner) facts or things: we need therefore to prize them off the world, to hold them apart from and against it, so that we can realize their inadequacies and arbitrariness, and can relook at the world without blinkers. Thirdly, and more hopefully, our common stock of words embodies all the distinctions men have found worth drawing, and the connections they have found worth marking, in the lifetimes of many generations: these surely are likely to be more numerous, more sound, since they have stood up to the long test of the survival of the fittest, and more subtle, at least in all ordinary and reasonably practical matters, than any that you or I are likely to think up in our armchairs of an afternoon—the most favored alternative method.

In view of the prevalence of the slogan "ordinary language," and of such names as "linguistic" or "analytic" philosophy or "the analysis of language," one thing needs specially emphasizing to counter misunderstandings. When we examine what we should say when, what words we should use in what situations, we are looking again not *merely* at words (or "meanings," whatever they may be) but also at the realities we use the words to talk about: we are using a sharpened awareness of words to sharpen our perception of, though not as the final arbiter of, the phenomena. For this reason I think it might be better to use, for this way of doing philosophy, some less misleading name than those given above—for instance, "linguistic phenomenology," only that is rather a mouthful.

To this we will add a brief comment on the formal logicians' special interest in ordinary language. It is well to remember that logic itself has largely arisen from a philosophical analysis of ordinary language. If, for example, people in law courts and legislative assemblies had not had some idea of which arguments using such words as "every" or "some" were valid and which were invalid, Aristotle could hardly have developed syllogistic logic. The formal logician thus has two sorts of interest in ordinary language. First, it offers him a possible source of new formal systems; second, it shows the limitations of his present machinery. For if there are (as, in fact, there are) many intuitively valid arguments which cannot be shown to be valid by the machinery of formal logic, the formal logician will be interested in discovering and systematizing the principles involved.

9.1 LOGICAL TRUTH, LOGICAL FALSEHOOD, AND LOGICAL NONSENSE

In a formal logical system, one can give examples of statements which are logically true or logically false and of procedures for deciding whether a given statement in that system is a logical truth or a logical falsehood. But, although statements in ordinary English do sometimes seem to be logically true or logically false, it is much more difficult to single out such statements and to give procedures which enable us to state with certainty that a given statement is logically true or logically false. Furthermore many statements which we might at first be inclined to say were logically false turn out on reflection to be not in any clear-cut way half-contradictory. Rather they are odd, inappropiate, absurd, nonsensical.

With some reservations, the logical truths of propositional logic, syllogistic logic, class logic, predicate logic, and modal logic probably remain logical truths when expressed in ordinary English.

Bannister either ran the mile in under four minutes, or he didn't.

If at least one person loves everyone, then at least one person loves himself.

If Bannister ran the mile in four minutes, then it is possible to run the mile in four minutes.

These statements are all logical truths if expressed in ordinary English, and they are instances of

$$p \lor \sim p \qquad (\exists y)\,(x)\,(Lyx) \supset (\exists z)\,Lzz \qquad p \dashv 3 \diamond p$$

The reservations which one must make have to do with cases in which apparent tautologies are, in fact, not being used as tautologies. If I say to a disappointed group of picnickers, "If it's raining, then it's raining," I don't simply mean to utter a tautology. I am saying, in effect, "The rain is a fact. You might as well accept it." Or if a father says to his son, "Abraham Lincoln did it, so it can be done," he may well mean, "You can do it if you try; come on, try!" rather than simply, "This is a fact, so it is logically possible."

Analytic Statements

Aside from these kinds of problems, however, there is a more interesting question. Are there logical truths expressible in ordinary English which are not logical truths in any system of formal logic? The answer to this question seems to be, "Yes." One large and interesting class of such statements is the class of *analytic* statements.

In the sense in which the term *analytic* was originally used by Kant, an analytic statement is a subject-predicate statement in which the predicate is "contained" in the subject. This seems to mean, in effect, that, if a full definition of the subject term is given, the predicate term will appear as part of the definition.

Thus the statement

All bachelors are unmarried.

is analytic because, if we define the term bachelor, we find that it means unmarried man. Thus, if we replace the term defined by the definition, the statement becomes

All unmarried men are unmarried.

The statement

All uncles are male.

is more complicated. "Uncle" is defined as "the brother of one's father or mother," and "brother" in turn is defined as "man or boy related to one by having the same parents in common," and finally "man" is defined as "an adult male human being" and "boy" as "a male child." The original statement now becomes (somewhat absurdly).

> All adult male human beings or male children who have the same parents as one's father or mother are male.

There are several difficulties in this standard account of analyticity. First, we have ignored senses of the words in question, for example, the sense in which "bachelor" means "holder of a B.A." or the sense in which "man" is used in legal documents to mean "human male or female." There is no practical difficulty in seeing which sense is meant in a given instance, but it is very difficult to give a satisfactory general account of how we do this. If we mix senses we can get this sort of absurdity:

1. Married student who has just received his B.A., to his wife: All bachelors are unmarried. I just became a bachelor, so, goodbye honey!
2. Fundamentalist wife beater: The Bible says "If a man strikes you on the right cheek, turn the other cheek toward him." I observe this religiously, but, if a *woman* strikes me, I hit her back.

Even if we can keep our senses unscrambled, there is another difficulty. This account suggests that what we do is to start with a statement of the form "All x are y," replace x with its definition yz to get a statement of the form "All yz are y" (for example, "All unmarried men are unmarried") which we somehow "see" immediately as analytic.

Not all statements of this general form, however, are analytic. For example, in the following pairs of statements, the first in the pair is analytic, but the second, superficially like it, is not.

1.	All fat cooks are fat.	2.	All white boats are white.
1'.	All pastry cooks are pastry.	2'.	All cattle boats are cattle.

Fairly obviously, "pastry" modifies "cook" in a different way than "fat" does, "cattle" modifies "boat" in a different way than "white" does. Again it is not easy to give a clear and general account of the difference which would enable us to see exactly which statements of the form "All xy are x" are analytic.

Furthermore, the very simple account which we have given of analytic statements fails to take into account even negative statements, much less other, more complicated, forms (yet Kant, and many others since, have said little more than what we have said so far). All of the following seem to be analytically true for reasons similar to those we have discussed above.

> No uncles are females.
> No uncles are mothers.
> No unmarried uncles are only children.
> All unmarried uncles have at least one sibling who has had children.
> All uncles have at least one relative.

Sticking to uncles for a moment, we can also give certain apparently logically true statements which do not seem to be analytic in the narrow sense:

> If he has a niece, then he is an uncle.
> If there is at least one uncle, then there is at least one parent.
> It is impossible for anyone to be both an aunt and an uncle.

Because of this sort of case it has become usual to define analytic more broadly than Kant did—to say that a statement is analytically true if it is true because of the meaning of the words which it contains.

Now, very similarly, there are contradictory statements in ordinary language. Some of them reflect statements which are contradictory in formal systems, for example,

> He is walking, but he's not walking.
> It's impossible to do it, but he did it.
> Everyone knows it, but he doesn't.

The problem, of course, is that such statements are uttered by people for various purposes, and people rarely mean them as self-contradictions. We can think of contexts in which all of the above statements would be quite meaningful and would convey something intelligible to an audience.

The same can be said of statements which seem at first to be false because of the meaning of the words contained in them, for example,

> He is a married bachelor.
> I have a female uncle.

With sufficient ingenuity we can think of situations in which such statements would make sense. For example, a husband who acted as if he were unmarried might be described paradoxically but vividly as a "married bachelor." A girl who plays the part of Uncle Vanya in a girl's school play with an all-girl cast might be called a "female uncle." It is, in fact, hard to give any expression, no matter how "obviously" self-contradictory, which could *never* be used in *any* conceivable context to convey information or produce understanding.

The same is true, within certain limits, of nonsensical statements. Pick a noun, verb, and adverb at random, for example, "Options fight sweetly." Nonsense? Imagine a Hollywood agent discussing ways of competing with his fellow agents. He describes with horror some of the methods of his fellow agents. His own method is to get options on all promising new talents.

This causes no bitterness and is fair to all. "Ah, yes," he chuckles, "options fight sweetly."

But perhaps that choice was not really random. Open a book at an arbitrary page and pick the first noun from the first line of that page, the first transitive verb from the next page, and another noun from the page after. You can add articles, make nouns agree, and so forth, since we are interested in grammatical sentences which are nevertheless nonsensical. Some examples:

1. case offended seance
2. waiters said afternoon
3. party closed murder

Examples 2 and 3, read as if they were telegrams or newspapers headlines, make a sort of sense. Even the first could be fitted into a story about a case at law which, when reported to a group at a seance, offended them.

Often examples of "logical nonsense" are given in which a predicate is applied to a subject to which it seems wildly inappropriate. For example, "Eternity is green," or "Saturday is in bed." But a context can make even these sensible: "Church art has a color for each basic idea: Death is black, eternity is green. . . ."

Of course, as the sentences get longer and more explicit, it becomes harder to give any reasonable context. Given a length of a paragraph and a certain amount of care you can devise an example which seems to be unsalvageably nonsensical.

Emptiness

But must a sentence be long or complex to be nonsensical? Surely not. In order to say why it is not, however, we must introduce a certain technical notion. We might call it ambiguity, but, since this has too many other associations, I will use the term "logically empty" or "empty" for short.

Emptiness will be defined in connection with a given language, L. (As in previous chapters, "expression" does duty for either "term" or "statement." An expression in L is *generally empty* in a given language L if, when it is presented to competent speakers of L without any context given, they either are unable to say what it means, or, if they do attempt to say what it means, they give random (unrelated, completely divergent) responses. An expression in L is *empty in a given context* C if, when it is presented to competent speakers of L in that context, they are either unable to say what it means or, if they attempt to say what it means, they give random responses.

Now plainly our earlier examples of nonsense are generally empty expressions. Take a representative sample of English speakers and present them with such expressions in English as "eternity" is green or "options fight sweetly." Ask them to explain what those expressions mean. You will either get no response or responses which are random—unrelated and completely divergent.

Emptiness in a given context is another sort of nonsense. Suppose in an oral examination for a Ph.D. candidate in philosophy the candidate is asked "What were Leibnitz's views on identity?" He replies, "Bears like honey." Or suppose a suspected racketeer is being questioned by a congressional committee about his whereabouts on July 14. He answers "Mother will be here later." Neither of these sentences is *generally* empty, but in the contexts given they are surely examples of nonsense. Thus, one can distinguish two sorts of nonsense, expressions which are generally empty and those which are empty in a given context.

Context

An extension of the notion of context may also help us with some earlier difficulties. The expression "married bachelor" if given without any context seems to be simply self-contradictory. As applied to Sam, who for the 172d consecutive night has come home to growl briefly at his wife as he changes clothes for a night out with the boys, it may seem apropos. Similarly "If a man has a wife, he is married" may seem to be a tautology if given with no context, but we could imagine a little episode in which it might convey significant information—and not just about language.

One problem that has consistently plagued attempts to define logical truth, logical falsity, and logical nonsense in ordinary language is the failure to distinguish utterances for which no context is given and utterances in a given context. Take nonsense for example: Any expression could be nonsensical in *some* context; probably very few expressions composed of English words in syntactically proper relationships are nonsensical in *every* context. But plenty of traditional examples, for instance, "eternity is green," are nonsensical in the sense of being generally empty. Similar things could be said about logical truth and logical falsity.

Much more could be said on this subject, but for present purposes we can conclude as follows. In this chapter, when we speak of an expression as being logically true or logically false, we will mean an expression which would be understood as true because of the meaning of the words contained in it if given without any specific context. By nonsensical we will mean generally empty.

EXERCISES 9.1

A.   Given the ordinary meaning of the word mother-in-law, which of the statements below are logically true? Which are logically false? Which are factually true or false?
1.   No mothers-in-law are childless.
2.   All mothers-in-law are female.
3.   All mothers-in-law are married.

4. All mothers-in-law have a relative who is married.
5. No mother-in-law is liked by any son-in-law.
6. Some mothers-in-law are male.
7. Some mothers-in-law have unmarried children.
8. Some mothers-in-law have only unmarried children.
9. Some mothers-in-law have neither sons-in-law nor daughters-in-law (alive or dead).
10. Some mothers-in-law have no sons-in-law.

B. Classify each of the following statements as logically true, logically false, or contingent. Justify your answer briefly. (Source: Plato, *Parmenides*.)

1. If there is a unit, this unit will not be many things; consequently, it cannot have parts.
2. Any part is a part of a whole.
3. A whole means that from which no part is missing.
4. If a thing has no parts, it cannot have a beginning or an end or a middle.
5. If a thing has neither beginning nor end, it has no limits.
6. If a thing has no limits, it has no shape.
7. If a thing has no parts, it cannot be anywhere in space.
8. If a thing changes, it becomes different from itself.
9. If a thing has no parts, it cannot move in space.
10. If a thing has no parts, it cannot be at rest.

9.2 EQUIVALENCE IN ORDINARY LANGUAGE

The notion of equivalence is one which is easy enough to manage in formal systems: Two propositions are materially equivalent if they are true and false under the same conditions; two classes are equivalent if they have the same members; and so on. On the other hand, the grounds for asserting or denying that two expressions in ordinary language are equivalent are by no means so clear. In what follows we will try to look at some reasons for saying that two expressions in ordinary English are or are not equivalent, hoping at least to begin the job of clarifying the notion of equivalence in ordinary language.

First, some preliminary clarifications: The only kind of equivalence which we will be considering is equivalence in meaning. If there are other kinds of equivalence in ordinary language, we will ignore them for present purposes. The things that have meaning are evidently linguistic entities of some kind, and we will use "expression" as our widest and vaguest term for whatever it is that has meaning. We will also speak of sentences— expressions which if uttered in appropriate circumstances would be true or false (or, if you prefer express true or false propositions). Also we will speak of concepts. The term concept is conveniently vague. It can refer to a word, to a phrase, (for example, losing control of oneself), or to a set of related terms (for example, a mistake, by mistake, mistakenly). Thus, if we said that the concept of mistake was equivalent in meaning to the concept of accident we would be saying that an accident meant the same as a mistake that "by accident" meant the same as "by mistake," and so forth.

Concepts

There seems to be good reason to think that equivalence of meaning between concepts is more basic than equivalence of meaning between sentences: If two sentences are equivalent in meaning it is because they contain concepts which are equivalent in meaning. Thus, consider the two sentences

It was an accident.   and   It was a mistake.

They are equivalent in meaning only if the concept of accident and the concept of mistake are equivalent in meaning. That is, we would not say that "It was an accident" means the same as "It was a mistake" unless we were prepared to say, "Accident means the same as mistake" or "Mistakes are the same as accidents."

As we will see, it is a great deal easier to show that two concepts are not equivalent than to show that they are. Therefore, we will begin by examining arguments to show that equivalence does not hold, hoping to gather what would be necessary to show that an equivalence in meaning does hold between two concepts.

J. L. Austin in "A Plea for Excuses" gives the following argument to show that the concept of accident is not equivalent in meaning to the concept of mistake.

You have a donkey and so do I and they graze in the same field. The day comes when I conceive a dislike for mine. I go to shoot it, draw a bead on it, fire: the brute falls in its tracks. I inspect the victim, and find to my horror that it is *your* donkey. I appear on your doorstep with the remains and say—what? "I say, old sport, I'm awfully sorry, etc. I've shot your donkey . . . *by accident*? or *by mistake*"? Then again, I go to shoot my donkey as before, draw a bead on it, fire—but as I do so, the beasts move, and to my horror yours falls. Again the scene on the doorstep—what do I say? " by mistake"? or " by accident"?

It seems quite clear to me, and to everyone else I have tried this story on, that in the first case I should say "by mistake" and in the second "by accident." It also seems quite clear that this is a very strong argument against the thesis that mistake and accident mean the same.

Why is this a strong argument against the equivalence of accident and mistake? Because, it would seem, this example gives us a case where it is clear that we should describe a situation as a mistake, and not as an accident, and another case in which it is clear that we should describe a situation as an accident and not as a mistake. Notice that I say "should," not "would"; in a perverse mood I may abuse language in any way I choose, but if I do so I am not using concepts in the standard, accepted way, the way that has been inculcated in me, as a native speaker of English, by example and correction.

Thus it would seem that we are prepared to deny that two concepts, A and B, are equivalent in meaning, just in case we can find some situation in which it is appropriate to apply A but not B, or vice versa. Nor does the situation have to be an actual one: We are examining "what we should say if" and not "what we do say when." There is not usually much difficulty in knowing "what we should say if" provided that we have a normal command of our language and are not just determined, for philosophical or other reasons, to be difficult.

Now, if it is true that we would deny equivalence in meaning between two concepts on the basis of one case where one concept applied and the other did not, it would seem that, if we say that two concepts *are* equivalent in meaning, we commit ourselves to the position that there is *no* case, real or imagined, where one concept would apply and the other would not. If this is what we mean by equivalence in meaning, then relatively few concepts will be so equivalent. One fairly trivial case where such an equivalence does seem to hold is between staircase and stairway. Although the etymology of the words might suggest that stair*case* implies enclosure and stair*way* does not, no such distinction seems to appear in the ordinary usage of these terms. They are as nearly interchangeable as any terms I know. It may be significant that they are single words and not clusters of related words; It might be argued that, if we have one set of related terms to mark a certain kind of case, we rarely have any use for a complete duplicate set. On the other hand, duplicate single words are somewhat less unlikely.

Not all supposed equivalences in ordinary language *seem* to be cases of meaning equivalence. Take the following example, freely adapted from Wittgenstein's *Blue Book*. What is it to imagine something? One rather common naive response is that imagining is "having pictures in your mind." But suppose instead of talking about what imagining is, you begin by talking about relative values and go on to say, "Now imagine that the White House is on fire and for some reason you are the only person present. What would you try to save, of all the things— Oh, wait one minute! Are you sure it's the *White House* you're imagining? Look carefully!" Now many people, if requested in this way to imagine, produce no interior imagery at all; others may have a mental picture, but a vague or fleeting one. In any case, one can see that the question, "Are you sure it is the White House you're imagining?" is quite unlike the question, "Are you sure this color picture is of the White House?" or even the question, "Do now have a clear, detailed, and correct mental image of the White House?" So "imagining" is not the same as "having pictures in your head."

In this example it is tempting to say we have distinguished two *things*, or that we are "talking about the world, not about words." However, it would be as true to say that we have distinguished the class of cases correctly described as "imagining" from the class of cases correctly described as "having a mental picture," just as earlier we distinguished the class of cases correctly described as "accidents" from the class of cases correctly described as "mistakes." Or, we could say about this example something parallel to what was said of the earlier one, that we have shown that the concept of "imagining" does not have the same meaning as the concept of "having a mental picture."

Finally, in this connection consider the following argument, again from Austin's "A Plea for Excuses." It is an argument to show that succumbing to temptation is not the same as losing control of oneself, and it goes as follows.

> I am very partial to ice cream and a bombe is served divided into segments, corresponding one-to-one with persons at the High Table: I am tempted to help myself to two segments and do so, thus succumbing to temptation. ... But do I lose control of myself? Do I raven, do I snatch the morsels from the dish and wolf them down, impervious to the consternation of my colleagues? Not a bit of it. We often succumb to temptation with calm and even with finesse.

There are several points of interest in this case. First a *phrase* "succumbing to temptation" is being compared to another *phrase* "losing control of oneself." Again, we can use the usefully ambiguous word "concept" and say that the concept of succumbing to temptation is being compared to the concept of losing control of oneself. But concept here does not mean "related group of terms" such as a mistake, by mistake, mistakenly. Rather it means a phrase which—what? Conveys a single idea? But this is no more help than talking of concepts. Perhaps it is a bit more help, but not much, to say that a single concept marks a single distinction or sets off one class of cases.

Second, although we are being presented, as in the previous examples, with a case in which the concept of succumbing to temptation does apply and the concept of losing control does not, we are partly convinced of this by being reminded of *certain things which it is appropriate to say about cases* which we would describe as cases of loss of control but which it is not appropriate to say about many cases of succumbing to temptation. Austin perhaps exaggerates somewhat for effect in this example, but, on being told that X lost control, we are not surprised to hear that he snatched, ravened, and so on: These words elucidate to what extent control was lost, rather than adding a new element. However, if we are merely told that X succumbed to temptation, we might be quite surprised to find that he did such things as snatch and raven, and it would seem that we were learning not just *how* he succumbed to temptation, but something besides the fact that he succumbed to temptation. Notice that, if we ask "To what extent did X lose control?" the answer, "He snatched and ravened" is appropriate. But if we ask, "To what extent did he succumb to temptation?" the appropriate answers might be something like "He took two pieces" or "He took half the bombe" or "He took the whole thing."

Applicability and Interchangeability

Both what Austin says and what I have just said about different answers to the question "to what extent?" indicate a further standard by which we would judge whether two concepts are equivalent: Not only must they apply to the same range of cases, but also they must be interchangeable in contexts of the kind which we have discussed.

Lastly, this is an example which makes it fairly clear why we are interested in equivalence in meaning between concepts, not simply because of interest in words as such, but rather because of interest in distinctions, marked by words, which may be philosophically useful to be clear about.

To sum up our results so far:

1. Two concepts are not equivalent if there are some cases in which one applies and the other does not.

2. One way of showing that there are cases in which one concept applies and another does not is to show that certain things can appropriately be said about cases to which the first concept applies but which cannot be said about the class of cases to which the second concept applies.

3. If we show that two concepts are not equivalent, we have shown that a class of cases described in a certain way is different in some respect from a class of cases described in another way, and this may be the philosophical point at issue.

These negative results suggest the following positive theses:

1. If two concepts *are* equivalent, then, for any case in which the one applies, the other will apply also.

2. If two concepts *are* equivalent, then anything which can appropriately be said about the class of cases to which the first concept applies can appropriately be said also about the class of cases to which the second concept applies.

3. If we show that two concepts are equivalent, we have shown that a class of cases described in a certain way is the same as a class of cases described in another way, and this may be philosophically important.

Let us call the suggested requirement that equivalent concepts apply to the same cases the *Applicability Criterion* and the suggested requirement that the same things should be sayable about cases to which equivalent concepts apply, the *Interchangeability Criterion*. If two concepts satisfy the Applicability Criterion we will say that they are *coapplicable*, while if they satisfy the Interchangeability Criterion, we will say that they are *interchangeable*. Now the claim that two concepts are coapplicable or interchangeable is a universal claim, and one counterexample can refute such a claim. But how can such a claim be supported?

One Word with Various Senses

One way which has often been suggested of finding whether two concepts, A and B, are equivalent in meaning is this: If A is equivalent in meaning to B, then it is absurd (or nonsensical, or logically odd, or even self-contradictory) to say that A applies to any case or cases but that B does not. Thus, if "puppy" and "young dog" are equivalent in meaning, then it would be absurd to say "This is a puppy but it is not a young dog." There is, however, a difficulty about this suggestion.

The difficulty involves different senses and uses of a single term. Thus even if it were true that "puppy" in the usual sense was equivalent in meaning to "young dog," someone might say "Baby seals are sometimes called 'puppies,' so 'puppy' does not mean the same as 'young dog.'" The immediate reaction of many people to this would be: "But that's not the kind of puppy I meant. I meant the kind that—well, the kind that *is* a young dog."

This seems like cheating, but, if we didn't make some distinction between senses of words, we would be in the absurd position of requiring that anything equivalent to "bark" as in "a dog's bark" must also be equivalent to "bark" as in "a tree's bark." This would lead to denying that certain terms had any equivalents even if we had satisfactory equivalents for each sense of these terms because no term would be equivalent to all of the senses of these terms.

A simple, but on the whole satisfactory, test of whether a word is being used in two senses is suggested by the medieval philosopher, Duns Scotus. We ask whether the term could be affirmed of a subject in one way and denied of the same subject in another without self-contradiction. Thus "bark" can be seen to have two senses, since a seal has a bark as in "dog's bark" but does not have a bark as in "tree bark." So also "puppy" has two senses, since an animal can without contradiction be a puppy (canine variety) and yet not a puppy (seal variety). It seems that along these lines we can distinguish different senses of terms and talk of equivalence only between terms taken in a single sense.

Absurdity

There still remain difficulties about the notion of absurdity and its application to equivalence in ordinary language, but these can perhaps be solved with the aid of the notion of emptiness introduced in Section 9.1. Take two terms that are probably equivalent in meaning, such as "staircase" and "stairway." Suppose that someone says, "This is a staircase, but it is not a stairway." This utterance would seem to be generally empty. When asked to say what was meant by it, competent speakers of English would not know what to say. This seems to be at least part of what is meant by saying that it is absurd or nonsensical to say that A applies but B does not, when A and B are equivalent in meaning.

EXERCISES 9.2

A. Which of the following concepts are equivalent in meaning, which are not? Support your answer briefly, using the methods discussed in this section.

1. accuse—charge	2. adjacent—adjoining
3. novice—neophyte	4. haughty—supercilious
5. candid—open	6. hateful—detestable
7. large—big	8. malice—spite
9. plot—conspiracy	10. rise—arise
11. diminish—decrease	12. grand—magnificent

13.	nomad—vagrant	14.	moral—ethical
15.	pleasant—agreeable	16.	position—situation
17.	quick—prompt	18.	receive—take
19.	roam—wander	20.	timely—opportune

B. The following statements can be considered as claims that two concepts are equivalent in meaning. Criticize them by the methods discussed in this section. (Source: Gilbert Ryle, *The Concept of Mind.**)

1. To be brittle is just to be bound or likely to fly into fragments in such and such conditions.

2. To be a smoker is just to be bound or likely to fill, light, and draw on a pipe in such and such conditions.

3. Strength of will is a propensity the exercises of which consist in sticking to tasks; that is, in not being deterred or diverted.

4. Weakness of will is having too little of this propensity (that is, that described in 3 above).

5. By "an effort of will" is meant a particular exercise of tenacity of purpose occurring when the obstacles are notably great or the counter-temptations are notably strong.

6. An action exhibits intelligence if and only if the agent is thinking of what he is doing while he is doing it and thinking what he is doing in such a manner that he would not do the action so well if he were not thinking what he is doing.

7. Feinting is the art of exploiting the possibility of misinterpretation by the onlooker.

8. When we say that someone could have avoided committing a lapse or error, we mean that he knew how to do the right thing but did not exercise his knowledge.

9. If a person feels a tickle, he has a tickle, and, if he has a tickle, he feels a tickle.

10. To enjoy doing something to want to do it and not to want to do anything else are different ways of phrasing the same thing.

9.3 IMPLICATION IN ORDINARY LANGUAGE†

In discussing implication in ordinary language we can begin by saying the same general sort of thing about implication which we said about equivalences; concept A will imply concept B it if is absurd or nonsensical to say that A applies to a case or cases while B does not, while at the same time it is not absurd or nonsensical to say that B applies and A does not. Thus, being an uncle seems to imply being male, since we would not know what to make of a claim that someone was an uncle but not a male, but we find no difficulty in saying that someone is a male but not an uncle.

* Quotes and paraphrases from Gilbert Ryle, *The Concept of Mind* (New York, Barnes and Noble), 1949. Used by permission of the author and publishers.

† Some of the ideas in this section were suggested to me by the work of Prof. Jon Wheatley, of the University of California, Santa Barbara, but the use I have made of these ideas is entirely my own. Prof. Wheatley's paper, "Logical Connections," in *American Philosophical Quarterly*, Vol. 4, No. 1, January, 1967, gives his own account of the matter.

However, there seem to be not one but several varieties of implication to be found in ordinary language. In order to distinguish these more precisely we will introduce some of the machinery of predicate logic. Instead of speaking of concepts, we will speak of predicates or qualities, and we will introduce a new operator, for which we will use the symbol @. This new operator will apply to propositions or propositional functions and @p will be interpreted as "It is absurd (generally opaque) to say that p." An expression such as (x) @ (Fx) will be read as "For anything whatsoever, it is absurd to say that that thing has the quality F," and other expressions with propositional functions will be read in a similar way.

Given this machinery, we can distinguish several types of implication. The strongest relation, which we will call *strong implication*, holds between two predicates which are such that in *every* case it is absurd that the first predicate should apply but that the second should not. Being an uncle seems to be related to being male by this strong implication, for it would always seem to be absurd to say that someone was an uncle when not of the male sex.

Indication and Suggestion

The next weakest relation, which we will call *indication*, holds between two predicates which are such that in at least some cases it would be absurd to say that the first predicate applied but that the second did not. Thus if a person promises to do something this *indicates* that he intends to do that thing, for in at least some cases it is absurd to say that someone promises to do a thing but does not intend to do it. One such case is the case when *I* say that I promise to do a thing. It would be absurd to add, "But I do not intend to do it."

An even weaker relation, which we will call *suggestion*, holds between two predicates which are such that it would be absurd to say that *in every case* the first predicate applied but the second did not. An example of suggestion would be the following: If someone asks a question this *suggests* that he wishes to know the answer to that question. It would be absurd to say that in every case in which someone asks a question he does not expect an answer, that is, that people *always* ask questions without wishing to know the answers to them.

Symbolically, we can define the three relations as follows. For any two predicates A and B, the relation of strong implication, symbolized as ⇒ will be defined as follows:*

$$((\lambda x)(Ax) \Rightarrow (\lambda x)(Bx)) = \text{def} (x) @ (Ax \cdot \sim Bx)$$

The relation of indication, symbolized as $>>$, will be defined

$$((\lambda x)(Ax) >> (\lambda x)(Bx)) = \text{def} (\exists x) @ (Ax \cdot \sim Bx)$$

* Those who have skipped Chapter 6 may simply read "$(\lambda y)(Ax)$" and "$(\lambda x)(Bx)$" as "the property of being A" and "the property of being B."

The relation of suggestion, symbolized as $> > >$, will be defined

$$((\lambda x)\,(Ax) > > > (\lambda x)\,(Bx)) = \mathrm{def}\ @\ (x)\,(Ax \cdot \sim Bx)$$

Relations of Strong Implication, Indication, and Suggestion

If we replace "absurd" by the modal notion "impossible" and treat the concepts in question as ordinary predicates, some interesting consequences follow. Strong implication can then be written as

$$(x) \sim \Diamond\,(Ax \cdot \sim Bx)$$

which is, of course, equivalent to

$$(x) \ \square\,(Ax \supset Bx) \qquad \text{and in turn to} \qquad (x)\,(Ax \dashv 3\ Bx)$$

This means that, if what is absurd is impossible, then strong implication is universalized strict implication. Even if the notions of absurdity and of impossibility are only analogous, strong implication will at least be analogous to universalized strict implication.

Even more interesting is what happens to indication. Written with "impossible" in place of "absurd" indication becomes

$$(\exists x) \sim \Diamond\,(Ax \cdot \sim Bx)$$

which is equivalent to

$$(\exists x) \ \square\,(Ax \supset Bx) \qquad \text{and in turn to} \qquad (\exists x)\,(Ax \dashv 3\ Bx)$$

Now, if there is at least one individual in the universe, this is the subaltern of

$$(x)\,(Ax \dashv 3\ Bx)$$

so that indication is implied by strong implication.

Finally, suggestion, with impossibility in place of absurdity, becomes

$$\sim \Diamond\,(x)\,(Px \cdot \sim Qx)$$

which by Modal Operator Exchange and Quantifier Exchange becomes

$$\square\,(\exists x) \sim (Px \cdot \sim Qx) \qquad \text{which is equivalent to} \qquad \square\,(\exists x)\,(Px \supset Qx)$$

Interestingly enough, if we accept one of the questionable quantifier–modal-operator inferences discussed in Chapter 8, namely the principle

$$(\exists w) \; \Box \, (\mathbf{Zw}) \; \mathbin{-3} \; \Box \; (\exists w) \, (\mathbf{Zw})$$

then suggestion is implied by indication.

Thus, for any two concepts A and B, there would seem to be some reason to suppose that

A strongly implies B

implies

A indicates B

which implies

A suggests B

This, in turn, means that, if A does not suggest B, A neither indicates or strongly implies B, while, if A does not indicate B, A does not strongly imply B, but A may suggest B.

All of this is illuminating for, prior to such analysis, it is not clear how strong implication, indication, and suggestion are related, and it may even be thought that suggestion is stronger than indication.

All three relations are transitive, that is, if $A >> B$ and $B >> C$, then $A >> C$, but indication and suggestion are too weak to allow analogies of such rules as MP, MT, CD.

Quasi-Implicative Relations

Now it seems likely that many philosophers who have talked about such relation as weak implication or presupposition have in fact been referring to what we have called indication and suggestion. It may, therefore, be possible to use the tools we have developed to clarify some statements made by philosophers (as we will see in Section 9.5).

However, besides strong implication, indication, and suggestion, there may be other interesting quasi-implicative relations to be found in ordinary language. For example, there is the relation which would hold between A and B if

$$(x) \, (\mathrm{A}x \supset @ \sim \mathrm{B}x)$$

This relation is, however, probably too strong to be generally useful, being analogous to the relation holding between A and B if

$$(x) \, (\mathrm{A}x \supset \Box \, \mathrm{B}x)$$

The relation which holds between A and B if

$$(\exists x)\,(Ax \cdot @ \sim Bx)$$

also has difficulties. By the ordinary rules of quantifier distribution and simplification, it implies

$$(\exists x)\,@\,(\sim Bx)$$

and statements of this form have a number of difficulties. They are, of course, analogous to such statements as

$$(\exists x)\,\square\,(Bx)$$

which seem to say that there are some things which have necessary properties. There are certainly trivial properties which a thing necessarily has or which it is absurd to say that it lacks, for example, the property of being self-identical. Whether there are any interesting properties which are essential or necessary properties is another and more controversial question.

It seems, then, that, of the logical relations which can be expressed by the simpler and more natural shufflings of the absurdity operator in quantified statements, only strong implication, indication, and suggestion hold promise of being philosophically interesting.

EXERCISES 9.3

A. In the following pairs of properties there seems to be some sort of implicative relationship between the first member of each pair and the second. For each pair give the strongest connection which seems to hold between the two. Support your answer briefly.
  1. being a mother—being female
  2. having a college degree—being intelligent
  3. being decorated for bravery—being brave
  4. being admired—being admirable
  5. being desired—being desirable
  6. being heard—being audible
  7. being seen—being visible
  8. expressing an opinion—holding that opinion
  9. holding a belief—acting on that belief.
  10. knowing P is true—acting as if P is true.

B. The following statements can be interpreted as asserting that some sort of implication holds between two concepts. Discuss which of the sorts of implication discussed in this section holds in each case. (Source: Ryle, *The Concept of Mind.**)

* Quotes and paraphrases from Gilbert Ryle, *The Concept of Mind* (New York, Barnes and Noble), 1949. Used by permission of the author and publishers.

1. A person's performance is described as careful or skillful if in his operations he is ready to detect and correct lapses, to repeat and improve on successes, to profit from the example of others, and so on.
2. If a skater keeps to the edge of the pond, calls his children from the middle, keeps an eye on the lifebelts, continually speculates what would happen if the ice broke, then he has qualms about whether the ice will bear.
3. When a person talks sense aloud, ties knots, feints, or sculpts, [these] actions are . . . things which he is intelligently doing.
4. To be intelligent is to apply criteria.
5. If I am competent to judge your performance, then in witnessing it I am on the alert to detect mistakes and muddles in it.
6. Where misunderstanding is possible, understanding is possible.
7. When a person does something voluntarily, . . . he is in some degree or in one fashion or other minding what he is doing.
8. When a person does something voluntarily, . . . it follows that, if linguistically equipped, he can tell without research or conjecture what he has been trying to accomplish.
9. To be in a lazy mood is . . . to tend to have sensations of lassitude in the limbs when jobs have to be done.
10. If a person is homesick, then he cannot help thinking and dreaming of home, resisting suggestions that he should prolong his absence, and being half-hearted about recreations of which he is ordinarily fond.

9.4 SOME VALID APPEALS TO ORDINARY LANGUAGE

Philosophers from Socrates to the present have appealed in various ways to ordinary language. Some such appeals are far from clear, and some are controversial or dubious or both. In what follows I wish to discuss several arguments based on appeals to ordinary language which seem to me to be quite clear and quite uncontroversial, at least as regards their form or pattern. Whether or not these forms or patterns can be applied in certain specific philosophical contexts *is* a matter of controversy. Nevertheless it is helpful to distinguish questions about the validity of the argument forms from questions about their applicability in specific cases.

Trading on Associations of Ordinary Sense

The first pattern or argument can be stated as an accusation which might be made against a philosopher, either with regard to a specific piece of philosophical writing or generally with regard to all of his work on a certain subject. I will call it Pattern A. It goes as follows:

1. You are not using this term as it is ordinarily used.
2. You have not given this term any clear nonordinary (special or technical) sense.
3. Therefore, this term, as you use it, is meaningless or nonsensical.

Added sometimes to Pattern A, though perhaps not properly part of it, is the additional accusation:

4. Your use of this term *seems* meaningful because you trade on the associations of the ordinary sense of the term.

I will first give a rather trivial example of this form of argument from ordinary life in order to make the point clear. Then I will discuss a somewhat more controversial application of the argument in philosophy.

Suppose that a student is given the privilege of making up an examination during a vacation period and is told to find his own proctor. He is told that the proctor may be a student because no faculty members are available. He turns in the examination.

"Who was your proctor?" he is asked.

"I proctored the exam myself," he answers.

"Nonsense," seems entirely appropriate as an answer.

A proctor, as the term is ordinarily understood, is a person, *other* than the examinee, who oversees the examination and guards against cheating. It seems to make no sense, then, to speak of proctoring oneself if the term is used in a standard way. One might *give* this term a sense, for example, by referring to examinations which are given on the honor system as self-proctored examinations. This would emphasize that each student must be responsible for his own honesty because there would be no overseer. Or the student might reply to the instructor's "Nonsense!"

"But I really did—I took a movie, with sound, of myself taking the exam, which proves that I didn't cheat."

Because some of the purposes of proctoring are served, this might be acceptable. In the absence of evidence that the verb "to proctor" is being used in some such special sense, however, the accusation, "You're talking nonsense," is surely justified.

The philosophical example is more controversial. Certain existentialists have used the term "responsible" in such a way that, while they place great importance on man's being responsible, it is clear that they do not mean that we are responsible *to* anyone or that we are subject to any penalty, even an internal penalty, in case of default. Now, it is at least arguable that the term "responsible" is ordinarily used in such a way that to be responsible is to be responsible *to* someone and to be subject to certain penalties if the responsibilities are not carried out. Thus "responsible, but responsible to no one" seems to be a self-defeating expression. We may sometimes speak somewhat metaphorically of being responsible to oneself, but this usually involves the idea of unpleasant consequences—pangs of conscience, self-punishment—in case of default. To talk of responsibility in the absence of *either* someone to be responsible to *or* penalties for default seems at least *prima facie* to be inconsistent with the ordinary use of the term.

If, in addition, it can be established that no clear special sense of "responsible" can be derived from the existentialist writings in question, then the accusation would seem to be justified that they are using this term without a clear meaning, and some support would be gained for the accusation of trading on the favourable emotional associations of the term as ordinarily used.

Equivocation between Ordinary and Technical Senses

The second pattern of argument which I will call Pattern B can similarly be stated as an accusation:

1. You are not using this term as it is ordinarily used.
2. You are using this term in a certain special or technical sense.
3. What you say is false if this term is taken in its ordinary sense.
4. What you say is trivially and uninterestingly true if this term is taken in the special or technical sense.
5. Therefore you have said nothing which is both true and either interesting or important.

Sometimes added to Pattern B, though it may not be essential to it, is the accusation:

6. Your point seems interesting or important only because of an equivocation between the ordinary sense and the special or technical sense.

I will give an example from ordinary life and one from philosophy.

Suppose that someone makes the startling claim, "Not a single wife in this city is faithful to her husband." Suppose, further, that it develops in the course of discussion that by a wife who is faithful to her husband this person means a wife who thinks of her husband every waking minute.

It would then be quite clear that he was not using the term "faithful" as it is ordinarily used, that he had given it a special sense of his own in which his statement was obviously but uninterestingly true, and that, in the ordinary sense of the term "faithful," his claim was false. Further, the shock value of his claim would depend on the confusion of his special and highly unusual sense of "faithful" with the ordinary sense. Once all this was clear, it could be seen that all this person had really done was to utter, in highly misleading form, the banality, "No wife thinks of her husband every waking minute." The only appropriate response seems to be something like, "So what?"

A philosophical example of some interest is the following. Suppose that a sceptic says, "We can never know the truth of any empirical statement." In the course of discussion the following points become clear: (a) He is using the term "know" in such a way that we cannot know the truth of a statement p if it is logically possible that p is false. (b) He is using the term "empirical statement" in such a way that, if p is an empirical statement, then it is always logically possible that p is false. (Note that we will not object to this: "Empirical statement" is a technical term, and this is a fairly standard sense of that term.)

It follows from (a) and (b) that it is true by definition that we never know the truth of any empirical statement. More arguable, but I think tenable, is the contention that the sceptic's use of "know" is not the ordinary use and that he is using "know" in a special sense of his own. The real hinge of this particular argument is the establishment of Point 3 of Pattern B: that in the ordinary sense of "know" it is false that we never know the truth of any empirical statement. If this can be shown, then all the sceptic has done is to show that if we define knowledge in a certain rather narrow way, then it follows by definition that certain things are not knowledge. Again the appropriate response seems to be, "So what?"

Now that we have some idea of what is involved in Pattern A and Pattern B we can raise these questions: (I) What do we mean by calling these patterns *valid*? (II) What counter moves are available?

First consider Pattern A. In its gross logical structure it would seem to be a simple propositional argument:

1. If this term is meaningful, it either is being used in the accepted sense or has been given a special or technical sense.
2. It is not being used in the accepted sense.
3. It has not been given a special technical sense.

Therefore this term is not meaningful.

Premises 2 and 3 can be established only in a particular case. Premise 1 would seem to be true by definition if the "either–or" clause exhausts the possibilities and it is intended to do so. Since the form is valid and Premise 1 is true by definition, then, in any case where Premises 2 and 3 are true of a term, the conclusion is true of that term.

Pattern B is slightly more complex in its gross structure:

1. Your statement is true only if the term is not taken in the ordinary sense.
2. Your statement is important only if the term is not taken in a special sense.
3. The term is either taken in the ordinary sense or in a special sense.

Therefore your statement is not true or not important.

The form is destructive dilemma and is, of course, valid. Premise 3 is not logically exhaustive since the term may be nonsensical. But if this is so we would apply Pattern A rather than Pattern B. So the truth of Premise 3 is a necessary condition for the applicability of Pattern B. The truth of Premise 1 can be ascertained only in specific arguments. Premise 2 holds true on the supposition that one would not be saying something of importance if one were using the term in question in a special sense, and this again can be established only in a particular case. So once more we have an either–or premise which is intended to be true by definition, and, since the form is valid if Premises 1 and 2 hold in a particular case, the conclusion follows.

The countermoves to Pattern A are fairly limited. The person under attack can reply:

a. "I am using the term in question in the ordinary sense, and what I say is true."
b. "I am using the term in question in the following technical sense. . . ."

Reply (a), if true, evades both patterns, but reply (b) to Pattern A leaves one open to an application of Pattern B.

The possible countermoves to Pattern B are more complicated. Aside from denying that one is not using the term in the ordinary sense, one could reply to Pattern B:

    c. "My use of the term in question is a technical one, but is so related to the ordinary sense that what I say is true even if the term is taken in its ordinary sense."

    d. "My use of the term is a technical one, and, if the term is taken in its ordinary sense, what I say is false, but what I say is nevertheless important."

Reply (c) might be offered by someone who claimed that in giving a term a special or technical sense he was only making more precise or clear the meaning of a term which was vague or carelessly used in ordinary usage. At least some sceptics, for example, have claimed this about their use of "knowledge."

Reply (d) is a more complicated countermove. If often goes with the position that the ordinary use of terms, or at least of the term in question, is so unsatisfactory that the term needs redefinition.

Unnecessary Redefinition

The reply to this countermove is sufficiently complex to be described as a new pattern. We will call it Pattern C, and it can be set down as follows:

    1. Your argument amounts to a proposal to redefine a term in ordinary usage.

    2. The ordinary sense of this term is perfectly satisfactory for its purposes.

    3. You have failed to establish that your special sense of this term is preferable to the ordinary sense.

Therefore, there seems to be no reason to adopt your proposal for a change in usage.

Often, but not always added to Pattern C is the statement:

    4. If the term in question was redefined, we would have to invent a new term to take the place of the redefined one, since we need a term with this meaning.

Again the pattern can be put as a simple deductive argument:

    1. A term should be redefined only if it is either unsatisfactory for its purpose or if the redefinition will enable that purpose to be served better.

    2. This term is not unsatisfactory for its purpose.

    3. The proposed redefinition will not enable that purpose to be served better.

Therefore, this term should not be redefined.

Premise 1 is not as watertight as the disjunctive premises in Patterns A and B. Its justification would seem to be that changes in definition should not be whimsical and should occur only if there is some good reason for redefinition. Good reasons for change can roughly be divided into cases where the present situation is unsatisfactory and cases where, although the present situation is fairly satisfactory, change will produce an improved situation. Thus, on the assumptions that change should not be whimsical and that the two cases divide the reasonable grounds for change. Premise 1 is true by definition.

Premises 2 and 3 will be true in specific cases, but establishing that a word is performing its linguistic function satisfactorily is a much more complex matter. (The argument that, if we did not have *this* word to mark a distinction or name a recurring situation, we would have to replace it by some other word which would serve the same purpose is relevant at this stage). However, if it can be established that Premises 2 and 3 are true, then surely the conclusion will be true.

Now, following the arguments as they have been presented here, there seems to be little doubt, that, if their premises are true, their conclusions will be true. Surely no one would agree to the premises and attempt to avoid the conclusions. In Pattern A, for example, he would have to admit that he was using the word in no ordinary or nonordinary sense, but deny that he was talking nonsense. Or, if he admitted the premises of Pattern C and still proposed to redefine the term in question, it would seem difficult to maintain that the proposed change was reasonable.

Why, then, have the patterns themselves not been more widely recognized, and attention paid to their applicability or nonapplicability in specific cases? Partly, I think, because unjustified generalizations of these arguments have been made. Instead of the relatively modest claims embodied in our Patterns A, B, and C, it has sometimes been claimed that *any* use of ordinary terms (for example, "knowledge") in nonstandard ways was nonsensical or at least that any special or technical sense of such terms was necessarily misleading and confusing or that attempted redefinition was always to be resisted as illegitimate. Especially some of Wittgenstein's remarks (such as "ordinary language is perfectly all right as it is") have been interpreted by some of his followers in this way.

However, if such sweeping claims are avoided and if each attempted application of Patterns A, B, and C is to be argued on its merits, some needed clarification might be added to debates about the legitimacy of appeals to ordinary language. We may well find that, in specific cases, the use of a term is indeed the ordinary one or a legitimate and interesting technical sense or a needed redefinition. But this must be shown and not either assumed or ruled out arbitrarily at the outset.

Finally, to facilitate discussion, I propose the following terminology, where the logical form of Patterns A and C is

$$p \supset (q \vee r)$$
$$\sim q$$
$$\underline{\sim r}$$
$$\sim p$$

and is sufficiently common in philosophy to need a name. Let us call this pattern "Excluded Alternatives." For Patterns A, B, and C, I propose the following names, based on political analogies:

Pattern C, where a change in established usage is resisted, I call "Defending the Incumbent."

Pattern B, where an alternative usage is rejected as trivial, I call "False Contender."

Pattern A, where no real alternative to ordinary usage is given, I call "No Contender."

That these arguments have been used in recent philosophy, I think is quite clear. Whether they have been successful can be decided only by getting down to cases.

EXERCISES 9.4

A. Which of the argument patterns discussed in this chapter would you be inclined to apply to the following arguments? Justify your answer briefly.
1. I am intelligent since I am a college graduate, and by "intelligent person" I *mean* "college graduate."
2. Joan of Arc is my mother! Yes she is, because I feel that a mother is someone who has this sort of special relationship to a person that Joan of Arc has to me.
3. Let us settle this absurd quibbling about whether computers can think. Of course they can, because anything that can do the complicated mathematical calculations that these machines can do is thinking!
4. God must exist for by God I mean the ground of being, and the ground of being is what must exist if anything exists.
5. Every action is selfish because a selfish action is one which a person gets something out of, and no action would be performed if the person performing it didn't get something out of it.

B. Which of the patterns of argument discussed in this section seem to be suggested by the following quotations? (Source: Ryle, *The Concept of Mind.**)
1. It should be noticed that, although ordinary folk, magistrates, parents, and teachers, generally apply the words "voluntary" and "involuntary" to actions in one way, philosophers often apply them in quite another way.
2. In this ordinary use it is absurd to discuss whether satisfactory, correct, or admirable performances are voluntary or involuntary. . . . But philosophers tend to describe as voluntary not only reprehensible but also meritorious actions.
3. In contrast with this ordinary use of lacuna expressions like "a patch of yellow . . ." and "a splash of crimson something or other," the Sense-Datum Theory recommends another idiom in which we are to say "I see a patch of White" [and not "I see a patch of white . . ."] or "he espied a two-dimensional, elliptical expanse of Blue" [and not "a flat-looking elliptical-looking blue something or other"]. What the Sense-Datum

* Quotes and paraphrases from Gilbert Ryle, *The Concept of Mind* (New York, Barnes and Noble), 1949. Used by permission of the author and publishers.

Theory has done is ... to talk as if it had found a new class of objects where it has only misconstrued a familiar range of statements, mentioning how otherwise unparticularized common objects are found to look.

4. The language of "volitions" [or "acts of will"] is the language of [a] para-mechanical theory of the mind. [But] ordinary men never report the occurrence of these acts, for all that according to the theory they should be encountered vastly more frequently than headaches or feelings of boredom ... ordinary vocabulary has no non-academic names for them ... we do not know how to settle simple questions about their frequency, duration or strength.

5. [There are a number of ways in which] the words "conscious" and "consciousness" are used, when uncommitted to special theories, in ordinary life. ... Philosophers, chiefly since Descartes, have in their theories of knowledge and conduct operated with a concept of consciousness which has relatively little affinity with any of [these uses].

9.5 PHILOSOPHICAL APPLICATIONS

In this section I will merely sketch some suggestions for applications of the notions developed in this chapter to current philosophical discussions. To do this in a really thorough and satisfactory manner would take more space than we have here, but each of the suggestions which I make are ones which have either been developed elsewhere or which I am confident can be developed in a satisfactory manner.

Logical Emptiness

Consider the notion of logical emptiness developed in Section 9.1. Now philosophers frequently state that some statement is nonsensical, logically odd, even self-contradictory in some extended sense. The notion of logical emptiness may help clarify some of these claims. For example, Norman Malcom in a paper entitled "Dreaming and Skepticism"* says:

The assertion "I am sound asleep" would be in a certain sense self-contradictory. The sentence "I am sound asleep" does not express a self contradiction in the way in which the sentence "A is taller than B and B is taller than A" expresses a self contradiction. If the latter sentence were written down in front of you, you could straight off deduce a proposition of the form "p and not p." You cannot do this with "I am sound asleep." But as soon as you bring in the notion of a person's *asserting* or *claiming* that he is sound asleep then you get a sort of self contradiction.

Is this "sort of self-contradiction" the same thing as general emptiness? It would seem so. If you asked any group of competent speakers of English what would be meant by the assertion "He claimed to be sound asleep,

* *Philosophical Review*, Vol. LXV, 1956.

and he was," it seems very likely that the members of this group would either be at a loss to say what was meant or else would give random responses. So this assertion is meaningless or nonsensical in the perfectly good sense that competent speakers of English would not know what to make of such a claim. On the other hand, Malcom goes on to say:

> The absurdity that I am trying to describe does not lie in my uttering the words " I am sound asleep " but in claiming or affirming or asserting that I am sound asleep. Whether I make the claim by using spoken or written words or by any other audible or visible signs is, therefore, irrelevant. If I use no physical signs but merely affirm in my mind that I am sound asleep (as I might affirm in my mind that my companion is a bore), it follows that I am not sound asleep. ... Not only is there a kind of self-contradiction in claiming or affirming that one is sound asleep: there is the same kind of self-contradiction in wondering or conjecturing whether one is sound asleep or in being in doubt about it. The proposition " He wonders if he is sound asleep " is absurd in the same way that the proposition " He claims he is sound asleep " is absurd.

Now if we apply the same test of logical emptiness to the statement " He affirmed in his mind that he was sound asleep, and he was " or " He wondered if he was sound asleep, and he was," we get a radically different answer. Present these statements to a group of competent speakers of English and you will get the same answer from virtually all of them, with only the normal variations due to such characteristics as stupidity, carelessness, or misplaced humor.

"The person in question was dreaming," they will more or less say. "It's quite possible to wonder if you're dreaming and find out that you are."

So, contrary to what Malcolm says, there is a radical difference between asserting by any means such as speech or writing that you are sound asleep and doing such things as thinking or wondering about the same subject. The lapse in Malcom's argument seems to occur in the second quotation where it is simply asserted without argument that it makes no difference whether we make audible or visible signs or not. This assertion would seem to be false. (Let me repeat that this is a mere sketch of an argument: I am quite sure that Malcom has made a serious error, but I am far from having shown this by what I have just said.)

A situation in which we are very often interested in finding whether two concepts are equivalent is the situation in which a philosopher has proposed a definition or analysis of an ordinary concept. For example, a perennially popular analysis of the concept of knowledge is one first proposed by Plato: Knowledge is true belief together with adequate reasons for the belief. A modern philosopher expressed this memorably as " being sure and being right on evidence which is conclusive."

However, another modern philosopher has proposed a counterexample, of which I give a modified version here.

"One of the girls in this office is getting married," suppose Jones says to his boss.

"You're right, but how did you know?" the boss replies.

Jones replies that he has seen Millie, the typist, trying on a wedding gown in a nearby store, heard her order a wedding cake on the phone, seen her wearing a diamond ring, and other such actions. The boss chuckles.

" Those are pretty conclusive reasons all right," he replies, "but it's my secretary, Joan, who's getting married. I'm keeping her so busy finishing her work and training a replacement that Millie has had to make all her wedding arrangements. Since they're exactly the same size and have exactly similar figures Millie even tried on Joan's wedding gown. Millie's ring is an heirloom; Joan has a much smaller diamond."

Now did Jones know or didn't he? He was right in what he *said*: One girl was getting married. He was sure: He had a belief, and that belief was in fact true. Furthermore, he had very good evidence. But I think it is very plausible to say that he did not, after all, know, despite being sure and being right on evidence that was "pretty conclusive." In fact, this counterexample, is one which it may be possible to rebut: Arguably the requisite conditions were not fulfilled. What he was sure of was that *Millie* was getting married though this is not what he said to the boss. And in what he was sure of, he was wrong. Furthermore, how much do we want to build into the word "conclusive"? In one sense the evidence can't have been conclusive since the conclusion to which it led Jones was false. Still, we are obviously investigating the question in a fruitful way: If "knowing" and "being sure" and "being right on evidence which is conclusive" are equivalent concepts, then they will be interchangeable in every context and coapplicable. This is what we try to ascertain by considering such counterexamples.

Implications in Ordinary Language

Let us turn now to possible applications of what was said about implication in ordinary language. In a paper entitled "Contextual Implication and Ethical Theory"* P. Nowell-Smith says, "Anyone who states p, whether or not he believes it, *does* imply that he believes it." By "imply" Nowell-Smith does not mean material or strict implication, for he recognizes that sometimes we do in fact state things which we do not believe. That is, since "n believes p" is sometimes false when "n states p" is true. Neither material nor strict implication can hold in general between these two statements for, of course, if "n states p" strictly or materially implies "n believes p," then, whenever "n states p" was true, "n believes p" would be true.

Now let us ask ourselves whether the relation between "n states p" and "n believes p" (let us call these "S" and "B" for short) is either suggestion or indication. Remember that suggestion and implication were defined for

---

* *Proceedings of the Aristotelian Society*, Vol. 36, 1962.

concepts rather than for statements, but analogous definitions can be given for statements. Indication can be defined as:

$$p >> q = \text{def in some case } @ (p \cdot \sim q)$$

Suggestion can be defined as:

$$p >>> q = \text{def } @ \text{ in every case } (p \cdot \sim q)$$

Consider the weaker relation first, if

$$S >>> B \qquad \text{then} \qquad @ \text{ in every case } (S \cdot \sim B)$$

But this is plainly true; it *would* be absurd if, in every case where a person stated p, that person disbelieved p. So it would seem that S does suggest B. Does S also indicate B? If

$$S >> B \qquad \text{then} \qquad \text{in some case } @ (S \cdot \sim B)$$

It would seem that this also is true; for in some cases it would clearly be absurd to say something and not believe it. In fact the "some" here can be stronger than "at least one": *Normally* when we state something we believe it.

G. E. Moore has pointed out the peculiarity of *stating* "p is true but I don't believe p," and a world or a language in which people did not normally believe what they said would be a world or a language far different from our own.

Remember that even indication is too weak to have analogues of *modus ponens* and *modus tollens*. This seems to be true in the case we are discussing also: Just because n doesn't believe p, we cannot deduce that he didn't say p, and we cannot in general safely infer that, if a person says p, he believes p. However, an analogue of Hypothetical Syllogism does hold for indication. Suppose (as is likely) that n, remembering he said p, does indicate that he said p.

$$R >> S \qquad \text{and} \qquad S >> B$$

We should be able to conclude:

$$R >> B$$

Is this intuitively satisfactory? A convincing case can be made: "Did I ever really believe that Brahms was a greater composer than Bach? Well, I remember saying it, and, if I said it, I suppose I believed it, so I must have once believed it." The cases which cause us intuitive difficulty are cases in which we have additional information which changes the situation: For example, I remember saying p, but also remember that I was lying. But since indication creates, in effect, only a probability, such additional information can affect the probability, a problem we will discuss further in the next chapter.

No Contender

Uses of the three appeals to ordinary language described in Section 9.4 are fairly common in modern philosophy. The No Contender argument, in which it is claimed that a term is not being used in the ordinary sense and not being given any clear nonordinary sense, is often used by analytic philosophers in attacking statements by philosophers of other schools which they claim to be obscure or metaphysical (in an unfavorable sense). An example of this type of argument can be found in a debate between Bertrand Russell and F. C. Copleston on the existence of God:*

Copleston: . . . I should maintain that, if there is a contingent being, it follows of necessity that there is a necessary being.

Russell: . . . The difficulty of this argument is that I don't admit the idea of a necessary being and I don't admit that there is any particular meaning in calling other beings contingent. . . . I can't find anything that [these terms] could mean. The word necessary it seems to me is a useless word except as applied to analytic propositions not to things. . . . I've not been able to see an interpretation of those particular terms.

Russell's argument here seems to be roughly: (1) Copleston is not using the word "necessary" in the ordinary logician's sense in which it can be applied only to propositions. (2) Copleston has not given any other clear sense of "necessary." (3) Therefore, Copleston is not using this term in a meaningful way.

Now Russell may, in fact, be mistaken in this particular application of No Contender. But it seems that this is a case of that argument, and, as we have seen, that pattern of argument seems, in general, to be valid.

False Contender

An interesting example of False Contender may be found in a paper by Paul Edwards criticizing certain arguments by Bertrand Russell. In this paper, "Bertrand Russell's Doubts about Induction,"† Edwards compares the stringent requirements that Russell attempts to lay down for inductive arguments to the way a man might use the term "physician" in such a way that only a doctor who invariably cured all of his patients instantaneously

---

* Originally a discussion on BBC, the British national radio service, this discussion can be found in print in many places, for example in *The Existence of God*, edited by John Hick (The Macmillan Company, New York), 1967.

† Most conveniently found in *Logic and Language*, edited by Anthony Flew, first series (Basil Blackwell & Mott, Ltd., Oxford, U.K.), 1952.

would be a physician. This is plainly not the way we use the term "physician." If we did use "physician" in this way, it would be trivially true that there are no physicians in New York. As we do, in fact, use the term, this is false. Edwards claims that Russell similarly defines "good inductive argument" in such a way that it is trivially true that there are no good inductive arguments while, as we ordinarily use this concept, it is false that there are no good inductive arguments. This would seem to be a case of a False Contender argument, and whether or not Edwards is correct in applying this argument to Russell, in general, this line of argument is a strong one.

Defending the Incumbent

Finally, what appears to be a Defending the Incumbent argument may be found in a paper by Keith Gunderson, "The Imitation Game,"* in which he argues that a proposal by A. M. Turing to restate the "ambiguous" question "Can machines think?" as "Can machines successfully play 'the imitation game?'" (which involves causing people to guess wrongly which of two concealed players is a machine, which a man). It is not proposed explicitly to redefine "thinking," but the problem may be looked at in this way. Gunderson argues that, by thinking, we mean so much more than the ability to succeed at the "imitation game" that no useful purpose is served by equating ability to play the "imitation game" with thinking. This seems to fall into the pattern:
1. Your argument amounts to a proposal to redefine the term "thinking."
2. The ordinary sense of this term is perfectly satisfactory for its purposes.
3. You have failed to establish that your special sense of this term is preferable to the ordinary sense.

Therefore, there seems no reason to adopt your proposal.

This, of course, is the Defending the Incumbent pattern, which, if applicable, is a satisfactory argument.

To sum up: we have in a very sketchy and unsatisfactory way shown how some of what we have said in this section can be applied to active philosophical controversies. Whether these techniques are in fact helpful can be settled only if the reader himself applies them to interesting problems.

DISCUSSION QUESTIONS

1. Is it ever important in ordinary life or in philosophy to decide whether two expressions are equivalent in meaning? If your answer is "yes," give examples, if "no," justify your answer briefly.

2. When we use expressions such as "Are you implying that . . ." or "The evidence suggests that . . ." or "His words seem to indicate that . . .," are we sometimes talking about indication and suggestion as defined in Section 7.3?

* In *Minds and Machines*, edited by A.R. Anderson, (Prentice-Hall, Inc., Englewood Cliffs, N. J.), 1964.

3. Discuss some cases where one might be accused of "talking nonsense" in nonphilosophical or philosophical discussion.

4. Where, outside of philosophy, might one find arguments such as those discussed in Section 9.4?

5. What sort of questions can be settled by appeals to the way in which we normally use words? What sort of questions cannot be settled by such appeals?

Chapter 10
TOOLS
OF
ANALYSIS

In this chapter we will take a brief look at some techniques related to logic, but which are not properly part of logic. Formal logic deals by means of symbols, rules, and proofs with statements and arguments in ordinary language. On one side, formal logic is related to mathematics and, on the other, to semantics and philosophy of language. In Section 10.1 and 10.2 we look at two topics, definition and theory of meaning, which are traditionally associated with logic but which perhaps belong more properly to semantics or philosophy of language. In Sections 10.3 and 10.4 we look briefly at two connected topics which are related in interesting ways to logical problems, probability theory and the scientific method. Finally in Section 10.5 we take a last look at some philosophical problems about logic.

As to the place of these topics in a book on logic, it is well to remind ourselves once more of the purpose of this book. We are acquiring logical techniques so as to be able to apply them to interesting philosophical problems. Even though the techniques discussed in this chapter may not be purely logical, we shall nevertheless try to show that they are useful tools for philosophical analysis.

10.1 DEFINITION

In the dialogues of Plato, which are often the first examples of philosophical discussion that are given to students, we find that Socrates is often trying to get a *definition* of some term such as "piety" or "justice" or "knowledge." Several things about his procedure are worth noticing. First, Socrates realizes very well that people ordinarily use such terms correctly and without difficulty or puzzlement. Thus in one sense we already "know what is meant" by such terms as "justice" or "knowledge." In fact, Socrates' whole investigation often depends on this implicit knowledge of what a word means, for he appeals to our ability to use words correctly when he asks whether a proposed definition does in fact agree with the way a word is used.

Second, Socrates is never satisfied with examples, with synonyms, or with technical jargon of the kind that he sometimes got from Sophists or their students. He is looking for a *clear and general description* of the way in which a word is used.

Finally, Socrates assumed that a clear and general account of how a key term such as justice, or knowledge was used would tell us something important and interesting, not just about language but also about the world. Thus, for example, if we could define justice, we would be able to learn when an act was just and when it was not. If we could define knowledge, we could discover when we really had knowledge and when we had only opinion or belief, for instance.

Criticisms of Socratic Definition

This last claim has been extensively challenged in recent years. Most modern textbooks are inclined to say that definition can give us information only about how words are used and not information about the world. Thus it might be objected that, even if we could get the sort of definitions of knowledge and justice which Socrates wanted, these definitions would tell us only whether we had in a given case the sort of thing which people ordinarily call knowledge or justice. So far, so good. But a number of confusions lurk behind these seemingly sensible remarks, as we shall see.

Another kind of criticism of Socrates' procedure is that it falsely assumes that a certain sort of clear and general account can be given of the meaning of words. Socrates often says that he is seeking the "common element" in all cases of knowledge or justice, and influential modern philosophers have argued that no such common element is to be found. Ludwig Wittgenstein used the metaphor of "a family resemblance": The members of a large family may have no single feature in common, but Jane may have Father's eyes and Mother's hair; Joe may have Father's nose and Mother's hair; Sally may have Father's eyes and Mother's nose; and so on. In fact, Wittgenstein and his followers would say, ordinary words are used in such a bewildering variety of ways that they have no exact boundaries, and no clear and general description can be given of how they are used.

Difficulties in Definition

One difficulty with the family-resemblance theory is that, although it may explain why we use the same word for different things, it presents difficulty in explaining why we use different words in different cases. If you take any group of things, no matter how diverse, they will have *some* overlapping characteristics. Unless the Wittgensteinians can give us (as never seems to have been done) an account of why some sorts of overlapping characteristics lead us to group things together and use the same name for all of them while other sorts of overlapping characteristics lead us to do no such thing, the theory fails. Furthermore, the family-resemblance theory only pushes the difficulty one step back. All the family members with Father's eyes seem to have *a* common characteristic, and so do all the family members who have Mother's hair, and so forth.

Wittgenstein may be quite right in thinking that we assume too easily that there must be a common characteristic because the same word is used. But in many cases there seems to be one statable common characteristic.

As with many other problems that we have considered, it seems better to get down to cases. One of Wittgenstein's famous examples is the word "game." He claims that there is *no* common characterisitic which all games have. But his efforts to find one seem curiously half-hearted. Perhaps with care and thoroughness a common characteristic could be given for all games.*

Two sorts of difficulties may have obscured this possibility. First, too many people have started off looking for the wrong things. For example, in defining "chair," one may look for some shape or design common to all chairs. Perhaps we should look at things like function as well as shape. Bertrand Russell once said that, with the aid of a good furnituremaker, he could create a counterexample to any proposed definition of "chair." Perhaps so, if the definition concentrates on shape, but one wonders how Russell and his furniture maker would know that the things they were creating were *chairs*.

The second difficulty is this: suppose we define chair as, for example, "a seat for one person which gives support to the back and supports the sitter some distance off the floor." Two kinds of counterexamples could be given:

---

* For example: Any activity such that its end result is not itself useful or valuable, so that the activity is indulged in only for the sake of recreation (one's own or others'). The end result may be achieved by skill or chance, but there must be some standard of success.

chairs in a doll house (which are not seats for any actual persons) and a chair of history at a university (not a physical chair at all).

The first use is a *derivative* use: Imitations, models, and the like are often referred to by the name of what they are copied from, for example, calling a stone statue of a horse a "stone horse" or even just "a horse." The second use we will call *metaphorical* ("metaphor" being the most commonly used term for a number of figures more closely distinguished by grammarians). The ways are complex in which "Chair of History" is related to "chair" or in which "Iron Horse" (locomotive) is related to "horse," but they seem to involve nonliteral uses of terms. A useful though sometimes tricky test of whether a term is being used in a nonderivative, nonmetaphorical way is the use of terms such as "ordinary" or "real." A dollhouse chair is not an ordinary chair, a chair of history is not a real or actual chair.

We have previously discussed problems having to do with different senses of words: derivatives and metaphorical uses of a term change the sense of the term in question (Duns Scotus' test, referred to in Section 9.2, applies here also). If we try to define only one sense of a term at a time, a good many apparent difficulties can be overcome.

To return to the first criticism of Socrates' search for definitions, let us grant for the sake of argument that at least some, perhaps most, descriptive terms in ordinary language can be defined by giving a common characteristic which are held by all things to which we correctly apply that word. If this is so, then at least sometimes this characteristic will be something objective, something "in the world." If we have never reflected about what it is that all things which we call chairs (or acts of courage) have in common and, by a process like that used by Socrates, discover that in each case we can find a common characteristic which is an objective feature of the world, then there seems to be reason to say that we have learned something about the world as well as about words.

Rules for Definition

The following traditional "rules" for definition are of limited but real usefulness in reminding ourselves of questions that we often want to ask about proposed definitions.

DR 1. A definition must not be obscure, figurative, or negative where it might be positive.

Comment: Obviously if we define in order to clarify or understand a term or concept, we defeat our own purpose if the definition is less well understood than the term to be defined. An attempt at definition which merely gives us a comparison, analogy, or metaphor is unlikely to be helpful. Finally, if we are to avoid obscurity, we will probably do well to avoid negative definitions where at all possible. Saying what a thing is not rarely gives us much idea of what it is.

All of these points, however, are relative. Technical terms are useful, but they may seem obscure to those not familiar with them. Terms such as "orphan" or "bald" can be best defined negatively. In some cases a metaphor or analogy may be the best or the only way of helping someone to understand an unfamiliar idea. Therefore, a definition which appears at first to break this rule may turn out to be a good one.

DR 2. A definition must not be circular.

Comment: Circularity in a definition is a more serious fault, since the basic objection to circular definition is that ultimately you are offered the term itself as a clarification or explanation of its own meaning. However, most dictionary definitions are circular to a greater or lesser degree. If you doubt this, look up some word. Then look up the definition of each key term in the definition, then each key term in the definition of the definition, and so on. You will sooner or later find yourself with a fairly small collection of terms such that if you start with the dictionary definition of any one of the group you will eventually be referred to the others. This is not a serious defect in dictionary definitions for two reasons. First, dictionaries are written for people who already speak a language. Somewhere in the group of terms he finds by looking up a dictionary definition, a competent speaker of a language will find some that are familiar to him. Second, dictionaries are often useful precisely because one can use them to determine the relation of a word to other related words. Somewhat similarly, a map or atlas can be used in two ways. First, it can show the relation of an unknown location to other locations and eventually to one with which you are familiar. Second, the map or atlas can show the relationship of a location to nearby locations. Just as a map is useless unless you have some reference point to relate it to, a dictionary is useless unless you can relate the words in it to something else than the other words in the dictionary. (Aristotle was making essentially this point when he argued that not every term can be introduced by verbal definition.)

DR 3. A definition must not be too broad.

Comment: The presupposition here is that there is an established usage for the word, a class of cases which, by imitation, being corrected, and so on, we have learned to associate with the term in question. A definition which is too broad would make the term to be defined apply to cases where competent speakers of the language would not employ that term. Since the sort of definition with which we are concerned is an attempt to describe how a term is used, not an attempt to revise or reform its usage, a definition fails if it is too broad.

DR 4. A definition must not be too narrow.

Comment: A definition which is too narrow would make the term to be defined not apply to cases in which competent speakers of the language would clearly apply it. Narrowness is a fatal defect in a definition for the same reason that being too broad is fatal. Notice that, if there are cases in which competent speakers of the language would not be sure whether or not to apply the term to be defined, these cannot be used as a basis for a charge that a definition is too broad or too narrow.

DR 5. A definition must not mention only trivial characteristics.

Comment: A characteristic or set of characteristics may single out exactly those cases to which a term applies without thereby helping us to understand what it is that those cases have in common. Thus, if we are trying to understand shape, it does not help us to be told that it is the only characteristic which always accompanies color. If we are trying to understand which characteristics men have in common, it does not help much to be told that man is the only creature which blushes. On the other hand, it is by no means easy to say what constitutes an important characteristic as opposed to a trivial one.

If we use the traditional rules of definition as a reminder of pitfalls in the way of attaining the objectives of definition rather than as ironclad requirements, they can be of considerable help. I will conclude by giving a brief summary of the rules, appending to each a question which might be asked (legitimately or not) in a philosophical context which seems to presuppose that rule.

A definition must not be:

1. obscure or figurative or unnecessarily negative
   "What do you mean by saying that God is a being whose existence is identical with its essence?"
2. circular
   "Doesn't your definition of *essence* contain the word *form*, which you earlier defined by using *essence*?"
3. too broad
   "In defining knowledge as perception, don't you include within your definition many things which we would not ordinarily call knowledge?"
4. too narrow
   "In defining knowledge as belief in propositions which are necessarily true, don't you exclude from your definition many things which we would ordinarily call knowledge?"
5. dependent on only trivial characteristics
   "Agreed that, if we define *man* as featherless biped, the definition is neither too broad nor too narrow, but does this state anything of importance?"

EXERCISES 10.1

A. Attempt a definition of the following terms which will avoid the pitfalls that are summed up in the traditional five rules of definition.

1. philosopher   2. statesman

3. hero
5. scholar
7. mistake
9. cynicism

4. coward
6. accident
8. knack
10. zany

B. Criticize the following definitions in terms of the five rules for definition. (Source: Hobbes, *Leviathan.*)
    1. Hope is the desire for something with a belief that we can attain it.
    2. Despair is the desire for something with a belief that we cannot obtain it.
    3. Fear is aversion from something with a belief that it may harm us.
    4. Courage is fear with a hope of avoiding the harm by resistence.
    5. Anger is sudden courage.
    6. Self-confidence is constant hope.
    7. Indignation is anger for an unjust injury to another.
    8. Ambition is desire for honor or power.
    9. Timidity is fear of things which can do us little harm.
    10. Jealousy is love with fear that the love is not returned.

C. Criticize the following definitions in terms of the five rules for definition. (Source: Spinoza, *Ethics.*)
    1. Desire is the actual essence of a man insofar as it is conceived as determined to a particular activity by some given modification of itself.
    2. Pleasure is the transition of a person from a less perfect state to a more perfect state.
    3. Pain is the transition of a person from a more perfect state to a less perfect state.
    4. Wonder is the thought of anything which brings the mind to a standstill because the concept in question has no connection with other concepts.
    5. Contempt is the conception of anything which touches the mind so little that its presence leads the mind to imagine these qualities which are not in it rather than those which are in it.
    6. Love is pleasure accompanied by the idea of an external cause.
    7. Hatred is pain accompanied by the idea of an external cause.
    8. Derision is a pleasure, arising from our thinking of the presence of a quality which we despise in the presence of an object which we hate.
    9. Hope is an inconstant pleasure, arising from the idea of something, past or future, about which we are uncertain.
    10. Fear is an inconstant pain arising from the idea of something, past or future, about which we are uncertain.
    11. Confidence is pleasure arising from the idea of something, past or future, of which we are certain.
    12. Despair is pain arising from the idea of something, past or future, of which we are certain.
    13. Joy is pleasure accompanied by the idea of something past which turned out to be better than hoped for.
    14. Disappointment is pain accompanied by the idea of something past which turned out to be worse than we hoped for.
    15. Pity is pain accompanied by the idea of an evil which has befallen someone else who we think is like ourselves.
    16. Approval is love toward one who has done good to another.
    17. Indignation is hatred toward one who has done evil to another.

18. Partiality is thinking too highly of anyone because of the love we bear him.
19. Disparagement is thinking too badly of anyone because we hate him.
20. Envy is hatred insofar as it induces a person to be pained by another's good fortune and to rejoice in another's evil fortune.
21. Empathy is love insofar as it induces a man to feel pleasure at another's good fortune and pain at his misfortune.
22. Self-esteem is pleasure arising from a man's contemplation of himself and his own power of action.
23. Humility is pain arising from a man's contemplation of his own weakness of body and mind.
24. Repentence is pain accompanied by the idea of some action which we believe we have performed by the free decision of our mind.
25. Pride is thinking too highly of oneself from self-love.
26. Honor is pleasure accompanied by the idea of some action of our own which we believe to be praised by others.
27. Shame is pain accompanied by the idea of some action of our own which we believe to be blamed by others.
28. Regret is the desire to possess something kept alive by the remembrance of that thing and at the same time held in check by the thought of other things which prevent our possessing it.
29. Gratitude is the desire to benefit one who has conferred a benefit on us.
30. Anger is the desire to injure someone whom we hate.
31. Cruelty is the desire to injure someone whom we love or pity.
32. Timidity is the desire to avoid a greater evil, which we dread, by undergoing a lesser evil.
33. Daring is the desire which sets us on to do something that our peers are afraid to do.
34. Cowardice is a fear which prevents us from risking some danger which our peers dare to meet.
35. Courtesy is the desire to act in a way which will please others and to refrain from actions which will displease them.

10.2 THEORY OF MEANING

In this section we will examine briefly certain features of ordinary language. Generally speaking there are two major divisions of expressions in ordinary language: *referring expressions*, which name or point to what we are talking about, and *describing expressions*, which say something about things to which we have already referred. Similar distinctions exist in the restricted and artificial logical systems which we have discussed, for example, the distinction between names of individuals or definite descriptions and predicates in subject-predicate logic.

Referring Expressions

There are two common ways in which referring expressions gain meaning: (1) Arbitrary convention: If I call my dog Floyd, no amount of examination of the dog will reveal that this is his name; you must learn that I have more or less arbitrarily attached this noise to this animal. (2) Unique description: If I refer to the first president of the United States, you are able to pick out a specific individual even though I did not give you a name for that individual. An important thing to note is that uniqueness is relative to context: There may be hundreds of dogs named Floyd but if mine is the only one in the neighborhood no confusion arises. Similarly, if you knock on my office door and I say "Come in, the door is unlocked," the expression "the door" plainly refers to the door on which you have just knocked.

An important thing to remember is that ordinary language depends very heavily on context; if every time we used a name or description it had to be absolutely unique, language would be too cumbersome to be useful. Equally important is the fact that we *can* always be as specific as we wish (full name and address usually single out one individual; legal descriptions, for example, of a piece of property, uniquely describe the thing involved).

Descriptive Expressions

In contrast to referring expressions, descriptive expresions refer to a kind or *class* of cases. Often the class of cases is extremely wide: Consider the differences in the situations that face us when a door is open, a box is open, a glove compartment is open, a grave is open. Yet all of these are obviously one sense of "open," and the cases are closely related. Descriptive terms are "arbitrary" or "conventional," but in a somewhat different way than are names: In learning a name we relate a noise to a *thing*, by what J. L. Austin calls a "denotative convention." In learning a descriptive term we relate a noise to a *class of cases* by what Austin called a "descriptive convention."*

When we make a successful reference (actually name or point out something which does exist) and also make a successful description (use a predicate which can meaningfully be applied to the sort of thing to which we have referred), then we make a *statement*, either true or false. By statement, we will mean (as Austin does also) a sentence actually uttered (spoken or written) on a datable occasion.

The Basis of Meaning

Let us briefly note some of the connections between this very sketchy account of some key features of ordinary language and topics which we have discussed. Logical nonsense (general opacity) frequently arises when we fail to refer successfully, while falsehood usually results when we fail to describe successfully. Logical truth and logical falsehood in ordinary language, as well as many implications and equivalences in ordinary language, depend ultimately on the meaning of descriptive terms. When we "appeal to ordinary language,"

---

* "Truth," *Proceedings of the Aristotelian Society*, Supplementary Volume, 1963.

the appeal is generally to the meaning of a descriptive term. Since knowing the meaning of a descriptive term is knowing the class of cases to which it applies and since knowing the class of cases is knowing the common characteristic of that class, a great deal of our concern in the analysis of ordinary language is with these common characteristics. Talk of "essences" or "natures" or "principles" is out of fashion in current philosophy, but it is dubious that the central concerns of linguistic philosophers are seriously different from the central concerns of philosophers like Plato and Aristotle.

The word "meaning" has several related senses. Mixing these often leads to philosophical confusion. We will distinguish three major senses of meaning, using for each a word which suggests the peculiarities of that sense. By the *denotation* of a referring expression we mean the thing or things to which it is related by a referring convention. For example, the denotation of "Richard L. Purtill" is myself, the denotation of "the Presidents of the United States of America" is George Washington, John Adams, and so on to the present President.

By the *connotation* of a descriptive expression we mean the conditions which specify the class of cases to which the expression is related by a descriptive convention. Definitions usually give the denotation of an expression. Proper names do not have a connotation, but other referring expressions have a connotation because we can give a set of conditions which specifies the class whose members are the denotation of the term. By the denotation of a descriptive expression we mean the members of the class of cases to which it is related by a descriptive convention. Thus the denotation of a referring expression is usually an individual or individuals, while the denotation of a descriptive expression is a case or cases.

By the *associations* of a term, we mean those things which are called to mind by that term. Associations thus differ from individual to individual: The associations of the name "Betty" or the description "logical" are unlikely to be the same for you and for me. Language depends on the fact that denotation and connotation are more or less the same for all speakers of the language, but associations can and do vary widely. Denotation, connotation, and association are three different but related senses of meaning. To see this, the reader may examine these examples:

Denotation: In the last sentence, above, "the reader" means you.

Connotation: In the same sentence, "examine" means "read and think about."

Association: To you, "examination" may mean staying up all night and studying; to your teacher it may mean a lot of papers to grade.

Let me emphasize that the distinctions made in this section are extremely rough as well as incomplete. As with the other topics in this last part of the book, we examine only a small part of the theory of meaning, which is part of a yet wider topic, the philosophy of language. I hope, however, that even these simple and crude distinctions may help us to avoid certain widespread confusions about meaning.

EXERCISES 10.2

A. Do the following pairs of words or phrases have (1) the same connotation (2) the same denotation, (3) the same associations? Justify your answer briefly.

1. brother—male sibling   2. mother—female parent
3. my country—the nation of which I am a citizen
4. my home—my place of legal domicile
5. television set—boob tube   6. lawyer—attorney
7. teacher—pedagogue   8. policeman—cop
9. Irishman—Mick   10. Scotchman—Scot

B. Discuss the sense of meaning that is probably intended in each of the following sentences. (Source: Aristotle, *On Interpretation*.)

1. A noun is a sound which has meaning by convention, which has no reference to time, and of which no part has meaning by itself.
2. In the name "Goodsteed" the part "steed" has no meaning in and by itself, as it does in the phrase "good steed."
3. Simple names are different in this respect from compound nouns: in the former a part has no meaning, but in the latter the meaning of the part contributes to the meaning of the whole.
4. Thus in the word "pirate-boat," the word "boat" has no meaning which is independent of the meaning of the whole word.
5. A verb is that which, in addition to its proper meaning, carries with it the notion of time.
6. A sentence is a meaningful portion of speech, some parts of which have an independent meaning.
7. The word "human" has meaning but is not a proposition, either positive or negative.
8. But if we separate one syllable of the word "human" from the other it has no meaning.
9. Similarly in the word "mouse" the part "ouse" has no meaning by itself.
10. Every sentence has meaning, but not every sentence is a proposition.

10.3 PROBABILITY THEORY

In this section we will briefly examine a system closely related to logic in some respects but whose full development leads into mathematical realms far removed from logic. Just as in set theory we studied only that part of the theory useful for analyzing statements and arguments in ordinary language, so in the theory of probability we will observe the same restriction. The boundary between logic and mathematics is not clearly defined, but, roughly speaking, when one begins to manipulate numbers by processes such as addition or multiplication, one has probably crossed the line into mathematics. We will in fact, cross that line in this section, but only briefly and for the purposes we have mentioned, that is, in order to analyze statements and arguments in ordinary language.

So far all of the statements we have considered could be analyzed in terms of truth and falsity. In modal logic we distinguished between necessary and contingent truth and also spoke of statements being possibly true or false. Now for the first time we are going to speak of *degrees* of confidence in, or belief in a statement. By convention these degrees are represented as numbers between 0 and 1, with 1 representing complete certainty of truth and 0 representing complete certainty of falsehood. Numbers other than 1 and 0 are interpreted as incomplete certainty. For example $\frac{1}{2}$ or 0.5 will represent a situation in which we consider the statement in question to be as likely to be true as to be false.

Our way of writing statements of probability will be to put a statement in parentheses preceded by "Pr" and followed by an equals sign and a number between 1 and 0. Thus if

$$D \,\#\, \text{Aristotle is dead} \qquad A \,\#\, \text{Aristotle is alive}$$
$$C \,\#\, \text{Aristotle is mentioned in a book I have randomly selected}$$
$$\text{from my shelves}$$

we could write

$$\text{Pr (D)} = 1 \qquad \text{Pr (A)} = 0 \qquad \text{Pr (C)} = \tfrac{1}{2}$$

Presumably the first two statements are true; the third is more dubious. We will regard probability statements as straightforward true or false, ignoring the complication of possible "second order" probabilities, that is, the possibility that the third statement, above, has itself a certain probability.

Compound statements can occur within the parentheses after Pr, and certain general rules can be given for finding the probability of compound statements when the probability of their component simple statements is known. Since these apply to any statements, we will state them with the aid of the familiar propositional variables. The usual arithmetical symbols will be used $(+, -, <, \leqslant, >, \geqslant)$. For multiplication we will use $\times$, as being less likely to lead to confusion than other symbols.

The most general rule for the probability of "either–or" compounds is the following:

$$\text{Pr (p v q)} = \text{Pr (p)} + \text{Pr (q)} - \text{Pr (p} \cdot \text{q)}$$

The most general rule for the probability of "both-and" compounds is this:

$$\text{Pr (p} \cdot \text{q)} = \text{Pr (p)} \times \text{Pr (q/p)}$$

The expression Pr (q/p) does not mean "the probability of q divided by p" but rather "the probability of q *given* p," that is, "the probability of q on the assumption that p is true."

335

If p and q are *mutually exclusive*, that is, cannot both be true, then:

$$Pr\ (p \cdot q) = 0$$

so that the first formula then becomes

$$Pr\ (p \lor q) = Pr\ (p) + Pr\ (q)$$

If p and q are *independent*, that is, if the truth of q makes no difference to the truth of p and vice versa, then

$$Pr\ (q/p) = Pr\ (q)$$

and the second formula becomes:

$$Pr\ (p \cdot q) = Pr\ (p) \times Pr\ (q)$$

Since these formulas are simpler, let us begin with them as we illustrate these formulas by some simple examples.

The simplest kind of case to which probabilities can be attached is a simple coin-tossing situation. If I throw an ordinary coin in the air, we usually count on the coin's being as likely to land heads up as tails up. There is a remote possibility of other outcomes, such as that the coin might land on its edge and balance there or a bird might fly by and snatch it in midair. Also such factors as random variations in density of metal probably prevent the probability of heads and tails being completely equal. Still for all practical purposes, if

H ⧣ Heads will come up   and   T ⧣ Tails will come up

then

$$Pr\ (H) = \tfrac{1}{2} \quad \text{and} \quad Pr\ (T) = \tfrac{1}{2}$$

The outcomes H and T are independent and mutually exclusive so we can use the simpler formulas. On one throw of the coin:

$$\begin{aligned} Pr\ (H \lor T) &= Pr\ (H) + Pr\ (T) \\ &= \tfrac{1}{2} + \tfrac{1}{2} \\ &= 1 \end{aligned}$$

That is, either heads or tails is bound to come up. As we have remarked this is an idealization of the actual situation. If I throw the coin twice, I may be interested in the probability of getting two heads, that is, a head *and* a head or H · H.

$$Pr (H \cdot H) = Pr (H) \times Pr (H)$$
$$= \tfrac{1}{2} \times \tfrac{1}{2}$$
$$= \tfrac{1}{4}$$

If I throw the coin three times or more I simply group the conjuncts in such a way that I can use the rule repeatedly to get the solution:

$$Pr (H \cdot (H \cdot H)) = Pr (H) \times Pr (H \cdot H)$$
$$= Pr (H) \times (Pr (H) \times Pr (H))$$
$$= \tfrac{1}{2} \times (\tfrac{1}{2} \times \tfrac{1}{2})$$
$$= \tfrac{1}{8}$$

and so forth. (The same is true for disjuncts.)

To illustrate the more complicated formulas, consider a well-shuffled deck of cards. We ordinarily count on each card's being equally likely to be drawn from a well-shuffled deck. Since there are 52 cards in the deck, the probability of getting any given card is 1/52. Since 12 of these are "court" cards (J, Q, K in each suit), the probability of getting a court card is 12/52; since 12 cards out of 52 are court cards, we have 12 chances out of 52 of drawing a court card if each card is equally likely to be drawn. Now let

C ⫫ The card drawn is a court card   J ⫫ The card drawn is a jack

Consider one draw from a well-shuffled deck; the probabilities of drawing C and J are *not* independent:

$$Pr (C/J) = 1$$

(If the card is a jack, it's sure to be a court card) and

$$Pr (J/C) = 4/12$$

(If the card is a court card, there are four chances out of twelve of getting a jack, since four of the twelve court cards are jacks.) Consider first a single draw. What are the chances of getting a jack, which is a court card, that is, a jack *and* a court card:

$$Pr (C \cdot J) = Pr (C) \times Pr (J/C)$$
$$= \frac{12}{52} \times \frac{4}{12}$$
$$= \frac{48}{624}$$
$$= \frac{4}{52}$$

or

$$Pr\ (J \cdot C) = \frac{4}{52} \times 1$$
$$= \frac{4}{52}$$

The probability of getting a jack *or* a court card is:

$$Pr\ (J \vee C) = Pr\ (J) + Pr\ (C) - Pr\ (J \cdot C)$$
$$= \frac{4}{52} + \frac{12}{52} - \frac{4}{52}$$
$$= \frac{12}{52}$$

It is also true that, for any statement p, $Pr\ (\sim p) = 1 - Pr\ (p)$. For example, the probability of *not* getting a jack is:

$$Pr\ (\sim J) = 1 - Pr\ (J)$$
$$= 1 - \frac{4}{52}$$
$$= \frac{48}{52}$$

The probability of *not* getting a court card is:

$$Pr\ (\sim C) = 1 - Pr\ (C)$$
$$= 1 - \frac{12}{52}$$
$$= \frac{40}{52}$$

Bayes' Theorem

An important formula which tells us how to calculate the probability of a given statement if we are given the probability of another statement is Bayes' Theorem:

$$Pr\ (p/q) = \frac{Pr\ (p) \times Pr\ (q/p)}{Pr\ (q)}$$

Thus, for example, the probability of drawing a jack provided we have drawn a court card is, as we saw previously:

$$Pr\,(J/C) = \frac{Pr\,(J) \times Pr\,(C/J)}{Pr\,(C)}$$
$$= \frac{4/52 \times 1}{12/52}$$
$$= \frac{4}{12}$$

We can think of Bayes' Theorem as representing the probability of a hypothesis on given evidence and rewrite it using H and E to remind ourselves of this interpretation:

$$Pr\,(H/E) = \frac{Pr\,(H) \times Pr\,(E/H)}{Pr\,(E)}$$

We can read this formula as "the probability of a hypothesis on given evidence is equal to the initial probability of that hypothesis [i.e., the probability of the hypothesis before considering the evidence in question] times the probability of obtaining that evidence if the hypothesis were true, this product being divided by the initial probability of the evidence [i.e., the probability of the evidence considering all possible hypotheses]."

Maximum-Likelihood Argument

Sometimes it is not necessary to use the complete Bayes' formula since, if Pr (H) and Pr (E) are not too far apart, Pr (H/E) is related very closely to Pr (E/H). Thus, it is often sufficient to find which hypothesis gives the highest probability to the observed evidence. When we choose the hypothesis which gives the greatest probability to the observed evidence, over those which make the observed evidence less probable, we are using what is called a *maximum-likelihood* argument.

Suppose I have two coins, one a fair coin and one with two heads. I choose one at random. I then throw the coin three times, and it comes up heads each time. In this case I have two hypotheses

F ⧺ I have a fair coin   T ⧺ I have a two-headed coin

and the evidence

E ⧺ three heads thrown

Pr (F) and Pr (T) are both $\frac{1}{2}$ while Pr (E/F) is just the probability of getting three heads with a fair coin, $\frac{1}{2} \times \frac{1}{2} \times \frac{1}{2} = \frac{1}{8}$. Of course Pr (E/T) is 1, or certainty, since a two-headed coin is certain to give heads. It can be shown that Pr (E) is 9/16. Using Bayes' Theorem we can show that

$$Pr\,(F/E) = \frac{Pr\,(F) \times Pr\,(E/F)}{Pr\,(E)}$$
$$= \frac{1/2 \times 1/8}{9/16}$$
$$= 1/9$$

and

$$Pr\,(T/E) = \frac{Pr\,(T) \times Pr\,(E/T)}{Pr\,(E)}$$
$$= \frac{1/2 \times 1}{9/16}$$
$$= 8/9$$

But if we were only concerned with choosing one hypothesis or the other, we could simply pick the hypothesis which gave the highest probability to the evidence. In fact, in this simple case Pr (H/E) and Pr (E/H) are in the same ratio for both hypotheses. This occurs whenever the hypotheses being considered are equally probable. (When the probabilities of the hypotheses are approximately equal, this will be approximately true.)

If we think of propositional logic as being concerned with statements which have only values 1 or 0 (certainly true or certainly false), we get some interesting parallels between our familiar truth tables for · and v and the results of applying the formulas for probability given above. If Pr (p) = 1 and Pr (q) = 1 then

$$Pr\,(p \cdot q) = Pr\,(p) = Pr\,(q/p)$$
$$= 1 \times 1^{*}$$
$$= 1$$

If either Pr (p) or Pr (q) is 0, of course, Pr (p · q) = 0. If Pr (p) = 1 and Pr (q) = 1, then

$$Pr\,(p \vee q) = (Pr\,(p) + Pr\,(q)) - Pr\,(p \cdot q)$$
$$= (1 + 1) - 1$$
$$= 1$$

If Pr (p) = 1 and Pr (q) = 0 or vice versa, then we get Pr (p · q) = 0 and

$$Pr\,(p \vee q) = Pr\,(p) + Pr\,(q) - Pr\,(p \cdot q)$$
$$= 1 + 0 - 0$$
$$= 1$$

---

* The term Pr (q/p) is equal to 1 since we are assuming that p is true.

or else

$$Pr\,(p \vee q) = Pr\,(p) + Pr\,(q) - Pr\,(p \cdot q)$$
$$= 0 + 1 - 0$$
$$= 1$$

while if both $Pr\,(p) = 0$ and $Pr\,(q) = 0$

$$Pr\,(p \vee q) = 0 + 0 - 0$$
$$= 0$$

These results are, of course, the same as those for the matrix definitions of

MATRIX 10.1		
$\cdot$	1	0
1	1	0
0	0	0

MATRIX 10.2		
$\vee$	1	0
1	1	1
0	1	0

$\cdot$ and $\vee$, with 1 for T and 0 for F (Matrices 10.1 and 10.2). Thus, we can regard truth values as peculiar sorts of probabilities or probabilities as peculiar kinds of truth values. At any rate, where the two theories overlap they give the same results.

In philosophically interesting applications of probability theory we rarely have numerical probabilities to deal with. In fact, this absence of numerical value is almost the characteristic feature of philosophical applications of probability. However, the general *proportions* as laid out by the numerical theory of probability hold. For example, the more probable a hypothesis is, the less probable its denial is and vice versa, which is what is stated by

$$Pr\,(\sim p) = 1 - Pr\,(p)$$

Intelligent Design or Chance?

Of the philosophical arguments which are basically likelihood arguments, perhaps the most interesting is the argument for an intelligent designer of the universe. The argument is that the observed order and understandability of the universe is much more probable under the hypothesis of an intelligent designer than under any other hypothesis. This argument is often criticized on the mistaken assumption that it is an argument from analogy. In fact, it is a very bad argument from analogy, but a rather good likelihood argument.

If the meaningful alternatives can be reduced to chance or design (as arguably they can), then we can argue as follows. It is possible but extremely improbable that the observed apparent order and apparent understandability of the universe is due to chance, just as it is possible but extremely improbable for alphabet blocks spelled out at random to form some message, say, HELP ME. However, on the hypothesis of an intelligent designer who moreover wishes the universe to be understandable to us, the observed order and regularity is highly probable just as in the case of the blocks the hypothesis that they were arranged by an intelligent being makes it likely that they do convey a massege. Thus, if we follow maximum-likelihood reasoning, we will prefer hypothesis of design.

The chance hypothesis has two further embarrassing consequences. First, if the apparent order of the universe is due to chance, the order is only apparent, and we do not in fact understand anything about the universe, but only think we do. Furthermore on the chance hypothesis we would have no reason to expect the apparent order and understandability of the universe to continue to hold. We might compare the situation with that of trying to decode what we thought to be a coded message. As soon as we find that it is only a jumble of letters put together at random, we not only realize that we can have no further success in decoding it, we also realize that any apparent success we have had in decoding it is illusory.

EXERCISES 10.3

A. You have the following cards: the 2 and 3 of hearts, the 4, 5, and 6 of clubs, and the 7 of spades. You draw a card at random. Let

A # The card drawn has an even number
B # The card drawn is a heart
C # The card drawn is a spade

(1) In terms of this situation answer the following questions:
1. Are A and B independent?
2. Are $\sim A$ and B independent?
3. Are A and C mutually exclusive?
4. Are B and C mutually exclusive?
5. Are A and B mutually exclusive?

(2) Find the probabilities of the following:

1. A	2. B	3. C
4. $A \cdot B$	5. $A \cdot C$	6. $B \cdot C$
7. $A \vee B$	8. $A \vee C$	9. $B \vee C$
10. $A \supset B$	11. $A \supset C$	12. $B \supset C$
13. $(A \vee B) \vee C$	14. $(A \cdot B) \vee \sim C$	15. $(\sim A \vee \sim B) \vee C$

B. Consider a case where we have six bags with five marbles in each, with the following distribution of black and white marbles.

Bag 1.	BBBBB	Bag 4.	BBWWW
Bag 2.	BBBBW	Bag 5.	BWWWW
Bag 3.	BBBWW	Bag 6.	WWWWW

Let H_n be the hypothesis that we have bag n. We choose one bag at random, meaning that for any given bag $\Pr(H_n) = 1/6$. We choose one marble from the bag we have chosen, after shaking it thoroughly, and it turns out to be black. Take it as given that the probability of this event is $\Pr(E_1) = 1/2$, before you have begun the experiment.

1. Can we rule out any hypothesis without further ado?
2. What is the probability of the observed evidence for each hypothesis?
3. If you have answered Exercise 2 correctly you now have $\Pr(H_n)$, $\Pr(E_1)$, and $\Pr(E_1/H_n)$ for each H_n. Use these numbers and Bayes' Theorem to find $\Pr(H_n/E_1)$ for each H_n.
4. What is the relation between the likelihoods obtained in Exercise 2 and the probabilities obtained in Exercise 3?
5. In the light of your answer to Exercise 4 could a maximum-likelihood argument be used if you had to choose one H_n?

6–10. Suppose two black balls had been drawn. Take it as given that the probability of this event is $\Pr(E_2) = 1/3$. Attempt to answer Exercises 1–5 for this changed situation.

C. Are the following statements about probability consistent or inconsistent with the discussion of probability in Section 10.3? (Source: Hume, *Enquiry*.)
1. Though there is no such thing as chance in the world, our ignorance of the real cause of any event has the same influence on the understanding and gives rise to the same sort of belief or opinion [as if there were chance].
2. If a die were marked with one figure on four sides and another figure on the remaining two sides it would be more probable that the former would turn up than the latter.
3. If the die had a thousand sides marked in the same manner and only one side different, the probability would be much higher [that the figure marked on the thousand sides would turn up].
4. When the mind looks forward to discover the event which may result from the throw of such a die, it considers the turning up of each particular side as equally provable.
5. Finding [that] a greater number of sides lead to one event than to the other . . . gives rise immediately, by an inexplicable contrivance of nature to a belief and gives that event an advantage over the other. . . . Let anyone try to account for this operation of the mind . . . and he will be aware of the difficulty.

10.4 SCIENTIFIC INFERENCE

In this section we will say something about the purely logical features of the methods of inference used in the sciences. The detailed study of these methods belongs to the philosophy of science or perhaps to a separate discipline related both to logic and to philosophy of science. However, there is enough connection between these methods and logical techniques to make a brief look at scientific inference rewarding.

Confirming Scientific Hypotheses

Consider first the relatively simple case where we have a simple scientific hypothesis which can be written as a universally quantified conditional statement. For example, if we let

$$Mx \;\#\; x \text{ is a metal} \qquad Hx \;\#\; x \text{ is heated} \qquad Ex \;\#\; x \text{ expands}$$

then the hypothesis

$$(x)\, ((Mx \cdot Hx) \supset Ex)$$

might be advanced. Suppose that we found a metal, call it rigidium, which did not expand when heated. If we let

$$r \, \# \, \text{rigidium}$$

then we would know that

$$(Mr \cdot Hr) \cdot \sim Er \qquad \text{which implies} \qquad (\exists x)\, ((Mx \cdot Hx) \cdot \sim Ex)$$

which is equivalent to

$$\sim (x)\, ((Mx \cdot Hx) \supset Ex)$$

so that by a series of purely deductive steps we can show that the supposed existence of rigidium would disprove the hypothesis in question.

However, suppose that we do not find a metal which does not expand when heated. Suppose, instead, that we try metal after metal and each one expands when heated. It then would seem more and more likely that the hypothesis was true. Our confidence in the hypothesis would grow with each confirmation. Now obviously there is no deductive argument from statements such as "iron expands when heated" or "copper expands when heated" to

$$(x)\, ((Mx \cdot Hx) \supset Ex)$$

but the movement from confirming instances to confidence in a hypothesis is extremely important in science. Our problem, then, is to give a logical analysis of the relation between confirming instances of a hypothesis and our legitimate increased confidence in the hypothesis. If none of the systems of logic studied so far is adequate to analyze this relation, perhaps we need a new system of logic, an inductive logic.

It has been suggested that this relationship can be analyzed in terms of probability. Supposing that we can assign an initial probability to a proposed scientific hypothesis, an initial probability to the observed evidence, and find the probability of the evidence given the truth of the hypothesis, then Bayes' Theorem

$$\Pr(H/E) = \frac{\Pr(H) \times \Pr(E/H)}{\Pr(E)}$$

will presumably give us the probability of the hypothesis relative to that evidence. The difficulty is that it is extremely difficult to suggest any plausible way of assigning initial probabilities to scientific hypotheses and to the evidence for these hypotheses.

In the light of these difficulties, it has been suggested that the relation between a hypothesis and its confirming instances should be analyzed in terms of likelihood rather than probability. The likelihood of a hypothesis on certain evidence is the same as the probability of that evidence, given the truth of the hypothesis

$$L\,(H/E) \,=\, Pr\,(E/H)$$

As we noted in the section on probability, we are sometimes justified in using a *maximum-likelihood* technique for choosing between competing hypotheses. We choose the hypothesis with the maximum likelihood, or in other words, the hypothesis which gives the highest probability to the observed evidence. However, maximum likelihood has difficulties of its own. Suppose, for example, that on stepping out of his space capsule the first man on Mars observes a small green rabbit. The hypothesis which makes this observation most probable is that all living creatures on Mars are green rabbits. However, this hypothesis seems open to question on other grounds. Surely it is more reasonable to expect a variety of life forms on Mars supposing that there are any at all.

Such objections have led some philosophers of science to reject the use of probability or related notions in analysing the relation between a hypothesis and its confirming instances. It has been suggested that no hypothesis receives any positive weight from instances which confirm it but, rather, that each hypothesis exists on sufferance until disconfirmed; all we can say of a hypothesis which has been put to the test a hundred times and survived each test is that it has not been disconfirmed. Nothing positive can be said about it, only that it has survived so far and can be accepted provisionally until it fails a test.

Confirmation Theory

The difficulty here is that this theory seems not to make a distinction between some far-out hypothesis which has survived one test and a long-standing generalization which has survived thousands of tests and is accepted as a law. Such difficulties have led some of the initial supporters of the theory we are discussing to modify it in the direction of giving some positive weight to a hypothesis which has survived a number of tests. But they emphasize that this "corroboration" does not obey the laws of probability and is not to be regarded as a probability or likelihood.

Some logicians and philosophers of science are now working on interesting new analyses of the relation between a hypothesis and its confirming instances. Such concepts as the amount of information conveyed by a hypothesis or the degree of unexpectedness of a hypothesis or piece of evidence may play an important part in future analyses. This whole area is being increasingly recognized as a promising field of study and Confirmation Theory, as it is sometimes called, seems to be on its way to becoming an established part of the philosophy of science, a part which has obvious relations to logic.

Paradox of the Ravens

A problem which arises in most theories of confirmation is the so-called paradox of the ravens. It arises from the apparently reasonable requirement that logically equivalent hypotheses should receive the same confirmation from a given instance. If we let

$$Rx \text{ \# } x \text{ is a raven} \quad \text{and} \quad Bx \text{ \# } x \text{ is black}$$

then a possible hypothesis would be $(x) (Rx \supset Bx)$. This would presumably be confirmed by some positive instance Ra $\cdot$ Ba, where a is the name of some individual. However, the statement

$$(x) (\sim Bx \supset \sim Rx)$$

is equivalent to our hypothesis and presumably an instance $\sim Bb \cdot \sim Rb$, where b is the name of a white shoe or a red herring, would confirm this hypothesis. But if the instance confirms the equivalent hypothesis, it confirms the original hypothesis. Thus the observation of a white shoe or a red herring apparently confirms the hypothesis that all ravens are black, which seems highly paradoxical. A number of solutions have been suggested for this paradox, but none has been generally accepted.

Revolution in Scientific Theory

Our discussion so far has in fact been highly abstract and artificial since a given hypothesis is rarely so directly related to confirming instances. Typically a given observation is implied by the conjunction of a number of statements, one of which is the hypothesis which we are trying to test. Now if

$$((A \cdot B) \cdot C) \supset D$$

and we find that D is false, then all we can conclude is

$$(\sim A \lor \sim B) \lor \sim C$$

Now if C is a new and highly speculative hypothesis and A and B are well-established laws or generalizations, we may be confident that C has been refuted. However it may sometimes happen that C is true and the well-established B (or A) is in fact false. So we rarely have a direct confrontation of hypothesis with evidence.

In fact, as we investigate the actual procedure by which scientists confirm or accept hypotheses, we find that, at least in well-developed sciences such as physics, a whole complicated theoretical structure may be being tested. It has even been argued that the basic theories of a science partly determine what counts as evidence or what counts as an observation. There seems to be some exaggeration in this position but a study of the history of science shows that in fact a highly complex process goes on. A theory or set of theories which is well established rarely solves all the problems which arise in the area it covers. As time goes on anomalies, phenomena which cannot be explained by the accepted theories, become more and more troublesome. Eventually this may lead to a scientific revolution in which established theories are overthrown and replaced by new basic theories. With the new theories may come a new approach, new interests, new problems so that it is hard to even compare the scientific work before and after the revolution.

Perhaps enough has been said to suggest that, when we begin to look at the actual processes of scientific inference as they have actually gone on in the past history of science and are now going on, we have a very complex situation which seems far removed from simple hypotheses and their confirming instances. However, it is equally true that the complex arguments which have gone on in the history of philosophy and are now going on seem far removed from the relatively simple patterns of deductive logic. Just as Aristotle's syllogisms were only a first step in deductive logic, but were useful for some purposes and gave a good start to deductive logic, so the present work of confirmation theorists may apply directly to some simple cases and provide a starting point for deeper investigations.

EXERCISES 10.4

A. Symbolize Exercises 1–5 using the machinery of predicate logic. Give your own dictionary.
 1. All emeralds are green stones.
 2. All emeralds are green, hard stones.
 3. No stones which are not green are emeralds.
 4. The stone in my ring is a green emerald.
 5. The stone in my ring is a hard, green emerald.
 Using the symbolizations from 1–5, answer the following questions. Justify your answer briefly.
 6. Is 4 a confirming instance for 1? For 2? For 3?
 7. Is 5 a confirming instance for 1? For 2? For 3?
 8. Does 4 confirm 1 more highly than it confirms 3?
 9. Does 5 confirm 2 more highly than 4 does?
 10. It is generally true that an instance which confirms a hypothesis confirms hypotheses which are implied by that hypothesis?

B. (1) Mention a confirming or disconfirming observation for each of the following theories. (2) How important, historically, was the instance in confirming or disconfirming the theory?

1. The theory that the earth is round
2. Einstein's Theory of Relativity (Special or General)
3. The theory that the earth goes around the sun
4. The ether theory
5. Darwin's theory of natural selection

10.5 PHILOSOPHICAL DIFFICULTIES

This section will not discuss philosophical difficulties peculiar to the material in this chapter, many of which have at least been touched on in the sections, but will consider some general difficulties about the application of logic to philosophy.

If you take any textbook of readings in philosophy or a current issue of any philosophical journal, you may ask yourself how what you have learned in this book can be applied to actual philosophical arguments. Let me state the negative side first.

Value of Techniques of Logic

There are a good many philosophical arguments which cannot usefully be analyzed by the techniques of formal logic and, therefore, not by the techniques which you have learned from this book. In traditional philosophical material there is little of formal techniques and almost no symbolism. In modern philosophical papers you may find symbols, but you will rarely find extended proofs or formalized arguments. Thus if you expect everything you have learned to be immediately and easily applicable to most philosophical material, you will be disappointed.

But there is a good deal to be said on the positive side. As we have seen in some of the examples given in the sections on applications much material that does not explicitly employ formal techniques can nevertheless, be better understood by use of these techniques. Of the modern material which does use formal techniques, you should be able to understand any symbols and techniques used in general philosophical material, though not all of what appears in the journals devoted exclusively to mathematical logic. To aid you with this, Appendix C gives some of the different symbols which are used instead of those which we have used. The *Principia* notation used in this book could be vastly improved; it was used in this volume because it is the most widely used notation. There are suggestions for further reading in logic at the end of this section, as well as some further reading about some of the problems dealt with in this chapter.

Analysis of Philosophical Arguments

In concluding this book it is well to remind ourselves of what formal logic can and cannot do in the analysis of philosophical arguments. If an argument can be proved to be valid in an accepted system of logic, then we can be sure that, if the premises are true, the conclusion is true. Whether or not the premises are true is usually a matter for philosophical discussion and can rarely be decided by formal logic. On the other hand, if an argument seems to be an instance of an invalid pattern in some system of logic or if we can find no way of showing it to be valid in any system, this does not show that the premises do not imply the conclusion. There may be logical systems yet undeveloped which will show the validity of such an argument. We may even have missed some way of applying standard systems of logic to the argument.

Thus our attitude should be cautious toward philosophical arguments which cannot be shown to be logically valid in any accepted system but which are advanced by competent philosophers. We should not say, "This argument is worthless," but rather, "I cannot see the worth of this argument." Even an argument which seems to be an obvious fallacy may be salvageable in some way. Out of regard for the truth as well as out of fairness to an opponent we should always try to do full justice to any argument which we are considering.

Unlike the lawyer, whose duty to his client is to win the case and who may take any legal means to do it, the philosopher should be concerned with finding the truth rather than with winning or losing an argument. One of the memorable expressions of this attitude is found in the words of Socrates as reported by Plato in his dialogue, *Meno*: "Some things I have said of which I am not altogether confident. But that we shall be better and braver and less helpless if we think that we ought to enquire than we should have been if we had indulged in the idle fancy that there was no knowing and no use in seeking to know what we do not know:—that is a theme upon which I am ready to fight in word and deed, to the utmost of my power."

READING LIST

Two books from which one can learn a great deal about logic are
Kneale, W., and Kneale, M. *The Development of Logic* (Oxford University Press, New York), 1962.
Prior, A. N. *Formal Logic* (Oxford University Press, New York), 1962.
Both of them have been cited in previous reading lists. Two books which are valuable for the student who wishes to study logic as a formal system are
Church, Alonzo *Introduction to Mathematical Logic* (Princeton University Press, Princeton, N.J.), 1956.
Stoll, Robert *Sets, Logic and Axiomatic Theories* (W. H. Freeman & Co., San Francisco, Calif.), 1961.
Two interesting and important works in the philosophy of logic are the following:
Strawson, P. F. *Introduction to Logical Theory* (Methuen & Co., London, U.K.), 1962.
Geach, P. T. *Reference and Generality*, 2d edition (Princeton University Press, Princeton, N.J.), 1968.

Two introductory logic books whose coverage overlaps to some extent with this one but which go on to develop logic in other directions are

Copi, Irving   *Symbolic Logic*, 3d edition (The Macmillan Company, New York), 1967.

Suppes, Patrick   *Introduction to Logic* (Van Nostrand Reinhold Company, New York), 1963.

Finally, every student of logic should be familiar with Lewis Carroll's sprightly and amusing introductions to traditional logic, written for children, and his great classics of logic on holiday, the Alice books:

Carroll, Lewis   *The Game of Logic* and *Symbolic Logic* (Dover Publications, Inc., New York), 1955.

——— *Alice in Wonderland* and *Through the Looking Glass*, especially Martin Gardiner's annotated edition (Clarkson N. Potter, Inc., New York), 1960.

Appendix A
SIMPLIFYING COMPOUND PROPOSITIONS

Some fairly elaborate methods have been worked out by logicians for finding the simplest form of a compound proposition. The simple methods given in this appendix will probably be sufficient for any simplification problem which is likely to arise in a philosophical context. These methods depend on using truth tables and examining the pattern of T's and F's characteristic of each compound expression, rather than on manipulation of symbols.

TABLE A.1

((p	⊃ (~ p ∨ (p ≡ p))) • (~ p	⊃ (p • p))) ∨ p		
T T	F T T T T	T T F T	T T T T T T
F T	T F T F T	F F T F	F F F F F F
√ √	√ √ √ √ √	√ √ √ √	√ √ √ √ √

To begin with the simplest case, any propositional form which has only one variable will need a truth table with only two lines. If it has two T's in its remaining column it will be a tautology and equivalent to p ∨ ~p; if it has two F's, it will be a contradiction and equivalent to p · ~p. If it has one T and one F, then it will be equivalent either to p or to ~p. Thus, an elaborate statement like that in Table A.1 can be seen, after working out the truth table, to be equivalent to p.

With two variables there is greater complication. Any form with two variables will need a truth table with four lines. Again, any form with four T's will be equivalent to p ∨ ~p; any form with four F's will be equivalent to p · ~p. If a form has three T's in its remaining column it will be equivalent to one of the propositions in Table A.2. If a form has three F's, it will be

TABLE A.2

p	q		p ∨ q	p ∨ ~q	~p ∨ q	~p ∨ ~q
T	T		T	T	T	F
T	F		T	T	F	T
F	T		T	F	T	T
F	F		F	T	T	T

equivalent to one of the propositions in Table A.3. If a form has two T's

TABLE A.3

p	q		p · q	p · ~q	~p · q	~p · ~q
T	T		T	F	F	F
T	F		F	T	F	F
F	T		F	F	T	F
F	F		F	F	F	T

and two F's, it will be equivalent to one of the propositions in Table A.4.

TABLE A.4

p	q		p	~p	q	~q	p ≡ q	p ≡ ~q
T	T		T	F	T	F	T	F
T	F		T	F	F	T	F	T
F	T		F	T	T	F	F	T
F	F		F	T	F	T	T	F

This makes sixteen forms counting the tautologies and contradiction forms, and any form with two variables will be equivalent to one of these sixteen forms. Thus by truth table we discover that the form in Table A.5 is simply equivalent to p · q.

TABLE A.5

p	q	$((p \vee (q \cdot \sim p)) \cdot (p \vee (p \cdot q))) \cdot (q \cdot (p \vee \sim q))$
T	T	TTTFFT TTTTTT TTTTTFT
T	F	TTFFFT TTTTFF FFFTTTF
F	T	FTTTTF FFFFFT FTFFFFT
F	F	FFFFTF FFFFFF FFFFTTF
		√ √ √ √ √ √ √ √ √ √ √ √ √ √ √ √ √

For forms with three variables there are 256 possible patterns of T's and F's which can occur in the final column. Thus, if we make some fairly arbitrary decisions as to simplicity (such as, is $\sim p \vee q$ simpler than $p \supset q$?) we can find and list 256 "simplest" forms. This has been done by myself and my students, using computers to do most of the work, and the result is printed in this book as Appendix B.* To use the list in Appendix B for simplification follow this procedure:

1. Set up a truth table for the form to be simplified and find the pattern of T's and F's in the last column remaining after all the crossing out has been done.

2. Convert this column to a column of numbers by the instructions in Table A.6.

TABLE A.6

If line 1 has T write 128	
2 ,, ,, ,, 64	
3 ,, ,, ,, 32	
4 ,, ,, ,, 16	If the line has F, write 0
5 ,, ,, ,, 8	
6 ,, ,, ,, 4	
7 ,, ,, ,, 2	
8 ,, ,, ,, 1	

3. Add the column of numbers.

4. Look up the number thus obtained on the list in Appendix B. The form listed next to that number is the simplest form equivalent to the form you started with. Let us do this for a complex form (Table A.7). Number 234 on our list is $r \vee (p \cdot q)$. Therefore this is the simplest form equivalent to

$$((p \cdot q) \vee (q \cdot r)) \vee ((p \cdot r) \vee r)$$

* For a description of the computer methods used, see my paper, "Doing Logic by Computer," *Notre Dame Journal of Formal Logic*, Vol. X, No. 2, April, 1969.

TABLE A.7

	p	q	r	$((p \cdot q) \vee (q \cdot r)) \vee$		$((p \cdot r) \vee r)$
1.	T	T	T	T T T T T T T	128	T T T T
2.	T	T	F	T T T F T F F	64	T F F F F
3.	T	F	T	T F F F F F T	32	T T T T T
4.	T	F	F	T F F F F F F	0	T F F F F
5.	F	T	T	F F T F T T T	8	F F T T T
6.	F	T	F	F F T F T F F	0	F F F F F
7.	F	F	T	F F F F F F T	2	F F T T T
8.	F	F	F	F F F F F F F	0	F F F F F
				√ √ √ √ √ √ √	234	√ √ √ √ √

For forms with four or more variables, this procedure is impractical since there would be 65,536 simplest forms for four variables and 2^{32} simplest forms for five. For forms that are this complex, one must employ methods which involve manipulating the symbols by rules such as Distribution, Association and eliminating superfluous expressions by means of such rules as Repetition, together with principles such as

$$p \equiv (p \vee (q \cdot \sim q)) \qquad \text{and} \qquad p \equiv (p \cdot (q \vee \sim q))$$

I have never found such methods to be of the slightest use in philosophical applications of logic, and will, therefore, content myself with giving you some references to books where such methods are discussed in detail.

REFERENCES

Copi, I. *Symbolic Logic* (The Macmillan Company, New York), 1967, Appendix A.
Quine, W. V. O. *Methods of Logic* (Holt Rinehart & Winston, New York), 1959, pp. 52–63.

Appendix B
THE 256
SIMPLEST
FORMS

Since this list was produced by computer, a minus sign was substituted for the symbol ∼, and = was substituted for ≡. This has been changed, but for technical reasons the spacing of the computer list has been preserved. The second number from the left is the number of lines of an eight-line truth table for which the expression at the right is true.

0	0		(	P	·	∼P)
1	1	∼P	·(	∼Q	·	∼R)
2	1	∼P	·(	∼Q	·	R)
3	2		∼P	·	∼Q	
4	1	∼P	·(	Q	·	∼R)
5	2		∼P	·	∼R	
6	2	∼P	·(	Q	≡	∼R)
7	3	∼P	·(	∼Q	v	∼R)
8	1	∼P	·(	Q	·	R)
9	2	∼P	·(	Q	≡	R)
10	2		∼P	·	R	

		Formula
11	3	$\sim P \cdot (\sim Q \lor R)$
12	2	$\sim P \cdot Q$
13	3	$\sim P \cdot (Q \lor \sim R)$
14	3	$\sim P \cdot (Q \lor R)$
15	4	$\sim P$
16	1	$P \cdot (\sim Q \cdot \sim R)$
17	2	$\sim Q \cdot \sim R$
18	2	$\sim Q \cdot (P \equiv \sim R)$
19	3	$\sim Q \cdot (\sim P \lor \sim R)$
20	2	$\sim R \cdot (P \equiv \sim Q)$
21	3	$\sim R \cdot (\sim P \lor \sim Q)$
22	3	$(\sim P \cdot (Q \equiv \sim R)) \lor (\sim R \cdot (\sim Q \cdot P))$
23	4	$(\sim P \cdot (\sim Q (\lor \sim R)) \lor (\sim R \cdot (\sim Q \cdot P))$
24	2	$(P \equiv \sim Q) \cdot (P \equiv \sim R)$
25	3	$(\sim P \lor \sim Q) \cdot (Q \equiv R)$
26	3	$(\sim P \lor \sim Q) \cdot (P \equiv \sim R)$
27	4	$(\sim P \cdot R) \lor (\sim Q \cdot \sim R)$
28	3	$(\sim P \lor \sim R) \cdot (P \equiv \sim Q)$
29	4	$(\sim P \cdot Q) \lor (\sim Q \cdot \sim R)$
30	4	$P \equiv (\sim Q \cdot \sim R)$
31	5	$\sim P \lor (\sim Q \cdot \sim R)$
32	1	$P \cdot (\sim Q \cdot R)$
33	2	$\sim Q \cdot (P \equiv R)$
34	2	$\sim Q \cdot R$
35	3	$\sim Q \cdot (\sim P \lor R)$
36	2	$(P \equiv \sim Q) \cdot (P \equiv R)$
37	3	$(\sim P \lor \sim Q) \cdot (P \equiv R)$
38	3	$(\sim P \lor \sim Q) \cdot (Q \equiv \sim R)$
39	4	$(\sim P \cdot \sim R) \lor (\sim Q \cdot R)$
40	2	$R \cdot (P \equiv \sim Q)$
41	3	$(\sim P \cdot (Q \equiv R)) \lor (R \cdot (\sim Q \cdot P))$
42	3	$R \cdot (\sim P \lor \sim Q)$
43	4	$(\sim P \cdot (\sim Q \lor R)) \lor (R \cdot (\sim Q \cdot P))$
44	3	$(\sim P \lor R) \cdot (P \equiv \sim Q)$
45	4	$P \equiv (\sim Q \cdot R)$
46	4	$(\sim P \cdot Q) \lor (\sim Q \cdot R)$
47	5	$\sim P \lor (\sim Q \cdot R)$
48	2	$P \cdot \sim Q$
49	3	$\sim Q \cdot (P \lor \sim R)$
50	3	$\sim Q \cdot (P \lor R)$
51	4	$\sim Q$
52	3	$(P \lor \sim R) \cdot (P \equiv \sim Q)$
53	4	$(P \cdot \sim Q) \lor (\sim P \cdot \sim R)$
54	4	$Q \equiv (\sim P \cdot \sim R)$
55	5	$\sim Q \lor (\sim P \cdot \sim R)$
56	3	$(P \lor R) \cdot (P \equiv \sim Q)$
57	4	$Q \equiv (\sim P \cdot R)$
58	4	$(P \cdot \sim Q) \lor (\sim P \cdot R)$
59	5	$\sim Q \lor (\sim P \cdot R)$
60	4	$P \equiv \sim Q$
61	5	$(\sim P \cdot \sim R) \lor (P \equiv \sim Q)$
62	5	$(\sim P \cdot R) \lor (P \equiv \sim Q)$
63	6	$\sim P \lor \sim Q$
64	1	$P \cdot (Q \cdot \sim R)$

```
65  2                                  ~R  ·(        P           ≡        Q)
66  2                 (      P    ≡     Q)   ·(       P           ≡     ~R)
67  3                 (    ~P    v    ~R)    ·(       P           ≡        Q)
68  2                                        Q        ·        ~R
69  3                                  ~R  ·(      ~P        v        Q)
70  3                 (    ~P    v     Q)    ·(       Q           ≡     ~R)
71  4                 (    ~P    ·    ~Q)   v(        Q           ·     ~R)
72  2                                        Q   ·(      P           ≡     ~R)
73  3  ( ~P  ·( Q    ≡        R))     v(    ~R      ·  (        Q           ·       P))
74  3                 (    ~P    v     Q)    ·(       P           ≡     ~R)
75  4                               P    ≡ (       Q           ·     ~R)
76  3                               Q    ·(      ~P        v        ~R)
77  4  ( ~P  ·( Q    v     ~R))     v(    ~R      ·  (        Q           ·       P))
78  4                 (    ~P    ·     R)    v(       Q           ·     ~R)
79  5                                  ~P   v(        Q           ·     ~R)
80  2                                        P        ·        ~R
81  3                                  ~R  ·(        P           v     ~Q)
82  3                 (      P    v   ~Q)    ·(       P           ≡     ~R)
83  4                 (      P    ·   ~R)    v(     ~P          ·      ~Q)
84  3                                  ~R  ·(        P           v        Q)
85  4                                                        ~R
86  4                               R    ≡ (      ~P          ·      ~Q)
87  5                                  ~R  v(      ~P          ·      ~Q)
88  3                 (      P    v    Q)    ·(       P           ≡     ~R)
89  4                               R    ≡ (      ~P          ·        Q)
90  4                                        P        ≡        ~R
91  5                 (    ~P    ·    ~Q)   v(        P           ≡     ~R)
92  4                 (      P    ·   ~R)    v(     ~P          ·        Q)
93  5                                  ~R  v(      ~P          ·        Q)
94  5                 (    ~P    ·     Q)    v(       P           ≡     ~R)
95  6                                         ~P        v        ~R
96  2                               P    ·(       Q           ≡     ~R)
97  3  (    P  ·( Q    ≡     ~R))    v(    ~R      ·  (      ~Q          ·       ~P))
98  3                 (      P    v   ~Q)    ·(       Q           ≡     ~R)
99  4                               Q    ≡ (       P           ·     ~R
100 3                 (      P    v    Q)    ·(       Q           ≡     ~R)
101 4                               R    ≡ (       P           ·     ~Q)
102 4                                        Q        ≡        ~R
103 5                 (    ~P    ·    ~Q)   v(        Q           ≡     ~R)
104 3  (    P  ·( Q    ≡     ~R))    v(    R       ·  (        Q           ·       ~P))
105 4                               P    ≡ (       Q           ≡     ~R)
106 4                               R    ≡ (      ~P          v      ~Q)
107 5  ( ~P v( Q (≡     ~R))    ·(     R      v (      ~Q          v       P))
108 4                               Q    ≡ (      ~P          v     ~R)
109 5  ( ~P v( Q    ≡     ~R))    ·(    ~R      v (        Q           v       P))
110 5                 (    ~P    ·     Q)    v(       Q           ≡     ~R)
111 6                                  ~P   v(        Q           ≡     ~R)
112 3                               P    ·(      ~Q          v     ~R)
113 4  (    P  ·( ~Q v    ~R))    v(    ~R      ·  (      ~Q          ·       ~P))
114 4                 (      P    ·   ~R)    v(     ~Q          ·        R)
115 5                                  ~Q  v(        P           ·     ~R)
116 4                 (      P    ·   ~Q)    v(       Q           ·     ~R)
117 5                                  ~R  v(        P           ·     ~Q)
118 5                 (      P    ·   ~Q)    v(       Q           ≡     ~R)
```

```
119 6                                        ~Q        v       ~R
120 4                           P   ≡ (      ~Q        v      ~R)
121 5 (   P v (   Q  ≡      R))    · (    ~R       v  (    ~Q       v     ~P))
122 5           (       P    ·    ~Q)    v (        P       ≡    ~R)
123 6                           ~Q  v (        P       ≡      ~R)
124 5           (       P    ·    ~R)    v (        P       ≡    ~Q)
125 6                           ~R  v (        P       ≡     ~Q)
126 6           (       P    ≡    ~Q)    v (        P       ≡    ~R)
127 7                           ~P  v (      ~Q        v      ~R)
128 1                           P    · (       Q       ·       R)
129 2           (       P    ≡     Q)    · (        P       ≡       R)
130 2                           R    · (        P       ≡       Q)
131 3           (     ~P    v      R)    · (        P       ≡       Q)
132 2                           Q    · (        P       ≡       R)
133 3           (     ~P    v      Q)    · (        P       ≡       R)
134 3 ( ~P · (   Q   ≡     ~R))    v (      R       ·  (       Q       ·       P))
135 4                           P   ≡ (       Q       ·       R)
136 2                                       Q         ·       R
137 3           (     ~P    v      Q)    · (       Q       ≡       R)
138 3                           R    · (     ~P        v       Q)
139 4           (     ~P    ·    ~Q)    v (       Q       ·       R)
140 3                           Q    · (     ~P        v       R)
141 4           (     ~P    ·    ~R)    v (       Q       ·       R)
142 4 ( ~P · (   Q   v      R))    v (      R       ·  (       Q       ·       P))
143 5                           ~P  v (       Q       ·       R)
144 2                           P    · (       Q       ≡       R)
145 3           (       P    v    ~Q)    · (       Q       ≡       R)
146 3 (   P · (   Q  ≡      R))    v (      R       ·  (     ~Q       ·     ~P))
147 4                           Q   ≡ (       P       · )      R)
148 3 (   P · (   Q  ≡      R))    v (    ~R       ·  (       Q       ·     ~P))
149 4                           R   ≡(        P       ·        Q)
150 4                           P   ≡ (       Q       ≡       R)
151 5 ( ~P v (   Q  ≡      R))    · (    ~R       v  (     ~Q       v       P))
152 3           (       P    v     Q)    · (       Q       ≡       R)
153 4                                       Q         ≡       R
154 4                           R   ≡ (     ~P        v       Q)
155 5           (     ~P    ·    ~Q)    v (        Q       ≡       R)
156 4                           Q   ≡ (     ~P        v       R)
157 5           (     ~P    ·      Q)    v (       Q       ≡       R)
158 5 ( ~P v (   Q  ≡      R))    · (      R       v  (       Q       v       P))
159 6                           ~P  v (       Q       ≡       R)
160 2                                       P         ·       R
161 3           (       P    v    ~Q)    · (                ≡       R)
162 3                           R    · (       P       v     ~Q)
163 4           (       P    ·      R)    v (      ~P        ·     ~Q)
164 3           (       P    v      Q)    · (       P       ≡       R)
165 4                                       P         ≡       R
166 4                           R   ≡ (       P       v     ~Q)
167 5           (     ~P    ·    ~Q)    v (        P       ≡       R)
168 3                           R    · (       P       v       Q)
169 4                           R   ≡ (       P       v       Q)
170 4                                                         R
171 5                           R   v (     ~P        ·     ~Q)
172 4           (       P    ·      R)    v (      ~P        ·       Q)
```

```
173  5              (      ~P    ·      Q)    v (        P      ≡      R)
174  5                              R   v (      ~P      ·        Q)
175  6                                        ~P          v      R
176  3                              P   · (      ~Q      v      R)
177  4              (      P    ·      R)    v (        ~Q      ·    ~R)
178  4 (   P · (  ~Q   v      R))    v (      R      ·  (        ~Q      ·    ~P))
179  5                            ~Q   v (        P      ·      R)
180  4                              P   ≡ (      ~Q      v      R)
181  5              (      P    ·    ~Q)    v (        P      ≡      R)
182  5 (   P v (   Q   ≡    ~R))    · (      R      v  (        ~Q      v    ~P))
183  6                            ~Q   v (        P      ≡      R)
184  4              (      P    ·    ~Q)    v (        Q      ·      R)
185  5              (      P    ·    ~Q)    v (        Q      ≡      R)
186  5                              R   v (        P      ·    ~Q)
187  6                                        ~Q          v      R
188  5              (      P    ·      R)    v (        P      ≡    ~Q)
189  6              (      P    ≡    ~Q)    v (        P      ≡      R)
190  6                              R   v (        P      ≡    ~Q)
191  7                            ~P   v (      ~Q      v      R)
192  2                                        P          ·      Q
193  3              (      P    v    ~R)    · (        P      ≡      Q)
194  3              (      P    v      R)    · (        P      ≡      Q)
195  4                                        P      ≡      Q
196  3                              Q   · (        P      v    ~R)
197  4              (      P    ·      Q)    v (        ~P      ·    ~R)
198  4                              Q   ≡ (        P      v    ~R)
199  5              (      ~P    ·    ~R)    v (        P      ≡      Q)
200  3                              Q   · (        P      v      R)
201  4                              Q   ≡ (        P      v      R)
202  4              (      P    ·      Q)    v (        ~P      ·      R)
203  5              (      ~P    ·      R)    v (        P      ≡      Q)
204  4                                                  Q
205  5                              Q   v (        ~P      ·    ~R)
206  5                              Q   v (        ~P      ·      R)
207  6                                        ~P          v      Q
208  3                              P   · (        Q      v    ~R)
209  4              (      P    ·      Q)    v (        ~Q      ·    ~R)
210  4                              P   ≡ (        Q      v    ~R)
211  5              (      P    ·    ~R)    v (        P      ≡      Q)
212  4 (   P · (   Q   v    ~R))    v (      ~R      ·  (        Q      ·    ~P))
213  5                            ~R   v (        P      ·      Q)
214  5 (   P v (   Q   ≡    ~R))    · (      ~R      v  (        Q      v    ~P))
215  6                            ~R   v (        P      ≡      Q)
216  4              (      P    ·    ~R)    v (        Q      ·      R)
217  5              (      P    ·      Q)    v (        Q      ≡      R)
218  5              (      P    ·      Q)    v (        P      ≡    ~R)
219  6              (      P    ≡      Q)    v (        P      ≡    ~R)
220  5                              Q   v (        P      ·    ~R)
221  6                                        Q          v    ~R
222  6                              Q   v (        P      ≡    ~R)
223  7                            ~P   v (        Q      v    ~R)
224  3                              P   · (        Q      v      R)
225  4                              P   ≡ (        Q      v      R)
226  4              (      P    ·      Q)    v (        ~Q      ·      R)
```

```
227  5              (      P    ·      R)   v (        P      ≡      Q)
228  4              (      P    ·      R)   v (        Q      ·     ~R)
229  5              (      P    ·      Q)   v (        P      ≡      R)
230  5              (      P    ·      Q)   v (        Q      ≡     ~R)
231  6              (      P    ≡      Q)   v (        P      ≡      R)
232  4  (    P · (    Q    v      R))    v (    R      ·  (        Q      ·    ~P))
233  5  (    P v (    Q    ≡      R))    · (    R      v  (        Q      v    ~P))
234  5                              R    v (        P      ·      Q)
235  6                              R    v (        P      ≡      Q)
236  5                              Q    v (        P      ·      R)
237  6                              Q    v (        P      ≡      R)
238  6                                        Q        v        R
239  7                        ~P    v (        Q        v        R)
240  4                                                        P
241  5                        P    v (        ~Q        ·      ~R)
242  5                        P    v (        ~Q        ·       R)
243  6                                        P        v      ~Q
244  5                        P    v (        Q        ·      ~R)
245  6                                        P        v      ~R
246  6                        P    v (        Q        ≡      ~R)
247  7                        P    v (        ~Q        v      ~R)
248  5                        P    v (        Q        ·       R)
249  6                        P    v (        Q        ≡       R)
250  6                                        P        v       R
251  7                        P    v (        ~Q        v       R)
252  6                                        P        v       Q
253  7                        P    v (        Q        v      ~R)
254  7                        P    v (        Q   v    v       R)
255  8                                        P        v      ~P
```

Appendix C
ALTERNATE
NOTATIONS

ables C.1 and C.2 give alternate symbols for the operators and connectives used in this book, citing a book or paper in which this alternate notation is used. In many cases, such as that of the "Polish" notation used in Prior's *Formal Logic*, the notation is also used in many other books and articles; in other cases, the notation is rarely seen. Therefore, after each book title I have inserted a comment as to how widespread the notation is.

The Polish notation used by Prior has the interesting property of being parenthesis free. Connectives have "places" for two propositions, for example Kpq. If either gap (or both) is filled by another connective letter it is understood that the compound proposition formed by that connective letter is connected to the proposition in the other gap by the first connective. An "N" denies the proposition or compound that it stands before. Thus

$$\sim (p \cdot (q \vee r))$$

becomes

$$NKpAqr$$

and

$$p \supset (q \cdot (r \vee \sim s))$$

becomes

CpKqArNs

The other notations are not strikingly different from our modified *Principia* notation. The arrow instead of $\supset$ for material implication and $\wedge$ instead of $\cdot$ for "and" are probably really better symbols for their purposes, but I believe strongly that there should be one logical notation universally used and for this reason have used what comes closest to being accepted as standard logical notation.

TABLE C.1

Standard Symbols

Principia Symbol	$\sim p$	$p \cdot q$	$p \vee q$	$p \supset q$	$p \equiv q$
Alternate used in:					
Prior, *Formal Logic* (common)	Np	Kpq	Apq	Cpq	Epq
Hilbert and Ackerman, *Mathematical Logic* (rare, but historically important)	$\bar{p}$	$p \& q$	$p\,q$	$p \rightarrow q$	$p \rightleftharpoons q$
Kalish and Montague, *Logic* (fairly common, esp. in math books)	$\sim p$	$p \wedge q$	$p \vee q$	$p \rightarrow q$	$p \leftrightarrow q$
Suppes, *Introduction to Logic* (fairly common)	$-p$	$p \& q$	$p \vee q$	$p \rightarrow q$	$p \leftrightarrow q$

	$(x)\,(Fx)$	$(\exists x)\,(Fx)$
Prior	$\Pi x\,\phi x$	$\Sigma x\,\phi x$
Hilbert and Ackerman	$(x)\,F(x)$	$(\exists x)\,F(x)$
Kalish and Montague	$\wedge x Fx$	$\vee x Fx$
Suppes	$(\forall x)\,(Fx)$	$(\exists x)\,(Fx)$

TABLE C.2
Specialized Symbols

Our Notation	≡	p ⊰ q	A))B	A)(B	A((B	A()B
Alternative used in:						
Lewis and Lanford, *Symbolic Logic*	=	p ⊰ q				
DeMorgan,* *Lectures on the Syllogism*			A))B	A) · (B	A(· (B	A()B

---

* DeMorgan had a different system, which included separate symbols for such ideas as "Only A's are B." My notation was invented independently of DeMorgan's, but I am glad to acknowledge the prior invention of a similar notation by a great logician.

Appendix D
MANY-VALUED LOGIC

Some philosophers have raised the possibility of a so-called many-valued logic, for example, a logic with three values True, False, and Uncertain. Using ? for Uncertain, reasonable matrices for $\sim$, $\cdot$, $\vee$, and $\supset$ for such a three-valued logic might be Matrices D.1, D.2, D.3, and D.4.

MATRIX D.1

$\sim$	
T	F
?	?
F	T

MATRIX D.2

$\cdot$	T	?	F
T	T	?	F
?	?	?	F
F	F	F	F

MATRIX D.3

$\vee$	T	?	F
T	T	T	T
?	T	?	?
F	T	?	F

MATRIX D.4

$\supset$	T	?	F
T	T	?	F
?	T	?	?
F	T	T	T

One difficulty of such a system is that many of the logical truths of propositional logic would cease to be logical truths. For example, using the matrices above we can fill in tables for $p \vee \sim p$, $p \supset p$, and $\sim(p \cdot \sim p)$ as shown in Table D.1.

TABLE D.1

p ∨ ~p	p ⊃ p	~(p · ~ p)
T T F T	T T T	T T F F T
? ? ? ?	? ? ?	? ? ? ? ?
F T T F	F T F	T F F T F
√ √ √	√ √	√ √ √ √

Defenders of many-valued logic are sometimes willing to sacrifice p ∨ p (sometimes called "the principle of excluded middle"). But of course this involves sacrificing p ⊃ p and ~(p · ~p) also. Even if in a many-valued logic it is reasonable to deny that for any statement either it or its denial is true, it seems odd to deny that, if a statement is true, it is true or that it is always false that a statement and its denial are both true. Furthermore a great many other odd things happen in a three-valued logic. For example (p · q) ⊃ p is no longer a logical truth, nor is ((p ∨ q) · ~p) ⊃ q. In fact the whole structure of propositional logic seems to fall apart.

It might seem that all these peculiarities of many-valued logic could be taken care of by adding more values or tinkering with the matrices, but it does not seem to be the case that this can be done.* There are certain irreducible difficulties in any many-valued logic with a finite number of values. But this should remind us of the parallel difficulty in Chapter 7, about finite-valued tables for modal logic. The solution here as it was there is to introduce an infinite-valued logic.

It turns out, moreover, that we already have such an infinite-valued logic, and it is the theory of probability, which is briefly described in Section 10.3. The theory of probability obviously has discarded the so-called principle of bivalence, the principle that a meaningful proposition can only have the value True or False. In the theory of probability however, it turns out that the principle of excluded middle, p ∨ p, is still a logical truth. By a logical truth within a logic of probability we mean a statement which receives a value of 1 for any assignment of values to its components. Now consider any proposition, p, and call the probability of this proposition n. The probability of ~p will be $1 - n$, and p and ~p are obviously mutually exclusive. Thus we can use the simpler form of the addition rule.

$$\Pr(p \lor \sim p) = \Pr(p) + \Pr(\sim p) = n + (1 - n)$$

Obviously this will be 1 no matter what n is.

In general, it can be shown that any tautology of propositional logic will be a logical truth within probability theory.† Thus it seems to me that

---

* For a full discussion of the whole field of many-valued logic, see Nicholas Rescher's *Many Valued Logic* (McGraw-Hill Book Company, New York), 1969.

† Ibid., pp. 184–188.

despite the effort and ingenuity expended on it by many philosophers, many-valued logic is a dead end. Any finite-valued many-valued logic will face the difficulties discussed above, and for a satisfactory infinite-valued logic we need look no further than probability theory.

Appendix E
SOLUTIONS TO EVEN-NUMBERED EXERCISES

1.1 A

(1) *Note that auxiliary words have been added to make grouping clear.*

2. Alice minds the baby, and it cries, and also the Cheshire Cat makes trouble.

4. Alice minds the baby, and also it is not true both that the baby cries and that the Cheshire Cat makes trouble (*or,* Alice minds the baby, and also either the baby doesn't cry or the Cheshire Cat doesn't make trouble *but not* Alice minds the baby, and the baby doesn't cry *and* the Cheshire Cat doesn't make trouble).

6. If Alice minds the baby, it cries and besides that the Cheshire Cat makes trouble.

8. If Alice minds the baby, then it is not true both that it cries and the Cheshire Cat makes trouble.

10. Either if Alice minds the baby it cries or else the Cheshire Cat makes trouble.

(2) **2.** False   **4.** True   **6.** False   **8.** True   **10.** True

1.1 B

2. C ≡ (~A · ~B)

4. A ⊃ (B ∨ ~C)

1.1 C

S ╫ You are in condition of slave

C ╫ You can do what you like

H ╫ You will be happy

F ╫ Your father wants something read

W ╫ Your father wants something written

M ╫ Your mother wants something read

R ╫ Your mother wants something written

Y ╫ You would be the first summoned

B ╫ The son of the king has bad eyes

A ╫ The king will allow the son to touch his eyes

K ╫ The son has knowledge of medicine

U ╫ We understand the subject

T ╫ Everyone will trust us

P ╫ We may do as we please

I ╫ Someone will interfere with us

F ╫ Everyone will hinder us as far as he can

W ╫ The wise are seekers of wisdom

G ╫ The hardened in ignorance are the seekers

O ╫ Those who realize their own ignorance and wish to cure it are the seekers of wisdom

2. (S · ~C) ⊃ ~H   or   S ⊃ (~C ⊃ ~H)

4. ((F ∨ W) ∨ ((M ∨ R) ⊃ Y))

6. B ⊃ (~K ⊃ ~A)   or   (B · ~K) ⊃ ~A

8. (U ⊃ ((T · P) · ~I)) · (~U ⊃ ((~T · F) · ~P))

10. (~W · ~G) ⊃ (~(W ∨ G) · O)

EXERCISES 1.2

1.2 A

2. contingent   **4.** tautology   **6.** contingent   **8.** contingent

10. contradiction

1.2 B

B ╫ Alice is a boy   G ╫ Alice is a girl

A ╫ Alice is in the wood   W ╫ The White Knight is in the wood

2. B ⊃ ~G contingent B ⊃ ~~B would be a tautology, but *nonboy* does not mean the same as *girl*.

4. (A · W) ⊃ A tautology

1.2 C

W ╫ You think we're waxworks   P ╫ You ought to pay

A ╫ You think we're alive   S ╫ You ought to speak

2. $(((W \supset P) \cdot (A \supset S)) \cdot (A \vee W)) \supset (P \vee S)$ tautology

4, 6, 8, 10. Cannot be done in propositional logic because they depend on meaning of words inside the sentence.

EXERCISES 1.3

1.3 A

2. not equivalent   **4.** not equivalent   **6.** not equivalent

8. equivalent   **10.** not equivalent

1.3 B

H ╫ The Hatter had tea with milk

D ╫ The Dormous had tea with milk

A ╫ The Hare had tea with milk

T ╫ You eat only treacle

I ╫ You will be ill

2. (a) $H \cdot (D \vee H)$ (b) $(H \cdot D) \cdot A$ not equivalent

4. (a) $\sim(T \supset I)$ (b) $T \cdot \sim I$ equivalent

1.3 C

E ╫ The gods exist

J ╫ The gods are just

B ╫ x is the beginning of change

O ╫ x has a soul

W ╫ Soul is what is self-moving

I ╫ Soul is the origin of change

N ╫ One soul is the origin of good, another of evil

P ╫ The gods punish evildoing

S ╫ x is changed by something else

L ╫ x has life

M ╫ x is self-moving

C ╫ What is self-moving is the origin of change

G ╫ One soul is the origin of good and evil

2. **(a)** $E \supset (J \supset P)$ **(b)** $\sim(\sim E \vee \sim J) \supset P$ equivalent

4. **(a)** $S \supset \sim B$ **(b)** $B \supset \sim S$ equivalent

6. **(a)** $(N \supset S) \cdot (S \supset M)$ **(b)** $(M \supset S) \cdot (S \supset N)$ not equivalent

8. **(a)** $(W \cdot C) \supset I$ **(b)** $\sim(\sim I \cdot (W \cdot C))$ equivalent

10. **(a)** $G \vee E$ **(b)** $\sim G \supset E$ equivalent

EXERCISES 1.4

1.4 A

TRUTH TABLE 1.4A

b	a	$((b \equiv \sim a) \cdot \sim a) \supset b$
T	T	T F F T F F T T
T	F	T T T F T T T T
F	T	F T F T F F T F
F	F	F F T F F T T F
		√ √ √ √ √ √ √

2. Valid. Truth Table 1.4A provides an example.

4. valid   **6.** valid   **8.** valid   **10.** valid

1.4 B

2. B # Mock Turtle begins
C # Mock Turtle finishes

$\sim$B $\supset$ $\sim$F
$\dfrac{F}{B}$ valid

(Note: *Can* and *must* cannot be
adequately translated.)

4. Q # The Queen won
S # Someone was beheaded

Q v S
$\dfrac{\sim Q}{S}$ valid

1.4 C

L # The gods love courage
U # Euthyphro is pious
P # Euthyphro is pleasing to the gods
R # The gods profit
O # The gods owe us something
E # Socrates speculates about the heavens
W # Socrates makes a weaker case appear
    stronger
A # Others must not be as wise as they
    appear

C # Courage is pious
J # Euthyphro is just
S # Our services to the gods
    are like a slave's
I # Socrates is like the comic
    poet's philosophers
N # No one is wiser than
    Socrates
V # Socrates is very wise

  2. (L $\supset$ C) $\supset$ (C $\supset$ L)   invalid
  4. ((U $\supset$ J) $\cdot$ (J $\supset$ P)) $\supset$ (P $\supset$ U)   invalid
  6. (((S $\supset$ R) $\cdot$ (R $\supset$ O)) $\cdot$ $\sim$S) $\supset$ $\sim$O   invalid
  8. ((I $\supset$ (E $\cdot$ W)) $\cdot$ ($\sim$E $\cdot$ $\sim$W)) $\supset$ $\sim$I   valid
10. ((N $\supset$ (V v A)) $\cdot$ $\sim$V) $\supset$ A   invalid

EXERCISES 2.1

2.1 A

2.   1   D $\supset$ (R v L)
     2    $\sim$R $\sim$D
     3    $\sim$L
     4    $\sim$R . $\sim$L   2, 3, Conj, IR
     5    $\sim$(R v L)   4, DeM, RR
     6    $\sim$D   5, 1, MT, IR   Q.E.D

4.   1   L $\supset$ (I $\supset$ D)
     2    $\sim$D $\sim$I v $\sim$ L
     3   L
     4   I $\supset$ D   1, 3, MP, IR
     5    $\sim$I   2, 4, MT, IR
     6    $\sim$I v $\sim$L   5, Add, IR   Q.E.D.

6.   1   L $\supset$ (D $\supset$ E) } $\sim$L v $\sim$ D
     2    $\sim$E
     3   (L $\cdot$ D) $\supset$ E   1, Exp, RR

	4	~(L · D)	2, 3, MT, IR
	5	~L v ~D	4, DeM, RR Q.E.D.
8.	1	C ⊃ V	
	2	N ⊃ ~V	} N ⊃ ~C
	3	~V ⊃ ~C	1, Transp, RR
	4	N ⊃ ~C	2, 4, HS, IR Q.E.D.
10.	1	~P ⊃ ~R	
	2	P ⊃ S	} ~R
	3	~S	
	4	~P	2, 3, MT, IR
	5	~R	4, 1, MP, IR Q.E.D.

2.1 B

2.	1	(B ≡ ~A)	} ~B
	2	A	
	3	(B ⊃ ~A) · (~A ⊃ B)	1, DME, RR
	4	B ⊃ ~A	3, Simp, IR
	5	~ ~A ⊃ ~B	4, Transp, RR
	6	A ⊃ ~B	5, DN, RR
	7	~B	2, 6, MP, IR Q.E.D.
4.	1	~B ⊃ ~A	
	2	C ≡ A	} B
	3	C	
	4	(C ⊃ A) · (A ⊃ C)	2, DME, RR
	5	(C ⊃ A)	4, Simp, IR
	6	A	3, 5, MP, IR
	7	A ⊃ B	1, Transp, RR
	8	B	6, 7, MP, IR Q.E.D.

2.1 C

2. D # Death is the separation of soul and body

A # Soul can exist apart

F # Soul becomes free through death

1	D ⊃ (A ⊃ F) } ~F ⊃ (~D v ~A)	
2	(D · A) ⊃ F	1, Exp, RR
3	~F ⊃ ~(D · A)	2, Transp, RR
4	~F ⊃ (~D v ~A)	3, DeM, RR Q.E.D.

4. I # Impossible with body to know purely

N # True knowledge possible nowhere

A # True knowledge possible only after death

P # Partial knowledge had in this life

1	I ⊃ (N v A)	
2	P ⊃ ~N	} ~A ⊃ ~I
3	P	
4	~N	2, 3, MP, IR

5	I ⊃ (A v N)	1, Com, RR
6	I ⊃ (~ ~A v N)	5, DN, RR
7	I ⊃ (~A ⊃ N)	6, DMI, RR
8	(I · ~A) ⊃ N	7, Exp, RR
9	~(I · ~A)	4, 8, MT, IR
10	~I v ~ ~A	9, DeM, RR
11	~I v A	10, DN, RR
12	I ⊃ A	11, DMI, RR
13	~A ⊃ ~I	12, Transp, RR Q.E.D.

6. D ╫ Soul destroyed when body is
F ╫ Death to be feared
H ╫ There is hope

1	D ⊃ F	⎫	
2	~D ⊃ H	⎬ ~H ⊃ F	
3	D v ~D	⎭	
4	F v H	1, 2, 3, CD, IR
5	H v F	4, COM, RR
6	~ ~H v F	5, DN, RR
7	~H ⊃ F	6, DMI, RR Q.E.D.

8. R ╫ Recognize equal and unequal
K ╫ Know equality itself
A ╫ Acquire this knowledge by sense experience
S ╫ Nothing in sense experience same as equality
B ╫ We're born having knowledge

1	R ⊃ K	⎫	
2	S ⊃ (~K v ~A)	⎪	
3	~A ⊃ B	⎬ B	
4	R	⎪	
5	S	⎭	
6	K	4, 1, MP, IR
7	~K v ~A	5, 2, MP, IR
8	K ⊃ ~A	7, DMI, RR
9	~A	6, 8, MP, IR
10	B	9, 3, MP, IR Q.E.D.

10. S ╫ Soul immortal   F ╫ Fear out of place
O ╫ Soul outwears body but wears out   I ╫ Soul like Ideas

1	S ⊃ F	⎫	
2	O ⊃ ~S	⎬ ~O · F	
3	I ⊃ S	⎪	
4	I	⎭	
5	S	3, 4, MP, IR
6	F	5, 1, MP, IR
7	~ ~S	5, DN, RR
8	~O	7, 2, MT, IR
9	~O · F	8, 6, Conj, IR Q.E.D.

EXERCISES 2.2

2.2 A

2. Invalid with A, P, and C all false; example:

```
   F       T
F  TF     F   ⎫
(C · ~P) ⊃ A  ⎬  F
T F           ⎭  A
~P
```

4.
```
1    J ⊃ (W ⊃ ~P)  ⎫
2    G ⊃ W          ⎬  G ⊃ ~P
3    J              ⎭
4    W ⊃ ~P         1, 3, MP, IR
5    G ⊃ ~P         2, 4, HS, IR      Q.E.D.
```

6. Invalid with B, S, and E all false

8. Invalid with P and F false and N true

10.
```
1    ~C ⊃ ~F   ⎫
2    B          ⎬  ~F · ~C
3    B ⊃ ~C     ⎭
4    ~C         2, 3, MP, IR
5    ~F         4, 1, MP, IR
6    ~F · ~C    4, 5, Conj, IR      Q.E.D.
```

2.2 B

2.
```
1    A ⊃ (B v D) ⎫
2    ~B           ⎬  ~A      Valid
3    ~D           ⎭
4    ~B · ~D      2, 3, Conj, IR
5    ~(B v D)     4, DeM, RR
6    ~A           5, 1, MT, IR      Q.E.D.
```

4.
```
        T    T
    T   F    F
    A ⊃ (B ⊃ C)  ⎫  F T      Invalid
                 ⎭  ~A
    T F
    ~C
```

2.2 C Since some statements are repeated, refer to earlier dictionaries for
6, 8, 10.

2. I # Substance produced by something internal
E # Substance produced by something external
C # Substance is its own cause
```
1    I v E           ⎫  C
2    ~E · (I ⊃ C)    ⎭
3    ~E              2, Simp, IR
4    I ⊃ C           2, Simp, IR
5    I               3, 1, DS, IR
6    C               4, 5, MP, IR      Q.E.D.
```

4. P # Substance can be divided into parts
R # Parts retain nature of substance
L # Parts lose nature of substance

1	P ⊃ (R v L)	
2	~R	~P
3	~L	
4	~R · ~L	2, 3, Conj, IR
5	~(R v L)	4, DeM, RR
6	~P	5, 1, MT, IR Q.E.D.

6. S # Parts of divided substance are substances
U # Substance could be made of substances

1	~S ⊃ ~R	
2	S ⊃ U	~R
3	~U	
4	~S	3, 2, MT, IR
5	~R	4, 1, MP, IR Q.E.D.

8. Y # Substance could be destroyed

```
          F   T
     F  T     F        F T
1  (L · P) ⊃ Y    ~P      Invalid
     T F
2    ~Y
```

10.

1	P ⊃ (R v L)	
2	~R	~P
3	~L v ~P	
4	P ⊃ (L v R)	1, Com, RR
5	P ⊃ (~ ~L v R)	5, DN, RR
6	P ⊃ (~L ⊃ R)	6, DMI, RR
7	(P · ~L) ⊃ R	7, Exp, RR
8	~(P · ~L)	2, 8, MT, IR
9	~P v ~ ~L	9, DeM, RR
10	~P v L	10, DN, RR
11	P ⊃ L	11, DMI, RR
12	L ⊃ ~P	4, DMI, RR
13	P ⊃ ~P	12, 13, HS, IR
14	~P	14, Red, RR Q.E.D.

EXERCISES 2.3

2.3 A

2.

1	E ⊃ (F v G)	
2	~E ⊃ ~H	H ⊃ (~F ⊃ G)
*3	H	ACP
4	H ⊃ E	2, Transp, RR
*5	E	3, 4, MP, IR

*6	F v G	5, 1, MP, IR	
*7	~ ~ F v G	6, DN, RR	
*8	~ F ⊃ G	7, DMI, RR	
9	H ⊃ (~ F ⊃ G)	3–8, RCP	Q.E.D.

4.
1	((P v Q) · R) ≡ S	T ⊃ S	
2	T ⊃ (Q · R)		
*3	T	ACP	
*4	Q · R	3, 2, MP, IR	
*5	Q	4, Simp, IR	
*6	R	4, Simp, IR	
*7	Q v P	5, Add, IR	
*8	P v Q	7, Com, RR	
*9	(P v Q) · R	8, 6, Conj, IR	
*10	(((P v Q) · R) ⊃ S) ·		
	(S ⊃ ((P v Q) · R))	1, DME, RR	
11	((P v Q) · R) ⊃ S	10, Simp, IR	
*12	S	9, 11, MP, IR	
13	T ⊃ S	3–12, RCP	Q.E.D.

6.
1	A ⊃ (B ⊃ C)	(D · B) ⊃ C	
2	~ D v A		
*3	D · B	ACP	
*4	D	3, Simp, IR	
*5	~ ~ D	4, DN, RR	
*6	A	5, 2, DS, IR	
*7	B ⊃ C	1, 6, MP, IR	
*8	B	3, Simp, IR	
*9	C	7, 8, MP, IR	
10	(D · B) ⊃ C	3–9, RCP	Q.E.D.

8.
1	(~ J v ~ K) ⊃ ~ L	M ⊃ (J · K)	
2	~ M v L		
*3	M	ACP	
*4	~ ~ M	3, DN, RR	
*5	L	4, 2, DS, IR	
6	~ (J · K) ⊃ ~ L	1, DeM, RR	
7	L ⊃ (J · K)	6, Transp, RR	
*8	J · K	5, 7, MP, IR	
9	M ⊃ (J · K)	3–8, RCP	Q.E.D.

10.
1	(R v S) ⊃ U	S ⊃ V	
2	~ V ≡ ~ U		
*3	S	ACP	
*4	R v S	3, Add, IR	
*5	U	4, I, MP, IR	
6	V ≡ U	2, Compl, RR	
7	(V ⊃ U) · (U ⊃ V)	6, DME, RR	
8	U ⊃ V	7, Simp, IR	

*9	V	5, 8, MP, IR	
10	S ⊃ V	3–9, RCP	Q.E.D.

2.3 B

2. G ⫢ Gryphon right   T ⫢ Turtle right   S ⫢ Turtle has sorrow

```
       T  F   ⎞
          T  F  ⎟
 1     ~(G · T)  ⎟
          T      ⎟
       F   T  ⎞  F T      Invalid
 2     T ⊃ S  ⎟  ~S
       T      ⎟
 3     G      ⎠
```

4. E ⫢ Turtle could afford extras   F ⫢ Turtle can take French
W ⫢ Turtle can take washing

```
     T    T    ⎞
 T    F   T    ⎟  F T
 E ⊃ (F v W)   ⎟  ~E      Invalid
 T F           ⎟
 ~F            ⎠
```

2.3 C

2. S ⫢ Socrates will do wrong
E ⫢ Socrates will return evil for evil
B ⫢ Socrates breaks an agreement with state because unjustly con-
demned
M ⫢ Socrates makes escape

1	~S		
2	E ⊃ S	(M ≡ B) ⊃ ~M	
3	B ⊃ E		
*4	(M ≡ B)	ACP	
*5	(M ⊃ B) · (B ⊃ M)	4, DME, RR	
*6	(M ⊃ B)	5, Simp, IR	
7	~E	1, 2, MT, IR	
8	~B	7, 3, MT, IR	
*9	~M	8, 6, MT, IR	
10	(M ≡ B) ⊃ ~M	4–9, RCP	Q.E.D.

4. L ⫢ Socrates approved of Laws of Athens
F ⫢ Socrates would have immigrated from Athens
C ⫢ Socrates would have tried to have the Laws changed
O ⫢ Socrates agreed to obey the Laws

1	~L ⊃ (F v C)	
2	~(F v C) ⊃ O	~C ⊃ (L · O)
3	~F	
*4	~C	ACP
*5	~F · ~C	3, 4, Conj, IR

*6	~(F v C)	5, DeM, RR
*7	~ ~L	6, 1, MT, IR
*8	L	7, DN, RR
*9	O	6, 2, MP, IR
*10	L · O	8, 9, Conj, IR
11	~C ⊃ (L · O)	4–10, RCP Q.E.D.

6. A # Socrates avoids well-governed cities
    W # Socrates' life will be worth living
    T # Socrates goes to Thessaly
    L # Socrates becomes a laughingstock
    C # Socrates can bring up his children well
    E # Socrates escapes

1	A ⊃ ~W	} (E ≡ (T v A)) ⊃ (E ⊃ (W ⊃ ~C))
2	T ⊃ (L · ~C)	
*3	E ≡ (T v A)	ACP
*4	(E ⊃ (T v A)) · ((T v A) ⊃ E)	3, DME, RR
*5	E ⊃ (T v A)	4, Simp, IR
**6	E	ACP
**7	(T v A)	6, 5, MP, IR
**8	~W v (L · ~C)	7, 1, 2, CD, IR
***9	W	ACP
**10	W ⊃ (L · ~C)	8, DMI, RR
***11	(L · ~C)	9, 10, MP, IR
***12	~C	11, Simp, IR
**13	W ⊃ ~C	9–12, RCP
*14	E ⊃ (W ⊃ ~C)	6–13, RCP
15	(E ≡ (T v A))	3–14, RCP Q.E.D.
	⊃ (E ⊃ (W ⊃ ~C))	

8. D # Death is complete extinction
    N # Dead man feels nothing
    C # Death is change and migration
    S # Eternity like dreamless sleep
    B # Death is blessing
    P # Dead in place we migrate to
    G # We shall be with great men

1	(D · N) v C	} P ⊃ B
2	N ⊃ (S · B)	
3	(C · P) ⊃ (G · B)	
4	(D v C) · (N v C)	1, Distr, RR
5	N v C	6, Simp, IR
6	(P · C) ⊃ (G · B)	3, Com, RR
7	P ⊃ (C ⊃ (G · B))	6, Exp, RR
*8	P	ACP
*9	C ⊃ (G · B)	8, 7, MP, IR
*10	(G · B) v (S · B)	2, 9, 5, CD, IR

*11	B · (G ∨ S)	10, Dist, RR
*12	B	11, Simp, IR
13	P ⊃ B	8–12, RCP Q.E.D.

10. E # Evil can happen to living or dead good man
S # Socrates' death is an evil
W # Socrates' signal would have warned about trial
R # Socrates has reason for anger with accusers
T # Socrates has reason for anger with condemners

1	~E ⊃ ~S	⎫ C ⊃ E
2	~S ⊃ (~W · (~R · ~C))	⎭
*3	C	ACP
*4	~ ~C	3, DN, RR
*5	~ ~C ∨ ~ ~R	4, Add, IR
*6	~(~C · ~R)	5, DeM, RR
*7	~(~C · ~R) ∨ ~ ~W	6, Add, IR
*8	~((~C · ~R) · ~W)	7, DeM, RR
*9	~ ~S	2, 8, MT, IR
*10	~ ~E	9, 1, MT, IR
*11	E	10, DN, RR
12	C ⊃ E	3–11, RCP Q.E.D.

EXERCISES 2.4

2.4 A

2. Prove q ⊃ (p ⊃ q)

1	q ⊃ (p ∨ q)	Ax2
2	q ⊃ (~p ∨ q)	1, Subst ~p/p
3	q ⊃ (p ⊃ q)	2, D3, IR1

4. Prove (p ⊃ (q ⊃ r)) ⊃ (q ⊃ (p ⊃ r))

1	(p ∨ (q ∨ r)) ⊃ (q ∨ (p ∨ r))	Ax4
2	(~p ∨ (q ∨ r)) ⊃ (q ∨ (~p ∨ r))	1, Subst ~p/p
3	(~p ∨ (~q ∨ r)) ⊃ (~q ∨ (~p ∨ r))	2, Subst ~q/q
4	(p ⊃ (q ⊃ r)) ⊃ (q ⊃ (p ⊃ r))	3, D3, PIR 1

6. Prove (p ⊃ q) ⊃ ((q ⊃ r) ⊃ (p ⊃ r))

1	(p ⊃ (q ⊃ r)) ⊃ (q ⊃ (p ⊃ r))	Proved in 4 above
2	((q ⊃ r) ⊃ ((p ⊃ q) ⊃ (p ⊃ r))) ⊃ ((p ⊃ q) ⊃ ((q ⊃ r) ⊃ (p ⊃ r)))	1, Subst (q ⊃ r)/p, Subst (p ⊃ q)/q, Subst (p ⊃ r)/r
3	(q ⊃ r) ⊃ ((p ⊃ q) ⊃ (p ⊃ r))	Proved in Exercise 3
4	(p ⊃ q) ⊃ ((q ⊃ r) ⊃ (p ⊃ r))	2, 3, PIR 1

8. Prove p ⊃ p

1	(q ⊃ r) ⊃ ((p ⊃ q) ⊃ (p ⊃ r))	Proved in Exercise 5
2	((p ∨ p) ⊃ p) ⊃ ((p ⊃ (p ∨ p)) ⊃ (p ⊃ p))	Subst (p ∨ p)/q, Subst p/r
3	(p ∨ p) ⊃ p	Ax 1
4	(p ⊃ (p ∨ p)) ⊃ (p ⊃ p)	2, 3, PIR 1

5	q ⊃ (p ∨ q)	Ax 2
6	p ⊃ (p ∨ p)	5, Subst p/q
7	p ⊃ p	6, 4, PIR 1

10. Prove p ⊃ ∼∼p

1	p ∨ ∼p	Proved in Exercise 9
2	∼p ∨ ∼∼p	1, Subst ∼p/p
3	p ⊃ ∼∼p	2, D3, PIR 1

2.4 B

2. Prove q ⊃ (p ⊃ q)

*1	q	ACP
*2	q ∨ ∼p	1, Add
*3	∼p ∨ q	2, Com
*4	p ⊃ q	3, DMI
5	q ⊃ (p ⊃ q)	1–4, RCP

4. Prove (p ⊃ (q ⊃ r)) ⊃ (q ⊃ (p ⊃ r))

*1	p ⊃ (q ⊃ r)	ACP
*2	∼p ∨ (q ⊃ r)	1, DMI
*3	∼p ∨ (∼q ∨ r)	2, DMI
*4	(∼q ∨ r) ∨ ∼p	3, Com
*5	∼q ∨ (r ∨ ∼p)	4, Assoc
*6	∼q ∨ (∼p ∨ r)	5, Com
*7	∼q ∨ (p ⊃ r)	6, DMI
*8	q ⊃ (p ⊃ r)	7, DMI

6. Prove (p ⊃ q) ⊃ ((q ⊃ r) ⊃ (p ⊃ r))

*1	p ⊃ q	ACP
**2	(q ⊃ r)	ACP
***3	p	ACP
***4	q	3, 1, MP
***5	r	4, 2, MP
**6	p ⊃ r	3–5, RCP
*7	(q ⊃ r) ⊃ (p ⊃ r)	2–6, RCP
8	(p ⊃ q) ⊃ ((q ⊃ r) ⊃ (p ⊃ r))	1–7, RCP

8. Prove p ⊃ p

*1	p	ACP
*2	∼∼p	1, DN
*3	p	2, DN
4	p ⊃ p	1–3, RCP

10. Prove p ⊃ ∼∼p

*1	p	ACP
*2	∼∼p	1, DN
3	p ⊃ ∼∼p	RCP

2.4 C

2. C ⫓ A has something in common with B

U ⫓ A can be understood by means of B

∼C ⊃ ∼U

379

4. N # A has the same nature or attributes as B
S # A is the same as B
N ⊃ S

6, 8, 10. Complete answers cannot be given without 1, 3, 5
6. Hint: Use 2, 1 Transp, HS
8. Hint: Use 5, 4, 3, Transp, HS
10. Hint: Use 6, 9, Transp, HS

EXERCISES 3.1

3.1 A

2. (a) O   (b) greyhounds/fat (animal)   (c) fat (animal)
4. (a) A   (b) person in the house/ill (person)   (c) person in house
6. (a) A   (b) Englishman/(person who) likes plum pudding
(c) Englishman
8. (a) I   (b) old misers/thin (persons)   (c) none
10. (a) O   (b) judges/(persons who) exercise self-control
(c) (persons who) exercise self-control

3.1 B

2. No beer drinker is courageous.
4. Some dangerous person is a beer drinker.
6. Some beer drinker is an admiral.
8. Every dangerous person is a beer drinker.
10. David is a beer drinker.

3.1 C

2. Every eleven o'clock in the morning is a time when Pooh liked a little something.
4. Every wedged bear is a bear who is comforted by sustaining books.
6. Some Woozle is a hostile animal. *or* Some time is a time when Woozles are hostile.
8. Some bee is a creature which was suspicious.
10. Every little cloud is a thing which always sings aloud.

EXERCISES 3.2

3.2 A

(1) **2.** Every welcome creature is friendly.
4. Every ungreedy creature is not a black rabbit.
6. No uncrackable thing is an egg.
8. Every creature which fails to delight the eye is ungraceful.
10. No canary who is melancholy is a canary who sings loud.
(2) **2.** No unfriendly creature is welcome (not unwelcome).
4. No black rabbit is not greedy.
6. Every egg is crackable (not uncrackable).
8. No graceful creature fails to delight the eye.
10. Every canary who sings aloud is not melancholy.

3.2 B

2. False (contradictory)   **4.** True (obverse)   **6.** True (converse)
8. True (subaltern of converse)   **10.** False (obverse is contrary of converse)

EXERCISES 3.3

3.3 A

2. Valid   **4.** Valid   **6.** Breaks Rule Six   **8.** Breaks Rule Six
10. InValid *BREAKS RULE 4.*

3.3 B

2. Every case in which we know naturally properties of pure spirits is a case
in which we know naturally pure spirits.
No case is a case in which we know naturally pure spirits.

No case is a case in which we know naturally the properties of pure spirits.

4. Every case of contradiction is a case which terms are being used in the
same way.
Some argument between theologians and philosophers is a case of contradiction.

Some argument between theologians and philosophers is a case in which
terms are being used in the same way.

(Comment: "Every" is surely too strong in the minor premise.)

6. Every case in which a being uses an imperfect instrument is a case in which
the being in question is subject to the limitations of that instrument in
question.
Every case in which man uses his intellect is a case in which a being is
using an imperfect instrument.

Every case in which man is using his intellect is a case in which the being
in question (man) is subject to the limitations of the instrument in
question (his intellect).

(Comment: Note that the words in parentheses cannot be supplied by
purely syllogistic means.)

8. Every speculative acquired science is something which perfects the speculative intellect.
Metaphysics is a speculative acquired science.

Metaphysics is something which perfects the speculative intellect.

10. Every agent who acts knowingly is an agent which needs a distinct knowledge of his destiny or end.
Every man is an agent who acts knowingly.

Every man needs a distinct knowledge of his destiny or end.

EXERCISES 3.4

3.4 A

2. Senna is nasty.
4. Some Dons are not tall men.

6. John is happy.

8. Every book which suits feverish patients makes one drowsy (interpreting the minor premise as "every").

10. You and I can detect a sharper. (Can you make this into a standard syllogism?)

3.4 B

2. Ā))R   contrapose R̄))A   D))B

    B)(W   obvert B))W̄   B))W̄

              convert

    C̄)(A   contrapose A))C   D))W

    R))S   contrapose S̄))R̄   W̄))S̄

    D))B   D))S̄

    S))W   contrapose W̄))S̄   S̄))R̄

                           D))R̄

                           R̄))A

                           D))A

    Every one of my dreams comes true.   A))C

                           D))C

4. K))X̄   contrapose X))K   D))H̄

    D)(H   obvert D))H̄   H̄))Ā

    B))A   contrapose Ā))B̄   D))Ā

    K)(E   Ā))B̄

    H̄)(A   obvert H̄))Ā   D))B̄

    B̄))Y   B̄))X

                           D))X

                           X))K

                           D))K

    No donkey is easy to swallow.   K)(E

                           D)(E

6. R̄))M   contrapose M̄))R   D))M̄

    S))B   M̄))R

    M))D̄   contrapose D))M̄   D))R

    R))S   R))S

                           D))S

                           S))B

    Every plum pudding which is distin-   D))B
    guishable from soup has been boiled
    in a cloth.

8. Ḡ))B   P))Ḡ

    P)(G   obvert P))Ḡ   Ḡ))B

    S)(R̄   obvert S))R   P))B

R)(H   B))S
B))S   ‾‾‾‾
‾‾‾‾   P))S
                                        S))R
                                        ‾‾‾‾
                                        P))R
                                        R)(H
                                        ‾‾‾‾
No prize-winning fruit was grown in   P)(H
a hothouse.

10. L)(Ē   obvert L))E   P))T
     T̄)(P   convert, obvert P))T   T))W
     W))L   ‾‾‾‾
     E)(G   P))W
     T))W   W))L
                                        ‾‾‾‾
                                        P))L
                                        L))E
                                        ‾‾‾‾
                                        P))E
                                        E)(G
                                        ‾‾‾‾
No kitten that will play with a gorilla P)(G
is green-eyed.

3.4 C

2. Every being that can cause endless motion is a being that has infinite power.
   The First Being can cause endless motion.
   _____
   The First Being has infinite power.

4. Every being that has infinite effect in its power is infinite.
   The First Being has infinite effect in its power.
   _____
   The First Being is infinite.

6. Every being which can bridge infinite extremes has infinite power.
   Every being which can create something from nothing can bridge infinite extremes.
   _____
   Every being which can create something from nothing has infinite power.
   The First Being can create something from nothing.
   _____
   The First Being has infinite power.

8. Every being which can know an infinite number of things has an infinite mind.
   Every being which knows all that can be known knows an infinite number of things.
   _____
   Every being which knows all that can be known has an infinite mind
   God knows all that can be known.
   _____
   God has an infinite mind.

10. No absolutely perfect being can be excelled in perfection.
    God is an absolutely perfect thing.
    _____
    God cannot be excelled in perfection.
    Every finite being can be excelled in perfection.
    _____
    God is not finite.

EXERCISES 4.1

4.1 A

2. Animals which like either acorns or condensed milk
4. Honey-loving bears
6. Donkeys who like neither honey nor condensed milk
8. Friendly tigers who don't like thistles
10. Gloomy animals who are neither donkeys nor thistle eaters

4.1 B

2. $H \cap \overline{G}$
4. $G \cap \overline{(H \cup E)}$
6. $\overline{(G \cup H)} \cap E$
8. $(F \cap G) \cup (\bar{F} \cap H)$
10. $(\bar{F} \cap \bar{E}) \cup (\bar{F} \cup H)$

4.1 C

V ⫲ Very small animals	2. $V \cap S$ (Piglet)
S ⫲ Surrounded by water	
B ⫲ Brainy animals	4. $B \cap H$ (Rabbit)
P ⫲ Friends of Pooh	
R ⫲ Friends of Rabbit	6. $P \cap R$ (Piglet)
O ⫲ Bouncy animals	
H ⫲ Animals who like honey	8. $B \cap P$ (Owl)
	10. $O \cap \bar{H}$ (Tigger)

EXERCISES 4.2

4.2 A

2. No bear is either acorn loving or thistle eating.
4. There are no bears who like neither honey nor condensed milk.
6. Some donkeys are gloomy.
8. Some gloomy donkeys like neither honey nor condensed milk.
10. Every thistle-eating donkey is gloomy.

4.2 B

T ⫲ Tiggers	L ⫲ Learning
E ⫲ Extraordinarily good flyers	G ⫲ Reasons for going and seeing
O ⫲ Those who fly as well as Owl	everybody
F ⫲ Funny things	S ⫲ Cases of looking for Small
A ⫲ Accidents	E ⫲ Cases of organizing an
H ⫲ Things you never have till	expedition
you're having them	W ⫲ Things I want
R ⫲ Things Rabbit knows	T ⫲ Thinnish pieces of rope
	I ⫲ Thickish pieces of string

2. $T \subseteq (E \cap O)$ 6. $L \in R$
4. $A \subseteq (F \cap H)$ 8. $(S \cup E) \subseteq G$
10. $(T \cup I) \subseteq W$ (No way of expressing "if there isn't any")

4.3 A

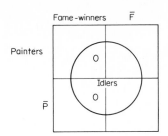

Fame-winners $\bar{F}$

Painters

Idlers

$\bar{P}$

2. See Figure. Not valid: the 1 could be $P \cap \bar{F}$.

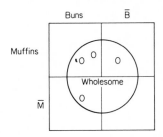

Buns $\bar{B}$

Muffins

Wholesome

$\bar{M}$

4. See Figure. Not valid: $(M \cap B) \cap \bar{W}$ could have members.

4.3 B

2.
1	$\bar{A} \subseteq M$	
2	$C \subseteq \bar{D}$	
3	$A \subseteq U$	$C \subseteq U$
4	$M \subseteq D$	
5	$\bar{A} \subseteq D$	1, 4, HSC
6	$D \subseteq \bar{C}$	2, Contrap
7	$\bar{A} \subseteq \bar{C}$	5, 6, HSC
8	$C \subseteq A$	7, Transp C
9	$C \subseteq U$	8, 3, HSC

4.
1	$\bar{R} \subseteq \bar{H}$	
2	$B \subseteq W$	$O \subseteq W$
3	$O \subseteq H$	
4	$\bar{B} \subseteq \bar{R}$	
5	$\bar{B} \subseteq \bar{H}$	4, 1, HSC
6	$H \subseteq B$	5, Contrap
7	$H \subseteq W$	6, 2, HSC
8	$O \subseteq W$	7, 3, HSC

4.3 C Note that "A is predicated of all B" means "Every B is A," etc.

2.
1	$B \subseteq \bar{A}$	$C \subseteq \bar{A}$
2	$C \subseteq B$	
3	$C \subseteq \bar{A}$	1, 2, HSC

4.
1	$B \subseteq \bar{A}$	$C \cap \bar{A} \neq \wedge$
2	$C \cap B \neq \wedge$	
3	$C \cap \bar{A} \neq \wedge$	1, 2, SSR

6.
1	$N \subseteq M$	$N \subseteq \bar{O}$
2	$O \subseteq \bar{M}$	
3	$M \subseteq \bar{O}$	2, Contrap
4	$N \subseteq O$	1, 3, HSC

8. 1 $N \subseteq M$ } $O \cap \bar{N} \neq \wedge$
    2    $O \cap \bar{M} \neq \wedge$ }
    3    $\bar{M} \subseteq \bar{N}$ 1, Contrap
    4    $O \cap \bar{N} \neq \wedge$ 2, 3, SSR

10. 1 $S \cap R \neq \wedge$ } $R \cap P \neq \wedge$
     2    $S \subseteq P$ }
     3    $R \cap P \neq \wedge$ 1, 2, SSR

12. 1 $S \subseteq \bar{P}$ } $R \cap \bar{P} \neq \wedge$
     2    $R \cap S \neq \wedge$ }
     3    $R \cap \bar{P} \neq \wedge$ 1, 2, SSR

14. 1 $A \subseteq \bar{B}$ } $C \cap \bar{A} \neq \wedge$
     2    $C \cap B \neq \wedge$ }
     3    $B \subseteq \bar{A}$ 1, Contrap
     4    $C \cap \bar{A} \neq \wedge$ 2, 3, SSR

EXERCISES 4.4

4.4 A

2. 1 $n \in C$ } $n \in (C \cup E) \cap D$
    2    $n \in D$ }
    3    $n \in (C \cup E)$ 1, AddC
    4    $n \in ((E \cup E) \cap D)$ 2, 3, ConjC

4. 1 $n \in ((G \cup H) \cup F)$ }
    2    $F = \wedge$ } $n \in H$
    3    $G = \wedge$ }
    4    $n \in \bar{F}$ 2, GenC
    5    $n \in \bar{G}$ 3, GenC
    6    $n \in (G \cup H)$ 1, 4, CDS
    7    $n \in H$ 6, 5, CDS

4.4 B

2. M # Class of those who make things in which there is evil, etc.
    B # Class of those who choose best
    W # Class of makers of world
    g # God
    1    $M \subseteq \bar{B}$ }
    2    $g \in W$ } $g \in \bar{B}$
    3    $W \subseteq M$ }
    4    $W \subseteq \bar{B}$ 1, 3, HSC
    5    $g \in \bar{B}$ 4, 2, DSC   Q.E.D.

4. I # Cases in which it is impossible not to sin
    U # Cases in which it is unjust to punish
    H # Human actions
    1    $I \subseteq U$ } $H \subseteq U$
    2    $H \subseteq I$ }
    3    $H \subseteq U$ 1, 2, HSC   Q.E.D.

6. F ⧺ Things future S ⧺ Things foreseen E ⧺ Events
C ⧺ Things following from causes
P ⧺ Things which are predetermined

$$
\begin{array}{lll}
1 & ((F \cap S) \cap C) \subseteq P & \\
2 & E \subseteq ((F \cap S) \cap C) & \\
\end{array} \bigg\} \; E \subseteq P
$$

3   E ⊆ P   1, 2, HSC   Q.E.D.

8. P ⧺ Producers of all real in sin
C ⧺ Causes of sin   g ⧺ God

$$
\begin{array}{ll}
1 & p \subseteq C \\
2 & g \in P \\
\end{array} \bigg\} \; g \in C
$$

3   g ∈ C   1, 2, DSC   Q.E.D.

10. G ⧺ Givers of means to goodwill to some only
S ⧺ Possessors of sufficient goodness
g ⧺ God

$$
\begin{array}{ll}
1 & G \subseteq \bar{S} \\
2 & g \in G \\
\end{array} \bigg\} \; g \in \bar{S}
$$

3   g ∈ S̄   1, 2, DSC   Q.E.D.

EXERCISES 5.1

5.1 A

2. Frodo asks questions of Gandalf, and, if Gandalf tells Frodo something, Frodo believes it.

4. Dwarves and elves don't believe each other.

6. At least one elf tells Frodo something.

8. At least one dwarf asks questions of every elf.

10. If Gandalf were a dwarf, then, if anyone believed Gandalf, that person would not be an elf.

5.1 B

2. Axy ⧺ x is the audience of y h ⧺ Ham Gamgee
Mxy ⧺ x is more attentive than y
$(\exists x)\, ((Axh \cdot \sim(\exists y)\,(Myx))$

4. Yx ⧺ x is young   Hx ⧺ x is a hobbit
Ix ⧺ x was included and present by parental permission
$(\exists x)\, ((Yx \cdot Hx) \cdot Ix)$
(Note the usual difficulty in expressing "many.")

6. Lx ⧺ x lives in Hobbiton   t ⧺ the time in question
Sxyz ⧺ x was seen by y after time z
$(x)\, ((Hx \cdot Lx) \supset \sim Sbxt)$

8. Gx ⧺ x is a parting gift
Hxy ⧺ x has a label written out personally by y
b ⧺ Bilbo
$(x)\, (Gx \supset Hxb)$

10. $\mathrm{M}x \# x$ was money
$\mathrm{J}x \# x$ was jewelry
$\mathrm{I}xy \# x$ is a sign of y
$\mathrm{E}xy \# x$ is a mention of y
$(x) ((\mathrm{M}x \vee \mathrm{J}x) \supset \sim(\exists y) (\mathrm{I}yx \vee \mathrm{E}yx))$

EXERCISES 5.2

5.2 A

(1) **2.** Everything causes everything to change something.
4. Something causes everything to change everything.
6. Something causes everything to change something.
8. Something causes something to change something.
10. For anything whatsoever, there is something which is caused by everything to change it.
12. For at least one thing there is something which everything causes to change it.
14. For anything at all there is something which is caused by something to change it.
16. Anything does not cause something to change everything.
18. Something does not cause something to change everything.
20. Anything does not cause something to change something.

(2) **2** implies **6,** and **2, 4,** and **6** imply **8** (answer incomplete).

(3) **8** is certainly true; so is **20.**
2, 4, 10, 12 are almost certainly false.
6, 14, 16, 18 are debatable and depend on one's metaphysical position.

5.2 B

* $(\exists x) (\mathrm{H}x \cdot \mathrm{A}x)$

2. $\sim(\exists x) (\mathrm{A}x)$ False because the starred statement implies $(\exists x) (\mathrm{A}x)$

4. $(\exists x) (\mathrm{A}x)$ True for the same reason

* $(x) (\mathrm{H}x \supset (\mathrm{B}x \cdot \sim \mathrm{W}x))$

6. $(x) (\mathrm{H}x \supset (\sim \mathrm{B}x \cdot \sim \mathrm{W}x))$ False because the starred statement implies $(x) (\mathrm{H}x \supset \mathrm{B}x)$, and this statement implies $(x) (\mathrm{H}x \supset \sim \mathrm{B}x)$, which are contraries

8. $\sim(\exists x) (\mathrm{H}x \cdot (\sim \mathrm{B}x \cdot \sim \sim \mathrm{W}x))$ True, equivalent to starred statement

10. $(x) ((\mathrm{B}x \cdot \sim \mathrm{W}x) \vee \mathrm{H}x)$ True because equivalent

EXERCISES 5.3

5.3 A

2.

1	$\sim(\exists x) (\mathrm{F}x \cdot \mathrm{G}x)$	$\left.\begin{array}{c}\\\end{array}\right\} \sim(\exists x) (\mathrm{H}x \cdot \mathrm{F}x)$
2	$(x) (\mathrm{H}x \supset (\mathrm{F}x \supset \mathrm{G}x))$	
3	$(x) \sim(\mathrm{F}x \cdot \mathrm{G}x)$	1, QE, RR
4	$\sim(\mathrm{F}\dot{x} \cdot \mathrm{G}\dot{x})$	3, UI
5	$\mathrm{H}\dot{x} \supset (\mathrm{F}\dot{x} \supset \mathrm{G}\dot{x})$	2, UI

	6	$(H\hat{x} \cdot F\hat{x}) \supset G\hat{x}$	5, Exp, RR
	7	$(F\hat{x} \cdot H\hat{x}) \supset G\hat{x}$	6, Com, RR
	8	$\sim F\hat{x} \vee \sim G\hat{x}$	4, DeM, RR
	9	$F\hat{x} \supset \sim G\hat{x}$	8, DMI, RR
	10	$\sim G\hat{x} \supset \sim (F\hat{x} \cdot H\hat{x})$	7, Transp, RR
	11	$F\hat{x} \supset \sim (F\hat{x} \cdot H\hat{x})$	9, 10, HS, IR
	12	$F\hat{x} \supset (\sim F\hat{x} \vee \sim H\hat{x})$	11, DeM, RR
	13	$F\hat{x} \supset (F\hat{x} \supset \sim H\hat{x})$	12, DMI, RR
	14	$(F\hat{x} \cdot F\hat{x}) \supset \sim H\hat{x}$	13, Exp, RR
	15	$F\hat{x} \supset \sim H\hat{x}$	14, Rep, RR
	16	$\sim F\hat{x} \vee \sim H\hat{x}$	15, DMI, RR
	17	$\sim (F\hat{x} \cdot H\hat{x})$	16, DeM, RR
	18	$(x) \sim (Fx \cdot Hx)$	17, UG
	19	$\sim (\exists x)(Fx \cdot Hx)$	18, QE, RR Q.E.D.
4.	1	$(x)(Fx \supset Gx)$	
	2	$(x)(Gx \supset \sim Hx)$	$(x)((Jx \cdot Fx) \supset Kx)$
	3	$(x)(Jx \supset Hx)$	
	4	$F\hat{x} \supset G\hat{x}$	1, UI
	5	$G\hat{x} \supset \sim H\hat{x}$	2, UI
	6	$J\hat{x} \supset H\hat{x}$	3, UI
	*7	$(J\hat{x} \cdot F\hat{x})$	ACP
	*8	$J\hat{x}$	7, Simp, IR
	*9	$F\hat{x}$	7, Simp, IR
	*10	$G\hat{x}$	9, 4, MP, IR
	*11	$\sim H\hat{x}$	10, 5, MP, IR
	*12	$H\hat{x}$	8, 6, MP, IR
	*13	$H\hat{x} \vee K\hat{x}$	12, Add
	*14	$K\hat{x}$	11, 13, DS, IR
	15	$(J\hat{x} \cdot F\hat{x}) \supset K\hat{x}$	7–14, RCP
	16	$(x)((Jx \cdot Fx) \supset Kx)$	15, UG Q.E.D.
6.	1	$(x)(Gx \supset Fx)$	
	2	$(x)(Fx \supset Hx)$	$(\exists x)(Hx \cdot \sim Gx)$
	3	$(\exists x)(Fx \cdot \sim Gx)$	
	4	$F\acute{x} \supset H\acute{x}$	2, UI
	5	$F\acute{x} \cdot \sim G\acute{x}$	3, EI
	6	$F\acute{x}$	5, Simp, IR
	7	$\sim G\acute{x}$	5, Simp, IR
	8	$H\acute{x}$	6, 4, MP, IR
	9	$H\acute{x} \cdot \sim G\acute{x}$	8, 7, Conj, IR
	10	$(\exists x)(Hx \cdot \sim Gx)$	9, EG Q.E.D.

(Note that premise 1 was unnecessary.)

8.	1	$(x)(Fx \supset Gx)$	
	2	$\sim (x)(Gx \supset Fx)$	$\sim (x)(Fx \equiv Gx)$
	3	$(\exists x) \sim (Gx \supset Fx)$	2, QE, RR
	4	$\sim (G\acute{x} \supset F\acute{x})$	3, EI

*5	$F\dot{x} \equiv G\dot{x}$	ACP	
*6	$(F\dot{x} \supset G\dot{x}) \cdot (Gx \supset Fx)$	5, DME, RR	
*7	$(G\dot{x} \supset F\dot{x})$	6, Simp, IR	
*8	$(G\dot{x} \supset F\dot{x}) \cdot \sim(G\dot{x} \supset F\dot{x})$	7, 4, Conj, IR	
9	$(F\dot{x} \equiv G\dot{x}) \supset ((G\dot{x} \supset F\dot{x})$ $\cdot \sim(G\dot{x} \supset F\dot{x}))$	5–8, RCP	
10	$\sim(F\dot{x} \equiv G\dot{x})$	9, Red, RR	
11	$(\exists x) \sim(Fx \equiv Gx)$	10, EG	
12	$(x) \sim(Fx \equiv Gx)$	11, QE, RR	Q.E.D.

(Note that Premise 1 was unnecessary.)

10.

1	$(\exists x)(Fx \cdot \sim Gx) \supset$ $(\exists x)((Hx \cdot Jx) \cdot Lx))$		
2	$(x)(Jx \supset Lx)$	$(x)(Fx \supset Gx)$	
3	$(Lx \cdot Hx) \supset Kx$		
4	$\sim(\exists x)(Lx \cdot Kx)$		
5	$(x) \sim(Lx \cdot Kx)$	4, QE, RR	
6	$J\dot{x} \supset L\dot{x}$	2, UI	
7	$(L\dot{x} \cdot H\dot{x}) \supset K\dot{x}$	3, UI	
8	$\sim(L\dot{x} \cdot K\dot{x})$	5, UI	
9	$\sim L\dot{x} \lor \sim K\dot{x}$	8, DeM, RR	
10	$\sim J\dot{x} \lor \sim(L\dot{x} \cdot H\dot{x})$	9, 7, 6, DD, IR	
11	$\sim J\dot{x} \lor (\sim L\dot{x} \lor \sim H\dot{x})$	10, DeM, RR	
12	$(\sim L\dot{x} \lor \sim H\dot{x}) \lor \sim J\dot{x}$	11, Com, RR	
13	$\sim L\dot{x} \lor (\sim H\dot{x} \lor \sim J\dot{x})$	12, Assoc, RR	
14	$(\sim H\dot{x} \lor \sim J\dot{x}) \lor \sim L\dot{x}$	13, Com, RR	
15	$\sim(H\dot{x} \cdot J\dot{x}) \lor \sim L\dot{x}$	14, DeM, RR	
16	$\sim((H\dot{x} \cdot J\dot{x}) \cdot L\dot{x})$	15, DeM, RR	
17	$(x) \sim((Hx \cdot Jx) \cdot Lx)$	16, UG	
18	$\sim(\exists x)((Hx \cdot Jx) \cdot Lx)$	17, QE, RR	
19	$\sim(\exists x)(Fx \cdot \sim Gx)$	18, 1, MT, IR	
20	$(x) \sim(Fx \cdot \sim Gx)$	19, QE, RR	
21	$(x) \sim\sim(Fx \supset Gx)$	20, NMI, RR	
22	$(x)(Fx \supset Gx)$	21, DN, RR	Q.E.D.

5.3 B

2.

1	$(x)(\sim Ux \supset Dx)$		
2	$(x)(Ex \supset \sim Qx)$		
3	$(x)(Dx \supset Qx)$	$(x)(Mx \supset \sim Bx)$	
4	$(x)(Bx \supset Kx)$		
5	$(x)(Mx \supset \sim Ux)$		
6	$(x)(Kx \supset Ex)$		
7	$\sim U\dot{x} \supset D\dot{x}$	1, UI	
8	$E\dot{x} \supset \sim Q\dot{x}$	2, UI	
9	$D\dot{x} \supset Q\dot{x}$	3, UI	
10	$B\dot{x} \supset K\dot{x}$	4, UI	
11	$M\dot{x} \supset \sim U\dot{x}$	5, UI	

12	K$\dot{x}$ ⊃ E$\dot{x}$	6, UI
13	K$\dot{x}$ ⊃ ~Q$\dot{x}$	12, 8, HS, IR
14	~Q$\dot{x}$ ⊃ ~D$\dot{x}$	9, Transp, RR
15	K$\dot{x}$ ⊃ ~D$\dot{x}$	13, 14, HS, IR
16	D$\dot{x}$ ⊃ ~K$\dot{x}$	15, Transp, RR
17	~U$\dot{x}$ ⊃ ~K$\dot{x}$	7, 16, HS, IR
18	K$\dot{x}$ ⊃ U$\dot{x}$	17, Transp
19	B$\dot{x}$ ⊃ U$\dot{x}$	10, 18, HS, IR
20	~U$\dot{x}$ ⊃ ~B$\dot{x}$	19, Transp, RR
21	M$\dot{x}$ ⊃ ~B$\dot{x}$	11, 20, HS, IR
22	(x) (Mx ⊃ ~Bx)	21, UG Q.E.D.

Note: Detailed solutions are not given for the rest, since soriteses involve only repeated HS and Transp steps.

4.
1	(x) (Mx ⊃ Tx)	
2	(x) (Dx ⊃ Gx)	
3	(x) (Ax ⊃ Wx)	
4	(x) (Yx ⊃ Mx)	(x) (Yx ⊃ Gx)
5	(x) (Tx ⊃ Ax)	
6	(x) (Wx ⊃ Dx)	

6.
1	(x) (Sx ⊃ Fx)	
2	(x) (~Mx ⊃ Cx)	
3	(x) (Fx ⊃ Tx)	
4	(x) (~Sx ⊃ Kx)	(x) (Hx ⊃ Kx)
5	(x) (Hx ⊃ ~Mx)	
6	(x) (Tx ⊃ ~Cx)	

8.
1	(x) (~Nx ⊃ Mx)	
2	(x) (Yx ⊃ Fx)	
3	(x) (Cx ⊃ Px)	
4	(x) (Fx ⊃ ~Bx)	(x) (Bx ⊃ ~Px)
5	(x) (Mx ⊃ Rx)	
6	(x) (Nx ⊃ Yx)	
7	(x) (Px ⊃ ~Rx)	

10.
1	(x) (Ox ⊃ Cx)	
2	(x) (~Mx ⊃ Px)	
3	(x) (Bx ⊃ ~Hx)	
4	(x) (Mx ⊃ Rx)	
5	(x) (~Ox ⊃ Nx)	(x) (Yx ⊃ Px)
6	(x) (Yx ⊃ Hx)	
7	(x) (Cx ⊃ Bx)	
8	(x) (Nx ⊃ ~Rx)	

5.3 C

2. Px ⧣ x has parts   Sx ⧣ x is a simple substance
Dx ⧣ x can be divided

1	(x) (~Px ⊃ ~Dx)	
2	(x) (Sx ⊃ ~Px)	(x) (Sx ⊃ ~Dx)

3	$\sim P\dot{x} \supset \sim D\dot{x}$	1, UI
4	$S\dot{x} \supset \sim P\dot{x}$	2, UI
5	$S\dot{x} \supset \sim D\dot{x}$	3, 4, HS, IT
6	$(x)(Sx \sim \sim Dx)$	5, UG Q.E.D.

4. $Sx \# x$ is a simple substance
$Cxy \# x$ is a cause of change in y
$Axy \# x$ changes by addition or rearrangement
$Ex \# x$ is an external cause of change

1	$(x)(Sx \supset (y)(Cyx \supset$ $\sim Ayx))$	$\left.\vphantom{\begin{array}{c}1\\2\end{array}}\right\}$ $(x)(y)(Sx \cdot Cyx) \supset \sim Ey$
2	$(x)(Ex \supset (y)(Cxy \supset Axy))$	
3	$S\dot{x} \supset (y)(Cy\dot{x} \supset \sim Ay\dot{x})$	1, UI
4	$S\dot{x} \supset (C\dot{y}\dot{x} \supset \sim A\dot{y}\dot{x})$	3, UI
5	$E\dot{y} \supset (y)(C\dot{y}y \supset A\dot{y}y)$	2, UI
6	$E\dot{y} \supset (C\dot{y}\dot{x} \supset A\dot{y}\dot{x})$	5, UI

(Notice the way in which instantiation had to be done to get the quasi names in the right relation.)

*7	$S\dot{x} \cdot C\dot{y}\dot{x}$	ACP
8	$S\dot{x}$	7, Simp, IR
*9	$C\dot{y}\dot{x}$	7, Simp, IR
*10	$C\dot{y}\dot{x} \supset \sim A\dot{y}\dot{x}$	4, 8, MP, IR
*11	$\sim A\dot{y}\dot{x}$	10, 9, MP, IR
*12	$C\dot{y}\dot{x} \cdot \sim A\dot{y}\dot{x}$	9, 11, Conj, IR
*13	$\sim(C\dot{x}\dot{y} \supset A\dot{y}\dot{x})$	12, NMI, RR
*14	$\sim E\dot{y}$	6, 13, MT, IR
15	$(S\dot{x} \cdot C\dot{y}\dot{x}) \supset \sim Ey$	7–14 RLP
16	$(x)((Sx \cdot C\dot{y}x) \supset \sim E\dot{y})$	15, UG
17	$(x)(y)((Sx \cdot Cyx) \supset \sim Ey)$	16, UG Q.E.D.

6. $Sx \# x$ is a soul $Ux \# x$ is a simple substance
$Px \# x$ has many properties $Rx \# x$ has many relations

1	$(x)(Sx \supset Ux)$	$\left.\vphantom{\begin{array}{c}1\\2\end{array}}\right\}$ $\sim(x)(Ux \supset \sim Px)$
2	$(\exists x)(Sx \cdot (Px \cdot Rx))$	
3	$S\dot{x} \supset U\dot{x}$	1, UI
4	$S\dot{x} \cdot (P\dot{x} \cdot R\dot{x})$	2, EI
*5	$(x)(Ux \supset \sim Px)$	ACP
*6	$U\dot{x} \supset \sim P\dot{x}$	5, UI
7	$S\dot{x}$	4, Simp, IR
*8	$U\dot{x}$	3, 7, MP, IR
*9	$\sim P\dot{x}$	8, 6, MP, IR
10	$P\dot{x} \cdot R\dot{x}$	4, Simp, IR
11	$P\dot{x}$	10, Simp, IR
*12	$P\dot{x} \cdot \sim P\dot{x}$	11, 9, Conj, IR
13	$(x)(Ux \supset \sim Px) \supset P\dot{x} \cdot \sim P\dot{x}$	5–12, RCP
14	$\sim(x)(Ux \supset \sim Px)$	13, Red, RR Q.E.D.

8. Nx ⧣ x is a soul in narrower sense
Cx ⧣ x has clear perception   Mx ⧣ x has memory
Sx ⧣ x is a simple substance

1	$(x)(Nx \supset (Cx \cdot Mx))$	
2	$(x)(Sx \supset (\sim Cx \cdot \sim Mx))$	$(x)(Sx \supset \sim Mx)$
3	$N\dot{x} \supset (C\dot{x} \cdot M\dot{x})$	1, UI
4	$S\dot{x} \supset (\sim C\dot{x} \cdot \sim M\dot{x})$	2, UI
*5	$S\dot{x}$	ACP
*6	$\sim C\dot{x} \cdot \sim M\dot{x}$	4, 5, MP, IR
*7	$\sim C\dot{x}$	6, Simp, IR
*8	$\sim C\dot{x} \vee \sim M\dot{x}$	7, Add, IR
*9	$\sim(C\dot{x} \vee M\dot{x})$	8, DeM, RR
*10	$\sim N\dot{x}$	3, 9, MT, IT
11	$S\dot{x} \supset \sim N\dot{x}$	5–10, RCD
12	$(x)(Sx \supset \sim Nx)$	11, UG Q.E.D.

10. Sx ⧣ x is a simple substance
Px ⧣ x is totally without perception
Ox ⧣ x is a soul   Ux ⧣ x is unconscious

1	$(x)(Sx \supset \sim Px)$	
2	$(x)(Ox \supset Sx)$	$(x)((Ox \cdot Ux) \supset \sim Px)$
3	$S\dot{x} \supset \sim P\dot{x}$	1, UI
4	$O\dot{x} \supset S\dot{x}$	2, UI
5	$O\dot{x} \supset \sim P\dot{x}$	3, 4, HS, IR
*6	$O\dot{x} \cdot U\dot{x}$	ACP
*7	$O\dot{x}$	6, Simp, IR
*8	$\sim P\dot{x}$	5, 7, MP, IR
9	$(O\dot{x} \cdot U\dot{x}) \supset \sim P\dot{x}$	6–8, RCP
10	$(x)((Ox \cdot Ux) \supset \sim Px)$	9, UG Q.E.D.

EXERCISES 5.4

5.4 A   Note: Dictionaries omitted when obvious

2.
1	$(x)(Bx \supset \sim Hx)$	
2	$(x)(Lx \supset Bx)$	$(x)(Lx \supset \sim Hx)$
3	F T F	T F
	$B\dot{x} \supset \sim H\dot{x}$	$L\dot{x} \supset \sim H\dot{x}$
4	T F F	
	$L\dot{x} \supset B\dot{x}$	Valid
	T	

4.
1	$\sim Lij$	
2	$(\exists x)(Fxi \cdot Lxj$	$(\exists j)(Liy \cdot (\exists x)(Fxi \cdot \sim Lyx))$
	T	
	T T	T F T F F
3	$F\dot{x}i \cdot L\dot{x}j$	$Liy \cdot (Fxi \cdot \sim Lyx)$

6. 1 $(x)\, Bx \supset Ix)$

2    $(x)\, (Mx \supset \sim Dx)$ $(x)\, (Bx \supset \sim Mx)$

3    $(x)\, (Ix \supset Dx)$ T F F T

                      $Bx \supset \sim Mx$

     T T T

4    $B\dot{x} \supset I\dot{x}$

     T T T F

5    $M\dot{x} \supset \sim D\dot{x}$

     T F F

6    $I\dot{x} \supset D\dot{x}$ Valid

8. 1 $(x)\, (Nx \supset Bx)$

2    $(x)\, (Dx \supset Fx)$ $(x)\, (Dx \supset Nx)$

3    $(x)\, (\sim Bx \supset \sim Fx)$ T F   F

                      $D\dot{x} \supset N\dot{x}$

     F T   T

4    $N\dot{x} \supset B\dot{x}$

     T T   T

5    $D\dot{x} \supset F\dot{x}$

     F   T T F T

6    $\sim B\dot{x} \supset \sim F\dot{x}$ Invalid

10. 1 $(x)\, (Dx \supset \sim Wx)$ $(x)\, (Mx \supset \sim Ox)$

2    $(x)\, (Ox \supset Wx)$ T F F T

3    $(x)\, (Mx \supset Dx)$ $M\dot{x} \supset \sim O\dot{x}$

     F T F   T

4    $D\dot{x} \supset \sim W\dot{x}$

     T T   T

5    $O\dot{x} \supset W\dot{x}$

     T F   F

6    $M\dot{x} \supset D\dot{x}$ Valid

12. 1 $(x)\, (Bx \supset \sim Px)$ $(\exists x)\, (Sx \supset \sim Bx)$

2    $(x)\, (Sx \supset \sim Cx)$ T   F F   T

3    $(x)\, (\sim Bx \supset Cx)$ $S\dot{x} \supset \sim \; B\dot{x}$

     T T T   F

4    $B\dot{x} \supset \sim P\dot{x}$

     T T T   F

5    $S\dot{x} \supset \sim C\dot{x}$

     F   T T   F

6    $\sim B\dot{x} \supset C\dot{x}$ Invalid

14. 1 $(x)\, (Tx \supset \sim Wx)$ $(x)\, (Tx \supset Ux)$

2    $(x)\, (Cx \supset Wx)$ T F   F

3    $(x)\, (Ux \supset Tx)$ $T\dot{x} \supset U\dot{x}$

     T T T   F

4    $T\dot{x} \supset \sim W\dot{x}$

     F T   F

5 C$\acute{x}$ ⊃ W$\acute{x}$
   F T T

6 U$\acute{x}$ ⊃ T$\acute{x}$ Invalid

5.4 B

2. 1 (∃x) (Bx · ∼Ax) (∃x) (Cx · ∼Ax)
  2 (x) (Cx ⊃ Bx)   F F T
            C$\acute{x}$ · ∼A$\acute{x}$

    T T T

  3 B$\acute{x}$ · ∼A$\acute{x}$
    F T T

  4 C$\acute{x}$ ⊃ B$\acute{x}$ Invalid

4. 1 (x) (Cx ⊃ ∼Bx) (∃x) (Cx · ∼Ax)
  2 (∃x) (Bx · ∼Ax)   F F T F
            C$\acute{x}$ · ∼A$\acute{x}$

    F T F T

  3 C$\acute{x}$ ⊃ ∼B$\acute{x}$
    T T T F

  4 B$\acute{x}$ · ∼A$\acute{x}$ Invalid

6. 1 (x) (Bx ⊃ ∼Ax) (∃x) (Cx · ∼Ax)
  2 (∃x) (Bx · ∼Cx) F F T F
            C$\acute{x}$ · ∼A$\acute{x}$

    T T T F

  3 B$\acute{x}$ ⊃ ∼A$\acute{x}$
    T T T F

  4 B$\acute{x}$ · ∼C$\acute{x}$ Invalid

8. 1 (x) (Nx ⊃ ∼Mx) (x) (Ox ⊃ ∼Nx)
  2 (x) (Ox ⊃ ∼Mx) T F F T
            O$\acute{x}$ ⊃ ∼N$\acute{x}$

    T T T F

  3 N$\acute{x}$ ⊃ ∼M$\acute{x}$
    T T T F

  4 O$\acute{x}$ ⊃ ∼M$\acute{x}$ Invalid

10. 1 (x) (Ox ⊃ ∼Mx) (∃x) (Ox · ∼Nx)
  2 (∃x) (Nx · Mx)   F F F T
            O$\acute{x}$ · ∼Nx

    F T F T

  3 O$\acute{x}$ ⊃ ∼M$\acute{x}$
    T T T

  4 N$\acute{x}$ · M$\acute{x}$ Invalid

EXERCISES 6.1

6.1 A

(1) **2.** Everything has some relation to everything.

   4. At least one thing has every relation to everything.

6. At least one thing has some relation to everything.

8. Something has some relation to something.

10. For anything there is something that has every relation to it.

12. There is at least one thing to which something has every relation.

14. For anything whatsoever, there is something which has some relation to it.

(2) 2 implies 6, and 2 and 6 imply 8

10 implies 12, and 10 and 12 imply 14 (answer incomplete)

(3) 8 and 14 seem obviously true

4, 10, and 12 seem false on the grounds that some relations are incompatible (father, son, father, mother)

2 and 6 are matters of controversy

6.1 B $Ixy \not\equiv x$ is identical with y

2. $(x)((\mathscr{F})(\mathscr{F}x) \supset \sim Ixx)$

4. $(x) \sim (\mathscr{F})(\mathscr{F}x)$ or $(x)(\exists \mathscr{F})(\sim \mathscr{F}x)$

6. The second form of 4 gives the antecedent of 1. Use MP.

8. Do these statements mean (a) every nonrelational property or (b) every property, relational or not?

10. If (b), 1 and 2 are trivially true; if (a), they are dubious.

6.1 C

2. $(x)(y)((\mathscr{F}x \equiv \sim \mathscr{F}y) \supset \sim (\exists \mathscr{F}z)(\mathscr{F}xy))$

4. $(x)(y)(\sim Ixy \supset (\mathscr{F})(\mathscr{F}x \equiv \sim \mathscr{F}y))$

6. Consequent follows by UI from antecedent

8. Seems to be false: You and I are not identical but both speak English, breathe, etc.

10. Since 4 seems false, the argument, even if valid, is not sound.

EXERCISES 6.2

6.2 A

2.

1	$(x)(Cx \supset \sim Dx)$	
2	Dm	$\sim Cn$
3	$m = n$	
4	$Cm \supset \sim Dm$	1, UI
5	$Dm \supset \sim Cm$	4, Transp, RR
6	$\sim Cm$	2, 5, MP, IR
7	$\sim Cn$	6, Id, Q.E.D.

4.

1	$(x)((Hx \cdot Jx) \supset Lx)$	
2	Hm	
3	Jn	$o \neq n$
4	$n = m$	
5	$\sim Lo$	
6	$(Hm \cdot Jm) \supset Lm$	1, UI
7	$Hm \supset (Jm \supset Lm)$	6, Exp, RR
8	$Jm \supset Lm$	2, 7, MP, IR

9	Jm	3, 4, Id
10	Lm	10, 9, MP, IR
11	Ln	10, 4, Id
12	o ≠ n	5, 12, Id Q.E.D.

6.2 B

2. s # Sam   f # Frodo   Hx # x is a hobbit

Sx # x was on the last stage of the journey

$((Hs \cdot Hf) \cdot (Ss \cdot Sf)) \cdot (x) ((Hx \cdot Sx) \supset ((x = s) \vee (x = f)))$

4. Dx # x can destroy y   r # the Ring

$Dfr \cdot (x) (Dxr \supset (x = f))$

6.2 C

2. Hx # x is discussing which foods are healthy

Bx # x is the best speaker

Wx # x is the worst speaker

Rxy # x recognizes y as the sort of speaker y is

$(\exists x) (\exists y) (\exists z) (((Hx \cdot By) \cdot Wz) \supset ((\exists w) (Rwy \cdot Rwz$
$\cdot (u) ((Ruy \vee Ruz) \supset (u = w)))) \vee (((\exists w) (Rwy)$
$\cdot (\exists u) (Ruz)) \cdot (w \neq u)))$

4. R # x is a better speaker   S # x is a worse speaker

$(x) (y) (z) (((Rx \cdot Sy) \cdot Rzx) \supset Rzy)$

6. Sxy # x says the same as y

Exyz # x explains what y says as well as he explains what z says

o # Homer   e # Hesiod   i # Ion

$Soe \supset Eieo$

8. Px # x is a poet $(\exists x) ((Px \cdot (x \neq o)) \cdot Sxo)$

10. Same as **4**

6.3 A

2.

	1	$C(\imath x) (Dx)$	
	2	$\sim Cj$ $\sim Dj$	
	3	$(\exists x) ((Cx \cdot Dx) \cdot (y) (Dy \supset (y = x)))$	1, DIO
	4	$(C\acute{x} \cdot D\acute{x}) \cdot (y) (Dy \supset (y = \acute{x}))$	3, EI
	5	$(C\acute{x} \cdot D\acute{x}) \cdot (Dj \supset (j = \acute{x}))$	4, UI
*6		Dj	ACP
	7	$Dj \supset (j = \acute{x})$	5, Simp, IR
	8	$C\acute{x} \cdot D\acute{x}$	5, Simp, IR
	9	$C\acute{x}$	8, Simp, IR
*10		$(j = \acute{x})$	6, 7, MP, IR
*11		Cj	10, 9, Id, IR
*12		$Cj \cdot \sim Cj$	11, 2, Conj, IR
	13	$Dj \supset (Cj \cdot \sim Cj)$	6–12, RCP
	14	$\sim Dj$	13, Red, RR
			Q.E.D.

4.
1	H($\imath x$) (Jx)	
2	(x) ($\sim$K$x \supset \sim$Hx)	$\sim$Jm
3	$\sim$Km	
4	($\exists x$) ((Jx · Hx) · (y) (J$y \supset (y = x)$))	1, DIO
5	(J$\dot x$ · H$\dot x$) · (y) (J$y \supset (y = \dot x)$)	4, EI
6	(Jx · H$\dot x$) · (Jm $\supset$ (m = $\dot x$))	5, UI
*7	Jm	ACP
8	Jm $\supset$ (m = $\dot x$)	6, Simp, IR
*9	m = $\dot x$	7, 8, MP, IR
*10	$\sim$K$\dot x$	9, 3, Id, IR
11	$\sim$K$\dot x \supset \sim$H$\dot x$	2, UI
*12	$\sim$H$\dot x$	10, 11, MP
13	J$\dot x$ · H$\dot x$	5, Simp, IR
14	H$\dot x$	13, Simp, IR
*15	H$\dot x$ · $\sim$H$\dot x$	12, 14, Conj, IR
16	Jm $\supset$ (H$\dot x$ · $\sim$Hx)	7–15, RCP
17	$\sim$Jm	16, Red, RR
		Q.E.D.

6.3 B

2. f = ($\imath x$) (Hx · Fxr)

4. ($\imath x$) (Hx · Fxr) $\neq$ ($\imath x$) (Rxr)

6.3 C

2. N$xy \,\#\, x$ nodded to y O$xy \,\#\, x$ went out and came back with y
B$xy \,\#\, x$ is a boy present at y's death
M$xyz \,\#\, x$ is a man who is to give y to z P$xy \,\#\, x$ is poison given to y
c $\#$ Crito   s $\#$ Socrates
Nc ($\imath x$) (Bxs) · O ($\imath x$) (Bxs) ($\imath x$) (Mx ($\imath x$) (Pxs) s)

4. T$xy \,\#\, x$ told y to lie down when his legs became heavy and stiff
T ($\imath x$) (Mx ($\imath x$) (Pxs)) s

6, 8, 10 cannot be done without **1, 3, 5.**

EXERCISES 6.4

6.4 A

2. The relation of being an ancestor is transitive.

4. The relation of fatherhood is not symmetrical.

6. The relation of brotherhood is symmetrical.

8. If the relation of being an ancestor were not transitive, it would not be symmetrical.

10. No relation which is not transitive is symmetrical.

6.4 B

2. $\sim$T^2 (λx) ($\sim$Ax)

4. $\sim$T^2 (λx) ($\sim$Ax) · S (λx) ($\sim$Ax)

6. 2 is true but 4 is false (incomplete answer)

8. Cannot both be true: 4 is a counterinstance to 5, if true

10. 2 and 4 are compatible, but 4 and 5 are incompatible (incomplete answer)

6.4 C

2. $Jx \mathrel{\#} x$ is just
$Ox \mathrel{\#} x$ is obedient to the rulers of the state
$S^2 \mathcal{FG} \mathrel{\#}$ quality $\mathcal{F}$ is the same as quality $\mathcal{G}$
$S^2 (\lambda x) (Jx) (\lambda x) (Ox)$

4. $Sx \mathrel{\#} x$ is strong
$Mx \mathrel{\#} x$ makes mistakes
$I^2 \mathcal{FG} \mathrel{\#}$ quality $\mathcal{F}$ is incompatible with quality $\mathcal{G}$
$I^2 (\lambda x) (Sx) (\lambda x) (Mx)$

6, 8, 10 cannot be done without **1, 3, 5.**

EXERCISES 7.1

7.1 A

2. Logically true	**4.** Not log. true	**6.** Log. true	**8.** Log. true
10. Not log. true	**12.** Log. True	**14.** Not log. true	
16. Not log. true	**18.** Log. true	**20.** Not log. true	

7.1 B

2. $H \mathrel{\#} x$ happens $I \mathrel{\#} x$ is $S \mathrel{\#} A$ sea fight takes place tomorrow

(1)	$\sim\Diamond \sim H \supset \Box\, H$	(2)	True
4. (1)	$\sim\Diamond \sim(H \vee \sim H)$	(2)	True
6. (1)	$I \supset \Box\, I$	(2)	False, except for determinists
8. (1)	$\sim(\Box\, (I \supset I) \equiv (I \supset \Box\, I))$	(2)	True
10. (1)	$\sim(\Box\, (S \vee \sim S) \equiv (\Box\, S \vee \Box \sim S))$	(2)	True

EXERCISES 7.2

7.2 A   **10** implies **6, 12** implies **8** (incomplete answer)

7.2 B

2. $\Diamond\, p$	$\sim\Diamond\, p$	contradictory
4. $\Box\, p$	$\sim\Box\, p$	contradictory
6. $\Diamond\, p$	$\Diamond\, p$	follows
	$\sim\sim\Diamond\, p$	follows
	$\sim\Box\, p$	doesn't follow
8. $\Diamond \sim p$	$\sim\Box \sim p$	doesn't follow
	$\sim\sim\Diamond \sim p$	follows
10. $\sim\Diamond \sim p$	$\Box\, p$	follows
	$\sim\Diamond \sim p$	follows

12. $\Diamond\, p$	**14.** $\sim\Box\, p$	not equivalent
16. $\sim\Diamond\, p$	**18.** $\Box \sim p$	equivalent
20. $\Diamond \sim p$	**22.** $\sim\Box \sim p$	not equivalent
24. $\sim\Diamond \sim p$	**26.** $\Box\, p$	equivalent

28. ~ ~◇ p   ~◇ p   contradictory

          ~◇ p   contradictory

30. ◇ p   ◇ ~p   subcontraries

7.3 A

For an S.3 system **8, 14, 16, 18,** and **20** could be logical truths; the rest could not (incomplete answer).

7.3 B

2. ◇ F ⊃ □ ◇ E   or   ◇ F ⊰ ◇ E

4. ◇ □ G ⊃ □ ◇ E   or   ◇ □ G ⊰ ◇ E

6. □ F ⊃ ◇ □ G

8. (◇ □ E ∨ ◇ □ F) ⊃ ~□ G

10. □ (G ⊃ F) ⊃ □ ◇ □ E   or   (G ⊰ F) ⊰ ◇ □ E

7.4 A

2. 1   ~F ⊰ ~P   ⎫
      2   ◇ ~F   ⎬   ~((◇ ~F · ~◇ ~P) ⊰ ~(~F ⊰ ~P))
      3   □ P   ⎭

      *4   (◇ ~F · ~◇ ~P) ⊰ ~(~F ⊰ ~P)   ACP
       5   ~◇ ~P   3, MOE, RR
       6   ◇ ~F · ~◇ ~P   2, 5, Conj, IR
      *7   ~(~F ⊰ ~P)   4, 6, MP, IR
      *8   ~(~F ⊰ ~P) · (~F ⊰ ~P)   7, 1, Conj, IR
       9   ((◇ ~F · ~◇ ~P) ⊰ ~(~F ⊰ ~P))   4–8, RCP
                ⊰ (~(~F ⊰ ~P) · (~F ⊰ ~P))
      10   ~((◇ ~F · ~◇ ~P) ⊰ ~(~F ⊰ ~P))   9, Red, RR
                                                 Q.E.D.

4. 1   E ⊰ □ E }   ~ ◇ (E · ◇ ~E)
      2   ~□ E ⊰ ~E   1, Transp, RR
      3   ◇ ~E ⊰ ~E   2, MOE, RR
      4   □ (◇ ~E ⊃ ~E)   3, DSI, RR
      5   □ ~ ~(◇ ~E ⊃ ~E)   4, DN, RR
      6   □ ~(◇ ~E · ~ ~E)   5, NME, RR
      7   □ ~(◇ ~E · E)   6, DN, RR
      8   □ ~(E · ◇ ~E)   7, Com, RR
      9   ~ ◇(E · ◇ ~E)   8, MOE, RR   Q.E.D.

7.4 B P # A perfect being exists

2. 1   □P ∨ □ ~P ⎫   ~P
      2   ◇ ~P   ⎭
      3   ~□ P   2, MOE, RR
      4   □ ~P   3, 1, DS, IR
      5   ~P   4, NE, IR

400

4. 1 $P \dashv \Box P$

     2    $\Diamond P$ $\Big\}$ P

     3    $(P \dashv \Box P) \dashv (\Diamond P \dashv P)$

     4    $\Diamond P \dashv P$ 1, 3, SMP, IR

     5   P   2, 4, SMP, IR

EXERCISES 8.1

8.1 A

2. For anything at all, it is possible that, if that thing is an author, it has broad interests.

4. Any author may have broad interests.

6. Any author necessarily has broad interests.

8. Any author has broad interests necessarily.

10. There is something that may be an author with broad interests.

12. Some author may have broad interests.

14. Something is necessarily an author with broad interests.

16. Some author has broad interests necessarily.

8.1 B

2. $Sxy \;\#\; x$ is similar to y $Hx \;\#\; x$ happens

     $(x)\,(y)\,(Sxy \supset (\Diamond Hx \supset \Diamond Hy))$

4. $Hx \;\#\; x$ is a house $Bx \;\#\; x$ is beautiful $Pxy \;\#\; x$ possesses y

     $(x)\,(y)\,(\Diamond ((Hx \cdot Bx) \cdot Pyx) \supset \Diamond (Hx \cdot Pyx))$

6. $Bx \;\#\; x$ begins $Ex \;\#\; x$ ends $(x)\,(\Diamond Bx \supset \Diamond Ex)$

8. $Lxy \;\#\; x$ loves y $Dxy \;\#\; x$ desires y

     $(x)\,(y)\,(\sim \Diamond Hx \supset \sim \Diamond (Lyx \lor Dyx))$

10. $Wx \;\#\; x$ is done by inferior, weak, or stupid men

     $Sx \;\#\; x$ is done by superior, strong, or intelligent men

     $(x)\,(\Diamond Wx \supset \Diamond Sx)$

EXERCISES 8.2

8.2 A

2. If n knows that p, then this implies that n knows that q materially implies p.

4. If n knows that p materially implies q and n knows that p, this implies that n knows that q.

6, 8, 10 cannot be done without **1, 3, 5.**

8.2 B

2. (a) $(x)\,(Px \cdot (y)\,(Oy \supset Kxy)) \supset (x = y))$

     (b)   True

4. (a) $(x)\,((Px \cdot (\exists y)\,(Oy \cdot \sim Kxy)) \supset (x \neq g))$

     (b)   True

6. 1 implies 4

8. Cannot be answered without 1

8.2 C

2. $\sim$Kap

4. Fap

6. False: our system says nothing about what follows from what we know.

8. False for the same reason, but this is parallel to the equivalence of Fnp and $\sim$Kn $\sim$p.

10. False for our system: the distinction that leads Hintikka to this conclusion may be a valid one, but is unnecessarily fine for most purposes.

EXERCISES 8.3

8.3 A

2. (a) If n is obliged to do (the action described by) p, then, if n is obliged to do (the action described by) q, he is obliged to do (the action described by) p.

(b) and (d) Sounds odd, but is simply a consequence of one of the paradoxes of material implication.

(c) If you are obliged to do this exercise, then, if you are obliged to refrain from murder, you are obliged to do this exercise.

4. (a) If n is obliged to do p and if doing p obliges him to do q, this implies that n is obliged to do q.

(b) and (d) This seems intuitively acceptable to me, but see the book by A. N. Prior mentioned in the Reading List at the end of Chapter 8.

(c) If you are obliged to love God and your neighbor and if loving God and your neighbor obliges you to ride a bicycle on a certain occasion, you are obliged to ride a bicycle on that occasion.

8.3 B

2. (F $\circ\!\!\!\to^n$ L) $\supset$ (OnF $\supset$ $\sim$Pn $\sim$L)

4. (PnF $\cdot$ $\sim$PnL) $\supset$ $\sim$(F $\circ\!\!\!\to^n$ L)

8.3 C

2. (a) OnOnp; (b) It is arguable whether doubled deontic modalities are necessary.

4. Dxy $\#$ x does (the action described by) y

(a) ((Dnp $\cdot$ $\sim$Dnp) $\dashv_3$ Dnp) $\supset$ ((Dnp $\cdot$ On $\sim$p) $\supset$ Onp)

(b) Since the antecedent of this conditional is a tautology, the truth value of the statement as a whole depends on the consequent. Since one conjunct of the antecedent of the conditional which is the consequent of the original conditional is the contrary of the antecedent, the antecedent and consequent of this "subconditional" cannot both be true. So if p does describe an obligatory action, it is trivially true; otherwise it is false.

EXERCISES 8.4

8.4 A

2. If n knows that p is logically impossible then n believes that he is not obliged to do p.

4. If n knows that he is obliged to do p, this implies that he knows p to be possible.

8.4 B

2. BbOaDaa ⊃ Bb ◇ Daa
4. (Mba · ∼◇ Daa) ⊃ (◇ Dba ⊃ ObBba)

EXERCISES 9.1

9.1 A

2. Log. true   4. Log. true   6. Log. false   8. Log. false
10. Log. false

9.1 B

2. Logically true, given the meanings of "part" and "whole"
4. Logically true since, if we can distinguish a beginning, end, and so on, we can regard them as parts
6. Logically true since a shape is a sort of limit
8. Contingent: If I lose one hair, I am still myself.
10. Contingent: Plato's reasons for this assertion are unconvincing.

EXERCISES 9.2

9.2 A   Arguably none of these pairs are equivalent. Consult a good dictionary for the shades of meaning involved.

9.2 B

2. A slip of Ryle's pen. What about cigarette smokers?
4. What about a man who gave in easily to temptation then bullheadedly pursued the object of his desires?
6. These conditions may be necessary but not sufficient. A thoroughly stupid action may be done with some attention. (Or do we want to say that even here *some* intelligence is exhibited?)
8. What about lapses or errors due to lack of knowledge that could easily have been remedied? (You *could* have avoided wrecking it by just looking at the instructions!)
10. I may be enjoying a lesser pleasure to which I would prefer some other pleasure which for some reason is not available.

(Note: None of these answers do full justice to Ryle. Read the book.)

EXERCISES 9.3

9.3 A

2. At least suggestion. It would be absurd to say that *no* college graduate was intelligent.
4. Probably indication. If there were not some admirable individuals, whom would hypocrites imitate?

6. Strong implication. If a thing is not audible it cannot be heard. Therefore if it is heard, it must be audible.

8. Probably indication, reasoning similar to 2 above.

10. Possibly strong implication. See discussion in Section 8.2.

9.3 B

2. At least suggestion, possibly indication. Though this behavior could be an act, it would be an imitation of genuine behavior.

4. Possibly strong implication if, as is arguable, intelligent behavior necessarily involves some kind of judgments, and judgments involve criteria.

6. Strong implication. Understanding and misunderstanding go together logically.

8. Probably indication. Though this may fail to be true in special cases, we are familiar with cases where it would be absurd to deny it.

10. At least suggestion, possibly indication. This sort of behavior is a typical indication of homesickness, though it may not always be associated with it.

EXERCISES 9.4

9.4 A

2. No contender. No meaning has been attached to the "special relationship."

4. False Contender. Trivially true in this special sense, debatable given the ordinary sense.

9.4 B

2. Possibly either False Contender or Defending the Incumbent, since an ordinary sense is being contrasted with a technical sense, which may be misleading or unnecessary.

4. Something like a No Contender argument since a technical usage is being accused of being unclear or empty.

EXERCISES 10.1

10.1 A

2. Plato suggested something like this: "A wise or skillful leader of a state or people who puts the interests of his people before his own interests"

4. A person who when faced with real or supposed danger is easily or excessively influenced by fear in such a way that he behaves unreasonably or contrary to duties or obligations

6. An event which is of a sort which is usually controllable or foreseeable but which, because of some special circumstances, occurs in a way which is at least partly unforeseen or beyond control

8. A special ability of a minor sort which is possessed by some individuals without training or acquired without intensive training

10. A person whose behavior is of an eccentric sort, bordering on the mildly insane but amusing and harmless

10.1 B

2. Too broad: I desire (mildly) a million dollars, and don't believe I'll get it, but despair is too strong for my feeling about this
4. Too broad: it is arguable whether one need feel fear to be courageous, but certainly not all courageous people hope to avoid harm by resistance (for example, martyrs)
6. Too broad: a religious person might have constant hope because of confidence in God, yet lack confidence in himself
8. Too narrow: one might be ambitious to accomplish a certain thing, not caring whether it gave one power or fame
10. Too broad: not everyone who fears that his love is not returned is jealous, though this fear may be characteristic of jealous people

10.1 C

2. Rule 1: meaning of "more perfect"?
4. Rule 3: not all cases fit this description
6. Rule 2: one might enjoy thinking of something without loving it
8. Rule 4: derision not always pleasurable
10. Rule 3: fails to distinguish fear from worry, etc.
12. Rule 3: fails to distinguish despair from remorse, etc.
14. Hard to fault
16. Rule 4: there are other grounds for approval
18. Hard to fault
20. Rule 4: fails to include desire for what another has
22. Rule 4: might arise from contemplation of possessions, position, etc.
24. Rule 3: fails to distinguish repentance from remorse, shame, etc.
26. No word in English has this exact shade of meaning
28. Rule 4: regret may fail to involve desires
30. Rule 4: anger may be directed at objects, facts, etc.
32. Rule 3: such a desire might be prudent rather than timid
34. Rule 4: some dangers might be unique

EXERCISES 10.2

10.2 A

2. Same connotation and denotation, not same associations
4. Since some legal domiciles are not homes, neither same denotation nor same connotation; obviously not same associations
6. Same denotation and connotation (in American English); since some lawyers prefer "attorney," presumably somewhat different associations
8. Same denotation; perhaps not same connotation since "cop" involves evaluative elements; Different associations

10. Same denotation and connotation, but, since Scots prefer "Scot," different associations

10.2 B

2, 4, 6, 8, 10. Connotation

2, 4, 8. Denotation would also be plausible

8. Only association plausible for "hu," not for "man"

EXERCISES 10.3

10.3 A

(1) **2.** Yes **4.** Yes

(2) **2.** 2/6 or 1/3 **4.** 1/6 **6.** 0 **8.** 4/6 **10.** 4/6

     12. 3/6 or 1/2 **14.** 5/6

10.3 B

2. $Pr(E_1/H_1) = 1$ $Pr(E_1/H_4) = 2/5$

    $Pr(E_1/H_2) = 4/5$ $Pr(E_1/H_5) = 1/5$

    $Pr(E_1/H_3) = 3/5$ $Pr(E_1/H_6) = 0$

4. The probabilities are $\frac{1}{3}$ of the likelihoods.

6. Rule out H_5 and H_6 because neither has two black balls.

8. $Pr(H_1/E_1) = 1/2$ $Pr(H_3/E_2) = 3/20$

    $Pr(H_2/E_2) = 6/20$ $Pr(H_4/E_2) = 1/20$

10. Yes

10.3 C

2. Consistent **4.** Consistent

EXERCISES 10.4

10.4 A

Gx ⧣ x is green Hx ⧣ x is hard

Ex ⧣ x is an emerald Rx ⧣ x is in my ring

Sx ⧣ x is a stone

2. $(x)(Ex \supset ((Gx \cdot Hx) \cdot Sx))$

4. $(\exists x)(((Sx \cdot Rx) \cdot (Gx \cdot Ex)) \cdot (y)((Sx \cdot Rx) \supset (y = x)))$

6. Yes for 1 and 3, debatable for 2

8. Debatable **10.** Debatable

10.4 B

2. Orbit of Mercury, confirming, important

4. Michelson-Morley experiment, disconfirming, very important

Final Note to Students: In many cases your answers may be correct even though they differ from those in this answer section. In case of doubt, consult your instructor.

Appendix F
FREQUENTLY USED FORMS AND RULES

IMPORTANT RULES

Replacement Rule (RR)

If we have a proof in which a proposition A occurs as a line or part of a line, we may write a proposition B as a line or part of a line which is otherwise the same as the line A is part of, provided that the logical form of the equivalence A ≡ B is one of the equivalences listed in Sections 1.3, 5.2, 7.2, 7.3, 8.1, 8.2, 8.3, or 8.4. The new line will be justified by citing the number of the line in which A occurs, the name of the equivalence, and RR.

Inference Rule (IR)

If we have a proof in which A (or A and B or A and B and C) are lines, then we may write a proposition D as a line provided that the logical form of A ⊃ D (or of (A · B) ⊃ D or of ((A · B) · C) ⊃ D) is one of the logically true implications listed in Sections 2.1, 4.4, 5.2, 5.3, 7.1, 7.2, 7.3, 8.1, 8.2, 8.3, or 8.4. The justification for the new line will consist of the number(s) of the line(s) A (or A and B or A and B and C), the name of the implication, and IR.

Rule of Conditional Proof (RCP)

At any point in a proof, any proposition, A, may be put down as a line of the proof with the justification Assumption for Conditional Proof (ACP), provided that an asterisk is placed to the left of the number of that line. (This will be called "starring" the line.) Each line which cites that line is similarly starred, and each line which cites a starred line is starred. Starred lines may also cite premises or previous lines obtained from the premises. The assumption may be "dismissed" after any starred line as follows: if the assumption is a proposition A and the last starred line is a proposition B we may write an *un*starred line, A ⊃ B, citing *all* starred lines so far (in the style: first starred line, dash, last starred line) and the justification Rule of Conditional Proof (e.g., 5–12, RCP). No starred line may be the conclusion of an argument and no starred line may be cited after its assumption is dismissed. For some restrictions on RCP see Section 8.4.

EQUIVALENCES

	Name	Symbolization
E 1	Double Negation (DN)	$p \equiv \sim\sim p$
E 2	Repetition (Rep)	$p \equiv (p \cdot p)$
E 3	Repetition (Rep)	$p \equiv (p \vee p)$
E 4	Consequentia Mirabilis (CM)	$p \equiv (\sim p \supset p)$
E 5	Negative Consequentia Mirabilis (NCM)	$\sim p \equiv (p \supset \sim p)$
E 6	Reductio (Red)	$\sim p \equiv (p \supset (q \cdot \sim q))$
E 7	Commutation (Com)	$(p \cdot q) \equiv (q \cdot p)$
E 8	Commutation (Com)	$(p \vee q) \equiv (q \vee p)$
E 9	De Morgan's Rules (DeM)	$\sim(p \cdot q) \equiv (\sim p \vee \sim q)$
E 10	De Morgan's Rules (DeM)	$\sim(p \vee q) \equiv (\sim p \cdot \sim q)$
E 11	Transposition (Transp)	$(p \supset q) \equiv (\sim q \supset \sim p)$
E 12	Definition of Material Implication (DMI)	$(p \supset q) \equiv (\sim p \vee q)$
E 13	Definition of Material Implication (DMI)	$(p \supset q) \equiv \sim(p \cdot \sim q)$
E 14	Negation of Material Implication (NMI)	$\sim(p \supset q) \equiv (p \cdot \sim q)$
E 15	Commutation (Com)	$(p \equiv q) \equiv (q \equiv p)$
E 16	Definition of Material Equivalence (DME)	$(p \equiv q) \equiv ((p \supset q) \cdot (q \supset p))$
E 17	Definition of Material Equivalence (DME)	$(p \equiv q) \equiv ((p \cdot q) \vee (\sim p \cdot \sim q))$
E 18	Complimentarity (Comp)	$(p \equiv q) \equiv (\sim p \equiv \sim q)$
E 19	Negation of Material Equivalence (NME)	$\sim(p \equiv q) \equiv (\sim p \equiv q)$
E 20	Negation of Material Equivalence (NME)	$\sim(p \equiv q) \equiv (p \equiv \sim q)$
E 21	Association (Assoc)	$(p \cdot (q \cdot r)) \equiv ((p \cdot q) \cdot r)$
E 22	Association (Assoc)	$(p \vee (q \vee r)) \equiv ((p \vee q) \vee r)$
E 23	Exportation (Exp)	$(p \supset (q \supset r)) \equiv ((p \cdot q) \supset r)$
E 24	Distribution (Dist)	$(p \cdot (q \vee r)) \equiv ((p \cdot q) \vee (p \cdot r))$

EQUIVALENCES—*continued*

Name	Symbolization
E 25 Distribution (Dist)	$(p \lor (q \cdot r)) \equiv ((p \lor q) \cdot (p \lor r))$
E 26 Absorption (Abs)	$((p \supset q) \cdot p) \equiv (p \cdot q)$

ARGUMENT FORMS

Variations of Modus Ponens

A 1   Modus Ponens (MP)
$$p \supset q$$
$$\underline{p}$$
$$q$$

A 2   Modus Tollens (MT)
$$p \supset q$$
$$\underline{\sim q}$$
$$\sim p$$

A 3   Disjunctive Syllogism (DS)
$$p \lor q$$
$$\underline{\sim p}$$
$$q$$

Other Conditional Arguments

A 4   Hypothetical Syllogism (HS)
$$p \supset q$$
$$\underline{q \supset r}$$
$$p \supset r$$

A 5   Constructive Dilemma (CD)
$$p \supset q$$
$$r \supset s$$
$$\underline{p \lor r}$$
$$q \lor s$$

A 6   Destructive Dilemma (DD)
$$p \supset q$$
$$r \supset s$$
$$\underline{\sim q \lor \sim s}$$
$$\sim p \lor \sim r$$

Convenient Transformations

A 7   Simplification (Simp)
$$\underline{p \cdot q}$$
$$p$$

A 8   Simplification (Simp)
$$\underline{p \cdot q}$$
$$q$$

A 9   Addition (Add)
$$\underline{p}$$
$$p \lor q$$

A 10   Conjunction (Conj)
$$p$$
$$\underline{q}$$
$$p \cdot q$$

409

INSTANTIATION AND GENERALIZATION RULES

Rule		*Formula*
Universal Instantiation (UI)	(a)	$\dfrac{(w)\,(Zw)}{Zo}$
Restrictions: Every **w** in **Zw** must be replaced by **o**, **ò**, or **ó** as the case may be; **(w)** must not be within the scope of a $\sim$ or of another quantifier; and the scope of **(w)** must extend to the end of the expression.	(b)	$\dfrac{(w)\,(Zw)}{Z\grave{o}}$
	(c)	$\dfrac{(w)\,(Zw)}{Z\acute{o}}$
Existential Instantiation (EI)		
Restriction: A new existential quasi name must be used for each application of EI; $(\exists w)$ must not be within the scope of a $\sim$ or another quantifier; and the scope of $(\exists w)$ must extend to the end of the expression.		$\dfrac{(\exists w)\,(Zw)}{Z\acute{o}}$
Universal Generalization (UG)		
Restrictions: Every **ò** must be replaced by **w**, and the scope of **(w)** must extend to the end of the expression; UG must not be used within a conditional proof on a universal quasi name which occurs in an assumption for that conditional proof; UG must not be applied to an expression which contains an existential quasi name introduced by EI.		$\dfrac{Z\grave{o}}{(w)\,(Zw)}$
Existential Generalization (EG)	(a)	$\dfrac{Zo}{(\exists w)\,(Zw)}$
Restrictions: Every **o**, **ò**, or **ó** as the case may be must be replaced by a **w**, and the scope of $(\exists w)$ must extend to the end of the expression.	(b)	$\dfrac{Z\grave{o}}{(\exists w)\,(Zw)}$
	(c)	$\dfrac{Z\acute{o}}{(\exists w)\,(Zw)}$

INDEX
OF FORMS
AND
RULES

NOTE: Page numbers indicate where forms or rules are introduced or listed. Those marked with an asterisk are given in full in Appendix F, immediately before this index. Of course, not every *use* of a form or rule is indexed.

INDEX
OF
SYMBOLS

NOTE: The first page number is the number of the page on which the symbol is first introduced. Subsequent page numbers, if any, are numbers of pages in which important changes or additions are made. Of course, not every *use* of the symbol is indexed.

INDEX

Universal instantiation, 178, 181, 207

Universe of discourse, 113

Validity, xxi

Variable, 14

Venn, J., 138

Venn diagram, 139

Von Wright, G. H., 232, 262

Whitehead, A. N., 66, 156, 203

Wittgenstein, L., 301, 326–327

70 71 72 73 74   7 6 5 4 3 2 1